SUPREMACY AT

T0357806

Evan Mawdsley is an historian and form[er professor of] history at the University of Glasgow. His [book] *The War for the Seas: A Maritime History of World War II* won the Anderson Medal for the best maritime non-fiction book of 2019.

Further praise for *Supremacy at Sea*:

"An excellent battle narrative . . . Using the lessons learned from this campaign, the U.S. Navy would become the dominant maritime power by the end of the war." Jerry D. Lenaburg, *New York Journal of Books*

"Evan Mawdsley deftly weaves together the human, technical, and logistical advances that forged this mighty naval warhammer, and then grippingly relates how the Americans wielded it during their victorious campaigns in the Pacific in early 1944. Highly recommended." Jon Parshall, author of *Shattered Sword*

"*Supremacy at Sea* tells of Task Force 58, the U.S. Navy's Big Blue Fleet, from inception to its great victory in the Battle of the Philippine Sea. Evan Mawdsley has an eye for what is important and his exploration of how TF 58 became the most successful and powerful naval force of World War II shines with insight and fresh perspective." Vincent P. O'Hara, author of *Struggle for the Middle Sea*

"In his masterful study of Task Force 58, Evan Mawdsley offers a deep and compelling account of the U.S. Navy's triumph in the Pacific War that looks beyond the battles and explains the foundation of eighty years of American naval supremacy." Joe Maiolo, author of *Cry Havoc*

"Mawdsley, with his trademark clarity and force, tells the story of Task Force 58, the most successful strike force in Second World War naval history . . . A tour de force." Phillips O'Brien, author of *How the War Was Won*

SUPREMACY AT SEA

TASK FORCE 58 AND THE CENTRAL PACIFIC VICTORY

EVAN MAWDSLEY

YALE UNIVERSITY PRESS
NEW HAVEN AND LONDON

For information about this and other Yale University Press publications, please contact:
U.S. Office: sales.press@yale.edu   yalebooks.com
Europe Office: sales@yaleup.co.uk   yalebooks.co.uk

Set in Adobe Garamond Pro by IDSUK (DataConnection) Ltd
Printed in Denmark By Nørhaven A/S, Viborg

Library of Congress Control Number: 2025930818
A catalogue record for this book is available from the British Library.
Authorized Representative in the EU: Easy Access System Europe, Mustamäe tee 50, 10621 Tallinn, Estonia, gpsr.requests@easproject.com

ISBN 978-0-300-25545-4 (hbk)
ISBN 978-0-300-28388-4 (pbk)

10 9 8 7 6 5 4 3 2 1

CONTENTS

PLATES, MAPS, FIGURES, AND TABLES

PLATES

1a. *Hornet* under attack during the Battle of Santa Cruz, October 1942. National Archives, 80-G-33947.

1b. *Enterprise* at the Battle of Santa Cruz, October 1942. National Archives, 80-G-30033.

2a. Admiral Chester W. Nimitz and Vice Admiral Raymond A. Spruance, February 1944. NH-62233 courtesy of the Naval History & Heritage Command.

2b. USS *Indianapolis* (CA-35), May 1943. 19-N-47561 courtesy of the Naval History & Heritage Command.

3a. Rear Admiral Charles A. Pownall, USN, October 1943. National Archives, 80-G-K-13643.

3b. Vice Admiral Marc A. Mitscher, USN, June 1944. National Archives, 80-G-236831.

4a. USS *Essex* (CV-9), July 1942. NH 54105 courtesy of the Naval History & Heritage Command.

4b. USS *Lexington* (CV-16), February 1943. National Archives, 80-G-35657.

5a. USS *Cleveland* (CL-55), later 1942. NH 55173 courtesy of the Naval History & Heritage Command.

5b. USS *Princeton* (CVL-23), January 1944. NH 95648 courtesy of the Naval History & Heritage Command.

6a. USS *Essex* (CV-9), May 1943. National Archives, 80-G-68097.

MAPS

FIGURES AND TABLES

ABBREVIATIONS AND TERMS

AA	Anti-aircraft
AAF	U.S. Army Air Force (USAAF)
Adm.	Admiral
AG	Air group (USN); carriers had a numbered air group with several squadrons
AKA	Attack cargo ship
AO	Fleet oiler
AR	Action report
ASP	Anti-submarine patrol [launched from task force]
APA	Attack transport
ATIS	Allied Translator and Interpreter Section [Australia]
BatDiv	Battleship division
BB	Battleship
Bde	Brigade
BuAer	Bureau of Aeronautics (USN)
BuNav	Bureau of Navigation (USN)
BuShips	Bureau of Ships
CA	Heavy cruiser
CAG	Commander, air group
CAP	Combat air patrol
Capt.	Captain
CarDiv	Aircraft carrier division

CCS	Combined Chiefs of Staff
Cdr	Commander
CenPac	Central Pacific
CIC	Combat Information Center
C-in-C	Commander-in-Chief
CincPac	Commander-in-Chief, Pacific Fleet
CincPOA	Commander-in-Chief, Pacific Ocean Areas
CL	Light cruiser
CNO	Chief of Naval Operations
CO	Commanding officer
COC	Combat Operations Center
Col.	Colonel
ComAirPac	Commander, Aircraft, Pacific Fleet
ComAirSols	Air Command Solomons
ComFifthPhibFor	Commander, Fifth Amphibious Force
CominCh	Commander-in-Chief, U.S. Fleet [formerly CincUS]
ComSubPac	Commander, Submarines, Pacific Fleet
CruDiv	Cruiser division
CV	Heavy carrier
CVE	Escort carrier
CVL	Light carrier
DD	Destroyer
DE	Destroyer Escort
Div.	Division
division	USN tactical air element, e.g. four fighter planes
DSM	Distinguished Service Medal
ELD	East Longitude Date (west of International Date Line, one day later than WLD)
FDO	Fighter director officer or flight deck officer
FRUPac	Fleet Radio Unit Pacific
Gen.	General
GM	General Motors
IFF	Identification Friend or Foe
IGHQ	Imperial General Headquarters (Japan)
IJN	Imperial Japanese Navy

JCS	Joint Chiefs of Staff
JICPOA	Joint Intelligence Center, Pacific Ocean Area
LCI	Landing craft, infantry
Lt	Lieutenant
Lt (jg)	Lieutenant (junior grade)
LSO	Landing signal officer
LST	Landing ship, tank
LVT	Landing vehicle, tracked (amtrac)
NAG	Naval Air Group (*Kōkūtai*) (IJN)
NAS	Naval Air Station (USN)
NGS	Naval General Staff (Japan)
NWC	Naval War College (USN)
NYSB	New York Shipbuilding
ONI	Office of Naval Intelligence
Oplan	Operation Plan
OTC	Officer in tactical command
POA	Pacific Ocean Areas (U.S. command)
RCT	Regimental combat team
RI	Radio intelligence
screw	Propellor (of ship). Twin-screw means two propellors
section	USN tactical air element, e.g. two fighter planes
ServRon	Service Squadron (unit of supply ships, e.g. tankers)
SoPac	South Pacific
SWPA	Southwest Pacific Area (U.S. command)
TBS	Talk Between Ships, VHF voice radio (USN)
TF	Task Force
TG	Task Group
TransDiv	Transport division
USAF	United States Air Force
USMC	United States Marine Corps
USN	U.S. Navy (as applied to personnel means regular Navy, not USNR)
USNA	U.S. Naval Academy (Annapolis)
USNR	U.S. Naval Reserve
USSBS	United States Strategic Bombing Survey
VB	Bomber squadron

VF	Fighter squadron
VT	Torpedo bomber squadron
WLD	West Longitude Date (east of International Date Line, one day earlier than ELD)
XO	Executive officer (deputy to CO)

AIRCRAFT DESIGNATIONS (U.S.)

B-24	Consolidated Liberator heavy bomber (PB4Y)
F4U	Vought Corsair fighter
F6F	Grumman Hellcat fighter
FM-2	General Motors Wildcat (Grumman design)
PB4Y	Consolidated Liberator heavy bomber (B-24)
SB2C	Curtiss Helldiver dive bomber
SBD	Douglas Dauntless dive bomber
TBF	Grumman Avenger torpedo bomber
TBM	General Motors Avenger torpedo bomber (Grumman design)

AIRCRAFT DESIGNATIONS AND ALLIED CODENAMES (JAPANESE NAVY)

Betty	Mitsubishi G4M twin-engined medium bomber
Emily	Kawanishi H8K four-engined flying boat
Frances	Yokosuka P1Y twin-engined medium bomber (*Ginga*)
Jake	Aichi E13A reconnaissance seaplane
Jill	Nakajima B6N torpedo bomber (*Tenzan*)
Judy	Yokosuka D4Y dive bomber (*Suisei*)
Kate	Nakajima B5N torpedo bomber
Myrt	Nakajima C6N reconnaissance plane (*Saiun*)
Val	Aichi D3A dive bomber
Zeke	Mitsubishi A6M fighter (*Zero-sen*)

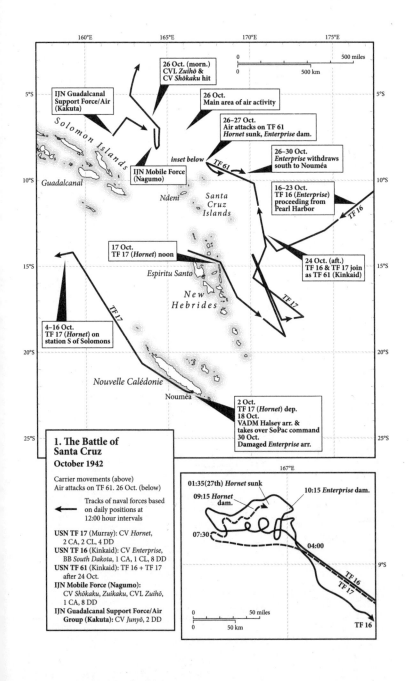

26 Oct. (morn.)
CVL *Zuihō* &
CV *Shōkaku* hit

IJN Guadalcanal
Support Force/Air
(Kakuta)

26 Oct.
Main area of air activity

26–27 Oct.
Air attacks on TF 61
Hornet sunk, *Enterprise* dam.

26–30 Oct.
Enterprise withdraws
south to Nouméa

inset below TF 61

IJN Mobile Force
(Nagumo)

16–23 Oct.
TF 16 (*Enterprise*)
proceeding from
Pearl Harbor

Solomon Islands

Guadalcanal

Ndeni

*Santa
Cruz
Islands*

TF 16

17 Oct.
TF 17 (*Hornet*) noon

24 Oct. (aft.)
TF 16 & TF 17 join
as TF 61 (Kinkaid)

Espiritu Santo

*New
Hebrides*

TF 17

TF 17

4–16 Oct.
TF 17 (*Hornet*) on
station S of Solomons

Nouvelle Calédonie

Nouméa

2 Oct.
TF 17 (*Hornet*) dep.
18 Oct.
VADM Halsey arr. &
takes over SoPac command
30 Oct.
Damaged *Enterprise* arr.

1. The Battle of Santa Cruz
October 1942

Carrier movements (above)
Air attacks on TF 61. 26 Oct. (below)

⟵ Tracks of naval forces based
on daily positions at
12:00 hour intervals

USN TF 17 (Murray): CV *Hornet*,
2 CA, 2 CL, 4 DD
USN TF 16 (Kinkaid): CV *Enterprise*,
BB *South Dakota*, 1 CA, 1 CL, 8 DD
USN TF 61 (Kinkaid): TF 16 + TF 17
after 24 Oct.
IJN Mobile Force (Nagumo):
CV *Shōkaku*, *Zuikaku*, CVL *Zuihō*,
1 CA, 8 DD
IJN Guadalcanal Support Force/Air
Group (Kakuta): CV *Junyō*, 2 DD

01:35(27th) *Hornet* sunk

10:15 *Enterprise* dam.

09:15 *Hornet*
dam.

07:30

04:00

TF 16
TF 17

TF 16

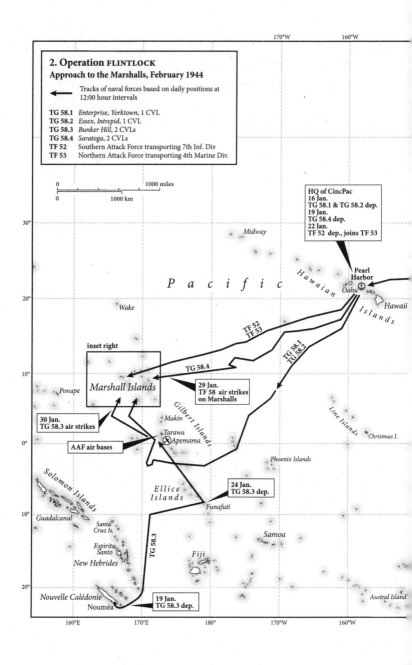

2. Operation FLINTLOCK
Approach to the Marshalls, February 1944

Tracks of naval forces based on daily positions at
12:00 hour intervals

TG 58.1 *Enterprise, Yorktown*, 1 CVL
TG 58.2 *Essex, Intrepid*, 1 CVL
TG 58.3 *Bunker Hill*, 2 CVLs
TG 58.4 *Saratoga*, 2 CVLs
TF 52 Southern Attack Force transporting 7th Inf. Div
TF 53 Northern Attack Force transporting 4th Marine Div.

0 — 1000 miles
0 — 1000 km

HQ of CincPac
16 Jan.
TG 58.1 & TG 58.2 dep.
19 Jan.
TG 58.4 dep.
22 Jan.
TF 52 dep., joins TF 53

P a c i f i c

Midway

Pearl Harbor
Oahu

Hawaiian Islands

Hawaii

Wake

TF 52
TF 53

TG 58.1
TG 58.2

inset right

TG 58.4

Marshall Islands

29 Jan.
TF 58 air strikes
on Marshalls

Ponape

30 Jan.
TG 58.3 air strikes

Makin

Gilbert Islands

Line Islands

Christmas I.

Tarawa
Apemama

AAF air bases

Phoenix Islands

Solomon Islands

Ellice Islands

24 Jan.
TG 58.3 dep.

Guadalcanal

Funafuti

Santa Cruz Is.

Samoa

Espiritu Santo

TG 58.3

Fiji

New Hebrides

Nouvelle Calédonie

19 Jan.
TG 58.3 dep.

Austral Island

Nouméa

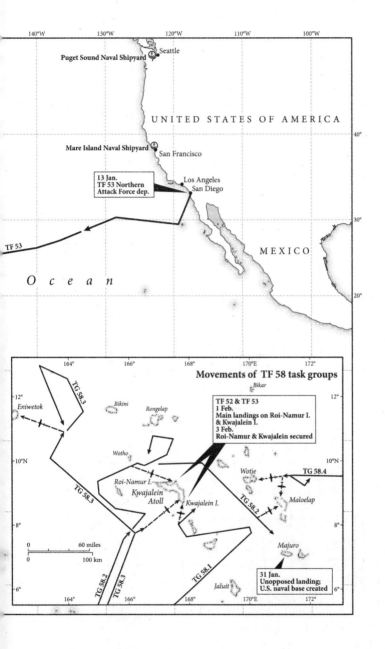

Puget Sound Naval Shipyard • Seattle

UNITED STATES OF AMERICA

Mare Island Naval Shipyard • San Francisco

Los Angeles
San Diego

13 Jan.
TF 53 Northern
Attack Force dep.

TF 53

MEXICO

O c e a n

Movements of TF 58 task groups

TG 58.3

Bikar

Eniwetok

Bikini

Rongelap

Wotho

TF 52 & TF 53
1 Feb.
Main landings on Roi-Namur I.
& Kwajalein I.
3 Feb.
Roi-Namur & Kwajalein secured

Wotje

TG 58.4

TG 58.3

Roi-Namur I.
Kwajalein
Atoll

Kwajalein I.

TG 58.2

Maloelap

0   60 miles
0   100 km

TG 58.2

Majuro

TG 58.2 TG 58.3

TG 58.1

Jaluit

31 Jan.
Unopposed landing;
U.S. naval base created

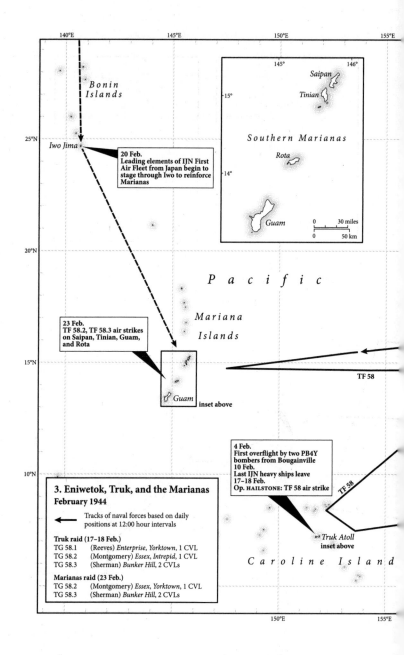

140°E 145°E 150°E 155°E

Bonin Islands

145° 146°

Saipan

15° *Tinian*

25°N

Iwo Jima

20 Feb.
Leading elements of IJN First
Air Fleet from Japan begin to
stage through Iwo to reinforce
Marianas

Southern Marianas

Rota

14°

0   30 miles
0   50 km

Guam

20°N

P a c i f i c

M a r i a n a

I s l a n d s

23 Feb.
TF 58.2, TF 58.3 air strikes
on Saipan, Tinian, Guam,
and Rota

15°N

TF 58

Guam   inset above

4 Feb.
First overflight by two PB4Y
bombers from Bougainville
10 Feb.
Last IJN heavy ships leave
17–18 Feb.
Op. HAILSTONE: TF 58 air strike

TF 58

10°N

3. Eniwetok, Truk, and the Marianas
February 1944

Tracks of naval forces based on daily
positions at 12:00 hour intervals

Truk raid (17–18 Feb.)
TG 58.1   (Reeves) *Enterprise, Yorktown*, 1 CVL
TG 58.2   (Montgomery) *Essex, Intrepid*, 1 CVL
TG 58.3   (Sherman) *Bunker Hill*, 2 CVLs

Marianas raid (23 Feb.)
TG 58.2   (Montgomery) *Essex, Yorktown*, 1 CVL
TG 58.3   (Sherman) *Bunker Hill*, 2 CVLs

Truk Atoll
inset above

C a r o l i n e   I s l a n d

150°E 155°E

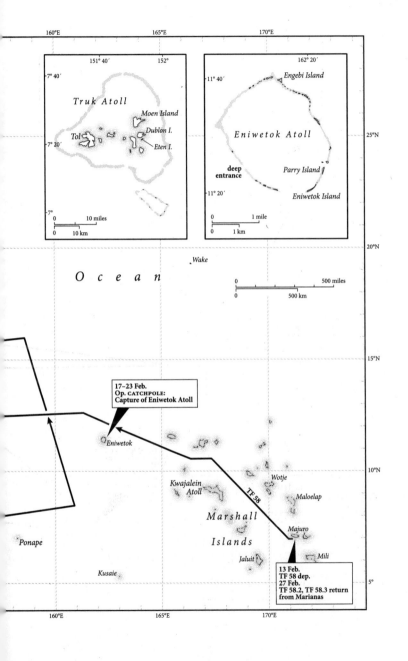

Truk Atoll

151° 40′   152°

7° 40′

Moen Island

Dublon I.

Tol

Eten I.

7° 20′

7°

| 0 | 10 miles |
| 0 | 10 km |

Eniwetok Atoll

162° 20′

11° 40′   Engebi Island

25°N

Parry Island

deep
entrance

11° 20′   Eniwetok Island

| 0 | 1 mile |
| 0 | 1 km |

20°N

O c e a n   · Wake

| 0 | 500 miles |
| 0 | 500 km |

15°N

17–23 Feb.
Op. CATCHPOLE:
Capture of Eniwetok Atoll

Eniwetok

Kwajalein
Atoll

Wotje   10°N

TF 58

Maloelap

M a r s h a l l

Majuro

· Ponape   *I s l a n d s*

Mili

Jaluit

13 Feb.
TF 58 dep.
27 Feb.
TF 58.2, TF 58.3 return
from Marianas

Kusaie   5°

160°E   165°E   170°E

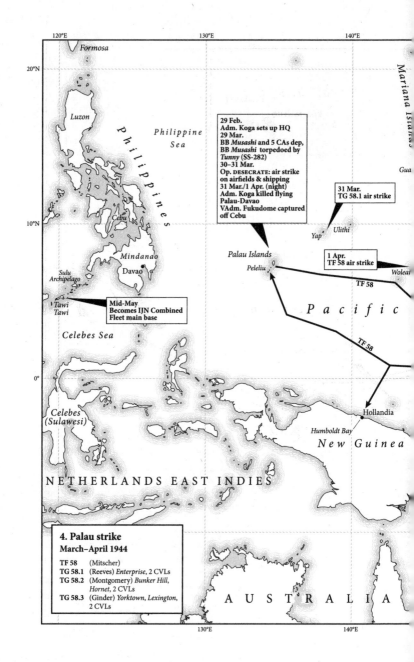

120°E **130°E** **140°E**

20°N

Formosa

Luzon

Philippine Sea

Cebu

10°N

Mindanao

Davao

Sulu Archipelago

Tawi Tawi

Celebes Sea

Mariana Islands

Gua[...]

Yap *Ulithi*

Palau Islands

Peleliu

Woleai

TF 58

P a c i f i c

TF 58

0°

Celebes (Sulawesi)

Hollandia

Humboldt Bay

New Guinea

NETHERLANDS EAST INDIES

AUSTRALIA

29 Feb.
Adm. Koga sets up HQ
29 Mar.
BB *Musashi* and 5 CAs dep,
BB *Musashi* torpedoed by
Tunny (SS-282)
30–31 Mar.
Op. DESECRATE: air strike
on airfields & shipping
31 Mar./1 Apr. (night)
Adm. Koga killed flying
Palau-Davao
VAdm. Fukudome captured
off Cebu

31 Mar.
TG 58.1 air strike

1 Apr.
TF 58 air strike

Mid-May
Becomes IJN Combined
Fleet main base

4. Palau strike
March–April 1944

TF 58   (Mitscher)
TG 58.1   (Reeves) *Enterprise*, 2 CVLs
TG 58.2   (Montgomery) *Bunker Hill*,
           Hornet, 2 CVLs
TG 58.3   (Ginder) *Yorktown*, *Lexington*,
           2 CVLs

130°E **140°E**

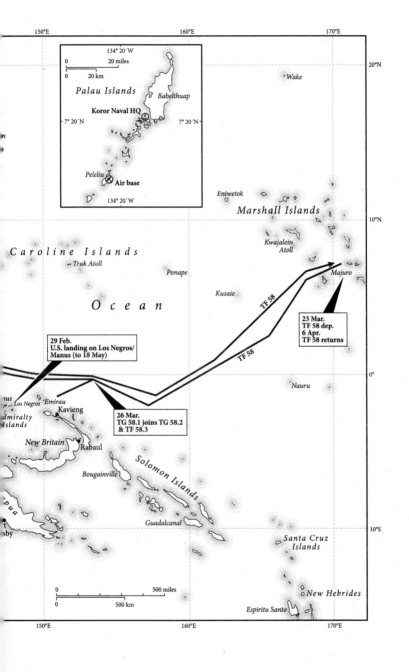

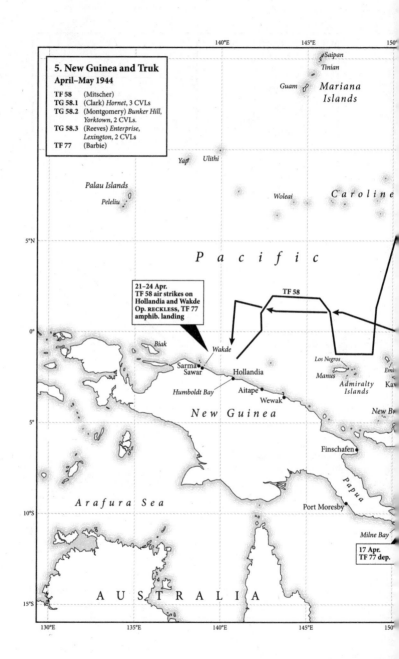

5. New Guinea and Truk
April–May 1944

TF 58   (Mitscher)
TG 58.1 (Clark) *Hornet*, 3 CVLs
TG 58.2 (Montgomery) *Bunker Hill*,
        Yorktown, 2 CVLs.
TG 58.3 (Reeves) *Enterprise*,
        Lexington, 2 CVLs
TF 77   (Barbie)

Saipan
Tinian
Guam *Mariana*
      Islands

140°E   145°E   150°

Yap *Ulithi*

Palau Islands
Peleliu

Woleai   C a r o l i n e

5°N

P a c i f i c

21–24 Apr.
TF 58 air strikes on
Hollandia and Wakde
Op. RECKLESS, TF 77
amphib. landing

TF 58

0°

Biak   *Wakde*

Sarma   *Hollandia*   *Los Negros* *Emi*
Sawar   *Manus*   *Ka*
Humboldt Bay *Aitape*   *Admiralty*
         Wewak   *Islands*

New B

N e w   G u i n e a

5°

Finschafen

A r a f u r a   S e a

Port Moresby

10°S

Milne Bay

17 Apr.
TF 77 dep.

A U S T R A L I A

15°S

130°E   135°E   140°E   145°E   150°

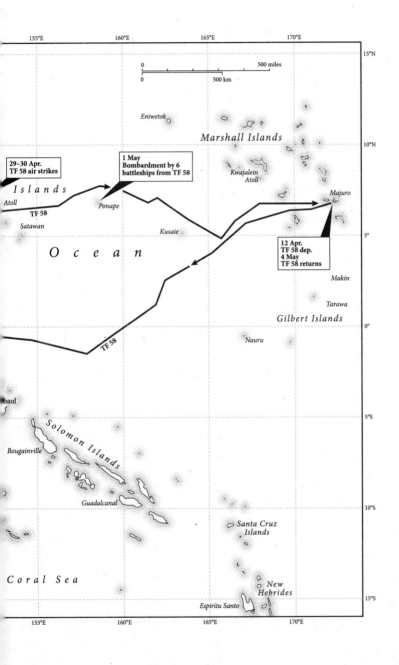

155°E 160°E 165°E 170°E

15°N

0   500 miles

0   500 km

Eniwetok

Marshall Islands

10°N

**29–30 Apr.
TF 58 air strikes**

**1 May
Bombardment by 6
battleships from TF 58**

*Kwajalein
Atoll*

I s l a n d s

Atoll

Majuro

TF 58

Ponape

Satawan

Kusaie

5°

**12 Apr.
TF 58 dep.
4 May
TF 58 returns**

O   c   e   a   n

Makin

Tarawa

Gilbert Islands

0°

Nauru

TF 58

baul

5°S

S o l o m o n   I s l a n d s

Bougainville

Guadalcanal

10°S

*Santa Cruz
Islands*

Coral Sea

*New
Hebrides*

15°S

Espiritu Santo

155°E 160°E 165°E 170°E

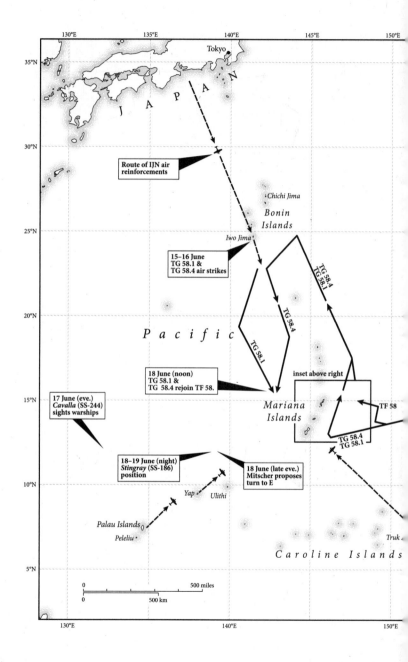

130°E · 135°E · 140°E · 145°E · 150°E

Tokyo

35°N

J A P A N

30°N

Route of IJN air reinforcements

·Chichi Jima

Bonin Islands

25°N

Iwo Jima·

15–16 June TG 58.1 & TG 58.4 air strikes

TG 58.4 / TG 58.1

P a c i f i c

20°N

TG 58.4

TG 58.1

inset above right

18 June (noon) TG 58.1 & TG 58.4 rejoin TF 58.

15°N

Mariana Islands

TF 58

17 June (eve.) *Cavalla* (SS-244) sights warships

TG 58.4 / TG 58.1

18–19 June (night) *Stingray* (SS-186) position

18 June (late eve.) Mitscher proposes turn to E

10°N

Yap · · Ulithi

Palau Islands ◦

Peleliu ·

Truk

C a r o l i n e   I s l a n d s

5°N

0 ——— 500 miles
0 ——— 500 km

130°E · 140°E · 150°E

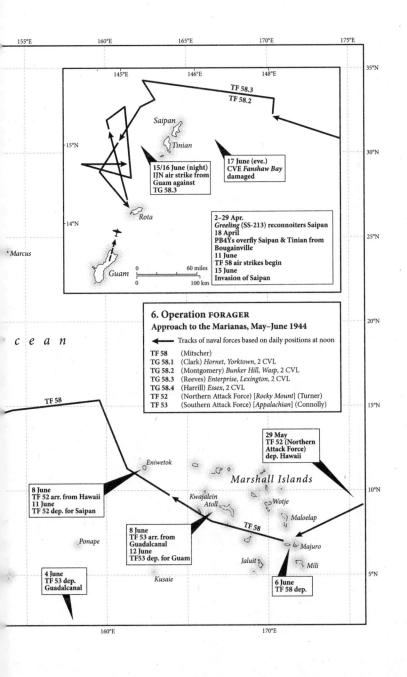

155°E 160°E 165°E 170°E 175°E

35°N
145°E 146°E 148°E

TF 58.3
TF 58.2

Saipan

Tinian

15°N 30°N

15/16 June (night) IJN air strike from Guam against TG 58.3

17 June (eve.) CVE *Fanshaw Bay* damaged

Rota

14°N 25°N

**2–29 Apr. *Greeling* (SS-213) reconnoiters Saipan
18 April PB4Ys overfly Saipan & Tinian from Bougainville
11 June TF 58 air strikes begin
15 June Invasion of Saipan**

Marcus

Guam

0 ——— 60 miles
0 ——— 100 km

6. Operation FORAGER
Approach to the Marianas, May–June 1944

20°N

⟵ Tracks of naval forces based on daily positions at noon

TF 58	(Mitscher)
TG 58.1	(Clark) *Hornet, Yorktown*, 2 CVL
TG 58.2	(Montgomery) *Bunker Hill, Wasp*, 2 CVL
TG 58.3	(Reeves) *Enterprise, Lexington*, 2 CVL
TG 58.4	(Harrill) *Essex*, 2 CVL
TF 52	(Northern Attack Force) [*Rocky Mount*] (Turner)
TF 53	(Southern Attack Force) [*Appalachian*] (Connolly)

c e a n

TF 58

29 May TF 52 (Northern Attack Force) dep. Hawaii

15°N

Eniwetok

Marshall Islands

**8 June TF 52 arr. from Hawaii
11 June TF 52 dep. for Saipan**

Kwajalein Atoll

Wotje

Maloelap

10°N

**8 June TF 53 arr. from Guadalcanal
12 June TF53 dep. for Guam**

TF 58

Ponape

Majuro

Jaluit

Mili

4 June TF 53 dep. Guadalcanal

Kusaie

6 June TF 58 dep.

5°N

160°E 170°E

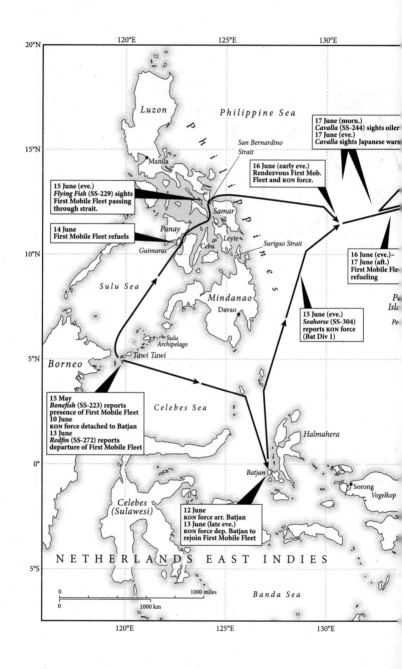

20°N

120°E · 125°E · 130°E

Luzon · *Philippine Sea*

17 June (morn.)
Cavalla (SS-244) sights oiler
17 June (eve.)
Cavalla sights Japanese wars[

15°N

San Bernardino Strait

Manila

16 June (early eve.)
Rendezvous First Mob. Fleet and KON force.

15 June (eve.)
Flying Fish (SS-229) sights First Mobile Fleet passing through strait.

P
h
i
l
i
p
p
i
n
e
s

Samar

14 June
First Mobile Fleet refuels

Panay

Cebu *Leyte*

Guimaras *Surigao Strait*

10°N

**16 June (eve.)–
17 June (aft.)**
First Mobile Fle[
refueling

Sulu Sea

Mindanao

Davao

P
Isl

Pe

15 June (eve.)
Seahorse (SS-304) reports KON force (Bat Div 1)

5°N

Sulu Archipelago

Tawi Tawi

Borneo

15 May
Bonefish (SS-223) reports presence of First Mobile Fleet
10 June
KON force detached to Batjan
13 June
Redfin (SS-272) reports departure of First Mobile Fleet

Celebes Sea

Halmahera

0°

Batjan

Sorong
Vogelkop

*Celebes
(Sulawesi)*

12 June
KON force arr. Batjan
13 June (late eve.)
KON force dep. Batjan to rejoin First Mobile Fleet

5°S

N E T H E R L A N D S   E A S T   I N D I E S

0 · 1000 miles
0 · 1000 km

Banda Sea

120°E · 125°E · 130°E

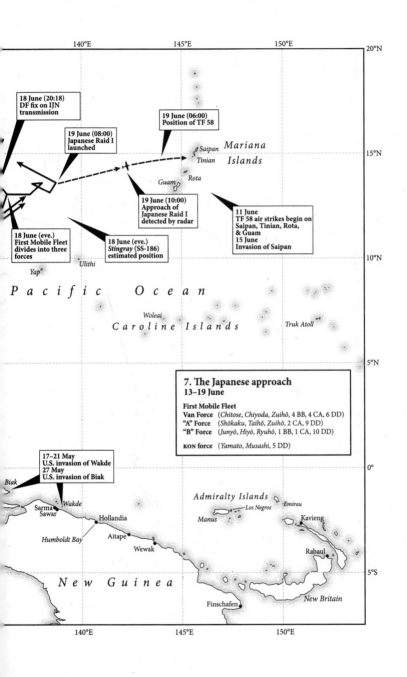

18 June (20:18)
DF fix on IJN
transmission

19 June (06:00)
Position of TF 58

19 June (08:00)
Japanese Raid I
launched

Saipan   *Mariana*
Tinian   *Islands*

Guam   Rota

19 June (10:00)
Approach of
Japanese Raid I
detected by radar

11 June
TF 58 air strikes begin on
Saipan, Tinian, Rota,
& Guam
15 June
Invasion of Saipan

18 June (eve.)
First Mobile Fleet
divides into three
forces

18 June (eve.)
Stingray (SS-186)
estimated position

Yap°   Ulithi

P a c i f i c   O c e a n

Woleai
C a r o l i n e   I s l a n d s   Truk Atoll

7. The Japanese approach
13–19 June

First Mobile Fleet
Van Force (*Chitose, Chiyoda, Zuihō,* 4 BB, 4 CA, 6 DD)
"A" Force (*Shōkaku, Taihō, Zuihō,* 2 CA, 9 DD)
"B" Force (*Junyō, Hiyō, Ryuhō,* 1 BB, 1 CA, 10 DD)

KON force (*Yamato, Musashi,* 5 DD)

17–21 May
U.S. invasion of Wakde
27 May
U.S. invasion of Biak

Biak   *Admiralty Islands*   Emirau

Wakde   Los Negros   Kavieng
Sarma
Sawar   Hollandia   Manus

Humboldt Bay   Aitape
Wewak   Rabaul

N e w   G u i n e a   *New Britain*

Finschafen

8. Sea/air engagement
19 June 1944

TF 58 (Mitscher) Inset below right shows disposition *c.* 11:00
TG 58.1 (Clark) *Hornet, Yorktown, Bataan, Belleau Wood,* 3 CA, 1 CL, 14 DD
TG 58.2 (Montgomery) *Bunker Hill, Wasp, Cabot, Monterey,* 4 CA, 12 DD
TG 58.3 (Reeves) *Enterprise, Lexington, Princeton, San Jacinto,* 1 CA, 4 CL, 13 DD
TG 58.4 (Harrill) *Essex, Cowpens, Langley,* 4 CL, 14 DD
TG 58.7 (Lee) 7 BB, 4 CA, 13 DD

First Mobile Fleet (Ozawa)
Van Force (Kurita) *Chitose, Chiyoda, Zuihō,* 4 BB, 7 CA, 8 DD
"A" Force (Ozawa) *Shōkaku, Taihō, Zuikaku,* 2 CA, 1 CL, 7 DD
"B" Force (Joshima) *Junyō, Hiyō, Ryuhō,* 1 BB, 1 CA, 8 DD

Philippine Sea

Van Force

08:00
Van Force launches Raid I

10:30

12:00

Raid II

05:30

Raid I

"B" Force

"A" Force

21:00 (18th)

Van Force

04:30

Raid III

08:45–09:02
"A" Force launches Raid II

08:07

"B" Force

"A" Force

10:00
"B" Force launches Raid III

05:30

Raid IV (Force "B")

03:00

09:10
Albacore* torpedoes *Taihō

Raid IV (Force "A")

11:35
Cavalla* torpedoes *Shōkaku

15:32
***Taihō* sinks**

15:01
***Shōkaku* sinks**

11:00
"A" Force and "B" Force launch Raid IV

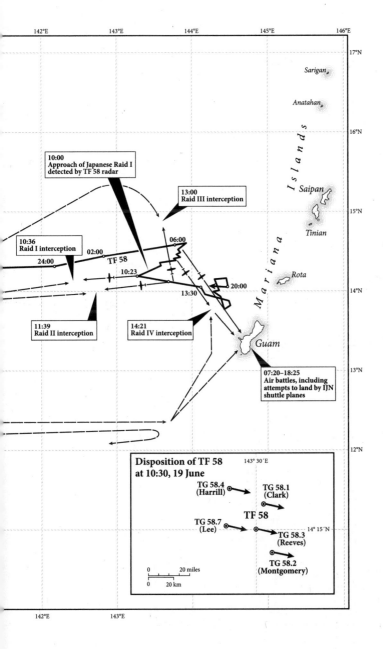

142°E 143°E 144°E 145°E 146°E

17°N

Sarigan

Anatahan

16°N

Mariana Islands

10:00
Approach of Japanese Raid I
detected by TF 58 radar

13:00
Raid III interception

15°N

Saipan

Tinian

10:36
Raid I interception

02:00

24:00   TF 58   06:00

10:23

Rota

20:00

13:30

14°N

11:39
Raid II interception

14:21
Raid IV interception

Guam

07:20–18:25
Air battles, including
attempts to land by IJN
shuttle planes

13°N

12°N

Disposition of TF 58
at 10:30, 19 June   143° 30´E

TG 58.4
(Harrill)   TG 58.1
(Clark)

TF 58

TG 58.7
(Lee)   TG 58.3
(Reeves)   14° 15´N

TG 58.2
(Montgomery)

0   20 miles

0   20 km

142°E   143°E

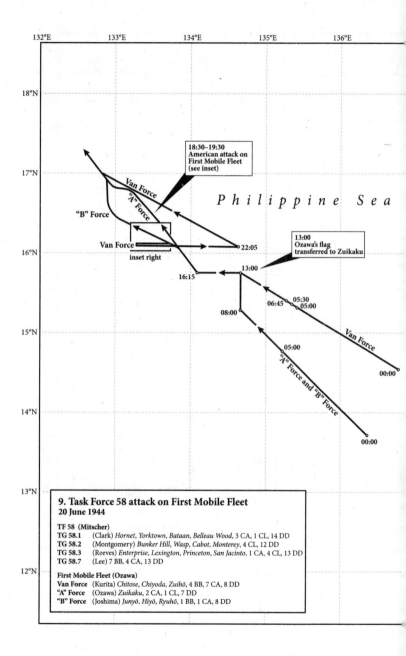

132°E   133°E   134°E   135°E   136°E

18°N

17°N

Philippine Sea

18:30–19:30
American attack on
First Mobile Fleet
(see inset)

Van Force

"A" Force

"B" Force

Van Force

inset right

16°N

22:05

13:00
Ozawa's flag
transferred to Zuikaku

13:00

16:15

13:00

08:00

06:45
05:30
05:00

Van Force

15°N

05:00

"A" Force and "B" Force

00:00

14°N

00:00

13°N

9. Task Force 58 attack on First Mobile Fleet
20 June 1944

TF 58   (Mitscher)
TG 58.1   (Clark) *Hornet, Yorktown, Bataan, Belleau Wood*, 3 CA, 1 CL, 14 DD
TG 58.2   (Montgomery) *Bunker Hill, Wasp, Cabot, Monterey*, 4 CL, 12 DD
TG 58.3   (Reeves) *Enterprise, Lexington, Princeton, San Jacinto*, 1 CA, 4 CL, 13 DD
TG 58.7   (Lee) 7 BB, 4 CA, 13 DD

First Mobile Fleet (Ozawa)
Van Force   (Kurita) *Chitose, Chiyoda, Zuihō*, 4 BB, 7 CA, 8 DD
"A" Force   (Ozawa) *Zuikaku*, 2 CA, 1 CL, 7 DD
"B" Force   (Joshima) *Junyō, Hiyō, Ryuhō*, 1 BB, 1 CA, 8 DD

12°N

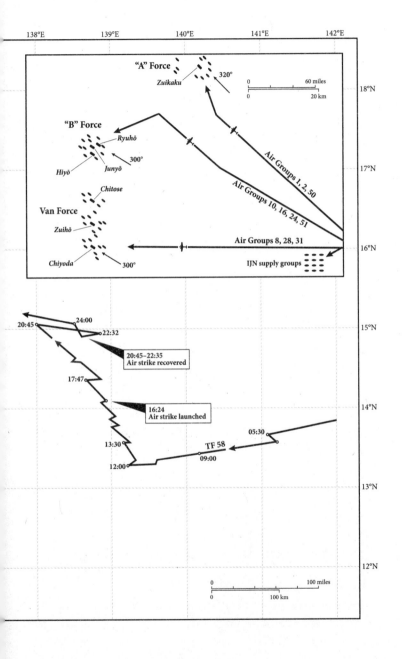

"A" Force
Zuikaku
320°

"B" Force
Ryuhō
Hiyō   *Junyō*
300°

Van Force
Chitose
Zuihō
Chiyoda
300°

Air Groups 1, 2, 50
Air Groups 10, 16, 24, 51
Air Groups 8, 28, 31
IJN supply groups

0 — 60 miles
0 — 20 km

24:00
20:45
22:32

20:45–22:35
Air strike recovered

17:47

16:24
Air strike launched

13:30
12:00

05:30
TF 58
09:00

0 — 100 miles
0 — 100 km

INTRODUCTION
Fourteen Months Earlier

Monday, 26 October 1942, had been a very hard test for the U.S. Navy. Now, in the dark Pacific night near the Santa Cruz Islands (northeast of Guadalcanal), USS *Hornet* had been reduced to a burning, abandoned hulk. The 20,000-ton aircraft carrier had been America's newest. Destroyers *Mustin* and *Arnold* stood by to finish her off, but sixteen torpedoes fired at point blank range missed or failed to detonate. In the early hours of Tuesday the grim task of destruction was efficiently completed by two pursuing Japanese destroyers; at 0135 on Tuesday the great ship finally slipped beneath the waves.

Meanwhile, the rest of Rear Adm. Thomas Kinkaid's Task Force 61 (TF 61) was "retiring" hastily to the southeast. The Imperial Japanese Navy (IJN) was left in command of the stretch of ocean north of the vital island battlefield of Guadalcanal.

Monday's battle had begun in the early morning.[1] TF 61, with Kinkaid as "officer in tactical command" (OTC), was steaming west in two groups, positioned initially about 20 miles apart. Each group was made up of a carrier, escorted by a few large surface ships and half a dozen destroyers. Each had its own task force designation, within the new TF 61. TF 16, commanded by Kinkaid himself, was organized around carrier *Enterprise*. TF 17, under Rear Adm. George Murray, was centered on the ill-fated *Hornet*. Kinkaid was operating under the overall command of Vice Adm. William F. ("Bill") Halsey, the new commander of the U.S. Navy's South Pacific (SoPac) "theater." Halsey and his headquarters were located far away, 900 miles to the south, at Nouméa in the French colony of Nouvelle-Calédonie.

A wholly new form of naval warfare had emerged in the Pacific in 1942. The weapons and tactics for sea/air carrier battles were the same for both the Japanese and the Americans. In traditional gunnery battles like Trafalgar, Tsushima, or Jutland, columns of ships had fought within visual range. Now they were 200 miles apart. In addition, the Battles of the Coral Sea and Midway in May and June 1942 had shown the limitations of fleet air defense. As one American newspaperman later put it, getting in close enough to deliver the first blow by means of a dawn attack was "as important in a carrier duel as it is in a barroom brawl."[2] Air search, especially at dawn, was crucial to locate the target, as a fast-moving fleet could change its position by 250 miles or more during the night.

Flight operations had begun in the early-morning darkness. On both sides search planes set off from carrier flight decks (the Japanese also catapulted floatplanes from their cruisers). Successful sightings of the opposing fleets were made by these scouts at about 0630, an hour after sunrise.[3] By 0740, two *Enterprise* search planes had actually succeeded in dropping bombs on the flight deck of a light carrier in the Japanese main force, preventing the takeoff and landing of her planes.[4]

Both sides launched their first big "deckload" strikes between 0700 and 0730. The attack planes were dive bombers and torpedo planes, with crews of two or three airmen. Smaller, single-seat fighter planes provided interceptor cover over the fleets (the "combat air patrol" or CAP) or escorted formations of attack planes. At 0830 Kinkaid was alerted by his own outbound aircraft that an enemy dive-bomber force was approaching. It was about 60 miles out, flying at 12,000 feet. Fifteen minutes later he sent out a warning: "Prepare to repel air attack."[5]

A coordinated attack on *Hornet*, situated furthest to the west of the two American carriers, began at 0910. About forty Japanese planes took part, deckload strikes from two carriers. Half were "Val" dive bombers and half "Kate" torpedo planes.[6] Four bombs and two torpedoes hit their target; in addition, two pilots actually crashed their Vals into *Hornet*, one of them hitting her superstructure. Floyd Beaver, a signalman stationed a dozen miles away to the east, on the bridge of *Enterprise*, later described his memory of the attack.

Dive-bombers plunged down on the writhing carrier, and torpedo planes seemed to crawl low over the water against her. Actually they were flying fast, but distance made everything seem slow and deliberate. Even the [AA] shells exploding over the *Hornet* seemed to explode slowly, their dark puffs seeming to appear out of nothing, like dropped ink on the pale blue cloth of the sky.[7]

Hornet was now on fire; nearly a hundred of her crewmen were dead, and many more were wounded. Her engines had stopped, electric power had cut out. The ship was unable to make headway or operate aircraft. Rear Adm. Kinkaid, too, could see the faraway column of black smoke; he sent a signal to Halsey in faraway Nouméa: "*Hornet* hurt."

For the Japanese, the attack on *Hornet* achieved its objective. But, pressed home through defending fighters and heavy AA (anti-aircraft) fire, the cost had been extremely high. From this first strike, seventeen out of twenty-one Vals and sixteen of twenty Kates would fail to return.[8] Fortunately for Kinkaid, *Enterprise* was not attacked at this point. Ten miles to the northeast, she and her task force were partly hidden by a rain squall.

Some 200 miles to the west of the burning *Hornet* was the main Japanese fleet. There the American deckload strike had arrived at about 0930. A squadron of Douglas SBD Dauntless dive bombers, launched from *Hornet* two hours earlier, dove on one of the enemy heavy carriers. Her flight deck was hit by four bombs. Like *Hornet*, the Japanese "flattop" was now unable to operate aircraft, but she was could at least still steam at full speed.[9]

The second deckload strike of Japanese attackers from their main force began arriving over Kinkaid's fleet an hour after the first, from about 1010. These planes had begun their launch at 0810. The enemy airmen were now hunting the undamaged *Enterprise*. Nineteen Val dive bombers took part in the first stage of this attack. The "Big E" was luckier than her sister ship, although she was hit just after 1015 by two small bombs. A second wave of sixteen Kates roared in thirteen minutes later, but these torpedo bombers failed to achieve any hits on the wildly maneuvering American carrier. Beaver, on the bridge of what was now the main target, recalled that the enemy "were strung out like tin ducks in a shooting gallery" and suffered heavy damage from the newly mounted 40-mm AA guns. The Kates "simply dipped into the sea and disappeared in a burst of white water." Total losses of the main-force second strike were again heavy: twelve Vals and ten Kates, as well as two escorting Zeros.[10]

A few minutes later, just after 1100, a deckload first strike of twelve Zeros and seventeen Val dive bombers arrived from a fourth Japanese carrier. This ship, operating independently from the other three, had originally been located 100 miles to the west of them. The planes attacked the *Enterprise* task force. Like the earlier strike they suffered heavy losses. Only the fighter escort and six of seventeen Vals returned to their carrier.[11]

Meanwhile, the American second strike, which *Hornet* had sent out at 0810 (before she was attacked), reached the Japanese main force at about 0950. The small group of nine SBD Dauntless dive bombers and eight bomb-carrying Grumman TBF Avengers was well short of "deck-load" strength. These planes did not succeed in attacking any of the Japanese carriers, although they damaged several cruisers. Meanwhile, the small first strike launched from *Enterprise*, beginning at 0747, caused no damage to the main enemy force. This strike group was made up of only seven TBFs and three SBDs, escorted by eight fighters. *Enterprise* did not have aircraft available for a second strike. After 1010, moreover, her crew would be preoccupied with recovering their own planes, and those of the more badly damaged *Hornet*.

The Japanese kept coming. One of the three carriers in their main force was still undamaged and she was now operating alongside the carrier that had been sailing independently.[12] Just after 1300 small attacks were launched, by Kate torpedo planes from one carrier, Val dive bombers from the other. About two hours later, at 1455, the Kates were spotted by *Hornet* and her escorts.

At 1335, an hour and a quarter before these attackers arrived, Kinkaid had pulled *Enterprise* away to the southeast. Damaged and overloaded with aircraft, it seemed necessary to lengthen her distance from the enemy, even if this meant abandoning *Hornet*. The admiral's war diary—written in the third person—gave his reasoning:

With the HORNET out of action, the extent of damage to the ENTERPRISE not fully determined, and the probability that there were one or two undamaged enemy carriers in the battle area which had not been sighted by our forces, the decision of Commander Task Force 61 [Kinkaid] to retire at high speed to the southeast was made without hesitation.[13]

Signalman Beach on the bridge of *Enterprise* saw that *Hornet* had become just a smudge of smoke over the western horizon. Alvin Kernan, a young rating aboard *Hornet*, watched from the opposite perspective. *Enterprise* disappeared to the east: "As she became smaller and then went hull down on the horizon, the war moved away from us, and with an awful feeling of loneliness we turned to the business of survival."[14] *Hornet*, ablaze, listing, and dead in the water, now had no air cover. Effective damage control had kept the ship from sinking after the first strike in the morning. Escorting destroyers, lying alongside, had sprayed water onto the fires burning within her hull. The big carrier was for a time towed slowly to the east by a cruiser. Some progress had been made in restoring power, but this had to be given up when, at 1523, a Kate dropped down in an end-game attack and put a fatal third torpedo into the crippled flattop. Three-quarters of an hour later, Vals hit *Hornet* with two more bombs.[15] The carrier's salvage was now impossible; in the next hour the remainder of her crew were taken off. Many Americans had lost their lives in the air attacks, but fortunately these made up only a comparatively small proportion of the ship's company, 118 out of about 2,200 men.

The naval battle of the Santa Cruz came near the turning point of the historic struggle for Guadalcanal Island. Japanese Army troops had seemed set to overrun the Henderson Field air base there. Two and a half weeks after Santa Cruz, on 14–16 November, U.S. Navy battleships, cruisers, and destroyers, supported by attack planes from the air base, would win two battles off Guadalcanal. Henderson Field held out, and three months later the Japanese were forced to evacuate their surviving forces from the island.

Taken on its own, however, the Battle of Santa Cruz was a major American naval defeat. The U.S. Navy lost one of its last two operational carriers in the Pacific, and the other suffered considerable damage; the Japanese lost no ships. The conclusion of the "Combat Narrative" prepared by the Office of Naval Intelligence (ONI) in Washington shortly afterward was understated but frank: "[T]he costly Battle of Santa Cruz, with the resultant reduction of our South Pacific carrier strength to one damaged vessel, was of dubious value to our cause." Fifty years later, in his authoritative account, the late Jon Prados came to the same conclusion: "[Japanese] Navy forces fought a pitched battle against an Allied fleet with several distinct advantages, and drove it from the field. The balance of losses was also unmistakable . . . The Imperial Navy's victory at Santa Cruz was a real one."[16] Several things explained this Japanese victory and the poor outcome for the Americans. Most obvious and most important, Kinkaid's fleet had been outnumbered. The United States was still fighting with its pre-war navy, the strength of which had been much reduced in the past eleven months. Of the carriers, *Lexington* had been lost in the Coral Sea in May, and *Yorktown* at Midway in June. *Wasp* had been sunk by a submarine near Guadalcanal in September, and *Saratoga* was in drydock at Pearl Harbor, undergoing repair for damage caused by a submarine torpedo. Despite the "decisive" defeat of the Japanese fleet at Midway, it was still capable of deploying more carriers and more planes. On 11 October five carriers of the Imperial Navy had been sent south toward Guadalcanal. On the 26th, 199 operational planes were available on the Japanese carriers; Kinkaid had only 130.[17]

Compounding this numerical weakness, the American command had limited information about the enemy's location and strength. At the earlier Battles of the Coral Sea and Midway American carrier task forces had benefitted from intelligence, primarily radio intelligence (RI). Japanese messages had been monitored and decrypted, providing the outnumbered American forces with the "priceless advantage" of being able to anticipate many of the enemy's movements. However, because the Japanese updated their ciphers and radio call signs in the late summer and autumn of 1942, this advantage had been temporarily nullified. In mid-October Japanese naval strength was seriously underestimated. In particular it had been thought that only two or three enemy carriers were on hand near the Solomon Islands, when in fact there were five. Another potential source of intelligence was the American submarine force, but in October 1942 not many modern boats were available and a number of them were being transferred from Pearl Harbor to Brisbane in eastern Australia. Task force movements before Santa Cruz were organized in haste, with no time to deploy the submarines in patrol lines.[18] In the methodically planned 1944 battles in the Philippine Sea and at Leyte Gulf, the numerous radar-equipped American submarines would provide priceless information about the enemy fleet and cause very significant damage.

In this situation, Halsey's orders as the theater commander were rash. The admiral had abruptly flown into his new South Pacific head-quarters (Nouméa) only a week before the Santa Cruz battle; this was on 18 October. His predecessor had been relieved for inactivity, and for his pessimism about the chances of holding Guadalcanal. The new "ComSoPac" was now eager to demonstrate that his ships and planes were playing an active role, and he hastily assembled TF 61 at sea.

Kinkaid's TF 16, with *Enterprise*, had actually left Pearl Harbor in Hawaii on 16 October, before Halsey's appointment. Meanwhile, Murray's TF 17, with *Hornet*, had departed for the north from Nouméa on 3 October. On 22 October Halsey sent orders to Kinkaid to make a "sweep" though the waters near the Santa Cruz Islands, once the two task forces had begun operating in tandem (the rendezvous took place only on the 24th). The eminent naval historian E. B. Potter argued that

> Halsey was undoubtedly trying to reproduce the conditions of the Battle of Midway which he had studied minutely. In that battle the American carrier commanders had achieved victory by learning the enemy's location before he learned theirs. This knowledge enabled the Americans to get the jump on the enemy while his planes, armed and fueled, were on deck.[19]

This assessment of Halsey's intentions may or may not be correct, but in any event ComSoPac did not make clear how far north TF 61 was to proceed.[20] Another able historian, John Lundstrom, has described Halsey's initiative as "a dangerous, even foolhardy gesture." Elsewhere Lundstrom judged that "Halsey was very lucky to escape total disaster had the *Enterprise* and all the carrier aircraft accompanied the *Hornet* to the bottom of the sea."[21]

Rear Adm. Kinkaid, who was executing Halsey's orders on the spot, had little experience in carrier aviation. He was a gunnery specialist, and in the early months of the war had commanded a division of four cruisers. His first direct carrier command had come after Midway, when the *Enterprise* task force (TF 16) was assigned to him. Rear Adm. Murray in TF 17 had twenty years' experience as a naval aviator but, as already mentioned, he and Kinkaid only began to operate together on 24 October (with the more senior Kinkaid as OTC). This was only two days before the battle. The two admirals had little chance to coordinate their plans before or during the fighting. Afterward, Murray was critical of some of Kinkaid's decisions. Vice Adm. John Towers, the newly appointed coordinator of Pacific Fleet aviation (ComAirPac) blamed Kinkaid for the loss of *Hornet*. In November Rear Adm. Frederick ("Ted") Sherman, an officer with greater aviation experience, took over as commander of TF 61. Kinkaid was apparently surprised by his relief, and angry. From hindsight the step seems justified.[22]

On the other side of the battle was the navy that invented the carrier task force. This was the *Kidō Butai* or "Mobile Force" which raided Pearl Harbor on 7 December 1941, with six aircraft carriers and over 400 planes. Kinkaid faced the most experienced carrier-fleet commanders in the world. Vice Adm. Nagumo Chūichi, with his aviator chief of staff, Rear Adm. Kusaka Ryūnosuke, had led the attacks on Pearl Harbor, Darwin (Australia), and Ceylon. In August 1942 they fought the Battle of the Eastern Solomons. Midway in June had been a disaster, but many lessons had been learned. Nagumo, with Kusaka, commanded the main Japanese carrier force at Santa Cruz. Rear Adm. Kakuta Kakuji, in charge of the smaller carrier force (with carrier *Junyō*) at Santa Cruz, had led carrier operations in the Philippines, the Bay of Bengal, and the Aleutians. Kakuta, Kusaka, and Nagumo would all be senior commanders in the 1944 Central Pacific campaign.[23]

Tactically, the enemy carrier force and its planes had out performed the American side. The Japanese lost more aircraft, but that was because, unlike their opponents, they were actually able to mount several—highly successful—air strikes. The coordinated attack by Vals and Kates—dive bombers and torpedo planes from two different carriers—on *Hornet* at 0910–0920 has been judged the most skillful of the whole

Pacific War.[24] The Americans, in contrast, launched only three relatively small and poorly coordinated strike waves (two from *Hornet* and one from *Enterprise*). Kinkaid's airmen managed just one dive-bomber attack on a big carrier. His torpedo planes failed to find the enemy carriers at all, let alone mount a coordinated attack with the dive bombers.

In 1942 American carrier aircraft were not better than those of the enemy. In particular, the Grumman F4F-4 Wildcat fighter was inferior to the Mitsubishi Zero in terms of range, rate of climb, maneuverability, and firepower. The Grumman TBF Avenger was larger and more modern than the Nakajima Kate, but the Douglas Dauntless and Aichi Val dive bombers were roughly comparable. In all cases the American planes had shorter range, although they could survive more damage.

The overall quality of Japanese pilots and other aircrew was still outstanding in late 1942. These men were well trained, some with nine months' experience of Pacific fighting, and a number who had fought in China. Many American aircrew were veterans, but some were untried. The replacement air complement of *Enterprise*, the new Air Group 10 (AG 10), had only joined the ship in Hawaii in September 1942. The air group (AG 8) aboard *Hornet* had seen more fighting, but the torpedo bomber squadron (VT-6), was new; the carrier's original "Torpedo Eight" (VT-8) had been wiped out at Midway.

The Kinkaid's ships had superior radar, and a radar-centered "fighter direction" system. This should have made possible interception of enemy air strikes at a safe distance from the carriers. Unfortunately, the CXAM air search radars aboard both *Hornet* and *Enterprise* were functioning poorly on 26 October. The fighter direcor officer (FDO) aboard *Enterprise*, who actually led the defense of both carriers, was an expert on radar technology but had never used it in battle. Admiral Nimitz—overall commander of the Pacific Fleet—later summed up the shortcomings:

> Our fighter direction was less effective than in previous actions. Enemy planes were not picked up until they were at close range, the radar screen was clogged by our own planes, and voice radio discipline was poor . . . Fighter direction against a number of enemy groups with our own planes in the air is a problem not yet solved.[25]

Thirty-seven Grumman Wildcat fighters were airborne over TF 61 when the first big Japanese strike arrived, but many of them had not climbed above 10,000 feet. When the enemy's second wave came in against *Enterprise*, fighter direction was also poor, and the CAP was still too low to intercept the high-flying Vals on their approach.

Santa Cruz was a low point in the fortunes of the U.S. Navy fast carriers. The Battle of Midway in June had been an outright American victory. At the Coral Sea in May, American carrier losses had been heavier than those of the enemy, but a strategic threat to New Guinea and Australia was blocked. In the battle of 26 October the U.S. Navy had been outnumbered and out-fought. An American carrier task force not only suffered heavier losses but was forced to withdraw from a vital sea area.

But the battle was also the end of an era for the enemy. The American offensive in the Central Pacific began fourteen months later, in January 1944, and the Combined Fleet did not come out to resist it. Santa Cruz was the last time the carriers of the Imperial Navy would actually take part in combat before June 1944. Partly this was because in 1943 Japan would go over to the strategic defensive. Partly it was because there would be few American carriers to fight. A decision was made in Tokyo to operate carrier planes from land bases. But it was certainly the case that in 1942 losses of aircraft and aircrew, and of sunk and damaged ships, had been heavy for Japan. Replacements were not available. And when the Japanese flattops did come out to fight again in 1944 the comparison with the American carrier fleet would be very different.

The communications officer of *Hornet*, who ended up swimming for his life with other members of the crew, recalled four days later a conversation he had overheard in the water: "Are you going to re-enlist?" "God Damn yes— on the new HORNET."[26] How and why the U.S. Navy recovered, how Task Force 58, the fast-carrier task force of January 1944, differed from Task Force 61 of October 1942, will be the subject of this book.

The Central Pacific campaign was a series of fleet operations carried out by U.S. forces in Micronesia from January to August 1944. In 1942–43, in the heroic first stage of the American-Japanese naval war, the battles—like Santa Cruz—had mostly been fought in the South Pacific, south of the equator (Pearl Harbor and Midway were, of course, important exceptions). In the winter of 1943–44 the action jumped north of the equator, into the Central Pacific.

The naval aspects of the Central Pacific advance have received relatively little attention by historians, even in the United States. They are overshadowed by the battles of Midway and Guadalcanal in 1942 and the sprawling Battle of Leyte Gulf in the Philippines in October 1944. In addition, no fleet-against-fleet action took place until toward the end of this Central Pacific campaign, with the Battle of the Philippine Sea of mid-June 1944. But even before that battle American naval forces had mounted a stunning naval advance in the Central Pacific, a chain of victories over the forces of the Japanese Navy's land-based air groups, extraordinary in its speed and depth, and decisive in its outcome. Remarkably, this victorious advance, including the Philippine Sea action, was won at very low cost, at least as far as the warships of the U.S. Navy and their crews were concerned.[27] This was certainly true compared to losses in 1942 or the year that followed October 1944, when the enemy adopted kamikaze ("suicide") tactics. Between the end of January and June 1944 no major American surface warship (carrier, battleship, cruiser, or destroyer) was lost or even put out of action. Fewer than a hundred members of the crews aboard the warships of TF 58 were killed in the fighting. Losses of naval aircraft and aircrew were higher, and a considerable number of aircraft were shot down or forced to "ditch." But downed aircrewmen were often rescued by surface ships, submarines, and seaplanes.

It was not just that TF 58 won a rapid and stunning success in the Central Pacific. This victory also marked, in the middle of 1944, the emergence of the U.S. Navy and especially its TF 58 fast-carrier spearhead, as the most powerful naval force in the world. In the 1890s the British Royal Navy still reigned supreme, and America's fleet had only just begun to compete in numerical terms with those in Europe. During World War I, despite ambitious plans, the top-heavy U.S. Navy was still considerably smaller than the naval forces of the British Empire and even Germany. In interwar arms-limitation treaties Britain accepted rough naval parity with the United States, but in 1939 the maritime potential of the British Empire was still superior in many respects. Especially important were the experience and tradition of the Royal Navy, the global base system provided by the Empire, and the much larger British merchant marine. But British wartime losses and the American ship-building program enabled the U.S. to catch up and overtake Britain.

Four of the six pre-war American aircraft carriers (CVs) operating in the Pacific during 1942 were lost. Then, between the summer of 1943 and the spring of 1944, the two Pacific survivors (*Saratoga* and *Enterprise*) were reinforced by no fewer than sixteen new "fast carriers." Seven of them were large, 27,200-ton "Essex" class CVs—including indeed a "new *Hornet*." Nine were 10,000-ton "Independence" class light carriers (CVLs). Meanwhile, a new generation of planes had reached the carrier air groups. The Hellcat fighter-bomber, developed extremely rapidly by Grumman, reached the fleet in the summer of 1943. It replaced the little Wildcat on the fast carriers and significantly outperformed the Japanese Zero. Fast torpedo planes and dive bombers were much more robust than their Japanese counterparts. All these U.S. Navy planes were now available in large numbers and flown by well-trained pilots and crewmen.

Accompanying the carriers was a fleet of fast battleships, cruisers, and destroyers, mostly very new and all bristling with anti-aircraft guns and sophisticated sensors (especially advanced radar). New radio systems allowed unprecedented effective communication between ships and aircraft; especially important were fighter direction systems. Sophisticated doctrine and tactics had been developed to exploit these advances. A quantity of fast fleet oilers supported the battle fleet with "underway replenishment," giving it better range and longer endurance than ever before. This vast assembly of ships and aircraft came into service after a massive industrial effort by the United States—begun in 1937 and greatly speeded up in mid-1940, eighteen months before Pearl Harbor.

In the decades that followed the war no other major power, including Soviet Russia, would ever come close to challenging the maritime supremacy achieved by the United States in 1944. The first six months of that year had seen the beginning of a new global era of sea power.

The time frame of this book requires a few further words of explanation. It was in January 1944—fourteen months after Santa Cruz—that the new fast-carrier force in the Central Pacific was redesignated as Task Force 58, and Rear Adm. Marc ("Pete") Mitscher became its commander. Mitscher's immediate superior at this time was Vice Adm. Raymond Spruance, who commanded the Central Pacific Force (later redesignated as the Fifth Fleet).

The main naval campaign fought by TF 58 lasted six months and essentially ended with the sea/air Battle of the Philippine Sea on 19–20 June 1944. That battle eliminated Japanese naval power in the Central Pacific, although ground fighting went on in the Marianas—on the islands of Tinian and Guam—until 10 August. Then, under what was termed the "platoon system," Bill Halsey took over from his close friend Spruance, the Fifth Fleet became the Third Fleet, and Task Force 58 became Task Force 38 (still under Pete Mitscher).

Halsey's Third Fleet operated from August 1944 to February 1945. It was made up of essentially the same ships as Spruance's Fifth Fleet—although they were very significantly reinforced. The Third Fleet (alongside Kinkaid's Seventh Fleet from the southwest Pacific) fought the Battle of Leyte Gulf in October 1944. The Fifth Fleet designation came back into use in February 1945, when Spruance made his scheduled rotation, relieving Halsey. Under Spruance, the Fifth Fleet and the revived TF 58 supported the invasion of Okinawa and mounted punishing air strikes against mainland Japan. Neither TF 38, nor the TF 58 of 1945 will be covered in the present book. Telling the whole history of the fast carriers would demand far too much space for a book of this length. It would also risk repeating the substance of two classic works, *The Fast Carriers* (1968), and *Titans of the Seas* (1975) written, respectively, by Clark G. Reynolds and by James and William Belote.

On the other hand, while looking at a relatively short (and decisive) time period, this volume brings in aspects of the U.S. Navy that made its supremacy possible and that are sometimes taken for granted in the story of the Pacific battles. Roughly speaking these aspects are personnel and logistics—people, bases, and supplies.

"Personnel" includes not only the well-known controversies within the senior ranks of U.S. Navy officer corps, including tension between "aviators" and "gun club" (the latter being specialists in the older branches of the service). The book also considers the hundreds of thousands of officers and enlisted men, the great majority landsmen, who had been recruited and trained to operate and maintain the U.S. Navy's new ships and aircraft on an ocean away from their homes. The strength of the pre-war Navy was multiplied by ten; the crews of TF 58 alone in 1944 numbered 100,000 officers and men.[28]

And, critical to the success of the front-line fast-carrier force was the revolutionary logistic capability of the "fleet train." In February 1944 the American forces rapidly established advanced naval bases in mid-Pacific, far to the west of pre-war establishments in Hawaii and on the U.S. West Coast. In these new advanced bases a growing number of supply and support ships of the "service squadrons" were positioned to serve the carriers and other ships. Meanwhile, the fighting ships were now supported by "task groups" of fast oilers and other vessels which could replenish them underway and keep them and their air groups at sea and in action for long periods. Not since the age of sail had any navy had such a capability. This resource, often unrecognized in "battle" histories, allowed the carrier task forces to keep up constant pressure and at a pace which overwhelmed the Japanese.[29]

Space does not permit discussion in the same depth of two other operational aspects of the U.S. Navy in the Pacific in the first half of 1944: amphibious operations and the submarine campaign against merchant shipping. This book does not detail the epic and heroic struggle of American marines and soldiers—on the ground—in island battles in the Marshalls and the Marianas, most notably at Kwajalein, Saipan, and Guam. These merit a new book of their own.[30] The events described here actually involved only two contested American landing operations, separated by about five months. These were in the Marshalls (Kwajalein and Eniwetok) in February 1944, and the Marianas (Saipan, Tinian, and Guam) in June, July, and August. The main advances in the months between were carried out essentially by naval and air forces. Indeed, one of the most important successes of the fast carriers of TF 58 was that their speed and flexibility made it possible to avoid the necessity of a bloody, exhausting, and time-consuming series of amphibious landings.

Likewise, there is only limited treatment here of the hugely important U.S. Navy submarine campaign against Japanese merchant shipping, which was expanding at the same time as the Central Pacific advance.[31] Nevertheless, the book does describe important "operational" successes of the submarine force in the Philippine Sea battle, acting as a vital scouting force and sinking two Japanese carriers. In preceding months they had, aided by radio intelligence, succeeded in limiting last-minute Japanese attempts to reinforce their island garrisons, especially in the Marianas.

To maintain the narrative flow and keep the American perspective, Japanese plans and operational details are largely confined to the endnotes. Developments are also outlined in Appendix II.

A few matters of form. Miles are nautical miles. Dates are local dates. This will usually be the ELD, East Longitude Date, since most of the events took place east of the Greenwich Meridian and west of the mid-Pacific International Date Line. Events in Hawaii, San Francisco, or Washington, all west of the Greenwich Meridian and east of the International Date Line, are dated using the WLD (West Longitude Date). Basically, the date in most of the Central Pacific (and Japan) is one day later than the date in Hawaii. (So, for example, the Battle of Santa Cruz took place on 26 October 1942 ELD, when the date was still 25 October WLD in Hawaii. The twenty-four-hour clock will be used, sometimes with the (local) date attached at the end for clarity's sake. Regarding names, following proper Japanese convention the surname-first form is used, e.g. Ozawa Jisaburō.

I am especially grateful to Heather McCallum and Joanna Godfrey at Yale University Press, who encouraged and then patiently supported the writing of this volume, partly as a kind of sequel to my previous Yale book, *The War for the Seas*. Another very special debt of thanks is owed to Vincent O'Hara. Without his help and advice about online sources during the Covid pandemic—when travel to archives and libraries, and travel in general, was so difficult—this book simply could not have been written. Vince also encouraged my virtual involvement with the outstanding Western Naval History Association, despite my base being in western Scotland rather than California. With his profound understanding of the Pacific War Richard Frank provided extremely valuable advice and encouragement—both at the beginning and the end of my writing process. Stephen Kepher kindly read several chapters and provided comments based on his deep understanding of World War II military planning and his hands-on experience of American carrier aviation.

My wife Gillian once again supported me and tolerated my preoccupation with a subject remote from her own professional world. This time, however, rather than simply living with Task Force 58, she set out to produce her own book. Beginning several years after me, she wrote and published a groundbreaking monograph on the Scottish legal system, while I was still slowly trundling my way across the Central Pacific.

This is certainly not the first book written in Britain about the U.S. Navy or its Pacific War. I do, however, still have a sense of writing it as an outsider, a "European" civilian. Many of the earlier books on the Pacific War were written by participants, or—in an intermediate golden age—by authors with both access to documents *and* the opportunity to interview senior veterans of the war. This book was written nearly eight decades after the event, outside the community of the U.S. Navy and, indeed, outside the United States. This situation presents challenges, but it also makes for a different perspective. My sincere hope is that readers in Britain, the United States, and elsewhere will find the end result thought-provoking.

CHAPTER 1

THE ORIGINS OF TASK FORCE 58

THE PACIFIC AND THE WAR

The Pacific is vast. As the U.S. Navy advanced toward Japan in 1943 and 1944, its planners divided the ocean into three zones, effectively east–west bands: North, Central, and South. The band of the "Central" Pacific (with the naval abbreviation "CenPac") extended from the equator north to the latitude of about 40°N, a distance of nearly 2,500 miles. The spread of the Central Pacific from east to west was less clearly defined, but the distance from west of Hawaii to Palau in the western Caroline Islands was 4,400 miles. The naval campaign in this vast theater of operations would last only six months, but it would change the course of World War II.

Four strategically placed groups of islands in the Central Pacific— which correspond roughly to Micronesia—were fought over. Nearly all had been controlled by the Japanese between the wars. The Marshall Islands were the nearest to American territory in 1941, but even so they lie on the far side of the International Date Line. The islands are some 2,400 miles to the west of Hawaii, and 4,400 miles southwest of California. The Marshalls are low coral atolls, each with a tiny land area. Typically, a ring of coral islets encircles and shelters a broad lagoon. The largest is Kwajalein Atoll. Eniwetok and Majuro atolls, along with Kwajalein, would be captured by the U.S. Navy in February 1944 and developed into crucially important advanced fleet bases.

The Gilberts (now Kiribati) straddled the equator to the south of the Marshalls. They were physically similar to the Marshalls but had been a British possession before 1941, rather than a Japanese one. The islands had not been part of pre-war American planning; operations there in late 1943 (notably at Tarawa) were a preliminary to the Central Pacific campaign rather than an integral part of it.

The Carolines stretch for about 2,000 miles from west of the Marshalls. There are some coral atolls but also "high islands" with (inert) volcanic peaks that rise well above sea level. Kusaie/Kosrae Island (at 163°E longitude) lies at the eastern extremity. Palau/Belau (134°E longitude) lies at the western one; it was the administrative center of the whole pre-war Japanese "Mandate." Near the middle part of the Carolines chain is Truk/Chuuk Atoll (152°E longitude), the Central Pacific base of the Imperial Navy.

The Marianas are located above the western Carolines at about 145°E longitude, and they run south to north for 500 miles. The largest islands, at the southern end of the chain, are Guam, Saipan, and Tinian. Compared to the Marshalls and the central and eastern Carolines, some of the individual islands in the Marianas are reasonably large, with heights reaching 1,500 feet above sea level. The Marianas were the most developed part of the Mandate, with a considerable population and significant economic development.

None of the islands of the Central Pacific had large populations, and many were uninhabited. Spain had taken nominal control of the region during the sixteenth and seventeenth centuries. The U.S. seized the Philippines in 1898 during the Spanish-American War, and Spain's Central Pacific islands were cast adrift. Guam in the Marianas went to the U.S. in the peace treaty. After a short period of ownership by Imperial Germany the remaining islands were put under the control of Japan as a Mandate by the League of Nations.

The islands had also been part of military planning before 1941. By the 1920s, at the latest, the Japanese and American navies had come to regard one another as potential enemies. Geography dictated that the Central Pacific, in particular the Marshalls-Carolines corridor, would be a theater of engagement if full-scale war ever broke out; one historian has termed it the "royal road."[1] Planning for a hypothetical war with Japan, the Americans had to consider an advance through the Mandate to reinforce their colony of the Philippines or—more likely—recapture it after it had been occupied. To prevail in this hypothetical war, the U.S. would then need to establish forward bases for a blockade of Japan. Map exercises were held at the U.S. Naval War College in the 1920s and 1930s, and the so-called ORANGE war plans developed. (Countries were assigned codenames based on a color; Japan was ORANGE, the USA was BLUE.) These plans envisaged in their final version a step-by-step American advance through the Mandate, establishing forward bases on captured islands as the fleet advanced. The plan would become a reality in 1944.

However, the actual Pacific naval war, up to the end of 1943, was different from pre-war expectations. Global war turned out not to be the same as the planned American-Japanese naval campaign. The Pearl Harbor attack and the devastation of the U.S. battleship fleet ended thoughts of an early offensive by American forces. After attacking Pearl Harbor, the Japanese Navy concentrated its activities in Southeast Asia and New Guinea, and for some months fighting in the Central Pacific was on a small scale. Immediately after 7 December 1941 the Japanese forces based in the Mandate had swept up weakly defended Allied outposts, including the British Gilbert Islands, U.S.-controlled Guam, and the remote mid-ocean U.S. possession of Wake Atoll. In February and March 1942 carriers and cruisers of the U.S. Navy did mount long-range hit-and-run raids against the Marshalls and the Gilberts and against Wake and the Japanese possession of Marcus Island. In terms of their effect, however, these were only pinpricks, and the basic American posture was defensive. The outpost at Midway Atoll and even the main Hawaiian Islands were under threat. The momentous Battle of Midway in June 1942, during which four enemy aircraft carriers were sunk (as well as the U.S. Navy's *Yorktown*), ended that danger. Midway also concluded—for a time—major naval combat operations by the surface ships of either side in the Central Pacific.

Unexpectedly, the South Pacific (south of the equator) became the major theater of American-Japanese naval combat. The stunning success of Japanese operations southward through Malaya, the Philippines, and Java to the approaches to Australia forced attention to the South Pacific among Allied planners. The Japanese had established an important forward base at Rabaul, after capturing the place from weak Australian forces in January 1942. Rabaul was on New Britain Island, north of Papua New Guinea. The Japanese attempted a further advance southeast from Rabaul in May 1942, taking control of undefended Tulagi and Guadalcanal in the British Solomon Islands. However, they were turned back in their attempt to capture Port Moresby on the south coast of Papua New Guinea. This setback was the result of the Battle of the Coral Sea—although that battle also resulted in the loss of the carrier *Lexington*.

A major feature of American operations, not foreseen before the war, was the setting up of a string of advanced bases on islands in the southeastern Pacific (Polynesia). These covered the supply line between the U.S. and Australia. A major center was established in March 1942 at Nouméa in the French colony of Nouvelle-Calédonie. However, the main Pacific Fleet base and Admiral Chester Nimitz, the commander-in-chief (CincPac), remained far to the north, at Pearl Harbor in Hawaii.

The Midway victory in early June 1942 provided the U.S. Navy with the opportunity to mount attacks in the South Pacific. The global strategy of the Allies was still based on the concept of "Germany First." Furthermore, a lack of ships, planes, amphibious forces, and auxiliary shipping ruled out for many months a major counter-offensive through the Mandate in the Central Pacific—along the lines of the ORANGE war plans. However, Admiral Nimitz and the U.S. Navy Commander-in-Chief (CominCh) in Washington, Admiral Ernest King, along with Gen. Douglas MacArthur in Australia, stressed the vulnerability of the South Pacific supply line. They were able to obtain permission from the Allied war leaders for "defensive-offensive" operations from the south against Rabaul.

The first stage of these operations was the counter-landing of an entire division of the U.S. Marine Corps (USMC) at Guadalcanal in the Solomon Islands in early August 1942. Six months of fighting ensued, which proved to be longer and more difficult than either side had expected. (The Battle of Santa Cruz, already outlined, was part of this.) Losses on both sides were very heavy, and by the start of 1943 neither the Japanese nor the Americans had more than one or two surviving heavy aircraft carriers available. The U.S. Navy lost carriers *Wasp* and *Hornet* in the Solomons, following the earlier sinking of *Lexington* and *Yorktown*. The fighting continued in the South Pacific even after the Japanese evacuated their starving troops from Guadalcanal in February 1943.

The strategic initiative was now passing to the Allies—gradually. In the course of 1943 greater resources became available. Successes mounted across the globe, especially in Russia and North Africa. Direct threats to the British Isles and to Australia and New Zealand had ended. The supreme American and British leadership now agreed to a limited offensive in the Pacific, going beyond the advance toward Rabaul. In May 1943 the American military command, the Joint Chiefs of Staff (JCS), even agreed to operations in the Central Pacific, at least into the Marshall and Caroline Islands.

The growing strength of the U.S. Pacific Fleet was a major reason why a Central Pacific offensive could now be planned. In the spring and summer of 1943 major reinforcements began to reach Pearl Harbor. New 27,200-ton "Essex" class heavy carriers (CVs) and 10,000-ton "Independence" class light carriers (CVLs) arrived. The first, on 31 May 1943, was USS *Essex* herself. A new *Yorktown* arrived in late June, a year after her namesake had been lost at Midway. The first of the new light carriers, *Independence*, reached Pearl Harbor in July. After completing their "work up" in Hawaiian waters the three carriers sailed together from Pearl Harbor in late August as Task Force 15, under the command of Rear Adm. Charles "Baldy" Pownall. The target was again (as in March 1942) Marcus Island. The place was too small and isolated to be well defended or developed into an American base, and Pownall's real objective was to give the new carriers and their raw air groups necessary combat experience.

Three more fast carriers arrived together at Pearl Harbor in August, the new *Lexington* and CVLs *Belleau Wood* and *Princeton*. In mid-September 1943, after their work-up, Pownall took them to sea as Task Force 16. This time the operation was a raid against Tarawa and Makin Atolls in the Gilberts. Toward the end of the same month the biggest carrier force the U.S. Navy had ever assembled departed from Pearl

Harbor for a strike against Wake. Task Force 14 was twice the size of the two U.S. task forces that had defended Midway, more than twice the size of the carrier force used to support the Guadalcanal landing in August 1942. Included were the first three "Essex" class and three CVLs—*Independence*, *Belleau Wood*, and the newly arrived *Cowpens*.[2] The attack took place on 5 October, and this time the fast-carrier air groups encountered enemy aircraft. The first of many successful air combats by new carrier-based Grumman F6F-3 Hellcat fighter planes took place, and a number of Japanese "Betty" twin-engined medium bombers were destroyed on the ground.

Despite these carrier raids the attention of Admiral Nimitz remained from February to November 1943 fixed on the South Pacific, and specifically the islands of the northern Solomons. They formed a "ladder" to be climbed toward Rabaul. In contrast to the extreme drama of Guadalcanal in the autumn of 1942 the advance of 1943 was a measured, rung-by-rung climb. It involved small cruiser-destroyer forces, and short hops by U.S. Army and Marine amphibious elements. Air power operated on both sides from land bases.

In the struggle for the skies over the Solomons, the American fighter and bombers—Navy, Marine, and Army (AAF)—grew rapidly in number and improved in quality. These planes steadily wore down the air strength of the Japanese Navy. The last Japanese air reserves were thrown in to deal with AAF bomber raids on Rabaul in October 1943 and to contest the landing which took place on nearby Bougainville Island on 1 November. Trained Japanese air squadrons were stripped from the Truk-based carrier fleet and rushed to airfields near Rabaul.

The biggest American carrier raids so far were mounted against Rabaul in the first and second weeks of November. On 5 November, Rear Adm. Frederick ("Ted") Sherman's TF 38 (*Saratoga* and CVL *Princeton*) launched the first strike from the east, and took part in a second attack six days later. This second strike was joined by Rear Adm. Alfred ("Monty") Montgomery's TF 50.3, which Nimitz had sent south from Pearl Harbor. TF 50.3 included *Essex*, CVL *Independence*, and the fourth and latest "Essex" class, *Bunker Hill*. Despite bad weather, damage was inflicted on Japanese aircraft, warships and merchant ships. Meanwhile, the much-feared counterattack by Rabaul-based planes failed to break through the air defenses of the American task forces, a complete contrast with the Santa Cruz battle fought thirteen months earlier.

For the Japanese the overall outcome of these actions was the worst possible. Rabaul soon ceased to function as an effective air or naval base. A ground force of 110,000 men was trapped in the Rabaul area, and another 60,000 on Bougainville (the survivors surrendered after the end of the war, in August 1945). And the effective air strength of the Japanese carrier force had been lost, without achieving anything.

The 1 November Bougainville landing and the carrier raids on Rabaul were part of a flurry of Allied operations in the Pacific at the end of 1943, before the main Central Pacific fighting began. The next step was Operation GALVANIC, the landings on Tarawa and Makin in the Gilberts, which lay about 1,200 miles ENE of Bougainville and Rabaul. The original sequence of operations in the Central Pacific, as proposed by the U.S. Joint Chiefs of Staff in Washington in May 1943, had been to begin with the Marshall Islands, carrying out a landing in mid-November 1943. This followed the logic of geography and pre-war American ORANGE plans. However, the Marshalls lay beyond the effective range of planes from the nearest American air bases. Admiral Nimitz decided that preliminary operations would be carried out to the south in the Gilbert Islands, where advanced airfields could be constructed.

Vice Adm. Raymond Spruance took command of GALVANIC. He had become commander of the Central Pacific Force (subordinate to Nimitz) in early August 1943, three and a half months earlier. Under Spruance three naval task forces converged on the Gilberts. TF 52 transported an Army division from Oahu to Makin Atoll, TF 53 took the 2nd Marine Division from New Zealand to Tarawa. Supporting both the invasion task forces were elements of TF 50, the fast-carrier force, still under Rear Adm. Pownall.

The story of the GALVANIC landings, which commenced on 20 November, need only be outlined here. A U.S. Army regiment took the lightly defended atoll of Makin with few casualties after a three-day fight. Events 100 miles to the south, at Betio Island in Tarawa Atoll, are much better known. The first of the atoll assault landings by the USMC, the Tarawa invasion was mounted against unflinching resistance of an enemy garrison numbering 4,000 uniformed troops, including 2,700 naval infantry. The Japanese were defending a flat island 2 miles long, 600 yards at its widest. They had had time to lay out defensive positions. Unable to retreat and unwilling to surrender, they fought almost to the last man.

On the American side pre-landing reconnaissance had been insufficient, and fatal miscalculations were made about tides. Many of the marines had to wade ashore through deep water under enemy fire. Initial air support from the carriers was late and of brief duration. The pre-landing shelling by gunnery ships lasted only two and a half hours. Bombs and artillery shells proved too little to achieve the planned paralysis of the defenders. The desperate battle ended with an American victory after three days, but at a high cost to the Marines. A total of 1,009 men had been killed, a three-day figure equal to half the ground-force losses suffered on Guadalcanal over six months. For a time it seemed to American planners that an island assault of this sort was too costly to repeat.

The fleet had provided direct and indirect support for GALVANIC. The fast carriers of Pownall's TF 50 had been broken down into several task groups, each assigned a specific role. TG 50.1 under Pownall himself, with carriers *Yorktown*, *Lexington*, and CVL *Cowpens*, steamed directly to a position between the Gilberts and the Marshalls, forming the "Interceptor Group." Their task was to attack airfields in the southern Marshalls and guard against movement by the enemy fleet from Truk. TG 50.2 (Rear Adm. Arthur Radford) looped south around the Gilberts with *Enterprise* and CVLs *Belleau Wood* and *Monterey* to a position west of Makin from which they could support the landing there. Montgomery's TG 50.3 with *Essex*, *Bunker Hill*, and CVL *Independence* came north from the advanced base at Espiritu Santo in the New Hebrides (now Vanuatu). They took up a station west of Tarawa, supporting the Betio landing.[3]

The invasion objectives were 2,000 miles from Pearl Harbor and 1,000 miles even from Espiritu Santo. This was the first operation where all ships had to refuel at sea. The carriers were operating a long way from their permanent bases and the "fleet train" was for the first time a vitally important element. Service Squadron 8 (ServRon 8) had positioned fleet oilers in escorted groups of two or three vessels at pre-arranged rendezvous points east of the Gilberts, allowing the carriers to replenish their fuel while underway. This involved a very large effort: a total of twenty-eight fleet oilers took part, shuttling back and forth to Pearl Harbor.[4]

The American aviator commanders, including Vice Adm. Charles Towers, did not approve of the way that the carriers had been used in GALVANIC. (Towers was Commander Air Force, Pacific Fleet—ComAirPac—under Nimitz in Hawaii.) The fast-carrier forces had been divided up, and those ships assigned to "direct support" of the landings on Makin and Tarawa had been made vulnerable to attacks by shore-based enemy aircraft and by submarines. The aviators had wanted, instead, concentrated offensive strikes against air bases in the Marshalls. However, the commanders of GALVANIC, Spruance and the amphibious force commander, Rear Adm. R. Kelly Turner, desired to complete the landings in the Gilberts as rapidly as possible, before the Japanese fleet could intervene (as it had at Savo Island in 1942). This ruled out a prolonged artillery bombardment by battleships and cruisers and required use of direct air support. With the support of Admiral Nimitz, their views had prevailed.

In the event, the role of the American fast carriers in the Gilberts was limited, although Towers' fears were to some extent justified. The Japanese did not send surface ships to defend the islands. Their carriers had been stripped of aircraft; their heavy-cruiser force weakened in the Bougainville fighting.[5] Long-range bombers and submarines of the Imperial Navy did, however, present a threat. Medium bombers attacked from bases in the Marshalls. The main air strike came in the evening of D-Day on Tarawa. (Although the term "D-Day" is popularly connected with the Normandy invasion of 6 June 1944, it was used throughout the war to denote the planned start-date of any operation.) Sixteen Bettys attacked Montgomery's TG 50.3, which was operating some 30 miles west of the atoll. Proper carrier-based night fighters were not yet operational. The enemy planes failed to hit *Essex* or *Bunker Hill*, but a group of five concentrated on CVL *Independence* and achieved one torpedo hit. Seventeen members of the crew were killed, and the ship had to return to the West Coast for six months of repairs.

As for the submarine threat, it became terribly concrete on the fourth day of the operation, 24 November. The escort carrier (CVE) *Liscome Bay* was torpedoed and sunk by *I-175* off Makin with very heavy loss of life; 644 men, including Rear Adm. Henry Mullinix, went down with the ship when she blew up. American escort ships did sink six of the Japanese submarines sent out to defend the Marshalls. The loss of *Liscome Bay*, however, showed the danger of exposing carriers off invaded islands for more than a few days and giving the enemy a chance to bring their slow-moving submarines into position.

The final episode in 1943 was a carrier raid on the Marshalls in early December. Rather than returning immediately to Pearl Harbor after GALVANIC, Pownall was ordered to refuel at sea and take two task groups of TF 50 to raid Kwajalein Atoll. The aim was to destroy enemy airfields and shipping and to take low-level aerial photos for the planned invasion. TF 50 was made up of four heavy carriers and two CVLs.[6]

A big air battle was fought over the Roi air base on the morning of 4 December, but the inexperienced strike leader did not attack a large group of Betty medium bombers on the ground. Sticking to the raid principle of "hit and run," Pownall decided not to launch a second strike, despite the strong arguments of Capt. J. J. ("Jocko") Clark, CO of the *Yorktown* (Pownall's flagship).[7] As TF 50 withdrew later in the day it came under sporadic attacks by single-engined torpedo planes. No hits were suffered. A spectacular series of photos taken from *Yorktown* featured in *Life* magazine in January; they showed a new Jill torpedo plane (Nakajima B6N) breaking up in flames after being hit by AA fire. In the evening a long and better-organized Japanese air attack developed. A torpedo hit *Lexington*, killing nine of her crew and damaging her steering. *Lexington* was able to limp out of the area, but she had to be taken to Puget Sound for repairs and returned only in early March 1944.[8]

TF 50 returned to Pearl Harbor on 9 December after a remarkable four-week operation. Pownall, however, now came in for heavy criticism, from above and from below. Capt. Clark ignored the chain of command and—in a remarkable act of insubordination—sent a memo criticizing his immediate superior's indecision. The memo was supported with aerial photographs showing undamaged enemy bombers on the

Roi airfield. This episode, and a number of earlier decisions made by Pownall, suggested that he was too risk averse.[9] Meanwhile, Rear Adm. Marc ("Pete") Mitscher was now available as a more senior and more aggressive replacement, and he had powerful friends and supporters. On 23 December Nimitz met privately with key members of his staff. Among them was Towers (ComAirPac), who urged the replacement of Pownall by Mitscher as the tactical commander of the fast carriers for the forthcoming invasion of the Marshalls. Nimitz—a non-aviator—accepted Towers' proposal, and Admiral King confirmed it. When Spruance was belatedly informed of Pownall's imminent departure he protested that his (Pownall's) performance had been wholly satisfactory. Spruance was not an aviator and had a sour relationship with Towers. He had—at the time—reservations about Mitscher's abilities. Nonetheless, Nimitz's decision stood.[10]

There had been earlier wartime arguments between aviators and non-aviators. That was not directly the central issue here. Pownall was a 1910 Annapolis graduate; he learned to fly in 1925–27. He served on carriers in the late 1920s and 1930s and was the first CO of *Enterprise*. He had missed Pacific front-line service in 1942,[11] but since his arrival at Pearl Harbor in August 1943 he had gained unmatched operational experience with the new fast carriers, including the four-week campaign in the Marshalls. This story is both an example of jostling for power at the higher levels of the U.S. Navy and a fascinating "might have been." Charles Pownall missed his chance to be the central figure in the Pacific carrier war. That role would go to another officer.

SPRUANCE AND MITSCHER

Two admirals were central to the story of Task Force 58 and the advance across the Central Pacific.

In May 1943 Raymond Spruance had been promoted to the rank of vice admiral.[12] Early the following month Admiral Nimitz told him that he would be given command of a new Central Pacific Force (CenPacFor), based at Pearl Harbor. His biographer, Thomas Buell, would describe Spruance as "the quiet warrior"—partly in contrast to some of his outspoken fellow wartime commanders. Another eminent naval historian, John Lundstrom, also summed Spruance up: "He was a very private person, unemotional and undemonstrative in public. To a great degree he was unconcerned about his image . . . His gods were logic and reason."[13] Spruance was a thinker with an academic knowledge of naval history and strategic thought, and he saw the long-term picture. Admiral King would later praise him as the most intelligent flag officer in the Navy. But Spruance was also a man of action, eager for seagoing command. In challenging combat operations he proved to be the efficient and effective leader of a team, with the ability to delegate and concentrate on essentials. And he was adaptable; very much brought up in the battleship navy, he would lead aviators to some of their most striking victories: at Midway in 1942, in the Central Pacific in 1943–44, and off Japan in 1945. In addition he would take overall charge of some the most challenging amphibious operations of the Pacific War.

Spruance formally took over his post on 5 August. He would be responsible for both Navy and Army forces in the Central Pacific. He was to be the seagoing commander of the most powerful naval force the U.S. had ever assembled. The Central Pacific Force included a squadron of fast battleships, a diverse amphibious armada and, above all, the growing "Fast-Carrier Force" (later Task Force 58). Spruance would go to sea with the assembled battle fleet and take direct command in major operations, including the invasion of the Gilberts in November 1943, the invasion of the Marshalls in January 1944, the raids on Truk and Palau in February and March, and the Battle of the Philippine Sea in June. His command would be redesignated as the Fifth Fleet on 26 April 1944.[14]

Spruance owed his position to his abilities and professional experience, but a healthy element of good fortune was also involved. He had begun the Pacific War as a rear admiral in a mid-level post, commanding Cruiser Division 5 (CruDiv 5), made up of four heavy cruisers. Once war with Japan began CruDiv 5 provided the surface-ship screen for Bill Halsey's TF 2, built around *Enterprise*. CruDiv 5 took part in the raids on the Marshalls and Gilberts in early February 1942, on Wake Atoll and Marcus Island in late February and early March, and on Tokyo in April.

The unpredictable now came into play. In late May Halsey was suddenly hospitalized at Pearl Harbor with severe dermatitis. The moment could not have been more critical. American codebreakers had learned that a huge Japanese fleet was about to descend on Midway. Halsey proposed that Spruance replace him in command of what was now TF 16 (*Hornet* and *Enterprise*), in order to ambush the oncoming Japanese. Nimitz concurred. Apparently both he and Spruance himself were surprised by Halsey's recommendation, in view of Spruance's lack of first-hand aviation service.[15] A supporting factor was probably the long and close friendship between Spruance and Halsey. This dated back to the early 1920s, when both men had worked closely together in the same destroyer division in the Pacific. Nimitz was convinced by Halsey's extremely favorable report about Spruance after the Pacific raids: "I consider him fully and superbly qualified to take command of a force comprising mixed types and to conduct protracted independent operations in the combat theater in war time."[16] Spruance raised his flag aboard carrier *Enterprise*. TF 16 now comprised *Enterprise* and *Hornet*, six cruisers and twelve destroyers. The CO of *Hornet* was Capt. Pete Mitscher.

Nimitz also decided that Rear Adm. Frank Jack Fletcher's TF 17 would operate together with Spruance's TF 16 if the damaged *Yorktown* could be successfully repaired at Pearl Harbor. In this event the more senior and experienced Fletcher would be in tactical command. This is indeed what happened. Spruance and TF 16 headed north from Pearl Harbor on 28 May 1942; Fletcher and TF 17 followed two days later.

For Spruance's career, chance events intruded even more dramatically in the great battle of Midway a week later. On 4 June dive bombers from *Enterprise* and *Yorktown* succeeded in fatally damaging three of the four enemy carriers in the Japanese advance force, before they could launch attacks of their own. The undamaged *Hiryū* was finally able to launch small but effective counterstrikes late in the morning. Spruance's TF 16 never came under air attack, but Fletcher's TF 17 did. *Yorktown* was badly damaged by dive bombers and torpedo planes and could no longer operate her aircraft. Fletcher decided to shift his flag to heavy cruiser *Astoria* during the afternoon. The impracticality of controlling movement of ships and aircraft from a cruiser became evident. In a momentous decision, Fletcher agreed to hand over tactical command. Spruance had signaled: "Have you any instructions for further operations?" Fletcher replied: "Negative. Will conform to your movements."[17]

Spruance was later given credit by historians for the Midway victory. This verdict was unfair to Fletcher, who maneuvered the fleet into its attack position, and whose *Yorktown* air group (in TF 17) performed effectively. The launch of strikes from *Enterprise* and *Hornet* in TF 16 had not been handled well. But at the very least Spruance confirmed his ability to command a fleet in battle. He was awarded a Distinguished Service Medal (DSM) with the following citation: "During the Midway engagement . . . his seamanship, endurance, and tenacity in handling his task force were of the highest quality." Fletcher was also awarded the DSM, as was Capt. Miles Browning, Spruance's chief of staff, who was an aviation specialist inherited from Halsey.[18]

In the event Spruance's initial experience as a seagoing fleet commander in 1942 was brief. He came ashore in June, shortly after Midway, to serve as Nimitz's chief of staff. This appointment had been arranged before the Midway emergency.[19] It was not Spruance, but Fletcher and Rear Adm. Kinkaid who would lead the carrier task forces in the difficult battles of late 1942 in the South Pacific.

There were a number of other factors aside from CruDiv 5 and Midway that enabled Raymond Spruance's successful progress up the chain of command. He had distinguished himself at the Naval Academy. Spruance came from a privileged middle-class background, with a family in America for many generations. A family business failure in the 1890s would eventually lead his influential mother to push him toward the tuition-free technical education provided by Annapolis. The young Spruance did not enjoy the Academy, finding the narrow program unchallenging. Nevertheless, he performed very well and graduated twenty-fifth out of 206, in the class of 1907.

Spruance's career in the Navy in the 1920s and 1930s had been solid and varied—although it did not include any aviation element. Early on, he had developed an expertise in electrical engineering systems, but he had moved away from that in order to spend more time at sea and further his career. Lt (jg) Spruance received his first command in 1913, five years after leaving Annapolis. This was destroyer *Bainbridge* (DD-1), based in the Philippines; his engineering officer was Carl Moore, who thirty years later would serve as his chief of staff. In 1914 he married Margaret Dean of Indianapolis, after a three-year courtship; theirs would be a long and happy relationship. As a full lieutenant and a lieutenant commander, Spruance held engineering posts ashore and was at home in staff posts before and during America's participation in World War I. He was rapidly promoted, reaching the rank of commander in September 1918 at the age of thirty-one. His second warship command was the new destroyer *Aaron Ward* in April 1919. *Aaron Ward* was part of DesDiv 32, commanded by "Billy" Halsey, and he and Spruance became, and remained, close friends. Command of *Aaron Ward* was followed by command of a succession of four other new "four-stacker" destroyers in the years up to 1925.

A central and important feature of Spruance's career, and an unusual one, was a long involvement with the Naval War College (NWC) in Newport, Rhode Island. The NWC offered an eleven-month course on naval strategy and decision-making and was considered a pathway to senior rank. Spruance first attended the Senior Course in 1926–27; in 1931–33 he returned as a member of staff and again, in 1935–38, as a captain. Latterly, he was head of the Operations Department. Another lifelong friendship was developed at the NWC, this one with Richmond Kelly Turner (Head of Strategy, and a brilliant lecturer). Turner would later be the most prominent commander of the U.S. Navy amphibious operations in the Pacific War—under Spruance and others. Carl Moore, Spruance's old shipmate from *Bainbridge* and his future chief of staff, was also at the NWC. (In February 1946, after the war, Spruance would become President of the College.)

As already mentioned, during World War II and the decades before it a degree of friction existed within the Navy between the dominant "gun club" and the challenging group of "aviators." (The two groups were also contrasted as "black shoe" and "brown shoe," based on their distinctive authorized footwear with uniforms.) Like the majority of the Navy's senior personnel, Spruance belonged to the former group. He was, literally, a "battleship admiral." He had a stint as XO of the 32,000-ton *Mississippi* in 1929–31. Then, as a captain, he was CO of the same ship from April 1938 to the beginning of 1940.

His other career experience was impressively broad, although with little time in Washington; a billet in the ONI in 1927–29 was his only posting there. Staff experience came from late 1931 as chief of staff to the "Commander, Destroyers, Scouting Force" in the Pacific in 1933–35. In 1940 he was appointed commandant of the new Tenth Naval District (Puerto Rico) in the Caribbean. In this post Spruance had frequent contact with Admiral Ernest King, who in December 1940 had become commander of the U.S. naval forces in the Atlantic. In the autumn of 1941 King was apparently sufficiently impressed by Spruance to request that he become his chief of staff. Spruance, who was already en route to take command of CruDiv 5, was eager for a seagoing post and took steps to avoid the posting.[20]

On 6 January 1944, Rear Adm. Marc "Pete" Mitscher was appointed de facto commander of the new Task Force 58 within Spruance's Central Pacific Force.[21] Although another "quiet warrior," Mitscher's appearance contrasted to the buttoned-down Spruance, and was effectively described by a journalist who interviewed him in late 1944: "Looking like a jockey in his long-billed, brown cloth cap, slender, wiry, tough little Vice Admiral Mitscher." The signature cap was to protect his eyes from the bright Pacific sun as he sat in a swivel chair watching flight deck operations from the flag bridge of his carrier. A biographer described Mitscher as "soft-spoken, slightly built, but tough and wiry."[22] Soft-spoken he was—sometimes to the point of inaudibility—but he was respected for his incomparable knowledge of naval aviation and the care that he felt his aviators were due.

These two quiet men were nearly the same age: Spruance was born in July 1886, Mitscher in January 1887. Their background, however, as they grew up in late nineteenth-century America and entered the U.S. Navy, would be markedly different.

When the war began in 1941 Capt. Mitscher was prominent among the "aviator" ("brown shoe") community. He was both a pioneer flyer and an officer with extensive command and administrative experience in naval aviation. Mitscher had since October 1941 been CO of the Navy's newest (and ill-fated) carrier, *Hornet* (CV-8), which was working up in the Atlantic. In March 1942 he took the big vessel through the Panama Canal and joined up in mid-Pacific with Halsey in *Enterprise*. The secret mission of TF 16 was an air strike against Tokyo. The sixteen twin-engined AAF bombers under the command of Lt Col. James Doolittle were launched from Mitscher's carrier.

Mitscher then commanded *Hornet* in the Battle of Midway. The epic sea/air battle made Spruance's career; ironically it almost terminated that of Mitscher, at least as a front-line combat commander. *Hornet* and *Enterprise* were still operating together at Midway as TF 16, but now under Spruance rather than Halsey. Mitscher's planes did not perform well. The fifteen planes of the *Hornet* torpedo bomber squadron (VT-8, "Torpedo Eight") were wiped out. During the critical morning of 4 June, the other three *Hornet* squadrons failed to find the enemy fleet at all, in what was later termed "the flight to nowhere." It was dive bombers from *Enterprise* and *Yorktown* that famously crippled the Japanese carrier force and won the battle. Mitscher sent the *Hornet* morning strikes out on the wrong bearing, west rather than WSW, on the hunch that the enemy flattops were operating in two groups. Afterward he tried to cover up his mistake by filing a misleading report. Spruance (who had been aboard *Enterprise*) did not openly challenge Mitscher's account, but he privately signaled Nimitz to base any appraisal on his own reports, rather than those of Mitscher: "Where discrepancies exist between *Enterprise* and *Hornet* reports, the *Enterprise* report should be taken as more accurate." He was clearly dissatisfied with the performance of Mitscher and his staff, and he communicated this to CincPac.[23]

Mitscher, now a rear admiral, was only briefly given command of a small carrier task force after Midway. He was then posted ashore to take command of Patrol Wing 2, a flying boat command based in Hawaii. Nimitz may have taken this decision partly based on Spruance's negative reports. In any event, Mitscher spent the second half of 1942 ashore in Hawaii; it was definitely his opinion that he had been "shelved" because of events at Midway.[24] In late December 1942 he was assigned to another support role as "Commander, Fleet Air, Nouméa" in Nouvelle-Calédonie, taking charge of shore-based (non-carrier) aircraft.

A little over three months later, in early April 1943, Mitscher returned to the air-combat front line. He moved to Guadalcanal and took command of a multi-service air group with the title of "ComAirSols" (Air Command Solomons). Halsey stated later, "I knew we'd probably catch hell from the Japs in the air. That's why I sent Pete Mitscher up there [to Guadalcanal], Pete was a fighting fool and I knew it."[25] The fighting over the Solomons remained the epicenter of the Pacific War in the spring and summer. This struggle was now carried out by shore-based aircraft on both sides, as most of the carriers had been sunk or heavily damaged. Admiral Yamamoto Isoroku, the C-in-C of the Combined Fleet, used all available aircraft, based at Rabaul and new air bases in the western and central Solomons, in his attacks. Yamamoto was shot down and killed by AAF fighters in mid-April, two weeks after Mitscher's arrival at Guadalcanal.

At the end of June 1943 the Allied offensive land campaign in the central Solomons opened with the invasion of New Georgia. For Mitscher, however, three months on hot, humid, and mosquito-ridden Guadalcanal had taken its toll. A man in his late fifties, he had been in poor health for some time and had lost weight. Now he was struck down with malaria and was in bed for two weeks.[26] He was replaced as ComAirSols by an AAF General. But the "fighting fool" was rightly judged to have welded together a highly successful air campaign using the three American services and the Royal New Zealand Air Force. He was awarded the DSM for this campaign. The citation stated that he had "achieved distinctive success in coordinating [. . .] various forces into a powerful offensive weapon . . . [which] inflicted tremendous losses upon the enemy, destroying more than five hundred Japanese aircraft and sinking more than twenty vessels."[27]

On his return home Mitscher was assigned to the post of Commander, Fleet Air, West Coast, with his headquarters at NAS (Naval Air Station) North Island in San Diego. This was a wide-ranging administrative post charged mainly with forming and training naval air squadrons. The organization seems to have been run by a large and efficient administrative staff. Mitscher himself was able to spend much of his five months in the post recuperating from Guadalcanal; this was evidently the intention of his superiors.

Pete Mitscher's appointment to replace Rear Adm. Pownall as commander of the fast carriers has already been discussed. King, Nimitz, and Halsey agreed that Mitscher was the best candidate. On 23 December 1943 Mitscher was informed of his appointment as Commander, Carrier Division Three (ComCarDiv 3), replacing Pownall. Two weeks later, on 6 January 1944 Mitscher was made commander of Task Force 58.[28]

As with Spruance there was an interesting back story. Unlike Spruance's genteel upbringing in gilded-age Indianapolis, Baltimore, and New Jersey, Mitscher had grown up in a wilder environment of frontier Oklahoma, grandson of a German immigrant and son of a merchant and local politician. Marc was a physically small child, but he thrived in this rough and tumble environment, riding a pony over the prairie. More importantly, his father Oscar Mitscher was able to obtain an appointment for him to Annapolis. Marc had no interest in the sea or a naval career, but he entered the Academy in the autumn of 1904, with the class of 1908.

His time in the Academy was much less successful than that of Spruance (who had been admitted in the previous year). Young Mitscher, called "Pete" by his fellow midshipmen, performed poorly. In the spring of his second year (1905–6), with continuing low grades and disciplinary demerits, he was "bilged"—forced to resign. Thanks to his father's influence he was able to reapply as a new entrant, now in the class of 1910. He survived the next four years, but remained poorly disciplined and academically weak. Mitscher left Annapolis in June 1910, 107th in a class of 130. He was now four years behind Spruance (who had graduated early, with part of his class, in September 1906).

Thankfully, Ensign Mitscher settled down—albeit not entirely—when he joined the working navy. He served for five years on cruisers, destroyers, and gunboats in the Pacific. This provided a grounding in conventional naval service that some later "aviators" would lack. He also married, in 1913, Frances Smalley of Tacoma, Washington. Theirs, like the Spruances', would be a long and happy union.[29]

His career would be defined by aviation, and he was almost in a different Navy from Spruance. He first applied to take part in the new aviation program in 1911, and was finally accepted in September 1915. An aviation training station had been established in January 1914 at Pensacola, a naval base and shipyard located in the Florida panhandle. In October 1915 Mitscher reported for duty there and learned to fly in primitive "box kites." He received his "wings" as a naval aviator (No. 33) in June 1916. He was twenty-nine years old; by the future standards of World War II this was an advanced age for a new pilot. Like Spruance, Mitscher did not go to Europe during World War I. He was occupied with aviation training establishments, notably as CO of NAS Miami, where in July 1918 he reached the rank of lieutenant commander.

Mitscher entered aviation history with the U.S. Navy's transatlantic flight of May 1919. This involved a group of three big Curtiss NC flying boats, one of which (NC-4) successfully flew from NAS Rockaway near New York City to Plymouth in Britain, via Nova Scotia and the Azores. Mitscher was pilot of NC-1, part of a crew of six. Flying low in heavy fog he was forced to land in the sea short of the Azores, as did the third plane, the NC-2 (flown by John Towers, then a commander). Nevertheless, Mitscher had undertaken a dangerous mission and was awarded his first medal, a Navy Cross for valor.

Mitscher's experience in the 1920s and 1930s was very different from Spruance's. Despite the episode of the transatlantic flight, promotion came slowly. Mitscher remained a lieutenant commander for a decade, and by the time he reached the rank of commander in 1930 he was twelve years behind Spruance in promotion terms. He became a captain in 1938, six years after Spruance. He did not command a ship until 1937, when he took charge of the seaplane tender *Wright* (AV-1) at the age of fifty. Spruance's first command had been in 1913, and since then he had been CO of four other destroyers; in 1938 he would take command of one of the Navy's capital ships. Mitscher had not attended the Naval War College—and later would declare himself proud of this gap in his career, which he regarded as retrograde and irrelevant.[30]

Yet his career was far from marginal. Mitscher's expertise and authority in the field of naval aviation was unmatched. Unlike Spruance he gained extensive experience in naval—and higher—politics in Washington D.C. while working in BuAer (the Bureau of Aeronautics), effectively as a technical advisor to Rear Admirals Moffett, King, (Arthur) Cook, and Towers. From September 1939 he was Assistant Chief of BuAer (under Towers). This was a glamorous and well-publicized part of the Navy, that had enjoyed rapid growth of personnel and aircraft.

Between postings in Washington Mitscher was directly involved in the creation of carrier aviation. In the 1920s the first three carriers joined the fleet, the experimental *Langley* (CV-1), and the huge converted battle cruisers *Lexington* (CV-2), and *Saratoga* (CV-3). Mitscher was, in succession, head of the Aviation Departments of

Langley and of *Saratoga*—and carried out the first landing on the *Saratoga*; he later would serve as XO of both ships. From 1934 he took charge of flying boat units and led a number of long-range group flights.

By January 1944 the command team of the Central Pacific Force (later the Fifth Fleet) and Task Force 58 was in place. Despite their contrasting backgrounds, Raymond Spruance and Pete Mitscher were not so very different in terms of their personalities. Both were taciturn men, although Mitscher was a more aggressive tactician, less averse to risk, while Spruance could be seen as a manager with a wide range of responsibilities and a longer-term perspective. Mitscher was more directly involved in combat and perhaps had an intuitive closeness to rank and file pilots and crewmen which Spruance lacked. Both had critics, among fellow officers during the war and among historians afterward. They were nevertheless each very able in their particular sphere. Before the war they would not have seemed destined to reach the highest ranks. Even in 1943 it could not have been predicted that they would work together well. But they would do both, and under them the U.S. Navy achieved a stunning run of victories.

CHAIN OF COMMAND

Admirals Spruance and Mitscher were in the middle of a chain of command. They were given general directives from above and translated them into action by their subordinate commanders. Their decisions, and those of their superior officers, were developed by staffs.

Only the structure is outlined here; Pacific strategy itself is covered in Chapter 3.[31] President Roosevelt was Commander-in-Chief, and made some key decisions about strategy, inter-service relations, and the selection of senior personnel. "FDR" was a strong supporter of the Navy and the Navy Department, having been Assistant Secretary of the Navy from 1913 to 1920. The Secretary of the Navy in Roosevelt's wartime Cabinet was Frank Knox, in office from July 1940 until his death in April 1944. Knox, a Republican newspaperman, was kept out of decisions on strategy and planning by Admiral King, the Navy's professional head.

Admiral King had his headquarters in Washington in "Main Navy," a giant ramshackle structure put up quickly in World War I and located in the Mall. After Pearl Harbor he became "CominCh" (Commander-in-Chief, U.S. Fleet), selected by the President and Knox.[32] In March 1942 King also received a parallel appointment as Chief of Naval Operations (CNO). This latter post was originally concerned more with planning and administration than with operations. As CominCh-CNO, and de facto directly under the President, King now had unprecedented control over operations and administration, although he concerned himself especially with the former. King had authority in strategic decisions affecting the operations and administration of the Navy and also in senior appointments and promotions. King's chief of staff as CominCh was Rear Adm. Richard S. Edwards. Rear Adm. Charles "Savvy" Cooke served as chief planner. Most aspects of logistics were dealt with by Vice Adm. Frederick J. Horne, who became the Vice Chief of Naval Operations (VCNO) in March 1942.

King was a tall, outwardly very blunt, and ambitious officer, sixty-two years old in December 1941. He had been passed over for appointment to CNO in 1939, but the outbreak of the European War saved him from final retirement as a vice admiral; in December 1940 he was made commander of U.S. naval forces in the Atlantic. King relished his hard-nosed reputation. As he put it himself, "When they get into trouble they always send for sons of bitches."[33] A working-class boy from Ohio, with immigrant parents (from Britain), he graduated fourth in his class from the Naval Academy in 1901. His naval career had been very varied, but his extensive experience in aviation was one aspect that prepared him for the Pacific War. Congress in 1926 had passed legislation requiring flight training for commanders of aviation ships and naval air bases. Capt. King passed the Pensacola flying course the following year, at the age of forty-nine. This qualified him in 1930–32 to command the giant new carrier *Lexington*. Between 1932 and 1936 King was head of BuAer in Washington; from 1936 he held major operational air posts in the fleet as "Commander, Aircraft," first in the Navy's Base Force and then in the Battle Force.

As CominCh-CNO King had a major role within the Joint Chiefs of Staff (JCS) committee, set up in Washington in February 1942. He served for most of the war alongside General George Marshall from the Army and General "Hap" Arnold from the Army Air Force. Indicative of Roosevelt's pro-Navy perspective, the chair of the JCS from July 1942 was an admiral; William Leahy was a former CNO—and personal friend of the President.[34] King and the JCS also had to interact with the military leaders of the British Empire through the Combined Chiefs of Staff (CCS). Historic decisions were negotiated at inter-Allied conferences which King took part in, not only the summit conferences at Casablanca, Tehran, and Cairo (and later at Yalta and Potsdam), but also at strategic planning conferences. Of the latter, three were relevant to the Central Pacific campaign: ARGONAUT (in Washington) in June 1942, TRIDENT (Washington) in May 1943, and QUADRANT (Quebec) in August 1943.

Although King was responsible for all the Navy's operations, including those in the Atlantic and the Mediterranean, his main focus in 1942–44 was on the eastern Pacific. It was an active front where the Navy and the Marines were the main forces involved. King flew every two or three months to San Francisco—and occasionally Hawaii—to meet directly with Admiral Nimitz, the C-in-C in the Pacific. Generally, however, King delegated decision-making and detailed planning to his fleet commanders. He accepted Nimitz's decisions, although privately he sometimes called him a "fixer," that is, an individual too prepared to compromise with (bureaucratic) opponents.[35]

Admiral Chester Nimitz was an affable—even folksy—Texan of German descent. On the surface, at least, he was quite unlike his severe boss. Like King, however, he was certainly capable of making firm decisions and accepting calculated risks. One of his subordinates later described him as "the resolute man with the white hair and the very blue eyes."[36] Seventh in his class at Annapolis, he was a highly capable administrator; his last pre-war post had been overseeing all naval personnel as head of the (confusingly named) Bureau of Navigation (BuNav). Nimitz was only fifty-six years old at the time of Pearl Harbor, and he still held the relatively low rank of rear admiral. He was six years younger than King, and only a year and a half older than Spruance. He had been catapulted into high operational command by the Pearl Harbor disaster; like King, he was selected by President Roosevelt and Secretary Knox. He passed over dozens of more senior candidates and was promoted directly to the four-star rank of full admiral. Although

Nimitz had broad experience, from submarines to battleships, he had—like Spruance—no aviation background.

From the time he arrived in Hawaii at the end of December 1941, Nimitz was always based ashore (unlike his Japanese counterparts). His headquarters were originally at the submarine base, but in the later summer of 1942 they were moved up Makalapa Hill to a new site overlooking Pearl Harbor. The bomb-proof CincPac building, two "decks" above ground and one below, was a big, white concrete structure, set among well-tended lawns and surrounded by other administrative buildings.[37] As CincPac the admiral commanded the ships, planes, and marines of the Pacific Fleet, but he also became C-in-C of the "Pacific Ocean Areas" (CincPOA); this was a command set up in the spring of 1942 by the JCS to take in non-Navy elements.

As CincPac-CincPOA, Nimitz commanded three widely separated areas in the huge expanse of ocean under his control. (Also directly under Nimitz's control was the submarine campaign led by the Commander, Submarines, Pacific Fleet (ComSubPac); from February 1943 this would be Rear Adm. Charles Lockwood.) The South Pacific, latterly under Halsey, was most active in 1942–43. By the end of 1943 and in 1944, most operations south of the equator were no longer under CincPac-CincPOA; they were in New Guinea, and under MacArthur's Australia-based Southwest Pacific Area (SWPA) command. (Operationally, Halsey was from the spring of 1943 subordinate to MacArthur—and established a good personal relationship with him; administratively, however, he answered to Nimitz.) The North Pacific, latterly under Kinkaid, was also remote from Hawaii, and although it involved actual American territory (in Alaska), fighting was limited. The local situation was effectively resolved after the recapture of Attu Island in the Aleutians in May 1943. Nimitz gave the commanders in the North Pacific and South Pacific considerable leeway to make their own decisions.

The Central Pacific was different. It was Nimitz's greatest concern, not least because it was closest to Hawaii, with CincPac headquarters and the main Pacific Fleet naval base beyond the West Coast. At Makalapa Nimitz had a large staff, large at least by the standards of the U.S. Navy. As already mentioned, Spruance was his chief of staff from June 1942 to August 1943. Nimitz had made this selection before

Midway, and the two officers worked very closely for nearly a year after that (and also took long hikes together in the countryside of Oahu). Each knew how the other thought, and Nimitz had full confidence in Spruance's abilities. Spruance was replaced as chief of staff by Rear Adm. Charles ("Soc") McMorris, another surface-ship specialist. In November 1943 an aviator, Rear Adm. Forrest Sherman, became Nimitz's assistant chief of staff for planning, and in March 1944 he moved up to the post of deputy chief of staff. Sherman had been CO of the carrier *Wasp* when she was sunk by a Japanese sub in September 1942; after that he became chief of staff to Towers (ComAirPac). A rapid advance lay ahead for Sherman after the war; he would serve as CNO from 1949 until his untimely death in 1951. Capt. Edwin Layton, who had played a major part in the Midway victory, served as intelligence officer.[38]

Among Nimitz's other subordinates was John Towers, who has been described as "the ultimate air admiral."[39] Promoted to vice admiral, he was sent out from Washington in October 1942 as ComAirPac; his relations with Nimitz (also with King and Spruance) were not warm. Nimitz worked better with Kelly Turner, an old friend who became his specialist in amphibious operations. Also important were Vice Adm. Calhoun, commander of the supply ships of the Service Force, and Vice Adm. Hoover, commander of the land-based air force, which included Navy and AAF long-range bombers. Lt Gen. Robert C. Richardson was commander of Army troops in the Pacific Ocean Areas (POA); their role was defending island bases and, with the Marines, assaulting Japanese-held positions. Richardson grumbled a great deal about what he perceived as the slights Nimitz and his staff dealt to him personally, and to the Army.

As well as the ambitious strategic task—crossing the Central Pacific—Nimitz and Spruance had to deal with the creation of an effective organization for the increasing strength of Army and AAF forces under their command in the POA. This was achieved effectively in September 1943, as the Central Pacific campaign began to roll out. At first a Fleet Staff and a Joint Staff existed side by side, both under Nimitz, and these eventually developed smoothly as an overall joint command. The Army played an especially important role in logistics. One of the best-known multi-service elements was JICPOA, the Joint Intelligence Center of the POA, which was set up in September 1943.[40]

Nimitz (with Spruance) also had to oversee the deployment of a naval force in a challenging situation. The fleet was now of an unprecedented size, but at the same time the mass of wartime personnel, both officers and "bluejackets," were much less experienced than those of the "old" Navy. They were now taking part in a radically different form of warfare, which demanded new tactical doctrines. Individual ships and aircraft were technically a great advance over their predecessors, and the main battle units were operated in a different way. Rather than being physically concentrated around a line of battleships, the main force was dispersed and highly flexible. Crucial elements, as far as the battle force was concerned, were the speed of the new ships, the centrality of aviation, and the development of methods for keeping task forces at sea for long periods of time. Meanwhile, amphibious warfare on a wholly unprecedented scale required a new range of weapons and tactics.

In the spring of 1943 Nimitz assembled a board to set out standard fleet procedures. This formalized his ad hoc but close attention in 1942 to the dissemination of immediate combat lessons. This resulted in a document entitled "Current Tactical Orders and Doctrine, U.S. Pacific Fleet" and known as PAC-10. Issued in June, its aim was "to provide, in the light of war experience, instructions both sufficiently inclusive and flexible to control the operations of Pacific Fleet task forces."

> The ultimate aim is to obtain essential uniformity without unacceptable sacrifice of flexibility. It must be possible for forces composed of diverse types, and indoctrinated under different task force commanders, to join at sea on short notice for concerted action against the enemy without exchanging a mass of special instructions.[41]

PAC-10 was drafted before the arrival of any of the new fast carriers. It came months ahead of the actual organization of fast-carrier task forces made up of the multiple task groups, each containing three or four carriers. Nevertheless, the procedures were tested successfully in the carrier raids (already mentioned) which began in August 1943, first against Marcus and the Gilberts, and then in the "dress rehearsal" in October, when two task groups raided Wake. Full-scale application came when four dispersed fast-carrier task groups deployed in Operation GALVANIC in the Gilberts in November. At the same time plans were developed for the flexible deployment of the new fast battleships, which now numbered six units.[42]

The most important command under Nimitz was that of Raymond Spruance and the Central Pacific Force. Spruance's staff was created in the summer of 1943.[43] As his chief of staff Spruance selected Capt. Charles ("Carl") Moore. As mentioned earlier, Moore was a long-standing navy comrade, with experience in surface ships and the Naval War College, but not in aviation. Moore's role was cut short by the decision made in early January 1944 that for future high-level commands with a major aviation element either the commander or his chief of staff should be an aviator. The same rule applied to major surface-ship elements. Spruance was a non-aviator, and so Moore did not have the required background. Nevertheless, he was only replaced on 1 August 1944, after the decisive campaign in the Marianas.[44]

In any event, in August 1943, Spruance had delegated the selection of most of his staff to Moore. Spruance later outlined his concept: "My ideas on staffs are that they should be composed of the smallest number of first class men who can do the jobs."[45] Spruance's staff in CenPac was only half the size of Halsey's in SoPac, although it should be kept in mind that Spruance also received a great deal of support from the Fleet and Joint Staffs with which his headquarters at Makalapa was co-located.[46] Unlike King and Nimitz (and Halsey from late 1942 to the middle of 1944), Spruance spent much of his time at sea and in the forward area. He usually chose a medium-sized vessel, the 10,000-ton heavy cruiser *Indianapolis*, as his flagship. The aim was to avoid tying down a major fleet unit, but it also brought the staff down to a size Spruance thought desirable. *Indianapolis* would be sunk by a submarine with very heavy loss of life in the last weeks of the war, but by that time she was no longer a flagship.

Key figures on Spruance's staff, in addition to Moore, were Emmet Forrestel as operations officer and Capt. Burton Biggs as logistics officer (the latter task representing a new development in wartime staffs). For operations Spruance had a number of other subordinates including Pownall (later Mitscher) with the fast carriers, Rear Adm. Willis Lee with the fast battleships, and Kelly Turner as commander from August 1943 of the new Fifth Amphibious Force (Fifth 'Phib).

Mitscher's staff, for TF 58, was smaller than that of King or Spruance, but it still eventually numbered 140 officers and men. His first chief of staff was Capt. Truman Hedding, an able aviator who had worked earlier under Pownall in TF 50. Mitscher and his staff were initially located aboard carrier *Yorktown* (CV-10); in March 1944 Mitscher transferred his flag to *Lexington* (CV-16). When the policy of balancing aviators and non-aviators in senior posts came into force, Capt. Arleigh Burke was assigned to replace Hedding. The actual replacement took place in March 1944. Burke was well known as a destroyer commander, but after a frosty start he and Mitscher worked very well as a team. Burke would have an even more striking career than Forrest Sherman, serving as CNO for two terms, from 1955 to 1961. Also prominent on Mitscher's staff of TF 58 was his operations officer, Cdr William J. ("Gus") Widhelm, who had been a dive-bomber pilot at Midway and Santa Cruz.

Mitscher's Task Force 58, in line with the PAC-10 doctrine, was subdivided into a number of task groups. These consisted of one or two heavy carriers, one or two light carriers, and supporting cruisers and destroyers (sometimes fast battleships were also attached). Each of the four task groups was larger than any of the carrier task forces that had fought in the battles of 1942. The four groups could operate near one another, as in the June 1944 Battle of the Philippine Sea, or one or two could be dispatched hundreds of miles away for separate operations. They also could take turns meeting fleet oiler groups for refueling. Likewise, flexible arrangements allowed the fast battleships to be divided up among the various fast-carrier task groups or kept together to operate as a battle-force main body.

Selection and preparation of commanders for new carrier task groups had begun in 1942 and 1943, anticipating the production and arrival of new ships and aircraft. All were aviators; most had combat experience. As the number of task groups increased, potential commanders were taken to sea to shadow more experienced task group commanders on a "makee-learn" basis. In mid-January 1944 Mitscher had as his immediate subordinates in Task Force 58 four rear admirals: John Reeves (TG 58.1), Alfred Montgomery (TG 58.2), Ted Sherman (not to be confused with Forrest Sherman) (TG 58.3), and Samuel Ginder (TG 58.4). Ted Sherman was an enthusiast for the cause of the "aviators," but was a "latecomer" himself, having transferred to flight training in 1935 with the rank of commander at age forty-seven. The other three were long-term career airmen who trained as pilots in the 1920s, shortly after graduation from the Naval Academy. All four had commanded carriers. Reeves was the first CO of the old *Wasp* (CV-7) and took her on two famous voyages ferrying Spitfires to Malta in the spring of 1942. Montgomery commanded *Ranger* in the Atlantic in 1940–41. Ted Sherman was in charge of the old *Lexington* (CV-2) in the Coral Sea battle. Ginder had taken over *Enterprise* when she returned from her repairs and refit in the spring of 1943 (after Santa Cruz).

OFFICERS AND ENLISTED PERSONNEL

Personnel—people—were, of course, a vital factor in the Central Pacific campaign. Many accounts of the U.S. Navy in the Pacific War tend to concentrate on admirals and "college-boy" pilots, leaving out a large human factor in the background. This was the junior officers and enlisted personnel of the ships from which aircraft operated and of other vessels which provided their essential escort.[47] Without these men naval supremacy would not have been achieved.

The pre-war U.S. Navy was top heavy, but in terms of capital ships it was the same size as the British Royal Navy, and the two fleets were the largest in the world. But it was certainly small in comparison with the wartime U.S. Navy of 1942–45. Enlisted numbers had been 80,000–85,000 in the 1920s and first half of the 1930s. There was a slight increase to 111,000 in 1939, and then a significant jump to 332,000 in 1941 as the American government responded to the European war and an aggressive Japan.[48] But in wartime the total number of enlisted personnel surged to 2,034,000 in 1943 and 2,808,000 in 1944, ending up nearly twenty or thirty times the figure of 1939. This can be compared with 5,977,000 in the U.S. Army ground forces and 2,314,000 in U.S. Army Air Force in May 1945.

As the Central Pacific campaign began, at the start of 1944, total personnel in the U.S. Navy (officers and enlisted) was about 2,300,000, of whom about 800,000 were actually serving afloat and outside the United States. The great majority of U.S. Navy personnel served in the Pacific area. The peak there (in August 1945) was 1,367,000, compared to the peak in the North Atlantic (in June 1944) of 150,000 or the Mediterranean (in August 1944) of 90,000. The fleet's spearhead was only a fraction of this in terms of personnel. As already mentioned, in January 1944 the number of personnel in the new Task Force 58 was about 100,000 officers and men. Total naval personnel in the Central Pacific numbered about 190,000 afloat in February 1944, with another 100,000 in shore postings.

Expansion was a complex process for both officers and enlisted personnel, albeit for different reasons. The enlisted personnel of the pre-war Navy were volunteers. In those years the Navy could pick and choose; recruits were of high quality, and were usually high school graduates. Minimum age of entry was seventeen. The term of service was initially for four years, but re-enlistment was encouraged. The Navy was generally seen by young men as an attractive service, providing some technical education and, hopefully, a chance to see the world. And the appeal of the Navy increased in the years of the Great Depression, when other jobs were scarce.

The beginning of the war in Europe in September 1939 and the surrender of France in June 1940 brought about major changes. Peacetime conscription—the "Draft" or "Selective Service"—began to develop slowly from September 1940. In its original form, all men between twenty-one and twenty-five were required to register for military service, initially with a lottery-based draft and one-year service. In 1941 and 1942, however, the draft only applied to the U.S. Army, and the Navy continued with voluntary enlistment. The Navy felt that its requirements were different from those of the Army. Younger men were wanted in the Navy, and it was argued that one year would not be adequate to prepare sailors for service in the fleet. Meanwhile, the Navy was able to attract the number of volunteers required for that time without compulsion. Behind all this was a powerful sense of Navy independence and identity, with an aversion to being submerged in an Army conscription system.

The volunteer principle continued after the attack on Pearl Harbor and the beginning of a global war. In the first months the Navy was swamped with patriotic volunteers. Promise of direct action, against an Asiatic enemy whose navy had attacked Pearl Harbor, was attractive to young Americans. The Navy opened new recruiting offices and ran an extensive advertising campaign. The President approved the Navy's policy of staying outside the Selective Service system, as indicated by a February 1942 memo to Secretary of War Stimson. As the Navy's administrative history later put it, "It would seem that the President's decision . . . was not based on nationwide manpower plans, or on an accurate study of the military performance of selectees, but rather on the traditional view as to what it takes to make a 'man-of-war's man.' " In the period up to February 1943 about 900,000 people (the great majority men) joined the U.S. Navy as volunteers.[49]

Women began to join the ranks in the "Woman's Reserve", also known as WAVES (Women Accepted for Volunteer Emergency Service), in September 1942. Input in 1943 was about 3,000 women a month. WAVES did not serve aboard combat ships, and indeed service was restricted to the continental United States and Hawaii. The only women serving in the Pacific theater were Navy nurses; the total of these in the USN as a whole was 11,000. On the other hand, the indirect impact of the WAVES in the combat theater was significant, because they freed up male officers and sailors for front-line service. In a more positive sense, women fulfilled a great many essential technical and administrative duties within the Navy in their stateside posts. They made a significant contribution to codebreaking, something which has only recently been given recognition. WAVES formed a relatively small part of total Navy personnel, some 80,000 in 1945—but that was comparable in size to the whole enlisted personnel of the Navy in the 1920s.[50]

At the end of 1942 the demands of global war forced a change of policy in the conscription system as a whole. A December 1942 Executive Order from the President directed that enlistment of personnel for the Navy, as well as the Army, should be done through the Draft and not independently. The two services were in future to specify how many men they required on a monthly basis, and these would be furnished by the Selective Service system. No man aged eighteen or over, or under thirty-eight, could be inducted into the armed forces—including the Navy—except through Draft. This change took effect in February 1943.

Nevertheless, loopholes remained for voluntary enlistment in the Navy, notably recruitment at age seventeen or older than age thirty-seven. Between February 1943 and March 1944, 780,000 personnel entered the Navy through the Draft, but another 200,000 entered the service as volunteers.

Overall, "input" of enlisted personnel into the Navy from civilian life was about 10,000 a month in the second half of 1941. The figure increased to 30,000–50,000 a month from December 1941 to the summer in 1942. Then input rose again, reaching 131,000 in October 1942, which was the highest month of the entire war—in a single month the growth of personnel was more than the pre-war strength of the entire Navy. In the first half of 1943—under the modified Selective Service enlistment system—intake was below that peak, at 60–70,000 a month, but it reached 100,000 a month in the second half of the year.

The unprecedented input of enlisted personnel put great demand on training facilities. In 1941 there were four Naval Training Centers for enlisted personnel: Newport (Rhode Island), Norfolk (Virginia), Great Lakes (Illinois, near Chicago), and San Diego (California). In the course of 1942 new training centers were opened, all named after historic admirals: "Bainbridge" in Maryland, "Sampson" in upstate New York, and "Farragut" in Idaho. These three were not located in traditional ports, but they were all near bodies of water, albeit small freshwater ones.

Recruit training—"boot camp"—was shortened during the war, from eight to four weeks.[51] But even before December 1941, training of "boots", who were mostly very young adults, far from home, involved marching with rifles and frequent inspections, and receiving a general introduction to Navy life and customs. Emory Jernigan, then a seventeen-year-old farm boy from Florida, went through boot camp at Norfolk in early 1941, with about a hundred recruits in Graduating Platoon 192. He later saw the value of this harsh induction, but he also felt that training staff, mostly experienced non-commissioned officers—chiefs and petty officers—were hard taskmasters:

[They] did anything to make you feel miserable and break your spirit so that you would not fail to do as you were told . . . The only thing they wanted you to learn in boot camp was to obey, keep your clothes neat, think good thoughts about the service and build self-respect. You learned to obey, no matter what happened.[52]

After basic recruit training about a third of the "boots" were assigned to special service schools for training as electricians, machinists' mates, and many other roles. This could lead to a "rate," i.e. to petty officer rank. The remainder, those consigned to relatively unskilled service in "deck" departments of ships or in the engine rooms, were granted ten days' leave and then went directly into the fleet. As replacements on big ships they were usually first assigned to "Z" Division for further training afloat, and to work out where on the ship their permanent station would be. A "seagoing goddam boot camp," was how one senior petty officer described this situation, even before Pearl Harbor.[53]

There were important developments in "operational" training, where the crew learned to work together (as opposed to the individual training at boot camp). Before the war the number of new ships was small and crews were made up of experienced officers and enlisted personnel. Operational training could be carried out aboard the new vessel. In wartime the rapid pace of construction and the very high percentage of inexperienced young sailors demanded a different procedure. Operational training was often carried out on shore, before the blue-jackets physically joined their assigned ship. They learned to work as a team, coordination was developed, and individuals were selected for specific roles.[54]

The hierarchy of the Navy's world, even for enlisted personnel, was complex. The lowest three ranks, of "non-rated" personnel, began with apprentice seaman (AS), leading to seaman 2nd class (S2/c) and seaman 1st class (S1/c). In the Engine Room Force, they could proceed from apprentice seaman to fireman 3rd, 2nd, and 1st class (F3/c, F2/c, F1/c).

Some sailors went directly from recruit training to a specialist school and joined the fleet as rated petty officers (roughly comparable to an Army sergeant). Other men, not selected for a training school, might later be selected as a "striker" and receive in-service training afloat for "rating" as a petty officer. Such promotions became more common as the fleet expanded. Three levels of petty officer existed. At the top were a small number of older veterans with the grade of chief petty officer (or "Chief"). Examples were chief boatswain's mate (CBM), chief gunner's mate (CGM), chief radioman (CRM), and chief machinist's mate (CMM). Ships were divided into divisions usually headed by a chief, formally alongside a junior and less experienced commissioned officer.

A chief boatswain's mate often served as master-at-arms, overseeing disciplinary matters for the whole ship and working closely with the commissioned executive officer (XO). Chiefs had better pay, a distinctive uniform and, on bigger ships, their own mess (i.e. catering facilities). Recalling his experiences in the engine room of *Washington*, in 1941–42, Emory Jernigan wrote:

> Chiefs are what keep the Navy going. They are the buffer between the officers and the men. They keep the Navy traditions alive, leading both the men and, in many ways, the officers. Neither good nor bad, they are the lifeblood of the Navy. Without them we would have been nothing.[55]

A small number of senior petty officers with a specialist skill could be promoted to the status of warrant officer.

In the U.S. Navy there was roughly one commissioned officer for ten enlisted personnel. The number of officers was 11,600 (plus 2,300 officer candidates) in 1939; in 1941 it had reached 38,600 (plus 1,500 officer candidates). The numbers of officers then grew very rapidly, reaching 118,000 in 1942, 219,300 in 1943, and 300,100 in 1944; in addition, officer candidates numbered 120,500 in 1943 and 84,600 in 1944.

The traditional source of career officers was the four-year course at the U.S. Naval Academy (USNA) at Annapolis, Maryland. This has already been touched on while describing the background of Spruance, Mitscher, and others. Founded in 1845, it featured an impressive campus with massive granite Beaux Arts buildings, erected in the early twentieth century as the U.S. began to build a big navy. In the 1920s and 1930s, graduating classes were relatively small, partly due to the surplus of officers trained for World War I. Indeed, in the early 1930s, during the depth of national funding cuts, some successful graduates were not awarded commissions.[56] The smallest graduating year was 1936, when the number shrank to 261. A more normal graduating class in the 1920s and 1930s, however, was 400–500 men. When America entered the war the size of Annapolis classes was 500–600. The length of the course was reduced from four years to three, and the midshipmen graduated a year early.

In the interwar years Annapolis had been supplemented by the new Naval Reserve Officers Training Corps (NROTC). This was set up initially in 1926 at half a dozen elite universities, and it provided training for a commission in the Naval Reserve (USNR).[57] By 1941 NROTC was producing about 200 USNR ensigns a year. Rapid expansion of the Navy after Pearl Harbor led to the setting up of procurement offices in key cities. By 1944 some 72,000 officers had been commissioned in the Naval Reserve directly from civilian life. These were often individuals with essential technical and administrative skills; an unusual example was the great naval historian Samuel Eliot Morison, who received a USNR commission as a lieutenant commander in May 1942. In addition, many enlisted personnel—warrant officers, chiefs, and petty officers—received commissions in the regular Navy in an initiative begun in February 1942, about 21,000 in 1943 alone. Some 60,700 such individuals were commissioned between Pearl Harbor and the end of 1944.

Then there were the young officers provided by the Naval Reserve Midshipman Program, also known as V-7. These were college students or graduates who took a three-month crash course at a Naval Reserve Training School to pass "through the looking glass" into the strange world of the Navy and its customs. As reserve midshipmen and under tight discipline they studied what were described as "naval science and indoctrination," and if successful they passed out as ensigns in the USNR. The program provided an overview of navigation, communications, first aid, gunnery, and seamanship.[58] These new officers were known in the fleet, with a degree of irony, as "ninety-day wonders," but they provided an essential element for the huge wartime expansion. The first four Reserve Midshipman Schools were established at the Naval Academy, and at the campuses of Columbia, Northwestern, and Notre Dame Universities. By the middle of 1943 two more schools had been established at Cornell and at Plattsburgh State University (both in upstate New York). Some 9,000 midshipmen were training in these schools at any one time.[59]

In wartime the Annapolis provided only 5 percent of the new officer personnel. Overall, some 85 percent of officers were in the USNR. The Navy's policy was to fill major command billets afloat with regular (USN) officers—mostly Annapolis graduates— and some reservists resented this. The logic, however, was that the regular officers generally had broad experience, they had chosen the Navy as career, and in addition they would be needed in the Navy after the war. As the war progressed USNR officers progressed to command some older destroyers, escort vessels, auxiliaries, and amphibious craft.

The total complement of an "Essex" class fleet carrier in 1943–44 was about 3,040: 270 officers and 2,770 enlisted men. Of these, 130 officers and 2,040 enlisted men formed the ship's crew, while 140 officers and 730 enlisted men were involved in operating and maintaining aircraft. If the carrier was the "Flag" of a task group another 30 officers and 130 enlisted men would be added.[60] The "Independence" class light carriers had a total complement about half that size, some 1,460: 140 officers and 1,320 enlisted. The crew of a fast battleship was somewhat smaller than that of a fleet carrier; the "South Dakota" class, for example, had a wartime complement of about 2,500. Among the most important escorts for the fast carriers were the new "Cleveland" class light cruisers; they had a complement of 70 officers and 1,115 enlisted men. The "Fletcher" class destroyers were the most numerous, large vessels for their type, with a wartime complement of 330 officers and men.

The commanding officer (CO) was in overall charge of the ship. Taking just major warship types, the CO of a carrier, battleship or cruiser normally held the rank of captain, while the CO of a destroyer would be a commander or lieutenant commander. The executive officer (XO), in charge of general administration, personnel and discipline, would be a commander in a big ship, or a lieutenant commander or lieutenant in a destroyer.

U.S. Navy ships were organized in a number of departments, with the officers and enlisted personnel assigned to related administrative "divisions." Again, details varied with the size, type, and function of a ship.[61] On a big ship the enlisted men of the Gunnery (or Ordnance) Department ("O") were organized into a number of "deck" divisions, each manning part of the armament, including AA guns; a battleship might have nine such divisions. The Engineering Department ("E") also had a large staff—known informally as the "Black Gang"—and would have several divisions. The Construction and Repair ("Hull") Department ("R") was under the "First Lieutenant" of the vessel. The Navigation ("N"), Communications ("C"), Supply ("S"), and Medical ("H") all had their own department and division(s). The divisions did give young bluejackets a valuable sense of structure, especially in a very big ship with a crew of 1,000 or more.

CHAPTER 2

FLINTLOCK

TF 58 and the Invasion of the Marshalls, January–February 1944

KWAJALEIN AND MAJURO

USS *Essex* began to launch her first strike against Kwajalein Atoll at 0537.[1] More than an hour and a half remained before sunrise as the first Hellcat fighter took off; sunrise would come at 0715. Conditions were still pitch black, with no visible horizon. The date was Saturday, 29 January 1944, two days before the first planned landings by American troops in the Marshall Islands, Operation FLINTLOCK.

Commanded by Capt. Ralph Ofstie, *Essex* was part of Task Group 58.2, one of four fast-carrier groups taking part in FLINTLOCK. *Essex* steamed with carriers *Intrepid* and *Cabot* at the center of a ring of escorting ships. A "plane guard" destroyer followed closely behind each carrier, ready to recover aircrew from takeoff accidents.

Strike ABLE from *Essex* was made up of nineteen F6F Hellcat fighters and six TBF Avenger bombers, led by Lt Cdr Herbert Houck USNR. Their mission that morning—alongside aircraft from *Intrepid* and *Cabot*—was to secure air superiority over the northern part of Kwajalein Atoll, especially Roi and Namur, two small islands joined by a causeway. Enemy planes were to be destroyed in the air and on the ground. Roi was small, but crammed into it was a triangle of runways making up the only operational air base in the atoll.

A pre-dawn launch was the standard tactic for the first attack on a fixed, island target. The hours of nighttime permitted the carrier or fleet

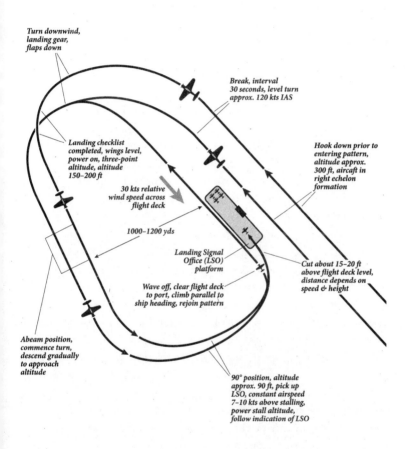

Turn downwind, landing gear, flaps down

Break, interval 30 seconds, level turn approx. 120 kts IAS

Landing checklist completed, wings level, power on, three-point altitude, altitude 150–200 ft

Hook down prior to entering pattern, altitude approx. 300 ft, aircaft in right echelon formation

30 kts relative wind speed across flight deck

1000–1200 yds

Landing Signal Office (LSO) platform

Cut about 15–20 ft above flight deck level, distance depends on speed & height

Wave off, clear flight deck to port, climb parallel to ship heading, rejoin pattern

Abeam position, commence turn, descend gradually to approach altitude

90° position, altitude approx. 90 ft, pick up LSO, constant airspeed 7–10 kts above stalling, power stall altitude, follow indication of LSO

Figure 2.1. Carrier landing procedure

unit to dash forward 150 miles or more, under cover of darkness and with little fear of enemy air attack. The distance to Roi was now 120 miles, well under an hour's flying time each way. The strike group from *Essex* were all airborne by 0604, and they arrived over their target at first light.

Launching a squadron or more of carrier planes was a highly complex procedure. Several hundred crewmen had worked through the night, positioning the planes of Strike ABLE at "flight three," the rear end of the flight deck. The flight deck crew (the V-1 division) wore color-coded vests (over dungarees) and helmets—white for the flight deck officer, brown for plane captains, blue for "plane handlers," yellow for plane directors (who supervised the plane handlers), green for men operating catapults and arresting gear, white (with red hats) for sailors handling ammunition, bombs and torpedoes, red jerseys for fire prevention; fuel handlers wore the standard dungarees, but with a red helmet.[2] At "flight three" the planes were loaded with fuel and ammunition. An enlisted "plane captain" was in charge of each F6F or TBF. The big radial engines needed to be run up for at least fifteen to twenty minutes to prepare for takeoff.

The single-seat fighters were usually "spotted" in the front rows of the parked aircraft at "flight three." On the big carriers they still had a clear deck of about 400 feet—rather more than a football field—for their takeoff run. The heavily loaded attack planes—dive bombers and torpedo bombers—were spotted furthest aft, as they needed a longer takeoff run. In general, planes on the flight deck had to be spotted aft or forward, with the opposite end clear. If planes were assembled too far forward they could not be launched. If they were assembled aft it was impossible to recover planes. There was, as a result, much movement back and forth. Fully loaded, with fuel and weapons, these planes weighed between 6 and 8.5 tons (comparable to an empty standard GMC six-wheel Army truck). They were towed into position either by a tractor or manhandled by numerous plane handlers of the deck crew.

Before the war the U.S. Navy had thought in terms of a "deckload" strike, launching all planes of a carrier—eighty or more—at one time. But the growing size of carrier aircraft and wartime experience led to the practice of using smaller groups of a "half-deckload" strength (half the air group) or less.

Essex was now facing into the wind. Noise and vibration from the ship's machinery, four turbines totaling 150,000 horsepower, increased as the vessel accelerated from cruising speed of about 15 knots to up to 30 knots for aircraft launch. A powerful headwind was needed to enable the safe launch of heavy aircraft, increasing the lift of their wings. For the plane handlers on deck a strong wind was now blowing to join the rumble of the ship's machinery and roar of airplane engines.

Sheltered from the man-made gale and the busy preparations above them, the pilots were seated in their "ready rooms" and received a pre-flight briefing. *Essex*'s Air Group 9 (AG 9) were an experienced team. They had taken part in five combat operations, beginning with the Marcus Island raid in August 1943. There was one ready room for each squadron in the air group. On a big carrier this was positioned directly under the flight deck, in a gallery above the hangar deck. When loud-speaker announcements ordered the pilots to "man your planes," they made their way up a companionway (stairway) to the flight deck.

The crews climbed aboard their planes. As the pilots restarted their engines the noise on deck greatly increased. With their wings folded the planes could be three or four abreast on the flight deck, but as they moved forward their wings were unfolded and locked. The pilots taxied them in turn to the takeoff spot. As the first Hellcat moved forward, the flight deck officer (FDO), wearing his distinctive white shirt, took a position off the starboard wing tip. There he made hand signals for the pilot to increase engine rpm. When the FDO was satisfied with the sound of the engine he waved a checkered flag and pointed toward the bow. The big fighter lurched forward and rolled faster and faster down the deck for takeoff.

As soon as he was airborne the pilot banked his plane into a left-hand (port) turn. All this happened quickly, and the second plane in the division had already reached the takeoff spot and was being sent off by the FDO. The following planes were normally only seconds behind the first two, and one by one they climbed quickly into the darkness. The lead plane and the ones behind would then climb to about 1,000 feet and enter a holding pattern, counter-clockwise above the carrier, following a racetrack circuit. The divisions of four or six planes flew together for tactical coordination. Once more elements had joined, they flew off toward their objective. This whole procedure was in no way simple, especially in the darkness; the launch of the twenty-five plane "half-deckload" of Strike ABLE took nearly half an hour.

As the first wave was being launched, planes of a second half-deck-load were in readiness below the flight deck, on the hangar deck. There they had been fueled and armed, and warmed up their engines. The elevators brought them up to the flight deck as soon as it was clear. On the larger carriers like *Essex* the planes were raised from the hangar deck, two at a time with their wings folded, on one of three elevators. Movement and spotting of the whole launch group would take twenty to thirty minutes of hectic activity.

This second launch group was—somewhat confusingly—designated as Strike No. 1. It was made up of seven Hellcats and eleven TBF Avengers, the TBFs carrying bombs for airfield attack rather than a torpedo. This launch itself was quicker; it began at 0635 and was completed by 0652. The process was repeated from 0720 with the big Strike No. 2, formed of eight Hellcats and twenty-eight SBD Dauntless dive bombers of VB-9. By the time Strike No. 2 had completed takeoff the sun had risen in the east.

The early-morning attacks against Roi airfield by *Essex* planes was coordinated with similar action by aircraft from *Intrepid*. Although Japanese radar on Roi-Namur had provided enough warning to get about thirty Zero fighters into the air, these were mostly shot down. Betty medium bombers were caught on the ground or destroyed while trying to escape to other Japanese bases. Overall the raid was highly successful, much more so than Rear Adm. Pownall's attempt with TF 50 on 4 December 1943. Afterward, the Roi airfield was inoperable. Japanese air strength there had been completely destroyed. Complete air control had been achieved over the whole of Kwajalein Atoll by midday. This was three days before the main landing on Roi-Namur itself on D+1 of FLINTLOCK. As the historian S. E. Morison described the events of 29 January: "the last Japanese fighter plane ever seen over Kwajalein was shot down at 0800."[3]

The *Essex* air group lost two planes and two pilots on that day. One was an "operational" loss, a Hellcat that blew up and crashed shortly after takeoff in Strike ABLE. A second fighter was damaged by AA fire during the airfield attack. The pilot was able to parachute into the lagoon. He was seen to get into his life raft, but search-and-rescue float-planes from the big surface ships were later unable to locate him.

The planes of Strike ABLE began to return at 0804 and the landings continued until 0825. "Recovering" aircraft formations and landing individual planes was the most complex part of carrier flight opera-tions—aside from air combat itself. The carrier would still be sailing into the wind (upwind) to reduce the air speed of the planes being recovered. Where possible, returning squadrons formed up in a holding pattern above their own carrier. In ideal circumstances one squadron would then drop into a counter-clockwise racetrack circuit above the ship. They flew upwind in the same direction as the carrier, passed ahead of it, and circled to port through 180°. They then entered a downwind leg in the opposite direction from the carrier, and about half a mile to port. The altitude of the returning group would now be about 500–1,000 feet, and from there it would break up into divisions.

Then came a descent to a lower level, still following the racetrack pattern, with individual planes flying one behind the other and about thirty seconds apart. They flew along the starboard side of the carrier on the upwind leg and then broke sharply to port and into the downwind leg on the port side of the carrier. At this point each pilot would lower his machine's tail hook and landing gear and make a final turn through 180° to port, into the final upwind approach onto the carrier. Landings were then made in very quick succession. For an experienced squadron one landing could be made every twenty or thirty seconds.

This last event was the stage that modern readers are probably most familiar with. In the last 200 yards astern of the ship the individual pilot came under the control of the landing signal officer (LSO). The LSO was an experienced pilot; he stood on a platform on the port side of the flight deck, facing astern and waving signal paddles to "coach" the returning planes into safe landings. The LSO confirmed that tail hook and flaps were lowered, retractable wheels were down. He informed the pilot with paddle signals if he was going too fast or too slow, and whether he was too high or too low for a safe landing.

Most critically the LSO could permit or forbid the landing. He could indicate a "cut" (moving the paddle in his right hand across his chest) at which point the pilot pulled the throttles back to idle, stalling the motor, and plumped down onto the flight deck for a successful landing. Or he could "wave off" a plane (waving the paddles over his head) to order it to complete another circuit.

After a successful approach, with the plane's wheels on the deck, its tail hook would normally engage one of the arrestor cables. On an "Essex" class, twelve arrestor cables ran athwart the rear third of the flight deck. In the unlikely event a pilot failed to snag a cable, the aircraft would (usually) be stopped by one of a series of transverse wire crash barriers, hopefully without suffering too much damage. The crash barriers protected aircraft that had landed earlier and the deck crew who were handling them. The recovery of the surviving twenty-three planes of Strike ABLE aboard *Essex* passed without incident.

At 0903, after all the recovered aircraft of Strike ABLE had been moved away from the forward part of the flight deck ("flight one"), *Essex* launched a CAP. This consisted of twelve Hellcats (three divisions) tasked to orbit the fleet at high altitude. These fighters could be controlled by the carrier's own fighter director officer (FDO), should radar detect inbound threats. The mission of the CAP was to protect the whole task group from air attack, not just the individual ship. (The long, often uneventful, patrols were known to the pilots as "eight-hour butt bruisers.")[4] Taking off after the CAP were six TBF Avengers, which were to carry out a defensive ASP (anti-submarine patrol) around the task group. (These were not the first defensive patrols put up by TG 58.2. First thing that morning, CAP and ASP had been provided by CVL *Cabot*. This ship had begun launching twelve Hellcats and six Avengers at 0630, shortly before sunrise. The main mission of the CVLs was routine protection of the task group; big offensive strikes were mostly mounted by the big carriers.) After the launch of the ASP Avengers from *Essex*, the recovery of Strike 1 and Strike 2 continued for an hour, from 0917 to 1022.

Essex launched smaller strikes, No. 3 and No. 4, in the early afternoon, from 1206; both had been recovered by 1634. Each consisted of two divisions of Hellcats (eight planes) and a handful of attack planes, some on photo recon missions. The last operation of the day from *Essex* was the launch, from 1750, of twelve Hellcats as another CAP. The evening period was the most dangerous for attacks by Japanese torpedo bombers, launched from distant bases like Truk. The last of the fighters and the ASP planes had been recovered by 1905, a few minutes after sunset.

The voyage of *Essex* and other ships of TF 58 to the Marshalls had begun two weeks earlier.[5] Rear Adm. Pete Mitscher took half the fast carriers of the newly formed TF 58 to sea from Pearl Harbor at midday on Sunday, 16 January 1944. They were organized as TG 58.1 and TG 58.2. The date was D-14, fourteen days before the date of the preliminary landings on Kwajalein Atoll, which was designated as D-Day.[6] (The main landings would take place on D+1.)

TG 58.1 comprised *Enterprise* and *Yorktown*, and CVL *Belleau Wood*, as well as escorting cruisers and destroyers. Mitscher's flagship was *Yorktown*. Rear Adm. Reeves, the task group commander, flew his own flag in *Enterprise*. TG 58.2 was similar—as already described—built around *Essex*, *Intrepid*, and CVL *Cabot*. The task groups passed through the narrow passage from Pearl Harbor, out the swept channel and into the open Pacific. Task Force 58 would not return to Pearl Harbor until the end of the Pacific War.

Operating close to one another, the ships made their way to the southwest, exercising in air operations and gunnery practice as they went. Ten days of steaming at 15 knots would take them to a position southwest of the newly captured Gilbert Islands. There, they were poised to strike, from the rear, the Marshalls and the Japanese island airfields.

On 19 January, TG 58.4 left Pearl Harbor. This third group included the veteran carrier *Saratoga*, as well as CVLs *Langley* and *Princeton*. Rear Adm. Samuel Ginder took these ships on a more direct route to a point east of the Marshalls. Meanwhile, the final fast-carrier task group approached from the opposite direction, the South Pacific. TG 58.3 was commanded by Rear Adm. Ted Sherman, and included *Bunker Hill* and CVLs *Cowpens* and *Monterey*. They had previously been engaged in strikes west of Rabaul; after that TF 58.3 had spent two weeks at Espiritu Santo before moving north via the new advanced base at Funafuti (now Tuvalu), south of the Gilberts.[7]

On 26 January *Indianapolis* joined TG 58.2. On board was Admiral Spruance, in charge of the whole Central Pacific Force, and overall commander of Operation FLINTLOCK. Spruance had hoisted his flag in Pearl Harbor on 18 January, and on the following day the cruiser had left without escort for a ready position at Tarawa in the Gilberts.

The Marshalls are the largest island group in the Pacific, containing over thirty sparsely populated low coral atolls. For the Japanese, the chain of atolls on the eastern side of the archipelago marked the very edge of their island empire. These atolls faced the direct and expected American approach route. The most important—running from north to south—were Wotje, Maloelap, and Mili. Each had an airfield, the most significant one located on Taroa island in Maloelap Atoll; Wotje had both an airfield and a seaplane base.

The western chain of the Marshalls included Kwajalein and Jaluit. Kwajalein, the more northerly, and the largest coral atoll in the world, lies more or less in the center of the whole island group. A major air base had been laid out on Roi Island on the northern side of the huge atoll; there was a seaplane base near Kwajalein Island on the southern side, and another airstrip was under construction there. Jaluit, the administrative center of the Marshalls before the war, covered the southern approaches and had bases for seaplanes and submarines. An outlier in the northwestern part of the Marshalls was Eniwetok Atoll, with an airfield and a large anchorage. Strategically placed, Eniwetok lay 350 miles northwest of Kwajalein and only 675 miles east of the big Japanese base at Truk.

The Marshalls had been a theoretical objective of American war planners for decades. Late in 1943, however, there were debates at the Pacific Fleet command about how best to capture them. Rear Adm. Kelly Turner, who had just returned from the Tarawa battlefield to Hawaii, preferred to attack first the eastern atolls of Wotje and Maloelap. In his view U.S. forces should capture the enemy air bases there and establish their own, before moving deeper into the Marshalls. Turner's close friend Spruance supported him, as did the Marine ground-forces commander, Major Gen. Holland Smith. The Tarawa experience had sobered all three and made them more cautious.

Admiral Nimitz, however, had a different and faster plan. He wanted to strike directly at Kwajalein in the center of the Marshalls, leapfrogging Wotje and Maloelap, as well as Jaluit and Mili. CincPac was supported by his chief of staff, "Soc" McMorris, and his influential warplans chief, the aviator Forrest Sherman. They knew from radio intelligence that the Japanese expected a landing in the eastern islands, and were reinforcing them with Army troops. They were confident, too, that the carriers of TF 58 and surface ships would be able to neutralize the Japanese air bases, aided by the continuing strikes against the southern Marshalls by AAF bombers from the Gilberts.

The final decision was made at a meeting at the Makalapa headquarters on 14 December. An affable man known for his folksy humor and the diplomatic treatment of his subordinates, Nimitz also had a hard side. One member of Spruance's staff recalled that the admiral listened to all the opinions and quietly announced his contrary decision: "Well, gentlemen, our next objective will be Kwajalein!" Nimitz gave his own recollection:

> I finally told Kelly [Turner]: "This is it. If you don't want to do it, the [Navy] Department will find someone else to do it. Do you want to do it, or not?" [Turner] smiled and said: "Sure I want to do it." And he did it to a T.[8]

One other change was now insisted on by Spruance. Majuro Atoll, some distance southeast of Kwajalein but apparently very lightly defended, would be added as an objective, in order to obtain a second big anchorage (in addition to Kwajalein). And so it was that on 16 December CincPac's Oplan (Operation Plan) 16-43 "(revised)" was adopted.

With Kwajalein Atoll now established as the main objective, the details could be worked out by Spruance's staff as Oplan Cen 1-44; this was completed on 10 January. Turner would command Task Force 51, the Joint Expeditionary Force.[9] Altogether, the assault and occupation force for the Marshall Islands totaled 50,000 assault troops and 30,000 garrison troops, more than twice the number which took part in the Gilberts. Landings would occur simultaneously on the northern and southern parts of the Atoll. The Japanese air base on Roi-Namur would be assaulted by the new 4th Marine Division with the Northern Attack Force (TF 53). Kwajalein Island would be the objective of the Army's 7th Infantry Division, with the Southern Attack Force (TF 52). Both forces had three naval elements: a transport group, a fire support group of older battleships, cruisers, and destroyers, as well as an escort carrier support group with several CVEs.

Transport of two ground-force divisions across thousands of miles of the Pacific demanded no small amount of what the planners called "lift." Five transport divisions (TransDivs) were required, each with half a dozen big transport ships. Coordination of movement was complicated. The first of the invasion forces to put to sea had been the troop transports of the Northern Attack Force. They left San Diego, with the Marine division, on 13 January (D-17). A two-week voyage took them across the Pacific to the Marshalls, bypassing Hawaii. The Southern Attack Force, with the Army's 7th Division, sailed directly from Hawaii on 22 January (D-9).

Before the two vulnerable transport armadas reached the final approaches to their objectives, enemy land-based air strength had to be eliminated. Accounts of FLINTLOCK often neglect the part played by Army bombers (unescorted B-24s and B-25s) operating from new bases at Tarawa and Apemama (Abemama) in the Gilberts. They were part the Seventh Air Force, commanded by Major Gen. Willis H. Hale USA, and under the overall command of Rear Adm. Hoover's Task Force 57. In December 1943 they began a six-week campaign to "soften up" the Japanese air bases in the Marshalls, especially the southern atolls of Mili and Jaluit. The AAF bombers were not very effective against ships at sea, but they were a powerful weapon against airfields, port facilities, and structures. The attacks on the eastern and southern islands also reinforced Japanese false expectations of where the landings would take place. Navy aircraft from the fast carriers joined the attacks throughout the Marshalls on 29 January. Some details have already been given of the preliminary strikes by *Essex* and other fast carriers of Mitscher's Task Force 58.

The "aviators" had complained about the scattered deployment of the fast carriers in the Gilberts in November 1943. In truth, the deployment in the Marshalls was not so different. Operating as four separate elements, the fast-carrier task groups launched initial strikes on 29 January (D-2) against the most significant centers of Japanese Navy air power in the Marshalls. Enemy strength was estimated to still number as many as 150 serviceable planes.

Kwajalein Atoll was hit from behind by planes from the six carriers of Montgomery's TG 58.2 and Sherman's TG.58.3, both approaching from the southwest. Similarly, the Taroa airfield on Maloelap was attacked from the southwest, by three carriers of Reeves' TG 58.1. Wotje was struck from the east by the three carriers of Ginder's TG 58.4.

On 30 January, after taking part in the first day of air strikes on Kwajalein Atoll, Sherman took TG 58.3 to the distant northwest corner of the Marshalls. His orders were to neutralize the airfield on Eniwetok Atoll and prevent enemy planes from flying in from the west. This task group also acted as a screen against any movement by the big ships of the Japanese fleet. It included the *Iowa* and *New Jersey*, brand-new 33-knot, 48,100-ton battleships that had just arrived in the Pacific. Meanwhile, Ginder and TF 58.4 remained on station to the east of the Marshalls, repeatedly hitting the airfields on Wotje and Maloelap.

Table 2.1. Fast-Carrier Operations during Operation FLINTLOCK

	TG 58.1 Reeves	TG 58.2 Montgomery	TG 58.3 Sherman	TG 58.4 Ginder
	Enterprise	*Essex*	*Bunker Hill*	*Saratoga*
	Yorktown	*Intrepid*		
	Belleau Wood	*Cabot*	*Cowpens*	*Langley*
			Monterey	*Princeton*
29 Jan.	Maloelap	Roi	Kwajalein I	Wotje
30 Jan.	Kwajalein I	Roi	Eniwetok	Wotje Maloelap
31 Jan.	Kwajalein I	Roi	Eniwetok	Wotje Maloelap
1 Feb.	Kwajalein I	Roi	Eniwetok	—

Source: Mor/7, p. 218.

Two days after the first naval air strikes, the old battleships, cruisers, and destroyers began to pound the islands of Kwajalein Atoll from close range to clear the way for the landings. Rear Adm. Richard Conolly, commander of the Northern Attack Force, earned the nickname "Close-In Conolly" for bringing the big ships of his fire support units so close to the enemy shore. On 31 January and 1 February bombardment continued in the northern and southern parts of the atoll, against Roi-Namur, Kwajalein Island, and nearby islets. The day and night bombardment exhausted the Japanese garrison before the main landings took place on 1 February. The weight of explosives delivered was much higher than at Betio in Tarawa Atoll.

Ground forces came ashore on Kwajalein Atoll for the first time on D-Day, Monday, 31 January (two days after the first air strikes), but these were still preliminary steps. American soldiers and marines landed on tiny islets near Roi-Namur and near Kwajalein Island. Their task was to put in place field-artillery support.

The main landings on Roi-Namur and Kwajalein Island took place on Tuesday, 1 February (D+1). The most important feature of these landings was that they did not repeat the errors at Tarawa and avoided heavy losses. The explanation was largely the weight and duration of preliminary bombardment by the ships of the Navy, and the artillery emplaced on the flanking islets. The air bombardment by the carriers of Montgomery's TG 58.2, already mentioned, had begun on the 29th, and continued on the 30th and 31st. The carriers of Reeves' TG 58.1 also took part, as well as the escort carriers (CVEs). However, tonnage of explosives delivered by warships and land-based artillery was much heavier than bombs dropped by aircraft. In addition, close-in reconnaissance had been much better than at Tarawa. Divers of the UDTs (Underwater Demolition Teams) determined that the beach approaches were clear of obstacles. Most of the initial assault force came ashore in amphibious tractors (amphtrac), also known as LVT-2s.[10] Amphtracs had also been used for the first time at Tarawa, but in smaller numbers.

Japanese strength on Kwajalein Atoll was slightly greater than at Tarawa. It was estimated at 8,675, although spread over a larger area. The 4th Marine Division faced 3,563 defenders on Roi-Namur and adjacent islets; these included only 400 combat troops, with the rest aviators, ground crew and support personnel. Roi, with its runways, was secured in the early evening of 1 February. The airstrip was very soon being put to use by American planes. Across the causeway, on adjacent and more built-up Namur, the fighting continued through the first night, but in the late afternoon of the 2nd that island too was declared secure.

Kwajalein Island, on the southern part of the atoll, was assaulted by the GIs of the Army's 7th Division, who had fought in the Aleutians and received extensive amphibious training at Hawaii. The landing was mounted on two beaches at the western end of the crescent-shaped island at 0930 on 1 February. The density of the 5,112 defending troops was less than on Roi-Namur but it included naval infantry and a battalion of Japanese Army troops who had arrived in November 1943.[11] Resistance on the island had ended by mid-afternoon on the 4th (Friday), when the GIs reached the eastern tip, although fighting continued briefly on nearby islets.

Total U.S. ground-force losses on Kwajalein Atoll were 486 killed and missing, the majority marines on Kwajalein Island. This compared with 1,009 U.S. ground troops killed at Tarawa. The Japanese fought desperately but their losses were 4,398 killed in the south (mainly on Kwajalein Island) and 3,472 in the north (mainly Roi-Namur). Among the dead was the commander of all Japanese forces in the Marshalls, Rear Adm. Akiyama Monzo. About a hundred Japanese were captured, along with 165 Korean laborers.[12]

No U.S. ships were sunk or badly damaged by the coastal batteries. In the Gilberts an escort carrier (*Liscome Bay*) had been lost, with 649 crew members, after a sub attack. Light carrier *Independence* had been put out of action for eight months by an aerial torpedo. In the Marshalls no U.S. ships were attacked from the air, although an AAF B-25 from Tarawa was shot down by Navy fighters by mistake on D+1. The only successful Japanese air strike was made after Kwajalein and Majuro had been secured. This was a night bombing on Roi on 12 February by flying boats from faraway Ponape. A lucky hit on an American bomb store caused a massive explosion which killed twenty to twenty-five men, destroyed most of the stores that had been landed on the small island, and sank two landing vessels in the lagoon.

Another feature of the Marshalls campaign was the weak reaction of enemy submarines. The operation plan of Spruance's Central Pacific Force (Oplan Cen 1-44) did identify a threat that "enemy submarines in strength will attack our surface forces in the Marshalls area [and] may operate on our lines of communications." However, the poorly organized Japanese submarine deployment in the Gilberts in November 1943 had led to the heavy loss of Japanese boats—six out of the nine boats involved. In addition a growing number of Japanese submarines had been diverted for the emergency supply of garrisons cut off in New Guinea, New Britain, and the Solomon Islands.[13]

The American command does not seem to have thought that intervention by the Japanese main fleet was likely, in view of its relative weakness. However, Oplan Cen 1-44 did note the possibility that "enemy naval forces in strength superior to any of our separated naval forces may attempt to prevent the seizure of our objectives." (Presumably "separated naval forces" was a reference to the four task groups of TF 58.) Spruance did prepare a special plan (Oplan Cen 2-44) for the conduct of a major fleet action involving carriers and battleships from the U.S. fleet, should one take place.[14] This did not prove necessary.

The capture of Majuro Atoll was in some respects even more remarkable than the battle of Kwajalein. Radio intelligence had suggested that Majuro was not well defended. The assault force arrived on 31 January, but Marine scouts found only one Japanese NCO, who surrendered. The Japanese had sent naval infantry to the island when the war began, but in November 1942 these troops were transferred to nearby Mili, which seemed more exposed. Majuro was reported secure at 1000 on 31 January. It became a functioning U.S. naval base extremely quickly. By 2 February two American fast battleships that had collided the day before were able to steam into the lagoon to begin repairs. By the following morning a big carrier, *Bunker Hill*, had berthed at Majuro, and by the afternoon of 4 February she had been joined by *Yorktown*, *Essex*, and others. A U.S. Army occupation garrison was quickly installed, and two airstrips laid out.

Another remarkable feature of Kwajalein and Majuro—and of the campaign—was that it did not matter that they were surrounded by enemy-held atolls. These were places that had had airfields and which still possessed sizeable garrisons. Mili, where one of the last Japanese reinforcement convoys had arrived in January 1944, was only 70 miles to the SSE of Majuro. Maloelap was 100 miles north of Majuro, and Wotje only 80 miles north. Some 120 miles to the southwest of Majuro lay Jaluit, completing the ring. After the capture of Kwajalein and Majuro the Americans effectively blockaded the Japanese-held islands and developed further the campaign of air attacks by AAF bombers operating from Tarawa and Apemama in the Gilberts, from Kwajalein, and from Majuro itself. Nothing demonstrated better the fragility of Japanese strategy. Majuro, one of the most important anchorages in the Central Pacific, was occupied with no resistance and speedily transformed into a vast base area. TF 58 would operate from here for the next six months.

By the middle of February the United States had won a very quick victory. The cost in American lives had been low—certainly compared to Tarawa. Doubts about continuing the advance to the west across the Carolines were now much reduced, and full support for this approach was evident in the key 12 March 1944 directive of the U.S. Joint Chiefs of Staff. The final dividend of FLINTLOCK was not just Majuro but the acceleration of the invasion of Eniwetok. This landing—Operation CATCHPOLE—will be described in the following chapter.

THE TWO-OCEAN NAVY

Leaders of the American armed forces argued for long months about how the war in the Pacific should be fought. What is sometimes lost sight of in discussing this controversy is the importance of the build-up of naval force, which was taking place 7,000 miles away in shipyards on the Atlantic coast. It was the stunning growth of the U.S. Navy's strength that confirmed the preferability of the strategic path through the Central Pacific. That growth came from decisions made as much as five years earlier. Particularly important construction work began in the middle of 1940, a year and a half before Pearl Harbor, and three and a half years before the Central Pacific campaign began.

The U.S. Navy had expanded by fits and starts since it emerged as a major force in the 1890s. The Spanish-American War of 1898 was followed by further fleet expansion, especially under President "Teddy"

Roosevelt. In 1916 another President, Woodrow Wilson, committed the (then neutral) United States to a "Navy Second to None." Sixteen huge new "capital ships" (battleships and battle cruisers) were planned, to reach a strength comparable to that of the British Empire. This development was cut short by the Washington Naval Treaty of 1922, which resulted from negotiations involving the biggest naval powers, the USA, the British Empire, and Japan, as well as France and Italy. The pointless post-war naval building race between the victorious Allies was ended by setting national limits on the total tonnage of capital ships and aircraft carriers for each signatory. The United States achieved parity with the British Empire in capital ships (battleships and battle cruisers), and a significant superiority over Japan.

For the USA and Britain 525,000 tons was the total capital ship limit; for Japan it was 315,000 tons. For aircraft carriers, a radically new type of warship not then regarded as a capital ship, the respective figures were 135,000 tons and 81,000 tons. The treaty also set limits for all navies on the displacement and guns of individual capital ships (35,000 tons and 16-inch guns) and aircraft carriers (27,000 tons for new-builds). No other warship should exceed 10,000 tons or have guns bigger than 8-inch. The total tonnage limit for capital ships was to remain in effect until 31 December 1936.

The London Treaty of 1930 continued the naval arms-limitation process. The three largest naval powers agreed not to exercise their right to replace ships over twenty years old before the end of 1936. (Replacement age for capital ships had in 1922 been agreed as twenty years from the ship's completion; in any event all replacements would have had to keep within the tonnage limits of an individual ship— 35,000 tons—agreed in 1922). In this treaty the USA, Britain, and Japan also agreed national tonnage limits running to the end of 1936 for cruisers, destroyers, and submarines, as well as limits on the numbers, size and armament of "heavy" and "light" cruisers, destroyers, and submarines. The treaty caused political controversy in Japan, where it was felt that the Imperial Navy had been put in a position of dangerous and long-term inferiority. In consequence, the Tokyo government indicated in 1934 that it would not take further part in the naval arms-limitation process after December 1936.

Despite the "building holiday" for capital ships that began in 1922, naval construction continued in the interwar decades. The U.S. had a big shipbuilding industry, and the world's largest steel production. The shipyards had been expanded during World War I. Most of them were located in the northeastern or mid-Atlantic states. Three private yards, the so-called "Big Three," were able to construct the largest ships. Bethlehem Steel's Fore River yard was at Quincy, Massachusetts, south of Boston. New York Shipbuilding (NYSB) was actually located at Camden, New Jersey, on the Delaware River opposite Philadelphia. Newport News Shipbuilding and Drydock Co. was located in Newport News, Virginia, near Chesapeake Bay. Three state-owned Navy Yards, which were also capable of building very big ships, were located at New York (Brooklyn), Philadelphia, and Norfolk (Virginia).

The main warship construction by the U.S. in the 1920s and early 1930s were the "treaty" cruisers, built initially to fit the 10,000-ton, 8-inch gun limitation of the Washington Treaty. The first, *Pensacola*, was laid down in 1926 and seventeen more followed, in five classes, by the end of the 1930s. Under the 1930 London Naval Treaty the U.S. Navy was also allowed to build nine 9,800-ton "Brooklyn" class light cruisers.

No destroyers were ordered until the middle of the 1930s, as a huge class of "four stackers" had been built for World War I. Then, half a dozen small classes of destroyers were built, and about seventy of these new vessels entered the fleet before Pearl Harbor. Space does not permit details about the overall design and construction of U.S. Navy surface ships. Nevertheless, it is clear technical improvements introduced and tested in the new destroyers were a factor in the achievement of American naval superiority during the war. One element was the provision of AA guns and their fire control systems. The "dual-purpose" guns of the 5-inch/38 caliber (5-in/38) design were first fitted to destroyer *Farragut* (DD-348), laid down in 1932, and would continue as the main secondary (and heavy AA) armament of U.S. Navy ships throughout the war.[15] The pre-war construction of the new destroyers also involved the development of turbines, boilers, and other machinery. *Mahan* (DD-364) and her sisters (laid down from June 1934) brought in civilian expertise, especially in propulsion machinery. These included improved high-pressure, high-temperature boilers, and compact, more efficient steam turbines. These changes allowed improvements in fuel economy and cruising range, which was especially valuable in the Pacific, with the very long distances involved.[16] It was also important that these improvements in armament and machinery were developed and thoroughly tested before the war. Another shipbuilding development in the 1930s was the increasing use of welding, at least for many parts of the ship's structure. This allowed for faster construction, saved weight and required less skilled labor.[17]

In 1936, as the treaty system started to break down, the United States prepared plans for new battleships as replacements for overage vessels. In late 1937 and mid-1938 the *North Carolina* and *Washington* were laid down. Keeping to the Washington Treaty size limits, they were 35,000-ton ships, armed with nine 16-inch guns. The first of the American "fast battleships," they could steam at 27 knots and were a substantial improvement over the older 21-knot battleships built at the end of World War I. The Navy took the calculated risk of equipping them with the improved machinery introduced in the new destroyers, high-temperature, high-pressure boilers and General Electric steam turbines. Their formidable battery of heavy AA guns consisted of twenty of the new 5-in/38 dual-purpose guns in twin mountings.

The U.S. Navy had not been allowed to lay down new battleships in the 1920s and early 1930s, but it did build aircraft carriers, working slowly toward the Washington Treaty limit. After the experimental *Langley* (CV-1), the next two were converted battle cruisers, the 37,700-ton *Lexington* (CV-2) and *Saratoga* (CV-3). These were followed in the 1930s by four ships designed as carriers from the keel up: *Ranger*, *Yorktown*, *Enterprise*, and *Wasp*. All the carriers were named after battles from the War of Independence or after sailing ships of the early U.S. Navy.

Carriers, battleships, cruisers, and destroyers designed in the "treaty" era formed much the largest part of the fleet with which the U.S. Navy entered the Pacific naval war and fought the battles of 1942. Only a small number of newest post-treaty ships took part in this fighting, late in the year and mainly around Guadalcanal.[18]

The fleet that fought in 1944 was very different, and much larger. The speed-up of American naval shipbuilding began in 1938 with the loosening of treaty restrictions, an international naval building race, and a generally more threatening international environment. Japanese aggression in China in July 1937 and the German annexation of Austria in March 1938 were important background events. The most significant legislation for naval construction was the Second Vinson Act of May 1938. It was named after Carl Vinson, an influential Democratic Congressman from Georgia, who was the chairman of the House of Representatives Naval Affairs Committee. The bill authorized expansion of the Navy's strength to a level 20 percent above its old Washington/London Treaty limits. Among other changes, capital ship tonnage was raised from 525,000 to 630,000, that for carriers from 135,000 to 175,000. At the same time very substantial government funds were now invested in shipyards, both state-owned and private. The yards were expanded, and improved equipment was installed (e.g. building slips, heavy-lift cranes, power plants). The Navy also adopted a policy of greater shipyard specialization. This would make possible the rapid building times for warships achieved during later years, with different yards concentrating on battleships, carriers, cruisers, destroyers, and submarines.[19]

This was still very much a "battleship navy." With the Second Vinson Act, work began on four more 35,000-ton fast battleships, similar to the two "North Carolina" class. The lead ship, *South Dakota*, was laid down in July 1939, and *Indiana*, *Massachusetts*, and *Alabama* followed. When the Washington Treaty tonnage limits were abandoned, the next battleships were the 48,100-ton *Iowa* and *New Jersey*, which were laid down in the summer and autumn of 1940. The first of these eight "fast" battleships would enter combat in late 1942, and all eight would be in the Pacific at the start of 1944. All would be equipped with nine 16-inch and twenty 5-in/38 guns. *Washington* and *South Dakota* took a decisive part in the night battle off Guadalcanal in November 1942, but the eight ships would never fight together in the long-expected duel with the Imperial Navy's battle line. However, with their high speed, efficient machinery, and powerful AA battery the new battleships were important for defending the carrier task forces. Their large fuel-oil capacity (6,200 to 7,600 tons) also made them invaluable for replenishing escorting destroyers at sea. Significant, but less important, was their role in the bombardment of land targets.

The Second Vinson Act also provided for a new cruiser and destroyer program. *Cleveland* was the first of what would eventually be a very large class of 11,700-ton light cruisers. She was laid down in July 1940. The first units of the class entered service in the Pacific early in 1943. The Navy also began construction of smaller (6,700-ton) light "anti-aircraft" cruisers (CLAA) of the "Atlanta" class, armed with sixteen 5-in/38 guns. The first four were laid down in 1940; *Atlanta* and *Juneau* were lost in the fighting around Guadalcanal. The first ship of a large new class of destroyers, the 1,800-ton *Benson*, was laid down in November 1939. The projected total was twenty-four ships. These were in service by the time of Pearl Harbor, as well as the first three of a repeat "Benson" class.

An even more striking growth spurt of the U.S. Navy began two years after the 1938 Act. The world situation now seemed much more dangerous. The European war began, and then came the unexpected and stunning success of Nazi Germany's May 1940 offensive in the Low Countries and France. The Naval Expansion Act was signed by President Roosevelt on 14 June 1940, two weeks after Dunkirk and a week before the surrender of France. It envisaged a further increase of 11 percent in the authorized total tonnage of the fleet. Only a month later, on 19 July, following the collapse of France and the entry of Fascist Italy into the war, Congress passed legislation bringing a much larger expansion. The Two-Ocean Navy Act authorized a 70 percent increase in tonnage to create a Navy able to fight a global war simultaneously in the Atlantic Ocean and the Pacific Ocean. Both the 1940 acts were long-term programs, with new ships planned to enter service as late as 1945–46. They foresaw construction in that period totaling 385,000 tons of capital ships, 279,500 tons of carriers, 486,500 tons of cruisers, and 250,000 tons of submarines. At the same time the authorized target for naval aircraft was raised to 15,000, from the existing figure of about 1,500.[20]

Cruisers were now to be built in unprecedented numbers. Combined with units begun under the 1938 Act, fifty-two "Cleveland" class cruisers would eventually be ordered, of which twenty-nine were actually completed as light cruisers and nine as light carriers (CVLs). Of the light cruisers, eighteen reached the Pacific by the middle of 1944. Two additional "Atlanta" class AA cruisers arrived in 1943; five more would be commissioned after mid-1944; the total was eleven. A new class of heavy (8-inch gun) cruisers began to enter service when the 14,500-ton *Baltimore* was commissioned in April 1943. Three more "Baltimore" class reached the fleet by the middle of 1944, where they served in the covering force for TF 58.

Also remarkable was the destroyer program. The need for escorts against the U-boats in the Atlantic eventually led to the ordering of another seventy-two ships of the repeat "Benson" class, the last two of these 1,800-ton ships were commissioned in April 1943 (for a grand total of ninety-six). This class would eventually form the bulk of the new American destroyers in the Atlantic and Mediterranean.

The succeeding "Fletcher" class was an even larger program, including twice as many vessels. Handsome, flush-decked ships with two funnels, these 2,300-ton destroyers had a main armament of five 5-in/38 in single mounts and ten torpedo tubes. They were 30 feet longer then the Bensons and had greater fuel capacity and more deck space for AA armament. The lead ship, *Fletcher* (DD-445), was laid down in October 1941 and commissioned in June 1942. A total of 175 Fletchers would be built. The class formed the bulk of the destroyer force in the Pacific from 1943 onwards, and the great majority of the escorts for the fast carriers.

Although it would have a great effect on the fighting in 1944, the Two-Ocean Navy Act was in some respects overtaken by events. Priorities changed radically with wartime experience. Preparations for five 64,000-ton "Montana" class battleships were halted in May 1942. Even more important, new types of warship, not envisaged in 1940, were built in huge numbers: transport ships and landing vessels for amphibious operations, escorts for convoy protection, and fleet oilers and other naval auxiliaries. But the Two-Ocean Act did provide for the huge number of carriers, cruisers, and destroyers that would be required to assure supremacy in the Pacific War.

The most important elements of the new navy—and of the Central Pacific campaign—would be the aircraft carriers. Two new "flattops" had been authorized in 1938, although not immediately ordered. One

(CV-8) became the ill-fated *Hornet*. To enable rapid construction, *Hornet* was a repeat of the 1933 "Yorktown" class design. The other carrier (CV-9) was to be of an improved type, and eventually became *Essex*.[21] The first three of this new "Essex" class were actually ordered from Newport News on 3 July 1940, on the basis of the 14 June 1940 Naval Expansion Act (not the 19 July 1940 Two-Ocean Act). These were *Essex* (CV-9), and ships with hull numbers CV-10 and CV-11.[22] *Essex* was named after an American sailing frigate, the first U.S. Navy vessel to visit the Pacific Ocean—under Commodore David Porter in 1813. Ten months would pass before the carrier was actually laid down; this would be on 28 April 1941. CV-10 and CV-11 began construction at Newport News on 1 December 1941, a week before Pearl Harbor.

Meanwhile, an even bigger carrier program was in the offing. This time there was a direct link to the Two-Ocean Act. In August 1940 contracts were signed for another eight "Essex" class carriers, four more (CV-12 to CV-15) to be built at Newport News, and four (CV-16 to CV-19) at the Fore River yard of Bethlehem Steel. The first two Fore River ships (CV-16 and CV-17/*Bunker Hill*) were laid down on 15 September 1941. As a result, by the time of the attack on Pearl Harbor on 7 December, five "Essex" class carriers were already under construction (three at Newport News and two at Fore River).

The accelerated delivery of the "Essex" class carriers had profound implications for the pace of the American offensive against Japan and especially in the Central Pacific. *Essex* was scheduled to be completed in March 1944; she actually reached the fleet in December 1942, fifteen months early. With their production rapidly accelerated, four of these ships would reach the Pacific Fleet between May and October 1943: CV-9/*Essex*, CV-10/*Yorktown*, CV-16/*Lexington*, and CV-17/*Bunker Hill*. A fifth carrier (CV-11/*Intrepid*) would arrive in January 1944. *Yorktown* and *Intrepid* were both seventeen months ahead of schedule.[23]

Two more "Essex" class from the August 1940 orders would reach the Pacific by June and July 1944—in time for the invasion of the Marianas and the Battle of the Philippine Sea. These were the fourth Newport News ship (CV-12/*Hornet*) and the third Fore River ship (CV-18/*Wasp*). Although twenty-four "Essex" class would eventually be commissioned, the first seven became the backbone of the U.S. Navy's fast-carrier force in the first half of 1944. Along with the earlier *Saratoga* and *Enterprise* and nine new light carriers (CVLs), they would win the air/sea war between opposing fleets in the Pacific.[24]

The 27,200-ton *Essex* was a very imposing ship. Measuring 820 feet at the waterline, she was 100 to 150 feet longer than the first six 35,000-ton fast battleships. *Essex* was also substantially bigger than the three "Yorktown" class carriers, from which her design had evolved. They had been 50 feet shorter and displaced only 19,900 tons. Unlike them, too, the "Essex" class were equipped with high-pressure, high-temperature boilers and Westinghouse turbines, which improved their range.

The most important features for air operations were the flight deck and, below it, the cavernous hangar deck. The flight deck of *Essex* measured 862 feet, with a maximum width of 109 feet. It consisted of thin steel plate with three-inch thick wood planking above it, laid across the width of the deck. As mentioned earlier, twelve arrestor cables were located on the aft third of the flight deck; ahead of them were the five wire crash barriers. Near the forward end of the flight deck was the H-II catapult; it could accelerate a 10,000-lb plane to 70 mph.[25] Most take-offs, however, were "rolling launches," using the length of the flight deck rather than a catapult. This enabled the faster launch of big strikes.

Essex was equipped with three giant elevators (lifts) to move aircraft from the hangar deck to the flight deck. The forward and aft elevators were on the center-line, the elevator amidships was situated on the port-side deck edge, opposite the island. Masts, from which radio aerials were strung, were set on the starboard side of the flight deck; they could be folded down, jutting out from the flight deck, during air operations.

Eighty years ago, observers were familiar with conventional big-gun ships of the "battleship navy," with their massive and complex superstructure and batteries of heavy artillery mounted in turrets fore and aft. They found it hard to admire the "flattops," slab-sided vessels, with a flight deck 55 feet above the waterline, and an asymmetric superstructure.[26] But *Essex* was handsome in an angular way, with a prominent "island" on the starboard side amidships. This structure was better proportioned than previous carriers, with a smaller funnel (thanks to more efficient boilers). Big Mk 37 directors for the 5-in/38 dual-purpose guns were set at either end of the funnel. Below them were new quadruple mounts for 40-mm AA guns. A forward 40-mm quad mount was situated above the ship's main "navigating" bridge. This in turn was set above the "flag" bridge, used if an admiral was on board. Between the funnel and the forward Mk 37 director rose a tripod foremast with a masthead platform carrying radar antenna, most notably the big "mattress" of the SK air search radar. As the war progressed this vertical forest of antennas would become more and more dense, and additional short-range 20-mm AA guns were added to the island.

The gymnasium-like hangar deck was 654 feet long, 70 feet wide and 18 feet high, from the surface of the hangar deck (the "main deck") to the braces supporting the flight deck above it. Additional accommodation, including aircrew ready rooms, was provided in a gallery deck hung under parts of the flight deck.

Unlike the "Yorktown" class, *Essex* had long-range AA guns mounted at flight deck level. These were 5-in/38 guns located on the starboard side, in two gun-houses forward of the island, and two gun-houses aft of it. Four more 5-in/38 in single mountings were located on the port side, in galleries below flight deck level. *Essex* was built with what was then regarded as a powerful battery of new medium-range 40-mm AA guns, in eight quad mounts (i.e. thirty-two guns). In addition to the four quad mounts on the island there were quad mounts at the bow and the stern, and two on the port side, below the flight deck level. As designed, forty-four 20-mm short-range AA guns were fitted in galleries set just below the level of the flight deck. The number of medium and short-range AA batteries would be much increased aboard *Essex* and her sisters as the war progressed.

Protection was limited. *Essex* had 2.5 inches of horizontal armor plate on her main deck (the floor of the hangar deck), but the flight deck was not armored. Unlike earlier carriers, *Essex* was equipped with two self-contained machinery units, fitted in tandem, each with two boilers and two turbine sets. This meant the ship could still remain underway even if one machinery unit was damaged There were four shafts turning four huge bronze propellors.

Essex had a fuel-oil capacity of 6,200 tons (for her main engines), stored in two tanks near the bottom of the ship, a third greater than the "Yorktown" class. She also carried 233,650 gallons (1,053,102 liters) of aviation gasoline ("avgas") in storage tanks, fore and aft just above the keel.

The preliminary design of *Essex* provided accommodation for 230 officers and 2,256 enlisted men, including 632 aviation personnel. Under wartime conditions ships of this class would carry a crew of as many as 3,000.

Essex was commissioned on 31 December 1942. Her first CO was Capt. Donald ("Wu") Duncan. Proceeding down the James River from the Newport News shipyard, *Essex* spent five weeks fitting out at the nearby Norfolk Navy Yard.[27] After that she proceeded out into the safe waters of Chesapeake Bay on 9 February 1943 to test her machinery and begin her "shakedown." That same week the Japanese completed their evacuation of Guadalcanal, and the decisive Allied victory on that island was completed. The first aircraft was launched from *Essex* on 17 February; this was a North American SNJ "Texan" training plane piloted by Cdr Lee, CO of the AG 9; on the 22nd, larger-scale aircraft landing operations began.

Trials and training continued in Chesapeake Bay until 15 March. After that *Essex* left the Norfolk naval base, steamed out into the Atlantic and proceeded south to the warmer waters of the Caribbean. The big carrier reached Trinidad, with the new American base leased in the British colony; this facility was created after the famous "destroyers-for-bases" deal of September 1940.[28] The Gulf of Paria was an eighty-mile-long lagoon between Trinidad and the coast of Venezuela, now enclosed by anti-submarine nets. There the *Essex* spent a week exercising; her aircraft operated ashore from the two airfields on Trinidad. She returned to the Norfolk Navy Yard on 9 April and was there for more than a month, making final preparations, before departing for the Pacific on 10 May.

Essex passed through the Panama Canal on 17–18 May. This was not a simple task, given the size of the ship and the narrowness of parts of the canal. Seven months later her sister ship *Intrepid* collided with the channel wall of the Gaillard Cut, and required several weeks of repair at the San Francisco Naval Shipyard (Hunter's Point).[29] Fortunately, the transit of *Essex* passed without incident. She proceeded directly to Hawaii without calling in at San Diego. A rendezvous at sea was made with battleship *Washington* on 30 May, and *Essex* steamed into Pearl Harbor on the following day.

Nearly three months of training in the Hawaiian area followed. During this time two more "Essex" class arrived at the Oahu naval base from the U.S. East Coast, *Yorktown* on 24 July and *Lexington* on 9 August. They had undertaken a similar shakedown process to *Essex*. *Yorktown* had been rushed to readiness by her energetic CO, Capt. J. J. ("Jocko") Clark, who would go on to serve as one of Mitscher's outstanding task group commanders.[30] *Independence*, first ship in a class of light carriers, had arrived at Pearl Harbor on 20 July; two more new light carriers arrived with *Lexington*. The U.S. Pacific Fleet was now much bigger than ever before. On 23 August 1943 *Essex*, *Yorktown*, and CVL *Independence* began raids deep into the Central Pacific; as already mentioned, their targets were the remote atolls of Marcus and Wake.

The light carrier *Independence* (CV-22) had been commissioned on 14 January 1943, two weeks after *Essex*.[31] Her CO was Capt. George Fairlamb. The commissioning ceremony took place at the Philadelphia Navy Yard, although the ship had been built across the Delaware in the huge NYSB yard, like all the later eight vessels of her class. *Independence* was the second of the new fast carriers to enter naval service, but she was very different from *Essex*. A 10,700-ton light carrier, she was less than half the tonnage of the "Essex" class ships. Her air complement was only a third the size, about thirty-four planes, as opposed to ninety.

Unlike the "Essex" class, *Independence* and her sister ships were not directly a product of the fleet-expansion legislation passed by Congress in June and July 1940. In the course of the later part of 1940 and 1941 it had become evident that more new aircraft carriers would be needed, and as soon as possible. The British Royal Navy had pioneered auxiliary, or "escort", carriers built on merchant-ship hulls, and the U.S. Navy had followed their lead. The first American-built escort carrier was *Long Island* (AVG-1, later CVE-1), commissioned in June 1941. She was built on a C3 merchant-ship hull, and with an 8,500 horsepower (hp) diesel motor she had a top speed of 16.5 knots. *Independence* was a similar improvisation, although she built on the hull of a cruiser, rather than a merchant ship.

One factor behind the "Independence" class was the intervention of President Roosevelt himself. In August 1941 the President had directed that two of the numerous new "Cleveland" class cruisers under construction be converted into carriers, but the specialists in the new Bureau of Ships (BuShips) had not supported the proposal. They argued that it would disrupt the cruiser program and result in small, costly ships that could be built little more quickly than the "Essex" class. Meanwhile, the aviators in the Bureau of Aeronautics (BuAer) were complaining that operations from a small fight deck would be "hazardous and difficult."[32] Five months later, after Pearl Harbor and with the need for carriers even more evident, the cruiser-conversion idea came back. It was now supported by Admiral Harold Stark, the CNO. On 2 January 1942 Stark sent a directive to BuShips ordering the first conversion; he noted the President's support and urged that additional conversions be considered.

The "Independence" class had many positive features, despite their size limitation. The first was that they were based on cruiser hulls and machinery. They had twice the speed of the CVEs (escort carriers) and could operate with the fast-carrier task forces. Their 100,000 hp steam turbines made them "fast carriers" capable of the same high sustained speed as the "Essex" class. Second, the design was inelegant, but it could be developed very quickly, helped by experience with the escort carrier program, especially the 10,500-ton "Sangamon" class; these had been based on the hull and machinery of a T2 fast oiler. Most importantly, thanks to the head start of the Two-Ocean Navy cruiser program, these light carriers could be completed quickly. In addition, the CVL program did not add to the load of the main "carrier" yards at Newport News and Fore River, where the available slipways were already full. By the end of 1943, seven "Independence" class had reached the Pacific Fleet, and only four "Essex" class; by June 1944 two more CVLs had arrived, and three more "Essex" class.

When the "Independence" conversion program began in the spring of 1942, eight "Cleveland" class light cruisers were on the stocks at the NYSB yard. CL-59/*Amsterdam*, the future CVL *Independence*, had been laid down in May 1941 and was rated as 40 percent complete when conversion began. The two other initial conversions were *Tallahassee/*

Princeton and *New Haven/Belleau Wood*.[33] The main additions required to the hulls were blister compartments to port and starboard, designed to improve stability. Three more conversions were ordered from NYSB at the end of March 1942, *Huntington/Cowpens*, *Dayton/Monterey*, and *Fargo/Langley*. The last ship had not even been laid down, so essentially she was built from the keel up as a light carrier rather than as a light cruiser. The design was the same as the earlier CVLs. The last batch was authorized on 4 June 1942 (coincidentally the date of the Battle of Midway). *Wilmington/Cabot* had been laid down in March 1942 as a light cruiser, and *Buffalo/Bataan* and *Newark/San Jacinto* were laid down as carriers.[34]

Independence lacked the imposing bulk and classic carrier lines of *Essex*. Her length overall was 683 feet, but the flight deck was only 552 feet long and 73 feet wide. The hangar deck was 55 feet wide and 285 feet long, considerably less than half the length of the *Essex* hangar deck. There were two elevators and one H-2-1 catapult. A boxy superstructure had been built above a sleek cruiser hull, giving the vessel a top-heavy appearance. This superstructure was basically a hangar deck, with the flight deck on top of it.

There was no centered "island" amidships, as on the big carriers. Rather, a small structure hung over the starboard side forward, with an open bridge and an enclosed pilot house. This was very like the superstructure of an escort carrier. Instead of the single funnel of *Essex* the design had four angular uptakes (from the four boilers) sticking out of the starboard side amidships. A stump mast was set between the two sets of funnels, carrying the antenna for the SK air search radar. Forward of the superstructure was a crane for lifting aircraft. *Independence* was designed to have dual-purpose 5-in/38 guns, one on the forecastle (above the bow) and one at the stern. These were replaced soon after commissioning by quad 40-mm mounts, which were more effective in the AA role. In addition she had twin 40-mm mounts on the gallery just below the level of the flight deck, four on the starboard side, and five to port.

"Cruiser" compartmentalization gave *Independence* enhanced survivability, certainly better than "escort" carriers with their merchant-ship hulls.[35] Not only were the CVLs much faster than the escort carriers and as a result more able to evade air attack, they also had some armor. Nevertheless, their smaller size made the "Independence" class more vulnerable than the big carriers. CVL *Princeton* would be sunk in a dive-bomber attack in October 1944 during the Battle of Leyte Gulf. None of the "Essex" class were lost.

Independence was launched in August 1942 and commissioned in mid-January 1943.[36] The crew of the "Independence" class was made up of about 1,600 officers and men. The ship spent five more weeks fitting out at the Philadelphia Navy Yard before proceeding 80 miles down the Delaware on 9 March. A dash into the open Atlantic around the Virginia Capes took her into Chesapeake Bay and the beginning of "shakedown" proper. On 23 March the planes of AG 22 were flown aboard. *Independence* left the Norfolk naval base on 9 April and arrived in Paria Bay (Trinidad) on the 14th. She remained there for two weeks and then returned to Philadelphia for her final fitting out.

Independence passed through the Panama Canal and arrived in California on 27 June. She spent two weeks in the Mare Island Navy Yard in San Francisco Bay, and departed for Hawaii on 15 July. On the evening of 20 July she docked at Pearl Harbor. Six weeks of hurried training in the Hawaiian area followed, before *Independence* joined *Essex* and *Yorktown* for the raid on Marcus Island on 1 September 1943.

The next two CVLs, *Princeton* and *Belleau Wood*, left the Camden shipyard in February and March 1943, respectively. They followed the same shakedown routine as the lead ship, and then reached Pearl Harbor together on 9 August, in company with the new "Essex" class *Lexington*. After them came *Cowpens* and *Monterey*, which arrived in time to take part in the November 1943 operations in the Gilberts. *Cabot* and *Langley* arrived before the end of 1943. The last of the "Independence" class were *Bataan* and *San Jacinto*. They reached Pearl Harbor in April and May 1944. By this time the operating base of the fast-carrier fleet had been moved forward from Hawaii to Majuro Atoll in the Marshall Islands, and the Marianas invasion was imminent.

CHAPTER 3

HAILSTONE

TF 58 Raids Truk, February 1944

ENIWETOK AND TRUK

The momentum of TF 58 was now rapidly gathering. The next decision, quickly made, was to bring forward the invasion of Eniwetok.
That atoll lay in the extreme northwest of the Marshalls. The strategically important anchorage there had featured in pre-war planning of
the U.S. Navy, but it was 350 miles northeast of Kwajalein and only
675 miles from Truk, where the Combined Fleet had its main Central
Pacific base.

On 2 February ELD Rear Adm. Kelly Turner, commander of the
Joint Expeditionary Force at Kwajalein, proposed that the Eniwetok
invasion be mounted at once. The capture of Roi-Namur and Kwajalein
Islands had been accomplished quickly. The reserve Marine landing
force had not been required, and was now available for a follow-on
attack. Admiral Nimitz himself arrived aboard a big Consolidated PB2Y
Coronado flying boat at Kwajalein lagoon on 7 February and immediately began discussing plans with Spruance and Turner. It was agreed
that the Eniwetok landing would begin on Thursday, 17 February. In
Nimitz's January 1944 GRANITE campaign plan (see below), the invasion of Eniwetok had been scheduled to begin on 1 May. This was three
months—not two weeks—after Operation FLINTLOCK at Kwajalein.

Eniwetok was much closer to Truk than Kwajalein, let alone Majuro.
Any invasion of Eniwetok would need protection against enemy air

attacks from Truk, and perhaps even against movements by the Japanese main fleet. Major elements of the Combined Fleet had actually made two sorties to Eniwetok from Truk in 1943, one in September, and one in October. As part of the Eniwetok invasion, the bulk of Task Force 58 would mount a covering air attack on Truk, hitting the Japanese base on 17 February, the same day as the planned landings. To carry this out the fast carriers sortied from their new forward base at Majuro on 12 February.

As with their efforts elsewhere in the Central Pacific, the Japanese had begun too late to strengthen the defenses of Eniwetok. Only in November 1942 (while the Guadalcanal battle was nearing its climax) had Japanese and Korean construction workers begun laying out an airstrip and refueling point on Engebi, a small triangular island on the northern side of the atoll. The facility was only completed in the late summer of 1943, and was little more than an intermediate landing strip for planes flying from the Carolines to the Marshalls. A few Betty medium bombers had been located here when FLINTLOCK began, but the airstrip had been quickly put out of action by the fast carriers of Sherman's TG 58.3.

The American invasion force of nine transports and various landing vessels departed from Kwajalein on 15 February.[1] The operation was codenamed CATCHPOLE, and D-Day was Thursday, the 17th. Valuable Japanese nautical charts had been captured earlier near Kwajalein, and the invasion fleet was able to pass safely into the Eniwetok lagoon from the south side and then steam the 10 miles across it. The tactics of Kwajalein were repeated, as field artillery was landed on D-Day on islets adjacent to Engebi Island. The landing on Engebi itself was then carried out by a Marine regiment on D+1 (18 February). The garrison of the island consisted of about 700 soldiers, nearly all of whom died in the fighting. The island was secured by the end of the afternoon, with the loss of only eighty-five men on the American side.

Then a reinforcement force of over 1,800 soldiers of the Japanese Army was discovered on the opposite side of the atoll from Engebi. These troops were hidden in abandoned coconut plantations on Eniwetok and Parry Islands, flanking Eniwetok Atoll's southern entrances; their presence had not been detected when the invasion fleet passed by them. Fortunately for the Americans the soldiers—like the troops on Engebi—were last-minute reinforcements from Manchuria who had arrived in early January 1944, with neither time nor materials to prepare proper defensive positions. Eniwetok Island was secured by the Marines on D+4, and Parry a day later (23 February); the fighting here was twice as costly for the Americans as on Engebi. Again, the enemy fought nearly to the last man. Overall, only sixty Japanese and Koreans were taken prisoner on Eniwetok Atoll, out of an original total of over 3,400.[2]

The Engebi Island airstrip would be quickly repaired and enlarged as a Marine fighter-plane base; a long AAF bomber runway was laid down on Eniwetok Island. Even more important, the lagoon would soon become a major advanced anchorage for the ships of TF 58 and the rest of the American Fifth Fleet, alongside Majuro.[3]

The rapid Marine victory on Eniwetok was overshadowed by the successful air attack on Truk Atoll, normally known as Operation HAILSTONE.[4] Truk (pronounced "Trook," now Chuuk) is a very large atoll in the center of the Caroline Islands. A huge lagoon, roughly 30–35 miles in diameter, is surrounded by a low barrier reef broken by four narrow passes, to the north, northeast, south, and west. Some of the "high" islands within the lagoon are much larger than the tiny coral islands in the Gilberts and the Marshalls. Japanese forces occupied Truk, then part of a German protectorate, in 1914, and after World War I it became part of the Mandate. Unlike other territories, there had been little Japanese civilian settlement or economic development here. The administrative capital of the Mandate was at Koror in the Palau group (western Carolines), and the main economic development and in-migration from Japan took place in the Marianas.

Under the terms of the 1922 Washington Treaty, Truk could not be fortified, and on the whole the Japanese abided by the treaty until 1936; even then little military construction took place at first. Nevertheless, Truk was closed to outsiders throughout the interwar period and speculation grew, especially in the U.S., about secret base development. The atoll certainly had potential. The barrier reef provided protection from submarine attack and close naval bombardment. The harbor was much more commodious than Pearl Harbor, and the land area much larger than that of the advanced bases the U.S. Navy would set up at Majuro and Kwajalein in 1944.

However, the Japanese really only began the development of Truk in early 1941, when the atoll became the headquarters of the Fourth Fleet, and a Base Force was deployed there. The main Japanese military facilities were developed on Dublon and Moen islands; little Dublon Town expanded. Then came the war with the Americans. Situated as it was between Japan and the fighting front in the South Pacific (Rabaul and Guadalcanal), Truk became an essential advanced base. Admiral Yamamoto, and Admiral Koga after him, made Truk the anchorage for the new super-battleships *Yamato* and *Musashi*, which served in turn as the Combined Fleet flagship. The passages were mined and coastal defense guns emplaced on Moen and some other islands. A base for the submarines of the Sixth Fleet was developed, with shore facilities and depot ships. In the hills of Dublon a tank farm for fuel oil was built, and tanker ships were moored in the lagoon. The naval base had only one small drydock, but many of the facilities for repairing and fueling ships were available afloat in auxiliaries. (Major repairs required shipyards in Japan.) Recognizing the importance of Truk as a destination for warships and cargo vessels, the U.S. Navy deployed submarines near the place from the early months of the Pacific War. They sank or damaged a number of ships on the approaches to the atoll.

Truk also served as a base and transit point for combat aircraft being ferried to the Empire's Pacific perimeter. Like the other facilities, those for aviation were built at a relatively late date. A station for flying boats and seaplanes had been set up at Dublon in 1939–40. Three airfields for land planes were put into operation by February 1944. These included a big new fighter field on the Eten Island, just south of Dublon Town. Bomber fields were located to the west of Dublon, on Param Island, and to the north, on Moen. Radar and direction-finding stations were also established.

Nevertheless, whatever was happening had been far beyond the range of American photo recon planes—at least until early February 1944. Mitscher was later reported as saying, "All I knew about Truk was what I'd read in the National Geographic, and the writer had been mistaken about some things."[5] The mysterious place developed a fearsome reputation as the Gibraltar of the Pacific. The American carrier pilots who suddenly learned, in February 1944, that their next destination would be Truk itself were both surprised and alarmed.

Long before the war, the U.S. Navy had been interested in Truk, because of its location and first-rate anchorage. Pre-war plans took in the possibility of establishing a mid-Pacific base here, and that continued after December 1941. The GRANITE campaign plan of January 1944 provisionally scheduled a multi-division amphibious invasion (Operation GYMKHANA) for August 1944. An earlier item on the GRANITE agenda was a large-scale carrier raid:

[T]he strongest practicable carrier striking force with available fast battleships and light forces in company will approach TRUK and deliver an all-out attack on available targets in the order: aircraft carriers, battleships, cruisers. Concurrently submarines will be concentrated in the approaches to TRUK for observation purposes and to attack enemy ships which may sortie during the operation.[6]

In fact, the fast carriers of Mitscher's TF 58 sortied from newly captured Majuro anchorage on Sunday, 13 February.[7] The moment was one of the most significant in the Pacific War. The fast carriers and the rest of the Central Pacific Force were no longer tied to Pearl Harbor and Hawaii. And Vice Adm. Spruance took to sea the largest concentrated fleet ever assembled by the U.S. Navy. More big ships had taken part in the FLINTLOCK in the Marshalls, but they operated as four widely dispersed groups. Three task groups were now sailing in close proximity: Reeves' TG 58.1 with *Enterprise*, *Yorktown*, and CVL *Belleau Wood*; Montgomery's TG 58.2, with *Essex*, *Intrepid*, and CVL *Cabot*; and Sherman's TG.58.3 with *Bunker Hill*, CVLs *Monterey* and *Cowpens*. Total aircraft embarked numbered nearly 590.[8]

Nimitz and Spruance had prepared for any kind of battle. Accompanying the carriers were fast battleships *Iowa*, *New Jersey*, *Alabama*, *Massachusetts*, *South Dakota*, and *North Carolina*. Spruance himself flew his vice admiral's three-star flag at the truck of the *New*

Jersey's mainmast. Supporting the carriers and battleships were five heavy cruisers, the new *Baltimore* as well as *Wichita*, *Minneapolis*, *New Orleans*, and *San Francisco*. Light cruisers were *Biloxi*, *Mobile*, *Santa Fe*, *Oakland*, and *San Diego*. The destroyer force totaled twenty-nine ships. In addition nine submarines were deployed to intercept fleeing Japanese ships and rescue downed aircrew.

TF 58 followed a circuitous course east of Eniwetok to avoid "snoopers" (enemy scout planes) from Truk. On 15 February, now northwest of Eniwetok, they refueled from five fleet oilers. That afternoon a patrolling Betty was sighted on radar and shot down by a Hellcat from *Belleau Wood*. Spruance's fleet then advanced rapidly, reaching the launching point northeast of Truk before dawn on 17 February.

The air attack on Truk was based on a plan worked out by Mitscher and his staff. The five heavy carriers launched an initial mass sweep by seventy-two Hellcat fighters. The four light carriers provided air cover over TF 58, and anti-submarine patrols around it. The attacking Hellcats engaged and overcame a smaller number of enemy fighters that were already in the air over Truk. They then took part in strafing attacks on the three airfields and the seaplane base. Following the Hellcats, TBF Avengers carried out airfield strikes, dropping cluster bombs and incendiaries. TF 58 quickly gained command of the air over Truk.

Cumulative losses of Japanese aircraft were high. Reliable figures give about 270 caught on the ground and fifty-five shot down in air battles. Many of the planes destroyed on the ground had been brought to Truk aboard transport ships or by ferry pilots and did not have crews; some had been withdrawn from Rabaul and were under repair. They were parked near the runways, often nose-to-tail.[9]

However, TF 58 did not achieve the decisive attack on the ships of the Combined Fleet which had been hoped for at the planning stage. As they approached the Japanese base, Spruance and Mitscher still anticipated that they might catch some major warships, as well as cargo ships and transports, but they no longer expected to inflict a decisive blow against the Combined Fleet as a whole. Two weeks earlier, on 4 February, two Marine PB4Y Liberators had carried out the first photo recon overflight of Truk. They came from a new air base near Bougainville and their flight lasted twelve hours. The aerial photographs, taken from

20,000 feet, revealed a battleship, two carriers, five or six heavy cruisers and four light cruisers, twenty destroyers, twelve submarines, and a large number of cargo ships. (Among the photos was the first image of a "Yamato" class super-battleship—*Musashi*). This was an impressive force, but it did not represent the main body. Moreover, Radio intelligence in the days after 4 February also indicated that many ships had left.[10]

The move away from Truk had actually begun well before the 4 February PB4Y overflight. The two best heavy carriers (*Shōkaku* and *Zuikaku*) had left Truk for Japan in December 1943, having expended their air groups in the defense of Rabaul. On 1 February five large surface ships had departed for Palau, 1,000 miles to the west. TF 58 had mounted air strikes against Kwajalein three days earlier, on 29 January, and it was now clear that American forces were committed to a full-scale attack on the Marshall Islands.

Nearly all remaining heavy ships left Truk on 10 February. This was a week after Kwajalein had been irretrievably lost and the other defended islands in the Marshalls cut off. Admiral Koga himself left for Japan aboard *Musashi*, accompanied by two light carriers, a light cruiser, and destroyers. On the same day, four more heavy cruisers and several destroyers departed for Palau.[11]

Even in the tactical sense, Operation HAILSTONE was not a surprise. The massive losses were partly a result of mistakes made by the defenders. According to a Japanese source, the command of the Fourth Fleet, under Vice Adm. Kobayashi Masami, was largely to blame. Major warships and the Combined Fleet headquarters had departed, but no systematic preparation of air units was made to defend the atoll or prepare counterattacks.[12] Nevertheless, approaching enemy forces were detected. Japanese fighter planes had been put on full alert on the morning before the strike, 16 February, but they were apparently stood down in the evening of that day.[13] The incoming attack on the 17th was picked up by Japanese radar thirty minutes before the shooting began, but only thirty or forty defending fighters had taken off.[14]

Likewise, despite the presence on paper of hundreds of aircraft, Truk had very limited attack plane and bomber capability even before the 17 February strike.[15] This was a singular failure of Japanese aviation. No large-scale attacks on TF 58 were mounted during daylight hours on 17

February. The CAP put up by the American light carriers was unnecessary, at least as far as Truk-based aircraft were concerned.

A general American attack on targets at Truk now began. The main effort was mounted by the aircraft of TF 58, but during the morning Admiral Spruance had organized Task Group 50.9, which was now deployed to sweep around Truk Atoll counter-clockwise and destroy any enemy shipping attempting to escape. The force included the pride of the battleship navy, the brand-new 33-knot *Iowa* and *New Jersey*, which had arrived in the Pacific in January. This task group was commanded by Spruance himself from the flag bridge of *New Jersey*. Accompanying the battleships were cruisers *Minneapolis* and *New Orleans* and four destroyers. Air cover was provided from a distance by CVL *Cowpens*.

Meanwhile, Mitscher's planes mounted a program of some thirty air attacks against shipping and military installations at Truk. These were carried out in squadron strength by SBD Dauntless, TBF Avenger, and SB2C Helldiver attack planes. The largest groups of Japanese transports, cargo ships, and auxiliaries were assembled in the anchorage east of Dublon. Some of these were vessels which had been damaged in earlier battles or submarine attacks, but the overall loss (over two days) would be five tankers, fourteen merchant-ship types of between 11,000 tons and 4,000 tons, and eleven smaller ocean-going vessels. Also lost were two big converted merchant ships that had served as support ships for the submarines of the Sixth Fleet. Nimitz's report later noted that "this anti-shipping assault was the heaviest ever delivered by Allied aircraft."[16]

Some ships had attempted to escape, either just before the attack or during it. The new light cruiser *Agano*, damaged by air attack in November 1943, had left Truk on the evening of 15 February, escorted by the old destroyer Oite. The following afternoon the cruiser was hit by a torpedo fired by submarine *Skate*, 160 miles north of Truk. Attempts to save the vessel failed, and she went down early on the 17th. *Oite*, carrying survivors back to Truk, was sunk by TF 58 aircraft on the morning of the 18th. Meanwhile, *Naka*, a second, older light cruiser, was sent out to assist *Agano*. She was caught underway west of Truk Atoll on the morning of the 17th and broken in half by a TBF torpedo.[17]

A third cruiser sunk was *Katori*, a training ship which had been headquarters of the 6th Fleet. With two destroyers she had been escorting a large merchant ship back to Japan. They went through the North Pass before dawn on 17 February and then came under air attack. The merchant ship was sunk, and *Katori* and one of the destroyers were damaged. In the afternoon the survivors were brought under attack by Spruance's battleship-cruiser force (TF 50.9). *Katori* and the damaged destroyer were sunk by gunfire.

Spruance's expedition was not without dangers. The battleships came under a small air attack, and *New Jersey* was the target of a torpedo fired by the surviving destroyer, *Nowaki*. Spruance's chief of staff, Carl Moore, thought an unnecessary risk had been taken and that the admiral just wanted to see the mountains of Truk. Even Spruance's biographer thought the reasons for the potentially risky operation were "obscure," but that the intention was to humiliate the Japanese.[18]

As mentioned already, the Japanese had not been capable of mounting a strike on Mitscher's carriers during the day. In the late evening, however, a small number of "bogies" were detected on radar, and just after midnight carrier *Intrepid* in TG 58.2 was hit by an aerial torpedo. The skillful attack suggested that the enemy had effective airborne radar. In any event the torpedo caused substantial damage. Eleven men were killed and *Intrepid* had to return to Pearl Harbor, before proceeding to the San Francisco Naval Shipyard at Hunter's Point for fuller repairs. She was now out of the Central Pacific campaign and would not return to the fleet until August 1944.[19]

During the night of 17/18 February a new tactic was employed by TF 58—night attacks using radar by twelve bomb-dropping TBF Avengers of VT-10 from *Enterprise*.[20] Further American air strikes were mounted on the morning of Friday the 18th. Now that no Japanese fighters were in the air the attackers concentrated on remaining shipping and shore facilities. One of the last targets was the tank farm on Dublon. This had been spared until then to prevent smoke from the burning fuel obscuring other targets.

American air losses were remarkably light: twelve Hellcats, seven torpedo planes and six dive bombers; eight of these were lost in accidents. As we have seen, Japanese fighters were quickly put out of action, and there were only about forty AA guns protecting Truk's installations. A total of twenty-nine crewmen were actually lost; a number of downed flyers had been picked up from the sea by seaplanes, some within the Truk lagoon itself. Seven U.S. Navy flyers met a tragic fate; falling into Japanese hands, they were tortured and beheaded.[21]

The successful American carrier strike had a powerful effect on the Japanese. The abandonment of Truk as an anchorage for major surface ships and as a full-strength air base meant giving up part of the "Absolute National Defense Sphere" laid out by the Imperial General Headquarters (IGHQ) and approved by an Imperial Conference on 30 September 1943. Rabaul, the Marshalls, and eastern New Guinea were east of the Defense Sphere; Truk was not. Unusually, the IGHQ publicly admitted heavy losses of 120 planes and thirteen merchant ships at Truk, although it was also claimed—falsely—that the enemy had lost a battleship, a carrier, two cruisers, and forty-four aircraft. Vice Adm. Kobayashi, the Fourth Fleet commander, was removed (and retired from the Navy in May). The removal of Admiral Nagano Osami, Chief of the Naval General Staff, took place on 21 February and was a result of Truk and earlier defeats. The massive recriminations aroused within the high command were such that it gained its own cover name in coded communications as the "T Affair" (*T jiken*).[22] The Imperial Navy had claimed the Pacific as its strategic domain, but the disastrous raid on Truk and the effective loss of the Marshalls woke the leaders of the Japanese Army to naval weaknesses in the Pacific that had not been admitted. Reinforcement of the western Carolines and the Marianas now, belatedly, became a national priority.

For the Americans, HAILSTONE had not been a "reverse Pearl Harbor," with the sinking of many major Japanese warships. It had, however, been a significant victory. One American account colorfully described 17 February as "a day when the Japanese lion had been bearded in his den and found to be only a scrappy alley cat."[23] The Combined Fleet was forced to fall back, initially to Palau and the Philippines. With that, its defensive capability to prevent further invasions was greatly weakened. The Japanese removal of the fleet from Truk also made clear that it was not necessary to take the big atoll. This allowed Admiral Nimitz to move directly toward the Marianas.

AMERICAN PACIFIC WAR STRATEGY, 1944

Kwajalein and Majuro had been quickly captured. A daring decision was made to advance northwest to Eniwetok, which resulted in another American success, achieved rapidly and at low cost. The carrier raid on Truk made clear that the overrated "fortress" had been abandoned by the main warships of the Japanese fleet; meanwhile, great success was achieved in destroying land-based aircraft and sinking merchant ships there. All of this would have a profound effect on the fighting in the Pacific for the rest of 1944

The invasion of Kwajalein had come about after a series of strategic decisions made at the highest levels of the Allied leadership. The longer-term strategy of the U.S. forces in the Pacific involved further choice and considerable controversy, involving headquarters in Pearl Harbor, Brisbane, and Washington. In particular, Nimitz's Navy-dominated Pacific Ocean Areas (POA) in Hawaii competed with MacArthur's Army-dominated SWPA, with its headquarters in Brisbane, Australia. Among the important resources at stake were manpower, aircraft, shipping, and supplies. Also debated was the overall role of the Navy. MacArthur argued for the isolation or capture of Rabaul and an advance along the north coast of New Guinea. This would then be followed by a turn north toward the Philippines, in the first instance to Mindanao Island. MacArthur and his staff wanted all resources in the Pacific to be devoted to this task, including those of the AAF and the Navy.[24]

The view of the U.S. Navy was at first less clear, although some version of a Central Pacific campaign was intended, and there was no question of subordination to MacArthur. Admiral King in Washington wanted an advance to the Mariana Islands by way of the northern Carolines. Control of these islands would sever the direct air and sea route from mainland Japan to the Central Pacific. Admiral Nimitz and his staff for a time supported an alternative drive through the *southern* Carolines, in cooperation with MacArthur's SWPA. The aim would be to establish an advanced fleet base west of Rabaul at Manus Island. Manus was the largest of the Admiralty Islands, and the location of the vast Seeadler Harbor. Nimitz's temporary rejection of the Marianas led

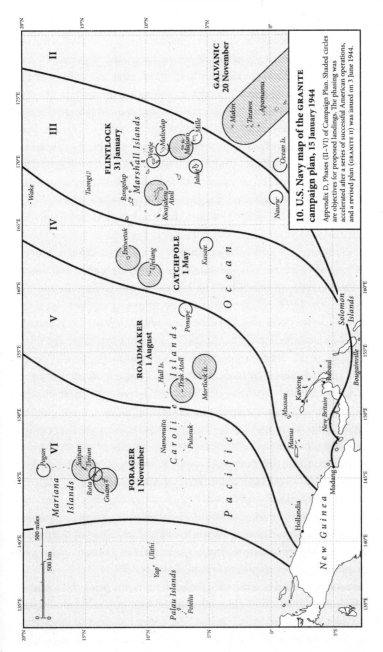

10. U.S. Navy map of the GRANITE campaign plan, 15 January 1944

Appendix D, Phases (II–VI) of Campaign Plan. Shaded circles are objectives for proposed landings. The phasing was accelerated after a series of successful American operations, and a revised plan (GRANITE II) was issued on 3 June 1944.

GALVANIC 20 November

FLINTLOCK 31 January

CATCHPOLE 1 May

ROADMAKER 1 August

FORAGER 1 November

II
III
IV
V
VI

Marshall Islands
Caroline Islands
Mariana Islands

Makin
Tarawa
Apamama
Ocean Is.
Nauru
Jaluit
Mille
Majuro
Maloelap
Wotje
Kwajalein Atoll
Rongelap
Taongi?
Wake
Eniwetok
Ujelang
Kusaie
Ponape
Hall Is.
Truk Atoll
Mortlock Is.
Namonuito
Pulusuk
Pagan
Saipan
Tinian
Rota
Guam
Yap
Ulithi
Palau Islands
Peleliu

Pacific Ocean

Solomon Islands
Bougainville
Rabaul
New Britain
Kavieng
Mussau
Manus
Madang
Hollandia
New Guinea

500 miles
500 km

to a brief, and unusual, tension in late January and early February 1944 between him and King.[25]

The clearest overall presentation of the intentions of the U.S. Navy in the Central Pacific over the course of 1944, after the capture of the Gilberts, had been in the "campaign plan," codenamed GRANITE. This was prepared by Nimitz's staff, under Rear Adm. McMorris. It was dated 13 January 1944, two weeks before the Marshalls invasion. Plan GRANITE followed on from a compromise "strategic concept" approved by the Allied Combined Chiefs of Staff (CCS) Committee. This involved a two-pronged advance, although one that gave somewhat more weight to the Central Pacific. The relevant document (CCS 417/2), dated 23 December 1943, had outlined the basic strategy:

> The advance along the New Guinea—N.E.I. [Netherlands East Indies]—Philippines axis will proceed concurrently with operations for the capture of the Mandated Islands [in the Central Pacific]. These two series of operations will be mutually supporting . . . When conflicts in timing and allocations of means exist, due weight should be accorded to the fact that operations in the Central Pacific promise at this time a more rapid advance toward Japan and her vital lines of communication; the earlier acquisition of strategic air bases closer to the Japanese homeland; and, of greatest importance, are more likely to precipitate a decisive engagement with the Japanese Fleet.
>
> The aim should be to advance . . . in time to launch a major assault in the Formosa-Luzon-China area in the spring of 1945 (i.e. before the onset of the typhoon season [May–November]), from a distant base.

Included was a stipulation to "[i]nsure that the sequence of operations remains flexible and that preparations are made to take any short cuts made possible by developments in the situation."[26]

Plan GRANITE laid out the specific operations involving the forces of the POA (Table 3.1). The first, after FLINTLOCK in the Marshalls, was supposed to be an air strike against the main Japanese naval base at Truk. Ideally this would be the Pearl Harbor raid in reverse, with a surprise attack on a large part of the Imperial Navy. It was provisionally planned for about 24 March 1944 and would coincide with the attack on Emirau and Manus islands, northwest of Rabaul.

The next phase of the plan was to involve a turn toward the northern Carolines. This was intended to follow the invasion of Eniwetok in the northwestern Marshalls, which was scheduled for 1 May. As we have seen, Eniwetok was actually captured in the second half of February. In the GRANITE timetable the amphibious assault on Truk Atoll in the central Carolines (Operation GYMKHANA), was to take place three months later, on 1 August. The invasion of Saipan, Tinian, and Guam in the Marianas (Operation FORAGER) would follow after another three-month gap, on 1 November 1944.[27]

The situation changed radically between mid-January (when Plan GRANITE was prepared) and early February (after the capture of Kwajalein and Majuro). In the January plan Majuro was to be "a supporting position including one or two airfields." Now it had become the major fleet advanced base; Manus was no longer the highest priority. The carriers and fast battleships of TF 58 did not return to Pearl Harbor and Espiritu Santo immediately after the invasion of the Marshalls (FLINTLOCK), as projected in the GRANITE plan. In a matter of days they began to use Majuro as a base, resupplying in the lagoon from the mobile "fleet train."[28] From there, fleet elements could strike directly

Table 3.1. Campaign Plan GRANITE [I], 13 January 1944

Objective	Region	Codename	Plan date	Actual date
Kwajalein	Marshalls	FLINTLOCK	31 Jan. 44	31 Jan. 44
Truk (raid)	Carolines	HAILSTONE	24 Mar. 44	17 Feb. 44
Emirau	Bismarcks	FOREARM	24 Mar. 44	20 Mar. 44
Manus	Admiralties	MERCANTILE [BREWER]	24 Mar. 44	29 Feb. 44
Eniwetok	Marshalls	CATCHPOLE	1 May 44	16 Feb. 44
Truk	Carolines	GYMKHANA	1 Aug. 44	Canceled
Mortlock	Carolines	ROADMAKER	1 Aug. 44	Canceled
Saipan/Guam	Marianas	FORAGER	1 Nov. 44	15 Jun. 44

Source: Campaign Plan GRANITE [I], p. 7.

west to raid Truk and the Marianas, rather than moving to the south-west (as in the GRANITE plan) to support landings at Emirau and Manus. This was a development of the greatest strategic importance.

Major developments had occurred: the relatively easy capture of Kwajalein and Majuro, the accelerated capture of Eniwetok, the successful suppression of the Japanese air threat from the bypassed Marshalls, the lack of effective resistance to the Truk raid, and the failure of the Japanese main fleet to take action. All these had a powerful impact on the American strategic debate. Above all, there was the growing sense that the fast-carrier force, TF 58, was an extremely powerful asset, and that land-based Japanese air groups were not the threat they had once been. An amphibious landing on Truk would not—it turned out—be required. Like the eastern Marshalls, Rabaul, and Bougainville, Truk could "wither on the vine." This final decision was made in JCS direc-tive 713/4, issued by the Joint Chiefs of Staff in Washington and dated 12 March 1944. It finally gave up the amphibious invasion of Truk and set the invasion of Saipan and Guam for the middle of June.[29] Meanwhile, to conciliate General MacArthur and the U.S. Army, Mindanao was kept as an objective, along with Palau in the western Carolines. The latter was set to be taken in September1944, after an accelerated advance by MacArthur's forces along the north coast of New Guinea.[30]

American leaders had a reasonable knowledge of capabilities of the Japanese enemy. It was evident that an effort was being made to rein-force the defenses of the western Carolines and the Marianas with ground defenses and air bases. Japanese Army reinforcements from mainland Asia were now playing a greater role.[31] What was lacking, from an American point of view, was a clear understanding of the enemy's strategic intentions, and especially whether the Japanese Navy would come out to fight a fleet action at this stage of the war.

U.S. NAVY AVIATORS

The mass training of aviation personnel was at the heart of the transfor-mation of the U.S. Navy and its victory in the Pacific. Especially impor-tant were pilots. The number trained each year had been low for much of the interwar period. It was under 170 a year between 1920 and 1935, with the exception of 1930 and 1931. Numbers began to rise in the second half of the 1930s. Some 212 pilots were trained in 1936, and 527 in 1937; in 1940 the figure reached 708. With war now being fought in Europe and after the passage of the Two-Ocean Navy Act, the figure for 1941 jumped sixfold to 3,112. Then, after Pearl Harbor, the annual number of pilots trained for the Navy grew at an astonishing rate, reaching 10,869 in 1942, 20,842 in 1943, and 21,067 in 1944.[32]

The Navy's first pilots were regular officers, Annapolis graduates like John Towers and Pete Mitscher. Initially, they were expected to undertake duties in conventional warships for two years before applying for aviation training. If accepted this was usually at NAS Pensacola, situated in the Florida panhandle. A training camp had been set up there in 1914, expanded during World War I. In the 1930s a number of quite senior officers undertook air training (not necessarily as pilots) at Pensacola in order to qualify for command of carriers, seaplane tenders, and naval air stations. Among them were Bill Halsey, Ernest King, John McCain, and Ted Sherman. Although the expectation was that only commissioned officers would *lead* air formations, a considerable number of senior enlisted men were offered training as Naval Aviation Pilots (NAPs), and indeed interwar legislation set a 30 percent limit for this category.

As the number of fleet aircraft grew in the late 1930s it became clear that not enough pilots could be drawn from the ranks of regular officers and enlisted men. A third source became increasingly important, which was a special classification for volunteers in the U.S. Naval Reserve designated as aviation cadets (AvCads); this program was also known as V-5. These men normally had a college degree or at least several years of college education, and were aged between twenty and twenty-eight. After a year at NAS Pensacola they served for three years in the fleet with the rank of aviation cadets, before being commissioned as ensigns in the Naval Reserve. It proved hard to hold on to these trained men, in competition with a growing civil aviation sector, and from 1939 they received commissioned ranks as ensigns as soon as they finished Pensacola, and were offered a seven-year term as commissioned officers, with possible promotion to lieutenant (jg). By the time of Pearl Harbor nearly half of Navy and Marine pilots were reservists.

Table 3.2. U.S. Navy Aviation Personnel on Active Duty, 1935–45

Year	Officers		Enlisted	
	Pilots	Other	Pilots	Aviation rates
1935	867	559	280	12,129
1936	963	502	297	13,055
1937	1,002	530	355	15,091
1938	1,059	580	447	19,463
1939	1,068	609	533	19,907
1940	2,203	145	349	5,924
1941	3,483	963	629	10,640
1942	9,059	5,716	732	27,286
1943	20,847	20,958	774	105,445
1944	37,367	26,596	575	183,886
1945	49,380	27,946	439	241,364

Source: Evans/Grossnick, *Naval Aviation*/1, p. 234. These figures exclude a considerable number of Marine aviation personnel. In 1944 the USMC figures were 10,457 pilots (nearly all officers) and 91,246 aviation rates.

The flyers of 1944 were different from what has aptly been described as the "first team" of 1942 (naval fighter pilots who had received their training before the war).[33] Not only were they now flying aircraft that were superior to those of their Japanese opponents, not only did they significantly outnumber those opponents, but they were also better trained. Naval flight training had been greatly expanded, as shown in Table 3.2. The original training air station at Pensacola was now joined by NAS Jacksonville in northern Florida, which was opened in the presence of President Roosevelt in October 1940. Another huge training base was commissioned in March 1941 in the form of NAS Corpus Christi in southern Texas, and in 1942 and later a large number of specialized training centers for flying personnel and maintenance staff entered service.[34]

The training of wartime carrier pilots was thorough and took considerable time. An example of the process was Ensign Alexander Vraciu USNR. Vraciu would be an unusually successful Hellcat pilot, but his path through the U.S. Navy's training establishment was similar to that taken by many of the future pilots of TF 58, and it is well documented.[35]

Born in 1918, Vraciu was the son of immigrants from Romania and grew up in the steel-industry town of East Chicago, Indiana. Like most wartime American pilots in World War II, he had been a "college boy," studying on a scholarship at DePauw University near Indianapolis. He graduated in June 1941 with a BA in Sociology. In the summer of 1940, between his junior and senior years at DePauw, Vraciu took flying lessons with the Civilian Pilot Training Program (CPTP) at Ball State University in Muncie. This initial program included fifty hours of flight instruction in little J-3 Piper Cubs and seventy-two hours of ground school.[36] Vraciu volunteered for the U.S. Naval Reserve in June 1941 at the time of his graduation from DePauw. This was partly because he had a low number in the Draft lottery and preferred naval duty to conscription into the U.S. Army. He was called up for naval service in October 1941. For his preliminary training Vraciu reported to NAS Glenview, north of Chicago. The course was open to men who had completed at least two years of college and were aged between twenty and twenty-eight. The intention was to identify those who had good flying aptitude (and eliminate those who did not). Vraciu already had a pilot's license and progressed without difficulty to the rank of Aviation Cadet (AvCad) on completing his six-month course.

After this, Vraciu was assigned to NAS Corpus Christi (others went to the older NAS Pensacola). Trainees at Corpus Christi progressed through "squadrons." Squadron 1 was primary training in biplanes, as well as ground school. Squadron 2 was basic training in obsolete operational planes in formation flying; at this stage a specialty was chosen, based on the trainee's ability (Vraciu opted for carrier fighters). Squadron 3 involved advanced training, including instrument flying, using modern trainers like the North American SNJ Texan. At Corpus Christi in August 1942 Vraciu earned his gold "wings," the insignia of a Navy pilot, and graduated as an ensign in the Navy Reserve; he was now aged twenty-three.

In the 1930s pilots had finished their training with the carrier squadrons to which they were being assigned. From the summer of 1941, however, a number of special training schools were established. Vraciu's final training and qualification involved coast-to-coast travel across the U.S. He moved to the Carrier Qualification Training Unit (CQTU) at

NAS North Island in San Diego, and the Advanced Carrier Training Group, Pacific Fleet, at NAS Melbourne in Florida. His carrier qualification was achieved by landing an F4F Wildcat aboard the newly converted training carrier USS *Wolverine* on Lake Michigan.[37]

In February 1943, now a qualified carrier fighter pilot, Ensign Vraciu was assigned to VF-3 squadron in the Hawaiian Islands, and he traveled there aboard an escort carrier. VF-3 was then based at the newly built NAS Puunene on Maui Island. "Fighting Three," originally the fighter squadron of *Saratoga*, was commanded by one of the heroes of 1942, Lt Cdr Edward "Butch" O'Hare. It was one of the first squadrons to receive the new Grumman F6F Hellcat.

VF-3 was redesignated VF-6 in July. VF-6 was assigned to AG 22 and the new light carrier *Independence* when she arrived at Pearl Harbor in late July 1943. In August 1943, a year and a half after beginning his Navy flight training, Vraciu took part in his first combat operation. This was during the raid on Marcus Island by *Essex*, *Yorktown*, and *Independence*, which was also the first carrier operation of the Hellcat. O'Hare carried out strafing attacks, with Vraciu flying as his wingman.[38] In October, now leader of a two-plane section, Vraciu took part in the raid on Wake, shooting down a Zero in air-to-air combat, and claiming a Betty and a Zero destroyed on the ground. In November he took part in the big raid on Rabaul and the invasion of the Gilberts; near Tarawa he shot down another Betty. After *Independence* was damaged by an aerial torpedo off Tarawa and forced to return to the U.S. for repairs, Vraciu transferred, with VF-6, first to *Essex* and then to the newly arrived *Intrepid*. In January 1944 he took part in the invasion of the Marshalls (where he shot down three Bettys) and the air strike on Truk in February, where he claimed four Zero fighters. After *Intrepid* was damaged he transferred to VF-16 aboard *Lexington* and took part in the Battle of the Philippine Sea.[39]

Training individual pilots and other aircrew was only part of the story. It was essential to create cohesive air units, both squadrons and air groups. Squadrons had a specific type of aircraft—fighter (VF), dive bomber (VB), or torpedo plane (VT). Each squadron was commanded by an officer with the rank of lieutenant commander; in 1944 the majority were still regular officers, although some were reservists. On carriers three or four squadrons trained to operate together in an air group. In the first half of 1944 all air groups were usually led by a commander who was a regular rather than a reservist.

Before the war one air group (aircrew and ground staff) was assigned to a specific carrier. For example, AG 6 was originally attached to *Enterprise* (CV-6). Prolonged wartime operations, with combat and attrition, led to air groups being rotated between ground bases and carriers, with experienced crews being returned to the U.S. to rest and share their expertise at a training base. Meanwhile, with so many new carriers under construction and entering commission, air groups had to be trained on shore, ready to be moved aboard carriers when their ships were ready. Training would begin on shore, first with individual squadrons working up at different airfields, and then air groups coming together on one airfield to train together before joining their carrier. As described in Chapter 2, in the run-up to 1944 new carriers would conduct air-group training round Chesapeake Bay and then Trinidad, and continue working up on the cruise to the Pacific and the early weeks of their operations in the Hawaiian area. When the crews had reached an acceptable level of training, they were given some combat experience, flying against isolated islands like Marcus or Wake. Only after that were they committed to operations against places where hostile enemy air opponents were more numerous and dangerous. Pacific air battles often involved large numbers of American pilots who had not been in air-to-air combat before, but the pilots had hundreds of hours of flying time, and had taken part in individual and group training which had been made as close to real combat as possible.

For most of the Central Pacific campaign, fighters of TF 58 engaged Japanese Navy island-based fighters over the Mandate and fended off relatively small-scale attacks by attack planes and twin-engined bombers. Mitscher's attack planes—TBF Avengers, SBD Dauntlesses, and SB2C Helldivers—were employed mainly in attacking airfields and other installations. Attacks on shipping, even at Truk, was mainly against small ships in harbors. They were not taking part in complex attacks on an enemy fleet at sea, of the type that had occurred in the carrier-versus-carrier battles of 1942. Only on one day (20 June 1944) would they have to deal with an enemy carrier fleet.

Training of enlisted personnel involved five times as many people. As is evident in Table 3.2, nearly 185,000 "aviation rates" were on active service in 1944. The enlisted ranks provided crewmen for the Navy's planes, but also a very large number of support personnel on carriers and ashore at land bases. They maintained engines and airframes, prepared armament, and looked after electronic equipment. The huge expansion of the number of Navy aircraft, which was first contemplated in 1940, led to the unprecedented development of training facilities. The pre-war system had been based on a scattering of small, specialized schools and "on the job" experience. Training was expanded after 1940, and by 1943 was concentrated at four very large Naval Training Centers (NTCs), established at Chicago, Jacksonville, Memphis, and Norman (Oklahoma), under the overall control of the Naval Air Technical Training Command (NATTC). Mass training of aviation machinist's mates (AMMs), aviation metalsmiths (AMs), and other technical rates was carried out in courses lasting four to six months. By 1943 output of skilled personnel was keeping pace with the very rapid growth in the number of carriers and carrier aircraft. Overall 300,000 aviation technicians would be trained in a network of sixty schools during the course of the war.[40]

The situation with regard to enemy aviation personnel also needs to be outlined, as it was an important factor in the events of the first half of 1944.[41] Most Japanese flyers were now lacking in training and experience, compared to their American opponents, and indeed compared to their own predecessors. This was in addition to now being repeatedly outnumbered by American carrier planes and often flying vulnerable aircraft which had become qualitatively inferior to those of their enemy.

In December 1941 and much of 1942, Japanese fighter, attack plane, and bomber crews had dominated the skies over the Pacific. Allied myths of Asiatic incompetence and even genetic myopia were dispelled by the run of victories. The situation with regards to aviation personnel and training in the Japanese Navy was different from the U.S. Navy, both before and during the Pacific War. Fighter pilots on the Japanese side were mostly warrant officers or petty officers, with a smaller proportion of junior commissioned officers. Even in January 1940 only about 10 percent of some 3,500 active pilots were officers.

In the 1930s, aside from a small proportion of regular officers, pilot candidates for the Japanese Navy came from enlisted sailors or specially recruited young men with a secondary education. The men from the fleet were young petty officers and seamen selected from a very large number of applicants in the Pilot Trainee Program. In the late 1930s, as the need for aircrew increased, the Imperial Navy began to recruit young civilians in their late teens. They were put through a program which mixed secondary general education and flight training; after successfully completing this they were sent to the fleet as enlisted aviators. This program was later supplemented by recruitment of secondary-school graduates. Pre-war training of individual pilots was rigorous, and selection and performance standards were very high. Unlike the wartime U.S. Navy, advanced carrier pilot training was carried out in fleet units, as was formation training.

This rigorous training system was effective, and it made Japanese naval aviation capable of striking victories. Outstanding examples occurred in December 1941, with the extraordinarily well-executed carrier strike on Pearl Harbor, the destruction of AAF air bases in the Philippines, and the sinking of two British capital ships by medium bombers off Malaya. A combination of selection and training and, early on, a degree of operational experience from 1937 in the Sino-Japanese war, meant that Japanese air units and individual pilots achieved remarkable success in early 1942, albeit against weak or unready opposition. This experience would also be evident in air-to-air combat and in coordinated attacks on the warships of the American fleet which took place during the carrier battles of 1942.

On the other hand, Japanese Navy air units suffered high attrition in 1942, including loss of formation leaders. The campaign in the Solomon Islands, notably in the October 1942 Battle of Santa Cruz, caused heavy losses of air personnel. This proved extremely hard—indeed impossible—to make up. American aircrew flew limited tours in the combat theater before being rotated home to recover and pass on their expertise by training replacements and reinforcements; this was less common in the Imperial Navy. In addition, with the American counter-offensive in 1943 many of the experienced Japanese ground crews, vital to a successful air effort, were killed in the fighting (at Roi and elsewhere) or had to be left behind at isolated bases like the eastern Marshalls, Rabaul, and Truk. During pilot training in wartime the Imperial Navy continued to maintain very high selection standards, which limited replacement of losses and the expansion of the naval service. This problem was only confronted during the belated attempt to rebuild the carrier fleet and, simultaneously, to raise a new cadre of land-based aircrew and aircraft in the form of the new First Air Fleet. Even in late 1943 and 1944 Japanese pilots demonstrated remarkable skill in night attacks, but only on a small scale. The demands of long flights over water, especially by single-seat aircraft, caused an unacceptable level of operational (non-combat) losses among inexperienced aircrew. The implications of all these shortcomings would become apparent in June 1944 during the attempted mass daylight attack over the Philippine Sea. The Americans would justifiably call this the "Turkey Shoot."

U.S. NAVY AIRPLANES

Another fundamental reason why the U.S. Navy gained supremacy in the sea/air war in the Pacific in 1944 was the number of aircraft it would throw into the air battles there. In each of the operations carried out from the middle of 1943 the carrier task forces overwhelmed the local defenses. This in turn was the result of the huge capability of the American aircraft industry. As already mentioned, the rapid expansion of the number of U.S. naval aircraft had begun eighteen months before Pearl Harbor, with the Two-Ocean Navy legislation authorizing procurement of 15,000 planes. The remarkable growth which followed is shown in Table 3.3. Most of the "combat" planes listed were destined for the Pacific.

The 22,116 combat aircraft available to the U.S. Navy (globally) in 1944 have to be contrasted with the 2,784 on hand in the Japanese Navy in April 1944. American numerical superiority was essentially ten-to-one.[42]

Battles of the sea/air war would be won by the side that had the most planes, but performance quality was also essential. Here the U.S. Navy also had the advantage in 1944. This was especially true for fighter planes, and the most important type in the Central Pacific campaign

Table 3.3 USN and USMC Aircraft on Hand, 1935–45

Year	Combat	Transport or Utility	Trainer
1935	1,041	67	170
1936	1,100	90	166
1937	972	113	161
1938	1,284	25	268
1939	1,316	150	262
1940	1,194	152	363
1941	1,774	183	1,444
1942	3,191	461	3,378
1943	8,696	878	7,021
1944	22,116	1,939	9,652
1945	29,125	2,897	8,370

Source: Evans/Grossnick, *Naval Aviation*/1, p. 93. This table excludes a small "miscellaneous" category.

was without doubt the F6F-3 Hellcat.[43] This was a fighter designed and built by the Grumman Aircraft Engineering Corporation of Bethpage, Long Island, New York. It was a big blunt-nosed aircraft, with very large angular wings spanning 42 feet.

Whatever the outstanding success in airframe design and production achieved by Roy Grumman and his team at Bethpage, equally important for the Hellcat was the development of the huge R-2800 Double Wasp engine by Pratt & Whitney Aircraft in East Hartford, Connecticut.[44] This was a twin-row radial engine, with nine cylinders in each row. Total displacement of the eighteen cylinders was 46 liters (2,804 cubic inches), making it the largest aircraft engine extant. It achieved an incomparable 2,100 hp.

The empty weight of the whole aircraft, without pilot, fuel, or ammunition, was 9,060 lb, loaded weight was 12,598 lb. (The only comparable single-engined fighter of the era, in terms of size, was the AAF's Republic P-47 Thunderbolt, also built on Long Island and also powered by the Pratt & Whitney R-2800.) The Hellcat was much bigger and had much better performance than either its predecessor, the F4F Wildcat, or its main opponent, the Mitsubishi A6M *Zero-sen*.

The empty weight of the F4F-3 was 5,238 lb; that of A6M-2 Zero was only 3,704 lb. The Pratt & Whitney R-1830 Twin Wasp of the F4F-3 displaced 30 liters and produced 1,200 hp. The radial engine of the A6M2 Zero displaced 27.9 liters, barely half that of the Hellcat's R-2800; power output was only 1,130 hp.

The Hellcat F6F-3 could fly at 335 mph at sea level (50 mph faster than the F4F-3), and 376 mph in the thinner air at 17,300 feet. The initial climb rate was 3,500 feet per minute (fpm), half again more rapid than the 2,265 fpm of the F4F-3. At Santa Cruz in 1942, the slow climb rate of the F4F-4s was one of the reasons the Japanese were able to break through to *Hornet* and *Enterprise*; the interceptors had not been able to reach the high-flying enemy attack planes in time to stop their approach.

The Hellcat was equipped with internal 250-gal. fuel tank under the pilot's seat; this gave the plane a range of 1,090 miles. Fitted with a 150-gal. "drop tank" under the fuselage the plane's range was extended to 1,620 miles.[45] The normal range of an F4F-3 Wildcat was only 845 miles. The Hellcat's endurance meant that it could be used as a long-range scout and could also carry out lengthy defensive patrols over the fleet in the CAP role.

In terms of firepower, the gun armament of the Hellcat was six 0.50-cal. machine guns in the wings, compared to the two slow-firing 20-mm cannon and two 0.30-cal. machine guns of the Zero. Another very important feature of the Hellcat, often not remarked upon, was that it could carry a large bomb load, two 1,000-lb bombs, one under each wing. The bomb load of the F6F was the same or better than that of the SBD and SB2C dive bombers, or the TBF torpedo bomber. This capability enabled the Hellcat to operate as a fighter-bomber—as indeed it did in the sweeps against the Marshalls and at Truk.

In general the Hellcat was much sturdier than the lightweight Zero. A bullet-proof windshield, 212 lb of armor to protect the pilot, oil tank and the oil cooler, as well as self-sealing petrol tanks were all features of the F6F which were not matched by the Zero. Grumman's Bethpage plant was given the nickname of the "Iron Works" for the sturdiness of its products.

The timely arrival of the Hellcat in the Pacific in the late summer of 1943 was not inevitable. Indeed, the Navy's original plan, before the war, had been to equip the carriers with the Vought F4U Corsair. The great potential of the Pratt & Whitney R-2800 Double Wasp was recognized, and the F4U had been designed around it. (Pratt & Whitney and Vought were both divisions of the United Aircraft Corporation.) The Corsair was the Vought entry in a competition for a new fleet fighter which BuAer had opened in February 1938, and it was the Navy's favorite. The XF4U-1 first flew in May 1940 and, after initial modifications to the design, a contract for 584 F4U-1 Corsairs was signed in June 1941.

In the same month, however, the Navy ordered a back-up design from Grumman. This step was motivated by the protracted development of the Corsair's airframe and the technical risks of its advanced R-2800 engine. The Grumman design was intended to be an improved F4F Wildcat, designated XF6F-1, and the engine was to be the more familiar R-2600 Twin Cyclone, manufactured by the Curtiss-Wright Corporation in Patterson, New Jersey. The Wright R-2600 was the same engine used to power two other projected carrier aircraft, the Grumman torpedo bomber (the TBF Avenger) and the Curtiss dive bomber (the SB2C Helldiver).

As it turned out, the XF6F-1 design team, led by Leroy Grumman and William Schwendler, had a different concept from that of the Navy. Rather than an improved F4F they designed the prototype of a completely new aircraft. It bore only a general resemblance to the F4F Wildcat, and at 4.5 tons was 60 percent heavier. As set out in the Navy's specification, the Wright R-2600 Twin Cyclone powered the prototype XF6F-1 when it was first flown on 26 June 1942, thirteen months after the XF4U-1, and three weeks after the Battle of Midway. The twelve-month development period from the beginning of design work to this first flight was in itself extraordinary. In fact, the Hellcat was the *only* operational single-engined American fighter plane of World War II to have its first flight after 7 December 1941. More remarkable, however, was the flight on 30 July 1942 of an even more powerful version of the Hellcat. This was the pre-production XF6F-3, fitted with the Corsair's Pratt & Whitney R-2800 Double Wasp. By the time of this late July test flight the Navy had already ordered the R-2800-powered Hellcat, and the first production F6F-3 flew on 4 October 1942.[46]

It is often stated that the F6F was designed to take on the highly maneuverable Japanese A6M2 Zero. In fact, the U.S. Navy had had little experience of combat with the Zero until midsummer of 1942, and the first Zero that could be inspected in detail (a crashed example from the Aleutians) only became available after the F6F-1 and F6F-3 had been designed and test-flown.

The first carrier unit to receive the F6F-3—on 16 January 1943—had been the VF-9 fighter squadron, at NAS Norfolk. This squadron was intended to operate from carrier *Essex*, which was fitting out at nearby Newport News. The Hellcat first went into combat on 28 August 1943 with land-based Navy squadron VF-33, operating from Guadalcanal. The first *carrier* combat operation by VF-5, VF-9 and VF-22 took place three days later, on 1 September, in the raid on Marcus Island. Only thirteen months had passed from first flight of the F6F-3 to combat operations.

Various explanations have been suggested for the replacement of the Corsair by the Hellcat.[47] The Corsair was somewhat faster than the Hellcat, and it would eventually remain in U.S. Navy carrier service considerably longer—into the Korean War. However, early evaluations of the Corsair had concluded that the type was—in unmodified form—not suitable for carrier operations by pilots of less than expert skill; this judgement was made after trials in the autumn of 1942. In contrast, the Hellcat turned out to have excellent low-speed performance and presented no special difficulties when landing aboard a carrier.[48]

Industrial efficiency was an additional factor in the choice of the Hellcat. Along with fast development of the design, Grumman also accomplished rapid mass production without major modifications. In the summer and autumn of 1942 work began on Plant No. 2 at Bethpage, Long Island. Grumman had had 813 employees in 1939 and 6,650 in 1941, but by 1943 the number had shot up to 25,094.[49] Thanks to the extremely efficient production set-up at Bethpage, ten F6F-3 fighters had been completed by the end of the 1942, and 2,547 would be delivered by the end of 1943. At that time Grumman was completing over 200 Hellcats a month, overtaking the F4U-1A Corsair in production numbers. In that year production of the other major Grumman types (the F4F and the TBF) had moved to Eastern Aircraft

Corp. plants, allowing Grumman to concentrate on the Hellcat; Eastern Aircraft was a subdivision of General Motors (GM).

Grumman may also have had better informal relationships with the Navy than Vought, thanks to positive experience with the Grumman FF1, F2F, and F3F biplane fighters, and with the F4F-3 and F4F-4 Wildcat. Probably most important, the Navy did not want to support two different fighter types on carriers. Since more of the carriers were equipping with Hellcats it seemed best to operate the Corsair from land bases by U.S. Navy and Marine squadrons. The F4U-1A Corsair did in fact begin combat operations in February 1943, six months before the Hellcat, but it was used from land bases in the South Pacific and was often flown by Marine pilots. In the period from January to August 1944 only a handful of F4U-2 Corsair night fighters would operate from the TF 58, fitted with a radar pod mounted on their starboard wing.

Fleet air defense, air combat, and airfield attack were the most important aspects of the air fighting of TF 58 in the first half of 1944 (up to the battle of 20 June), and in these actions the Hellcat was the main type involved. However, three carrier attack aircraft were also important: the Grumman TBF Avenger, the Douglas SBD Dauntless, and the Curtiss SB2C Helldiver.[50]

The TBF, with its angular wings, portly fuselage, and flat nose resembled the other Grumman planes, the Wildcat and the Hellcat. It carried a crew of three: pilot, radioman/bombardier, and rear turret gunner. Powered by the Wright R-2600 Twin Cyclone, the plane was somewhat bigger in wingspan and length than the F6F. The TBF could fly at 257 mph at sea level, 50 mph faster than its predecessor, the Douglas TBD Devastator. This was the case even though, at 10,555 lb (empty), it was twice as heavy. Unlike other torpedo bombers, the Avenger carried its lethal weapon in an internal weapons bay. Aircrew knew it as the "pregnant turkey." Alternative loads were a 2,000-lb bomb or four 500-lb bombs, as well as a 275-gal. long-range drop tank. The TBF was sturdily constructed, and it had considerable defensive armament: two forward-firing .50-cal. machine guns, and two guns firing aft—a power-operated dorsal turret with a .50-cal. gun, and a .30-cal. ventral gun. Range on internal fuel was 1,105 miles, or 1,390 miles with two 58-gal. underwing drop tanks.

The XTBF-1 prototype first flew in August 1941, but 286 production machines had been ordered "off the drawing board" the previous December. The first production aircraft followed in early January 1942, by which time the type had been assigned the name "Avenger." The first combat use of the TBF was in flights from Midway Atoll in early June 1942. The small detachment involved was nearly wiped out, but the ten-month gap between first flight and combat service was another remarkable development and production achievement by Grumman. The TBF-1 served aboard carriers from the time of the Guadalcanal landing in August 1942 and remained in use until the end of the war. In early 1944 production was moved from the Grumman plant at Bethpage to a giant Eastern Aircraft Corp. facility, a converted GM car plant in Ewing, New Jersey. GM-built Avengers were designated as TBMs, and a number of them had reached TF 58 by June 1944.

Two dive-bomber types operated with TF 58 squadrons in 1944, both two-seaters. The Douglas SBD-1 Dauntless had entered service with the Navy and the Marines in September 1940. The SBD-5 ("dash-5") version was still the main dive bomber in service when TF 58 was formed. The Dauntless was substantially smaller than the Hellcat and its wings did not fold. It was powered by a single-row Wright R-1820 Cyclone. The SBD had already become the most successful U.S. Navy aircraft of the war, when SBD-3s accounted for four Japanese carriers and a heavy cruiser at Midway. The SBD-5 version had an uprated (R-1820–60) motor delivering 1,200 hp and a top speed of 253 mph at 16,600 feet. There was a 75-gal. fuel tank in the fuselage and a 55-gal. tank inside each wing (total 185 gal.); two 58-gal. drop tanks could also be carried. Maximum range on internal fuel was 1,100 miles with a 1,000-lb bomb. The Dauntless could carry a 500-lb or 1,000-lb bomb in an external cradle; this allowed the bomb to be swung forward to clear the propellor while the aircraft was making a steep diving attack. It was equipped with two forward-firing .50-cal. guns, and two .30-cal. operated by the rear gunner. Robustly built, the SBD-5 was equipped with bullet-proof windshield, some armored protection, and self-sealing fuel tanks.

The Curtiss SB2C Helldiver, which the Navy introduced in late 1943 to replace the SBD Dauntless, was 80 percent heavier than its predecessor. The wingspan was 8 feet greater, but the wings could be folded. The Wright R-2600 Twin Cyclone (the same motor as that of the TBF) was much larger and more powerful than the Wright R-1820 Cyclone of the Dauntless. The SB2C-1C could fly at 281 mph at 12,400 feet and was somewhat faster than either the Dauntless or the Avenger.

The Helldiver was designed, like the Avenger (and unlike the Dauntless), to carry its main weapon load internally; this reduced aerodynamic drag. The plane normally carried a 1,000-lb bomb, although it could carry a 1,600-lb bomb, or two 1,000-lb bombs. Guns were two 20-mm cannon in the wings, firing forward, and two .30-cal. operated by the rear gunner. Both pilot and gunner had some armor protection.

The flying range of the Helldiver was disappointing, at 1,110 miles. This led to a practical combat radius, with a 1,000-lb bomb, of only 240 miles. A 110-gal. fuel tank was set in the middle of the fuselage, between the pilot and the gunner; there was also a 105-gal. tank in each wing (for a total internal capacity of 320 gal.).

The U.S. Navy's hugely ambitious aircraft procurement program was not flawless. The problem with operating the F4U-1 Corsair as a carrier fighter was one example. Even harder to carry through had been the development of the new dive bomber. Although the SBD-1 version of the Dauntless had first flown in May 1940, it was based on a design that had entered Navy service in 1938 (as the Northrop BT-1). In May 1939 the Navy ordered construction of the prototype of a big replacement "scout bomber" designed by Curtiss-Wright, the XSB2C-1. Powered, like the future TBF Avenger, by the Wright R-2600 Twin Cyclone, it first flew in December 1940. By this time the Navy's expansion program was well underway, and 200 SB2Cs had been ordered off the drawing board three weeks before the first test flight. The main construction plant was in Columbus, Ohio, but a few were also built at two plants in Canada. In the event, thirty-five months would elapse between December 1940 and the entrance of the SB2C-1 to combat service in November 1943; this contrasted with ten months for Grumman's TBF.

The SB2C would be known by pilots and maintenance personnel as "the Beast," and even as the "Son of Bitch, 2nd class" (SB2C). The overall design was flawed, with bad solutions to the challenge of creating a large aircraft with a powerful engine that could still fit into the confines of carrier hangar deck and elevator. The Curtiss design featured a very large wing and tail, but a short fuselage. It proved to be unstable in flight, and its low-speed characteristics, so important for carrier operations, were not good. The prototype suffered two crashes, in February and December 1941. Hundreds of corrective modifications had to be made by Curtiss. The SB2C-1 was still plagued with technical problems when it finally reached new squadrons being set up and trained in the spring of 1943. Equipment faults, which became evident during *Yorktown*'s shakedown in Trinidad in June 1943, led her CO, Capt. J. J. Clark, to urge that the SB2C by taken out of production. In the event the unreliable SB2Cs were put ashore at Trinidad and Norfolk, and Clark's carrier proceeded to the Pacific with its VB-5 dive-bomber squadron re-equipped with the familiar SBD-5.

Unlike *Yorktown*, *Essex* and *Lexington* had originally been equipped with the SBD, and they had sailed to war with that type. *Bunker Hill* was the first carrier to take the somewhat improved SB2C-1C Helldiver to the Pacific—ironically, leaving her F4U-1 Corsairs behind in Hawaii. The VB-17 dive-bomber squadron of *Bunker Hill* carried out the first combat operation of the Helldiver in November 1943, against Rabaul.

Gradually the situation with the Helldiver improved, as the worst "bugs" were ironed out. *Intrepid* arrived in Hawaii in January 1944 equipped with SBD-5s (VB-6), but *Hornet* came out in March with the SB2C-1C (VB-2), as did *Wasp* (VB-14) in April. By the time of the Philippine Sea battle in June 1944, the Helldiver SB2C-1C had replaced the SBD in most dive-bomber squadrons; the exceptions were those of *Lexington* and *Enterprise*. In the end the SB2C Helldiver was only slightly superior in speed, range, and bomb load to the SBD-5 and SBD-6 versions of the Dauntless (production of which ceased in July 1944). Improved versions of the Helldiver, the SB2C-3, and SB2C-4, with an uprated version of the R-2600 engine, entered service in the later months of the war. Roughly the same number of Helldivers and Avengers were built, some 7,000 in each case. In the end the SB2C was built in larger numbers than any other dive bomber, including the famous Ju 87 Stuka. But despite late-war service in the Philippine Sea and Leyte Gulf battles it remained the least satisfactory of the U.S. Navy's major wartime aircraft.

This is not the place to go into detail about Japanese aircraft developments.[51] The main point is that numerical and technical advantages so apparent in 1941–42 had been overcome by the Americans in 1943 and 1944. The planes of the Japanese Navy aircraft had been designed for an offensive role. Tactical potential and range had been achieved at the cost of survivability—sturdy construction, armor for the pilot, self-sealing fuel tanks, and sometimes even radios. The Mitsubishi Zero was the naval aircraft encountered in largest numbers in the Central Pacific. It flew from island airfields and (in June 1944) from carrier flight decks. The basic qualities of the little fighter have already been mentioned. Both in its A6M2 and (improved) A6M5 variants, it was highly maneuverable at low speeds and had a very good climb rate and (long) range capability. It was now outclassed by the Hellcat. Nearly 11,000 Zeros were manufactured over the course of the war, an impressive total, but the type was never replaced as a carrier-based fighter.

The Japanese Navy's two new single-engined carrier-based attack planes, the two-seat Yokosuka D4Y/Judy and the three-seat Nakajima B6N/Jill were both newer than the Zero; they had entered service in late 1942 and 1943. There were among the first naval aircraft to be given "popular" names by the Japanese: the D4Y was known as *Suisei* ("Comet") and the B6N as *Tenzan* ("Heavenly Mountain"). These planes were fast and could operate at long ranges, but they had little self-protection and were at first available only in small numbers. Some of the older attack planes were still encountered in 1944, the D3A/Val and B5N/Kate—both made famous at Pearl Harbor—but they were slower and even more vulnerable.

The main twin-engined bomber was still the Mitsubishi G4M/ Betty, which had good range but poor self-protection. A much superior bomber, the Yokosuka P1Y/Frances (with the popular name *Ginga* or "Milky Way"), was becoming available, but only in small numbers. The Japanese also had an excellent four-engined, long-range flying boat in the form of the Kawanishi H8K/Emily, but few were built and they were increasingly vulnerable to radar-controlled fighters. The other scout machine encountered in the Central Pacific was the Aichi E13A/

Jake. Entering service in 1940, this was a single-engined, three-seat floatplane catapulted from battleships and cruisers or operated from shore bases; it had an impressive range of 1,300 miles.

FLEET AIR DEFENSE

It is understandable to think about the air war over the Pacific as one of airplanes and pilots—Hellcats versus Zeros, courageous and skillful aviators in air-to-air combat. Beyond this, however, the essence of American fleet doctrine, especially against enemy air attack, was *layered* defense. "Air search" radar detected enemy scout planes and incoming strike formations as far as 100 miles out from the fleet. Interceptors orbiting over the fleet were vectored against an attack force now 70 miles away, directed by shipboard radar centers. Concentric rings of destroyers, cruisers, and even battleships surrounded the carriers, which were the center of a rapidly maneuvering formation. All of the ships were armed with long-, medium-, and short-range anti-aircraft guns. These provided mutual support and effectively engaged with barrage and direct fire those enemy planes which had penetrated the fighter screen. New forms of communication, especially VHF voice radio, were vital for all of these functions. This layered defense, combined with growing numbers of U.S. Navy ships and aircraft, became more and more effective at the end of 1943 and the beginning of 1944.

Radar was one of the key elements of World War II at sea. (Admiral Halsey, when ranking "the instruments and machines that won us the war in the Pacific," put submarines first, radar second, and planes only third.)[52] Especially important for the operations of TF 58 was the use of radar to give timely warning of the range and bearing of approaching enemy planes; this information eliminated the need for large standing patrols of fighters, which would not have been practical. The U.S. Navy began to develop radar systems in the late 1930s, but it also benefitted from gaining access in 1940 to British technology and experience. The British forces, specifically the RAF and the Royal Navy, had used radar and "fighter direction" under combat conditions.

The first major U.S. Navy radar system, designed to detect distant aircraft ("air search"), was designated CXAM. From 1941 it began to be fitted to battleships and aircraft carriers. This radar was notable for a large (17-ft × 17-ft) rotating "mattress" antenna positioned high on a ship's superstructure. It was tested in action aboard *Lexington* off Rabaul in February 1942, when enemy recon planes were detected, and a fighter director officer used radar information to coach F4F-3 Wildcats into the successful interception of enemy bombers. CXAM was further developed as the SK air search radar, which was carried by large ships for the duration of the war. SK could detect aircraft at a distance of about 100 miles and at an altitude as low as 1,000 feet. It could determine bearing and range, but not height (at least not directly); it could also not detect planes flying at a very low altitude. There were some worries that radar emissions might give away the position of the task force or ship, but in November 1942 Admiral Nimitz instructed that radar be kept on all the time: "Although the use of radar may possibly disclose our presence, the information to be gained from it, plus the warning of impending attack, will usually far outweigh the negative value of radar silence."[53]

SM "pencil-beam" microwave radar began to be fitted to big ships in late 1943, and this provided height information at about 50 miles out; SM also provided greater detail about the nature of the approaching "bogey." A vitally important feature of the system was radar identification, the ability to distinguish friendly interceptors from approaching enemy attack planes. Known as IFF ("Identification Friend or Foe"), this involved fitting transponders to friendly aircraft.[54]

In 1942 the radar and "fighter direction" was still far from perfect. U.S. Navy fighters did not successfully intercept the mass strikes of carrier aircraft against Kinkaid's TF 61 at Santa Cruz in October 1942. Progressively, however, things got better. Radar improved, along with the communications system, and teams of fighter director officers (FDOs) were trained. The FDOs had a hugely responsible task; they were usually USNR officers no higher in rank than a lieutenant, chosen for their aptitude and rigorously prepared. A month after Santa Cruz, Nimitz ordered that all ships be fitted with a "Combat Operations Center" (COC), with links to the fighter communications network and the ability to act as a center for radar information, especially for the FDO.[55]

Radar demanded space aboard ship to house equipment and personnel. The "old" *Hornet* (CV-8), commissioned in 1941, was the first carrier to have generous accommodation for electronics. This was built into the successor classes, from *Essex* onwards. By 1944 each American task group had its own long-range fighter defense system, coordinated at higher (task force) level. The COC was later redesignated as a "Combat Information Center" (CIC). Set up on large and small warships, it became essential to the conduct of operations. Meanwhile, rapid analysis of radar data was improved by the arrival of the PPI (Plan Position Indicator), which provided a radar display in a map/plan form.

All of this provided vital warning of the presence of "snoopers" which enabled their destruction and prevented early sightings of American task forces. It also helped TFG 58 to deal with mass attacks during daytime, and small-scale threat by bombers at night. However, defending the fleet against night attacks remained a problem, despite the arrival aboard the carriers of a small number of F4U-2 and F6F-3N night fighters fitted with AI radar pods.[56] Again, the large size of the Corsair and the Hellcat had allowed the addition of heavy radar equipment. Later, in 1945 off Japan, *Enterprise* would be fitted out as a night-defense carrier.

At Santa Cruz in 1942 the fighter defense of the task forces, even with radar and fighter direction, was for a variety of reasons not functioning properly, and it was overwhelmed. More successful, however, was the "local" air defense of the ships of TF 61. The AA guns of some of the American ships at Santa Cruz had been upgraded in the course of 1942, and they inflicted very high losses on the attacking Japanese dive bombers and torpedo planes. In 1943 and 1944, AA defense, while still not impossible to penetrate, had become even more formidable.

In the interwar years the major navies had put much effort into developing anti-aircraft systems.[57] The U.S. Navy's standard long-range 5-in/38 gun, which first went to sea in 1936, has already been mentioned. This 127-mm weapon was "dual purpose" (DP); it could fire at surface targets or be elevated to fire at aircraft. All new major warships from destroyers on up, and even some auxiliaries, were armed with these guns. Destroyers had four or five single 5-in/38 mounts; cruisers and battleships had multiple twin mounts to supplement their (single-purpose) main armament; fleet carriers, with more limited deck space, had single or twin mounts. A "Fletcher" class destroyer carried five 5-in/38, a new "Cleveland" class light cruiser carried twelve guns (in six twin mounts), a new fast battleship like *South Dakota* carried sixteen (in eight twin mounts).

Although in emergency the 5-in/38 gun mounts of the ships could fire independently, they were intended to operate together as part of a complex gun-direction system. Central rangefinders and "directors" had been introduced for the main armament of battleships before World War I. In some respects, however, the requirements of AA directors were even more demanding, as they operated in three dimensions against small, rapidly moving targets. This required a special AA fire control director, that could very quickly predict the future position of a plane or formation and provide firing information to all long-range AA guns that could bear on it. The standard U.S. Navy director for the 5-in/38 guns was the Mk 37; one or two systems were mounted high up at either end of the superstructure on heavy carriers, cruisers, and destroyers. The new fast battleships carried four in a diamond disposition, with one each fore and aft, and one on the starboard and port beam amidships. The highly sophisticated system comprised an optical rangefinder, an analogue "computer," and "slave" remote-control links to 5-in/38 gun mounts.

During the war the system of the 5-in/38 gun and the Mk 37 director was improved. Radar was added to the optical system, and in late 1942 the British-designed proximity (VT) fuse was introduced. Rather than the shell being exploded by actually hitting the target (an unlikely event), by a timer fuse, or by an altitude fuse, this shell included a tiny radar unit which caused the shell to explode, dispersing shrapnel, when an aircraft was detected within close proximity.

The 5-in/38 was most effective as an AA gun in barrage fire directed against formations of high-flying bombers or groups of low-flying torpedo planes. It was less effective against individual aircraft at close range, especially dive bombers. For this, ships were equipped with medium-range and short-range AA guns. In 1941 the newest pre-war

U.S. Navy medium-range AA gun had been the 1.1-in/75 (28-mm bore), which had entered service only two years earlier. This weapon was fitted in a "quad" (four-barrel) mounting to allow high rate of fire. However, the system was heavy, it was unreliable, and the individual shells were small. In 1942 the 1.1-in/75 began to be replaced in new and repaired/refitted ships by the Swedish-designed 40-mm Bofors gun. This weapon had a maximum effective range of 2,500 yards, and rate of fire of 120 shells per minute; each shell weighed 2 lb. The limitation of the 40-mm guns was that the shell was too small to carry a proximity fuse. The Bofors was produced in very large quantities for the U.S. armed forces by the automobile manufacturer Chrysler.

The 40-mm Bofors were fitted to all U.S. major warships, mostly in electrically powered quad or twin mounts. For example, the "Essex" class *Intrepid* was equipped in 1943 (in addition to eight 5-in/38 long-range guns) with forty 40-mm guns (ten quad mounts). In 1944 the number of these guns was increased to sixty-eight (seventeen quad mounts). The quad mount had a crew of eleven. The twin mount was also widely used. For example a "Fletcher" class destroyer in 1944 might carry as many as five 40-mm twin mounts (as well as six 20-mm single mounts). Groups of 40-mm mounts had their own Mk 51 director.

Short-range fire was delivered by the Swiss-designed 20-mm Oerlikon, usually in single mounts. These replaced the pre-war Browning 50-cal. (12.7-mm) machine gun. The Oerlikons could produce a wall of fire, but with an effective range of only about 1,000 yards and a shell weighing only a quarter of a pound they could not reliably stop an attacking plane before it had launched its bomb or torpedo. Nevertheless, they deterred enemy pilots from making too close an approach, and they boosted the morale of the ship's crew. In 1943 *Intrepid* carried fifty-five 20-mm guns, increased to seventy-six in 1944.

Beyond individual ships and their AA systems, special air defense tactics were developed for the task group as a whole, which operated in a circular formation. In the days of Trafalgar, Tsushima, and Jutland the battleships fought in a "line of battle," albeit supported by cruisers and flotillas of destroyers. These battleships fought in visual contact with an enemy fleet that was in a similar linear formation. In contrast, in Pacific War carrier operations, task groups consisted of a series of concentric rings. The most valuable ships were in the center; a ring of fast battle-ships and/or cruisers surrounding them in a second ring, and destroyers formed an outer ring. Small numbers of radar picket destroyers were sometimes deployed well outside the defensive ring, in the direction of the main enemy air threat; their mission was to give advance warning of air raids. Earlier—as at Santa Cruz—the carriers had operated sepa-rately, relying on dispersal to escape the attention of enemy attackers. By late 1943 and 1944 they were concentrated in formations standard-ized by the USF-10A fighting instructions. Voice radio and radar facil-itated the (relatively) safe changes of course that were required. Low-flying enemy planes had to pass through rings of defensive fire (and there were instances of ships coming under "friendly fire" from their neighbors). The ring formation, coupled with frequent ASP from the carriers, was also a safeguard against submarine attack (although in reality Japanese submarines did not prove to be a danger for fleet carriers in 1943–45).

Finally, it must be emphasized that the attacking planes were trying to launch their bombs and torpedoes to hit ships which were moving at between 20 and 30 knots and able to maneuver violently. This was much more difficult than attempting to hit a stationary target. This was, of course, a problem for both sides. Although the American air groups had considerable experience striking stationary targets like airfields and other static installations, they were undergoing a new and more challenging experience when they attacked the fast-moving Japanese fleet during the Battle of the Philippine Sea on 20 June 1944.

In any event, by the end of 1943 the task of attacking American task groups was much harder than in the previous year. The Japanese had failed to mount effective counterattacks against the carriers raiding Rabaul in November 1943. Four waves of carrier aircraft, about seventy-five planes in all, were launched from land bases against TF 38 on 11 November; they hit no ships and suffered very heavy losses.[58] The last significant land-based daylight air attack was during Rear Adm. Pownall's TF 50 raid on Kwajalein in early December 1943. Despite the Pownall's apprehensions, Japanese air activity during the day on 4 December had no effect, although during the night *Independence* was damaged by a torpedo. The new situation allowed the end of "hit-and-run" raids by the fast carriers. In place of that, Mitscher could now report that he was going to "fight his way in," relying on the powerful air defense system. The U.S. Fleet could now operate close to Japanese air bases with a degree of impunity, at least as long as the enemy was using conventional (non-kamikaze) tactics. The ultimate test in our period would be the attempted Japanese strikes against TF 58 on 19 June 1944, during the Battle of the Philippine Sea.

CHAPTER 4

SEVEN-LEAGUE BOOTS

TF 58 Raids the Marianas, February 1944

THE MARIANA ISLANDS: "WE WILL FIGHT OUR WAY IN"

Kwajalein, Majuro, and Eniwetok—the key positions in the Marshall Islands—had been captured. The Japanese had withdrawn their surface fleet from their main Central Pacific stronghold at Truk in the Carolines; that place had been attacked by Spruance and Mitscher with TF 58 and "neutralized" as a major air or naval base. Now, still only in the third week of February, the operations of Mitscher and TF 58 continued, with an extraordinary long-range carrier strike against the Mariana Islands, 700 miles west of Truk, 1,600 miles west of Majuro, and 3,200 miles west of Pearl Harbor. The fast carriers were now racing ahead with unmatched power and "seven-league boots."[1]

The original intention of Nimitz and Spruance had been to follow the Truk raid with further strikes on the Japanese air bases at Ponape and Jaluit. Ponape was in the eastern Carolines, and Jaluit in the southern Marshalls. The objective would have been to secure the newly captured atolls in the Marshalls from long-range Japanese air attacks. Now the success of TF 58 at Truk—and the evidence there of Japanese weakness—convinced Nimitz to mount a much more daring strike against the Marianas.[2] Nimitz had questioned the wisdom of invading the Marianas after the bloody battle on Tarawa in November, but successes in the Marshalls and at Truk had changed his mind. He was now in full agreement with Admiral King in Washington about the importance of the islands.

On Friday, 18 February, Nimitz signaled Spruance, who was in the second day of strikes on Truk, with the change of plan. He proposed that part of TF 58 should now proceed even further west, attacking the Marianas. Spruance (aboard *New Jersey*) and Mitscher (aboard *Yorktown*) were observing radio silence, but they discussed Nimitz's proposal by signal lamp and agreed to it.

The raid against the Marianas was so quickly conceived that it had not even been assigned a codename. It was carried out under Mitscher's hastily drafted Oplan 3-44. Spruance did not take part in the Marianas strike himself. Still flying his flag in *New Jersey* and escorted by only one destroyer, he returned to the newly captured anchorage at Kwajalein, arriving on 21 February. At Kwajalein he took part in a staff conference and an inspection of base development, a vital issue. He then he proceeded south aboard his flagship to Majuro to rejoin the fleet, arriving on the morning of the 26th.

Mitscher led the striking force of TF 58 on his own, still flying his flag in *Yorktown*. Significantly, the operations of the past weeks in the Marshalls and Truk had given Nimitz and Spruance confidence in the acting fast-carrier commander. The ships advancing toward the Marianas under Mitscher were designated as Task Force 58, although it did not now include all the fast carriers. The three heavy carriers and three light carriers of this force were divided into two task groups, which operated close together. Task Group 58.2 was now made up of *Yorktown*, *Essex*, and CVL *Belleau Wood*, four light cruisers and seven destroyers; it was reinforced by fast battleships *Alabama* and *South Dakota* as it neared the Marianas. *Essex* remained the flagship of the admiral commanding TG 58.2, Rear Adm. "Monty" Montgomery. Task Group 58.3 was still commanded by Rear Adm. Ted Sherman in *Bunker Hill*; Sherman's two other carriers were still CVLs *Monterey* and *Cowpens*. Accompanying Sherman's carriers were now fast battleships *Iowa*, *North Carolina*, and *Massachusetts*, three heavy cruisers and nine destroyers. Total air strength of the two task groups was about 370 planes.[3]

After withdrawing to the east from Truk, TF 58 made a rendezvous with fleet oilers SSW of Eniwetok on Friday, 19 February. TG 58.2 refueled from *Kaskaskia*, *Neches*, and *Sabine*; TG 58.3 from *Cimarron*,

Guadalupe, and *Platte*. To avoid recon planes from Truk, the two task groups then proceeded to the north, before turning west on the 21st for the run-in toward their objective.

The distant destination was a long string of islands named in honor of Queen Mariana (regent for Carlos II) when Spain took formal control of them in the 1670s.[4] They stretch north and south for some 425 miles, but Saipan, Tinian, and Guam all lie at the southern end. These islands are small in absolute terms, but they were considerably larger than those in the atolls of the Marshalls and the Carolines. Guam, the largest, is nearly 30 miles long, and nearly twice the area of Malta. Unlike the Marshalls, Truk, and the Palaus, none of the Marianas possessed a harbor large enough to accommodate a large number of big ships, let alone substantial port facilities.

Guam became an American possession as a result of the Spanish-American War of 1898. The Germans bought the other islands in the Marianas from Spain after the war, only to lose them to the Japanese in 1914 (they became part of the Mandate in 1919). By 1944 the islands had substantial garrisons and space for tactical maneuver; they were also relatively near Japan and ports in China. Japanese troops from Saipan had captured unfortified Guam quickly in December 1941. After that, the Marianas were deep in the Japanese Empire, shielded by the Marshalls and the Carolines.

In particular, information was not available about new Japanese airfields. There were in fact three on each of Saipan and Tinian, the most northerly of the islands attacked (and adjacent to one another). Guam, the former American possession in the south, had two uncompleted airfields.[5] Rota, between Tinian and Guam, still had only a rough landing strip which was under development.

The advancing TF 58 was spotted by a patrolling Betty medium bomber in the afternoon of Tuesday, 22 February. Attempts to shoot the plane down failed, and a sighting report it sent was intercepted. Mitscher made the critical decision to proceed despite this and broke radio silence: "We have been sighted by the enemy. We will fight our way in."[6] In light of the recent successful attack on *Intrepid* off Truk, this was a weighty decision. And unlike what happened on the eve of the Kwajalein invasion and before the Truk raid, the Japanese were able to attempt a number of air attacks against the incoming task force during the night of 22/23 February and early the following morning. These began after dusk and were concentrated against Montgomery's TG 58.2, which was steaming parallel to Sherman's TG 58.3, but further north.

Mitscher decided to defend the task groups using the radar-controlled gunfire of the escort ships rather than night fighters. The shells of their 5-in/38 guns were partly conventional and partly fitted with proximity (VT) fuses. Because the Japanese intruders could be tracked on air search radar the task groups could turn away from them to avoid contact. Radar and VHF voice radio also made possible radical changes of course during the night, without collisions. In the event, the Japanese were only able to carry out attacks by individual aircraft, at least until morning. After that, small formations of Judy dive bombers were broken up without getting into an attack position. Nevertheless, they delayed for a short time the launch of strike aircraft from TG 58.2. No American ship was hit, although *Alabama* and cruiser *Mobile* suffered minor damage from "friendly" AA fire, and one Hellcat was shot down by accident. A total of eight enemy planes were claimed shot down by TG 58.2 and two more (after sunrise) by the CAP of TG 58.3. Overall, however, Japanese losses in these confused operations were considerably higher than those of the Americans.[7]

Mitscher launched his own deckload strikes at 0745 on Wednesday, 23 February. His carriers were now about 100 miles east of the various targets in the Marianas.[8] Planes from *Essex*, *Yorktown*, and *Belleau Wood* (TG 58.2) attacked the largest islands, Saipan and Guam. Those from *Bunker Hill*, *Monterey*, and *Cowpens* (TG 58.3) struck Tinian and Rota.

Some Japanese fighters attempted to intercept the raiders, but with little success. A generally reliable Japanese source (published in 1990) gives a figure of thirty-six Japanese Navy fighters engaged over the Marianas, of which eleven were shot down.[9]

Mitscher's TF 58 had two objectives. The first was to obtain aerial photographs of the southern Marianas. This would contribute to planning for what would be one of the most important amphibious landings of the Pacific War. The second was to weaken Japanese air strength by destroying aircraft and damaging ground facilities.[10] The photography went well, despite mixed weather. Excellent photographs were obtained of the primary objective, Saipan, and there were also good images of nearby Tinian. Guam seems to have been less successful, although there were visual sightings of the airfields there.[11]

The strafing and bombing of Japanese aircraft on the ground was also extremely successful. Based on pilot reports and aerial photographs, six single-engined planes and seven twin-engined planes were claimed destroyed on airfields on Saipan, as well as three four-engined flying boats and five floatplanes. Twelve single-engined and thirty-two twin-engined planes were claimed destroyed on Tinian, and two single-engined and five twin-engined planes on Guam. The claims were only of aircraft that had clearly been destroyed, and the total of those put out action by strafing was believed to be considerably higher.[12] At 1630 operations ceased, and TF 58 began its retirement; there were no more targets to hit.

It was especially important that many of the aircraft destroyed on 22 and 23 February were from the First Air Fleet. Elements of this new formation had just been rushed to Saipan and Tinian from Japan. This was an emergency response to the attacks on the Marshalls and Truk, and to the withdrawal of major warships west to Palau and north to mainland Japan. The First Air Fleet (*Dai-ichi Kōkū Kantai*) was a major shore-based formation that had been created on 1 July 1943 to defend the Central Pacific. It was commanded by Rear Adm. Kakuta Kakuji.[13] While being set up, equipped, and trained in mainland Japan it was directly under the command of the Navy Minister rather than part of the Combined Fleet. However, on 15 February 1944, during the crisis in the Marshalls, Kakuta's command was subordinated to the Combined Fleet, and the first units to be formed were thrown prematurely into battle. The movement of First Air Fleet aircraft from Japan began on 20 February; some planes stopped for fuel or shelter at Iwo Jima in the Bonins.[14]

The premature commitment of the first air groups seriously dislocated the training schedule of the whole First Air Fleet, and in addition many aircraft and crews were lost. As one Japanese officer put it under interrogation after the war, "the advance echelon had arrived on 20 February, just in time to have its protruding nose flattened."[15] The results would still be painfully evident when the full-scale battle for the Marianas began in June.

In contrast, the cost of the Marianas strikes to the U.S. Navy side was very low. Only five Hellcats and an Avenger torpedo bomber were lost on this day of air strikes, mostly from AA fire.

After completing the strikes on the Marianas, TF 58 completed a four-day passage back to the new forward base at Majuro. There were no significant incidents, although a patrolling Japanese bomber (probably from Truk) was shot down on the 24th. Mitscher followed a course north of Eniwetok and Bikini and then south to Majuro. The big ships had enough fuel for the return trip, and the destroyers were refueled from the battleships on the 25th. On the morning of Sunday, 27 February Mitscher led the triumphant TG 52.2 and TG 52.3 into the Majuro lagoon, carriers first, then battleships and cruisers.

With this ended an extraordinary series of operations. When Admiral Nimitz met President Roosevelt in the White House in March he jokingly described the Marianas raid as an "encore." (On 6 March Nimitz appeared on the cover of *Life* magazine.) February had been a very successful month for both Spruance and Mitscher. After the Marianas raid Spruance was promoted to the rank of full (four-star) admiral. Mitscher was promoted to vice admiral and given the title Commander, Fast Carrier Force, Pacific Fleet. Something even more profound had been achieved. As the eminent naval historian Clark Reynolds later put it: "The Truk-Marianas raids by Task Force 58 revolutionized naval air warfare."[16]

THE FLEET TRAIN: ADVANCED BASES AND SERVRONS

The Central Pacific campaign is remembered for strikes by U.S. Navy carrier task forces and air battles—like the raid on the Marianas—and for amphibious landings. But behind the American success were logistic capability and the extremely rapid development of major new advance bases.[17] Especially important were Majuro, Kwajalein, and Eniwetok, which were nearly 3,000 miles west of Pearl Harbor and 1,900 miles north of Nouméa (the U.S. Navy's advance base in the South Pacific).

The demands of the Pacific campaign for American forces were unique. One element, of course, was the vast distances involved, which were much greater than those involved in the Atlantic crossing to Europe.

Other challenges, especially in the Central Pacific, were the small land area of the island objectives, the negligible size of the population there, and the lack of labor, food, and even water. Multiple logistical challenges had to be faced. Assault troops had to be transported across an ocean to storm fanatically defended objectives. It was also necessary to bring in and supply "follow-on" forces assigned to garrison and protect newly captured territory. Personnel were required to serve at air bases and other rapidly constructed installations. Forward of Pearl Harbor, Australia, and New Zealand, almost all locations lacked modern infrastructure in the form of berths, lighters, dockside cranes, and storage facilities, as well as railways or proper roads to take goods inland. All this demanded a huge amount of shipping, which only became available in late 1943 and 1944. Also required was long-term planning. As one history of Pacific logistics put it: "[T]he development of amphibious assault tactics, which marked such a tremendous advance in naval warfare, was accompanied by equally important, if less spectacular, progress in methods of logistic support. Together they made possible the strategy of our advance across the Pacific." Admiral Spruance later recalled, "Without these Mobile Service Squadrons we could never have had the rapid movement of our fleet to the westward at ever increasing distances from Pearl Harbor and its continued operation as a fleet in these waters."[18]

A specific factor, directly relevant to the theme of this book, was the logistics of American naval operations. Especially important was the so-called "fleet train" of auxiliary vessels working from advanced bases. Before the war the leadership of the U.S. Navy devoted little attention to "supply," as compared to operations, even at the Naval War College. The planners had toyed with the idea of mobile bases for the advancing battleship fleet, but they had done little to actually build the necessary auxiliary vessels or even to set out an organizational structure.[19] Little preparation was done to incorporate the U.S. Merchant Marine in a future conflict. However, a small "Base Force" had existed between the wars. In February 1942 it was renamed the Service Force, Pacific Fleet. Its head from late 1939 and throughout the war was Rear Adm. (later Vice Adm.) William L. ("Uncle Bill") Calhoun.

In any event, in the interwar years the Navy had been based mainly on either coast of the continental United States. The Hawaiian Islands are today thought of as the "rear" of the Pacific naval offensive of 1942–45, but even they lay 2,000 miles west of California. Pearl Harbor was essentially still an "advance" base when the battle fleet was moved there in the summer of 1940—in the hope of deterring further Japanese aggression. Admiral Richardson, the fleet commander, was replaced in February 1941 after complaining that forward-basing in Hawaii was impeding the effective build-up of his forces. Far from home bases at San Pedro (near Los Angeles) and San Diego in southern California, Pearl Harbor had only limited facilities for servicing, repairing and even refueling warships, and training personnel. The Pearl Harbor Navy Yard did have two large drydocks (one built in 1940) and a submarine base. The Hawaiian Islands also had considerable land area for base development and training facilities, especially on Oahu. As one historian put it, by the end of 1943 "Pearl Harbor was on the way to becoming the mighty base a complacent America public had assumed it to be in 1941."[20]

In late 1941, before the Japanese attack, minor works had begun to garrison and develop small U.S. island possessions in the Central Pacific west of Hawaii, at Wake, Johnston, Palmyra, and Midway. None of these specks in the ocean were (or would be) of much value as bases even for individual surface ships. Advance base development, when it came in 1942, would be where the fighting was, in the South Pacific. It began in February 1942 with a fueling station at Bora Bora (codenamed BOBCAT), near Tahiti. This was a link in the supply chain to Australia, which was so vital in 1942 at the time of the greatest Japanese threat. It was at this time that the Navy's later famous Construction Battalions (CBs or "Seabees") began to be deployed. By end of 1943, 120,000 Seabees would be in service outside the continental U.S.

Nouméa, a port on the southern end of the French island possession of Nouvelle-Calédonie, was developed as the main advanced base of the U.S. Pacific Fleet during the Solomons campaign. As the months passed, service ships were moved to Nouméa to provide supplies and repair facilities for the battle fleet that was fighting further north around Guadalcanal. A floating drydock, ARD-2, arrived to deal with repair and maintenance of destroyers and submarines. Among the big ships repaired at Nouméa were *Enterprise* and *South Dakota*, which came in for initial repairs after the Battle of Santa Cruz.

The island of Espiritu Santo in the New Hebrides (now Vanuatu), north of Nouméa, was also built up. The most striking arrival here was a huge floating drydock. Sections built in the U.S. were towed across the Pacific and assembled at the end of 1943; ABSD-1 (Advanced Base Sectional Dock) could accommodate a ship as big as a battleship for refit or repair and was fitted with traveling cranes. (A similar unit, ABSD-2, would be assembled at Manus, but it was not operational until the autumn of 1944.)

Even in the first six months of 1943, after Guadalcanal was secured, the South Pacific remained the center of Admiral Nimitz's logistic effort. Shipments of "ordnance and combat materials" there came to 100,000 tons, as compared to 34,000 tons to the Central Pacific; the contrast in petroleum products was even more striking, 214,000 tons versus 15,000 tons.[21] CincPac's administrative headquarters, however, had remained at Hawaii. And by the late summer of 1943 Pearl Harbor again served as the main concentration of American naval power in the Pacific. From here would come the main movement of warships for the invasions of the Gilberts and Marshalls, although some other elements would set out from bases developed in the South Pacific, especially Nouméa and Guadalcanal.

Plans for a mobile advance base force were realized in the early autumn of 1943 with the deployment of new mobile Service Squadrons in the Central Pacific. The fleet train began to take a much more flexible form. In the course of 1943 the number of service vessels at Hawaii and other locations in the Central Pacific had risen from 77 to 358.[22] The advanced bases in 1942 had been set up on relatively large islands (like Nouvelle-Calédonie and Espiritu Santo) with an existing friendly civilian population and some port facilities. The small, sparsely inhabited islands of the Central Pacific—the Marshalls and the Carolines—needed something different.

Service Squadron Four (ServRon 4), the first mobile base, began to function in November 1943, on the eve of the Gilberts invasion. It was located at Funafuti Atoll in the Ellice Islands (now Tuvalu), a British possession lying south of the equator and between Samoa and Gilberts. Funafuti was small and sparsely inhabited, and the Japanese had not continued on here after they occupied the Gilberts in December 1941.

American marines from Samoa only arrived in October 1942, during the Guadalcanal campaign. A year later, ServRon 4 comprised the 9,000-ton destroyer tender *Cascade* (newly built on a C3 hull), and repair ships *Vestal* and *Phaon*, as well as twenty-one smaller vessels, including tugs and barges.[23] ServRon 4, in particular *Vestal*, carried out important preliminary repair work on CVL *Independence* after she was torpedoed off Tarawa.

The really important role of these ServRons was the rapid development and utilization of *captured* harbors. This involved the establishment of a second mobile base organization, ServRon 10, which had been set up at Pearl Harbor in November 1943. ServRon 10 arrived at Majuro in the Marshalls at the start of February 1944, within days of that atoll's seizure. Commanded by Capt. Worrall Carter, ServRon 10 allowed the immediate use of Majuro's sheltered lagoon, providing secure fueling and repair facilities. The first of the fast carriers entered the lagoon on 4 February. As already mentioned, battleships *Washington* and *Indiana*, damaged in a collision, were able to begin their repairs by ServRon 10 within a day of the accident. From Majuro, Task Force 58 would very soon sortie for the raid on Truk and the Marianas. The base facilities in the Marshalls were further developed when ServRon 4 was moved up from Funafuti to Kwajalein at the end of February and was then absorbed into ServRon 10.

In early June 1944, as soon as TF 58 had sortied to deliver its air strikes on the Marianas, the headquarters of ServRon 10 moved on to Eniwetok. This atoll, while still in the Marshalls, was considerably nearer Saipan and Guam. By this time the floating strength of ServRon 10 included four destroyer tenders: *Cascade*, along with 16,500-ton *Prairie*, the C3-based USS *Markab*, and LST *Phaon*. There were also six repair ships, including *Vestal* and the new 16,000-ton *Ajax* and *Hector*, three repair-shop barges, and six small or medium-sized floating drydocks. In addition thirteen ammunition barges, fifteen barges for crucial stores, twenty-three storage barges for fuel oil and gasoline, and fifteen tugs were located at Majuro, and oilers moored in the lagoon provided a floating tank farm. Majuro became mainly a base for submarines and for replacement carrier aircraft.[24]

After August 1944, as the American fleet advanced into the western Pacific, the floating-base system was developed even further.[25] Even

Eniwetok and Majuro were now too far from the front line. In September 1944 Ulithi, a giant atoll in the western Carolines, would be occupied without enemy resistance. It was quickly transformed into the main advance fleet base for the invasion of the Philippines and Okinawa, using the resources of ServRon 10, still commanded by Worrall Carter, now a Commodore.[26] At the same time advanced repair facilities were developed at Manus's Seeadler Harbor.

Advance shore bases also played an important support role in the carrier air war. The task of maintaining carrier aircraft could take place at forward bases without their ships having to return to Pearl Harbor or the West Coast. In wartime maintenance personnel remained at sea with the air department of one carrier, which meant that air groups required separate facilities and maintenance personnel ashore while preparing to join the fleet, or when flying to land bases after months at sea. This was formalized in the spring of 1944 with the creation of the Carrier Aircraft Service Units (CASUs), facilities ashore which could be moved forward rapidly. Some seventy were eventually in service in the Pacific. Meanwhile, increasing use was made of special escort carriers based at Majuro and elsewhere to deliver replacement aircraft to the front-line carriers and transfer out flyable but worn-out or damaged aircraft ("duds").[27]

THE FLEET TRAIN: UNDERWAY REPLENISHMENT

New advanced bases, attended by the growing number of vessels in the Service Force, were essential to the Central Pacific campaign. However, the most directly important element was the fleet oilers and their capability to resupply the fast carriers and other warships at sea, especially in the middle of long-range operations like the raids on Truk and the Marianas. The process involved is normally known as "underway replenishment" (abbreviated as "unrep").[28] The new American warships with their high-pressure/high-temperature machinery had been designed for long-range operations, but more than anything else, it was underway replenishment that made possible the seven-league boots of TF 58. In contrast, the British Royal Navy, with a large number of imperial ports available, was more "base-minded" and did not develop a similar "underway" capability.

As already mentioned, in Chapter 2, a weakness of the U.S. Navy in the interwar period was that only a small number of auxiliary ships had been commissioned. This shortcoming included the lack of vessels able to transport the heavy fuel oil that nearly all ships burned to heat their boilers. (Fuel oil had suddenly begun to replace coal in warships in the period just before and during World War I, and by the 1920s it was used in nearly all U.S. Navy warships.) America did not have defendable overseas colonies or bases. Any naval operations in the Western Pacific by battleships—still the core of the fleet—and their escorts (especially destroyers) would require tankers bringing their vital fuel oil. By the late 1930s, however, the oilers in service consisted of slow and relatively small vessels. For the most part these were twenty years old or more, and they were not in good repair.

USS *Cimarron* (AO-22), launched in January 1939, was the first of the modern U.S. Navy "fleet oilers." The Navy officially used (and still uses) the term "oiler" to differentiate its fueling ships from civilian "tankers." The fleet oilers did not look very different from classic civilian tankers with their "engines aft/bridge-amidships" layout. The funnel, superstructure, and machinery were located near the stern, and the bridge was situated on an "island" amidships, with two well decks forward and aft of it. Indeed, during the war many fleet oilers were built on the same basic (T2) design as the "civilian" tankers, nearly 500 of which were completed at that time.

Nevertheless, fleet oilers, especially those put into Navy service in World War II, were different in important respects. Their engines were more powerful, much more so in the case of the "Cimarron" class, which had 13,500 shp (shaft horsepower) steam-turbine machinery driving two shafts (and two propellors). These particular ships were able to operate at 18 knots; this matched the cruising speed of contemporary warships, including the fast carriers. This was well above the "economical" speed of a normal civilian tanker. Even the slower newbuild fleet oilers would be able to keep up with most of the Navy's warships. (All these ships were sometimes called "fast oilers".)

Fleet oilers were also different because they were not intended simply for bulk transfer of fuel oil from port to port—although they were sometimes consigned to that role. Their mission was to refuel other warships while underway at sea, and to do this they were equipped with pumps, hoses, kingposts, and elaborate tackle. In addition, they mounted a considerable defensive armament. Typically this consisted of four longer-range guns (5-in/38 or 3-in/50) in single mounts and a number of medium (40-mm) and light (20-mm) AA guns. A final difference was that the fleet oilers had accommodation for as many as 300 officers and men, about four or five times the crew of a civilian tanker.

Cimarron was laid down in April 1938 at Sun Shipbuilding & Drydock Co. in Chester, Pennsylvania; Chester is 15 miles down the Delaware River from Philadelphia. At this time Sun was one of America's biggest shipyards, with much experience in the construction of civilian tankers. The short designation of the "Cimarron" class, assigned by the U.S. Maritime Commission, was T3. The ships were 553 feet long. "Light" displacement was 7,470 long tons, increased to 24,830 when fully loaded with fuel. The total fuel-oil capacity of *Cimarron* was 146,000 barrels (bbl), equal to 6,100,000 (U.S.) gallons.[29]

Like all U.S. Navy oilers, AO-22 was named after a river. The Cimarron is a tributary of the Arkansas River. The ship was launched by the wife of Admiral Leahy, the CNO; the role of Elizabeth Leahy in this event was indicative of the high importance the Navy was beginning to attach to this type of vessel. Commissioned two months later, in March 1939, *Cimarron* was dispatched to carry oil between the West Coast and Pearl Harbor; she would not be fully "navalized"—with full armament and fuel-transfer equipment—for some time after that. Two sister ships, *Neosho* (AO-23) and *Platte* (AO-24), were commissioned later in 1939.

More and more fleet oilers were ordered or acquired, especially after the enactment of the Two-Ocean Navy program in June 1940. The Navy had subsidized construction of further "Cimarron" class fast tankers for civilian oil companies, like Standard Oil of New Jersey (Esso), and these now began to be taken into naval service. SS *Esso Albany* was commissioned as USS *Sabine* (AO-25) in December 1939, and seven more "Cimarron" class had been commissioned into the Navy by July 1941. Most of these would not be ready for operational refueling at sea for some months after December 1941. Nevertheless,

Cimarron and *Sabine* would later accompany and refuel the carrier task force that attacked Tokyo in the April 1942 Doolittle Raid.

The outbreak of the Pacific War in December 1941 brought a further planned increase in fleet oiler numbers. The second type were the six vessels of the "Kennebec" (AO-36) class. The Maritime Commission had designated these as the T2 type tanker (T2 came from size, i.e. smaller than T3). The pre-war construction of these ships had also been subsidized by the Navy. The first three were originally operated as tankers by civilian oil firms, and they were taken into naval service in the first nine months of 1942. They were single-screw ships, slower (16.5 knots) and slightly smaller than the "Cimarron" class. Five more classes of T2 fleet oilers—thirty-six ships—would be acquired during the war. These were commissioned in 1942–44, but only about half were active in the Central Pacific; others took part in the war in the Atlantic, the Mediterranean, and the southwest Pacific.[30]

More important, as far as the fast carriers of TF 58 were concerned, was the second batch of the "Cimarron" class (T3-S2-A2). *Ashtabula* (AO-51), laid down in October 1942 and commissioned in August 1943, was eventually followed by thirteen sister ships. Six fleet oilers of this sub-class were sent to the Central Pacific and were operating there by June 1944.

Although fleet oilers like *Cimarron* could be used for bulk transport of fuel from port to port, or to serve as fixed refueling stations at advanced bases, their main function would be underway replenishment. They did this while steaming at considerable speed side by side with one or more "receiving" warships; this maneuver was termed "broadside" refueling or "riding abeam." Although it is sometimes suggested that the U.S. Navy pioneered this capability, its eventual opponent (Japan's Imperial Navy) had more fast oilers available in 1941, and more experience in broadside refueling. Indeed, this capability played a major role in the success of the Pearl Harbor raid (which was supported by seven fleet oilers). It was also used in later Japanese operations in 1941 and 1942, including the Indian Ocean raid (on Ceylon) and the Battle of Midway.[31]

The U.S. Navy had used underway replenishment for smaller ships during World War I; destroyers were fueled underway as they were being transferred across the Atlantic to bases in Ireland. Lt Cdr Chester

Nimitz, the future CincPac, was directly involved in these operations as XO of the oiler USS *Maumee* (AO-2). Experimentation continued sporadically after the war, still in the battleship era, but the technique only began to be taken seriously in the late 1930s. Broadside refueling for large warships (i.e. larger than destroyers), was initially regarded in the U.S. Navy as impractical because of the danger of collision, and in any event no fast oilers were available. (The alternative was the "astern method," in which the tanker towed the receiving ship and fueling hoses were run over its stern, but this meant that both vessels were moving at an unacceptably slow pace.) However, more naval funding was now available and the requirements of the new carriers and their escorts were becoming evident. Launch and recovery air operations had to be carried out at fuel-burning high speeds, and at the same time supplies of aviation gasoline aboard carriers had to be constantly topped up. The Navy also belatedly adopted at this time the technique of broadside refueling of battleships and cruisers. Nimitz, now a rear admiral, was again involved in the development and testing of the technique in 1939.

Along with the launching and recovering of aircraft, refueling at sea was one of the most difficult and important activities carried out by the fast-carrier force. The big flattops (and their escorting destroyers) expended large amounts of fuel oil when operating aircraft, in high-speed runs into their targets and, of course, while under attack. They needed to refuel at speed as they began the approach to enemy air bases and naval forces. The tankers and warships being refueled could steam at 12 knots, while only 70 to 120 feet apart. Heated fuel oil was passed to big ships through six-inch diameter hoses. Great skill was required to keep two big ships at the correct distance, and to use cranes, lines, and saddles to prevent the hose from breaking or dipping into the ocean water; this would cool down the fuel oil and delay refueling.

As already mentioned, a "Cimmaron" class fleet oiler could carry 146,000 barrels (bbl) of fuel oil, equivalent to 6,100,000 (U.S.) gallons. The capacity of later fleet oilers was similar. Other petroleum-based products were regularly transported and transferred. During the Gilberts campaign, for example, each fleet oiler typically carried 80,000 bbl of fuel oil, 18,000 bbl of aviation gasoline ("avgas"), and 6,782 bbl of diesel oil.[32]

This needs to be compared to the capacity of "receiving" ships. The design storage capacity of an "Essex" class carrier was about 42,000 bbl of fuel oil and 5,500 bbl (231,000 gal.) of avgas. These ships also carried about 1,200 bbl of diesel oil. Fuel oil consumption of an "Essex" class at cruising speed, about 19 knots, was 1,700 bbl a day. High speeds could quadruple consumption: a day's steaming at 31 knots would expend 6,300 bbl.[33]

The fast carriers operated with escorts, and those ships needed to be refueled too. There might be twelve destroyers in the screen of a carrier task group, and each required frequent refueling, either from a fleet oiler or from one of the bigger warships. A "Fletcher" (DD-445) class destroyer, the most numerous type in the Pacific, had a design fuel capacity of about 3,400 bbl of fuel oil. The destroyers had to steam at least as fast as the carriers they were escorting. At 19 knots—roughly task-force cruising speed—the destroyer would burn 460 bbl a day, so this speed could be kept up for a week. At 31 knots, however, fuel burned would be 2,100 bbl a day; this could be sustained without refueling for only a day and half.[34]

As already mentioned, in the first months after December 1941 the U.S. Navy possessed only a handful of fast oilers ready for underway replenishment service in the Pacific. Individual ships nevertheless made possible the campaign of long-range, hit-and-run carrier raids in the first half of 1942. Civilian tankers and Navy oilers were used to transport fuel oil 2,000 miles and more from southern California and the Caribbean (through the Panama Canal) to Hawaii. This was organized by the pre-war Base Force, later ServRon 8 of the Service Force. In December 1941 Pearl Harbor was the location of a recently built "tank farm," in which the above-ground tanks held 4,500,000 bbl of fuel oil.

In the course of 1942 and 1943 the Navy built up its force of fast oilers and gained experience and confidence in their use. In the Solomons in late 1942 and early 1943 warships had often fueled and received service, repairs and supplies at hastily built advanced bases at Espiritu Santo, Nouméa and elsewhere in the South Pacific, with fuel oil brought in from Pearl Harbor and the West Coast.

The Gilberts invasion in November 1943 was the first operation in which all ships refueled at sea. More than a dozen fleet oilers took part.

They were detached, in groups of two or three, escorted by some of the newly arrived destroyer escorts (DEs). Rendezvous points were assigned, where groups of three oilers could meet and refuel carrier task groups. After emptying their tanks they shuttled back to Pearl Harbor to refill. By this time a huge underground facility had been built there to store fuel oil for the Pacific Fleet. It was buried 100 feet underground at Red Hill, east of Pearl Harbor. Total capacity of the twenty storage tanks was 6,000,000 bbl. Construction had begun in December 1940 and was completed in September 1943. Fuel stored at Red Hill was then transferred by tankers from Pearl Harbor to forward bases at Majuro and Eniwetok. From there, fleet oilers—the "Cimarron" class and others—took it to supply the active operations of Task Force 58 and other elements of the Pacific Fleet using underway replenishment.

During the Marshalls invasion in February 1944 a similar procedure was followed, although the number of fleet oilers involved had grown to twenty-eight. The procedure developed further once the Marshalls became the advance base and the newly formed ServRon 10 began to organize oiler movements. The fleet oilers and civilian tankers of ServRon 8 could now bring fuel directly from the West Coast and the Caribbean to Majuro, Kwajalein, and Eniwetok, where it could be trans-shipped to fleet oilers operating in more dangerous waters. During the raid on Palau in March some fleet oilers operated from Manus.

By June 1944, with the invasion of Saipan and the climactic Battle of the Philippine Sea, this system would be even more highly developed. No fewer than thirty fast oilers were operating in the Central Pacific. The movements of USS *Guadalupe* (AO-32), a "Cimarron" class fleet oiler, provide a good example of what was involved.[35] On 17 May 1944 *Guadalupe* returned to Majuro from Pearl Harbor, loaded with fuel, and became part of ServRon 10. On 20 May, while stationary at Majuro, she provided 2,000–3,000 bbls of fuel oil to each of four cruisers; a week later battleships *Washington* and *North Carolina* each received 6,000–8,000 bbls. Still situated at Majuro, *Guadalupe* then topped up her tanks with 51,700 bbl of fuel oil from the civilian tanker SS *Perote*, and with 8,000 bbl of diesel fuel from another civilian tanker.

On 6 June *Guadalupe* left Majuro with fleet oilers *Platte* and *Caliente* and several destroyer escorts in a refueling group (Task Unit 16.7.4).

Guadalupe was now carrying 90,100 bbl of fuel oil, 8,000 bbl of diesel fuel, and 391,000 gallons (9,300 bbl) of avgas. Three days later she refueled light carriers *Monterey* and *Cabot* and five destroyers, transferring 13,000 bbl of fuel oil and 15,000 gallons of avgas. Three more escorts were refueled on 10 June, and on the following day five cruisers and a destroyer. Five days later *Guadalupe* refueled battleships *Washington* and *New Jersey*, and two destroyers with 39,000 bbl of fuel oil. Her fuel-oil tanks now near empty, *Guadalupe* returned to Eniwetok on 19 June, where she filled up again from two station tankers.

Despite their flammable cargo and their operations close to the fighting, the fleet oilers suffered remarkably few losses. Indeed, they seldom came under attack from enemy aircraft or submarines. The two Pacific wartime sinkings, both of "Cimarron" class ships, took place outside our period. *Neosho* (AO-23) survived the Pearl Harbor attack but was sunk by dive bombers during the Battle of the Coral Sea in May 1942 (having been mistaken for a carrier). *Mississinewa* (AO-46) was struck by a submarine-launched suicide torpedo (*Kaiten*) while anchored at the advanced base of Ulithi in November 1944. As will be described in Chapter 8, one fleet oiler unit did come under Japanese air attack east of Saipan during the Battle of the Philippine Sea, but the result was only minor damage to three vessels.

The advanced bases and the fleet oilers together formed the fleet train, which played a decisive and essential role in the U.S. Navy's achievement of supremacy in the Pacific, especially the mobility of the fast-carrier task forces. Capt. Carter could rightfully claim that his men and ships at Majuro were crucial: "The Fast Carrier Force . . . remained in the advanced areas and received its servicing from Squadron Ten as it repeatedly struck and advanced, to the consternation and confounding of the enemy." Admiral Spruance later made the same point: under Nimitz and with Calhoun's Service Force, "we had a combination that could—and did—go anywhere in the Pacific."[36]

CHAPTER 5

DESECRATE

TF 58 Raids Palau, 30–31 March 1944

THE PALAU STRIKE AND THE DEATH
OF ADMIRAL KOGA

The operations of Mitscher's Task Force 58 were paused for over three weeks, after near-continuous activity from the end of January to the end of February. Then, on 23 March the fleet departed from Majuro to mount air strikes against the Palau group of islands in the western Carolines. The attacks took place on 30 and 31 March, and the operation was assigned the codename DESECRATE.[1]

Palau was the location of Koror Town, the administrative center of the whole Japanese Pacific Mandate in the interwar years.[2] Babelthuap, the main island, was the second largest in the Central Pacific, after Guam. The U.S. had little recent intelligence about the place, but they knew it had capacious anchorages. A fine fleet anchorage existed in the form of the Kossol Roads at the north end of Babelthuap and, further south, good harbors were available at Koror and Malakal. These were used by convoys supplying Kavieng and Rabaul. Nevertheless, Palau is one of the less well-known locations in the Pacific War, essentially because the main islands, Koror and Babelthuap, were never invaded by Allied forces.[3]

For the Americans, Palau was a challenging objective. It was a very long distance even from their new bases in the Marshalls; Palau was over 2,100 miles west of Majuro. It was also strategically placed, in the center of a ring of Japanese forces, in the Philippines, the Marianas, and western New Guinea.

One purpose of DESECRATE was to support the amphibious landing planned by General MacArthur's forces at Humboldt Bay (often referred to as Hollandia). This was situated nearly 700 miles southeast of Palau on the New Guinea coast, and deep in the rear of the Japanese Army operating there. Codenamed RECKLESS, MacArthur's operation was scheduled for 24 April (it actually took place two days earlier). TF 58 would prevent the enemy from using Palau as a shipping hub and air base to threaten RECKLESS. There was also a major new enemy airfield on Peleliu Island (at the southern end of the Palau group), and another field was believed to be under construction on Babelthuap.

Probably Nimitz, Spruance, and Mitscher were less interested in MacArthur's campaign than in the pursuit of the Combined Fleet, much of which had transferred to Palau after the effective abandonment of Truk in February 1944. The intelligence assessment on Japanese strength at Palau in late March indicated the presence of one to three battleships, four to six heavy cruisers, one or two light cruisers, fifteen destroyers and "possibly (though unlikely) one or more carriers."[4]

Although Spruance had had confidence in Mitscher's ability to lead the carrier strike against the Marianas on his own, he rejoined the massive fleet (again formally designated TF 50) for the deep expedition to Palau. On 23 March Spruance departed from Majuro, riding again in the new battleship *New Jersey*. The main strike element force was still TF 58. Mitscher, for his part, flew his flag in the now-repaired *Lexington*, which was part of Task Group 58.3.

The Palau strike was even more ambitious than the raid on the Marianas in late February. The fast-carrier force was now made up of three fast-carrier task groups with a total of some 460 planes. The intelligence estimate in late March was that 170 Japanese planes were based in Palau; this turned out to be a substantial overestimate. Nevertheless, a further 500–600 planes were thought to be available in the Carolines as a whole (also an overestimate). In addition to that, enemy air reinforcements could be expected to arrive rapidly from the Marianas, New Guinea, and Netherlands East Indies.[5] Because there was also the possibility of an engagement with heavy surface ships of the Combined

Fleet, TF 58 included a very large gunnery force: six fast battleships, ten heavy cruisers, and five light cruisers. A "major action plan" for a full-scale surface engagement had been drafted.[6]

The main part of Spruance's and Mitscher's ships left Majuro on 24 March. TG 58.2 comprised carriers *Bunker Hill* and *Hornet*, with CVLs *Monterey* and *Cabot*. This task group was now commanded by Rear Adm. Montgomery, aboard *Bunker Hill*. Accompanying Montgomery's carriers were the new battleships *New Jersey* (Spruance's flagship) and *Iowa*, six heavy cruisers, and fifteen destroyers. Rear Adm. Samuel ("Cy") Ginder commanded TG 58.3 which, when fully assembled, included *Yorktown*, *Lexington*, and CVLs *Princeton* and *Langley*. The powerful escort force for Ginder's task group comprised fast battleships *Alabama*, *Massachusetts*, *North Carolina*, and *South Dakota*, four heavy cruisers, a light cruiser, and sixteen destroyers. TG 58.1 was smaller, made up of *Enterprise*, *Belleau Wood*, and *Cowpens*, accompanied by four light cruisers and seventeen destroyers. In command was Rear Adm. John W. ("Black Jack") Reeves. This task group had come up from the South Pacific; it joined the Majuro force on 26 March for refueling at sea.[7]

The distances involved and the size of the American armada meant that fuel supply was a vital consideration. The main Support Force (TG 50.15), sailing from Majuro, was made up of four large escort carriers (*Chenango*, *Sangamon*, *Santee*, and *Suwanee*, with about 120 planes), three heavy cruisers, twelve destroyers, and fleet oilers *Platte*, *Sabine*, *Kaskaskia*, and *Guadalupe*. Fleet oilers *Atascosa*, *Ashtabula*, *Escambia*, *Kankakee*, *Neches*, *Suamico*, and *Tappahannock*, coming up from Espiritu Santo, took part in the refueling of the various elements of TF 58 on 26 March, along with *Cacapon* and *Chikaskia*.[8]

Meanwhile, seven Pacific Fleet submarines were deployed around Palau, waiting to catch any Japanese warships or merchantmen that tried to escape; two more were in "lifeguard" positions near Yap and Woleai, ready to rescue aviators whose planes went down during raids planned there.[9]

The command structure for DESECRATE was essentially the same as that for FLINTLOCK in the Marshalls. Capt. Charles Moore was still Spruance's chief of staff. Mitscher, however, had been assigned a new chief of staff aboard *Lexington*, when aviator Truman Hedding was replaced by surface-ship veteran Capt. Arleigh Burke. Hedding was temporarily assigned to *Lexington* in the same task group (TG 58.3), working with the staff of Rear Adm. Ginder. A destroyer brought Burke to his new assignment on 27 March, in the middle of the operation.[10] Burke had been an aggressive and highly successful destroyer-squadron commander in the Solomons. The new policy of combining a non-aviator and an aviator in major commands was not something that pleased either Mitscher or Burke, and at first their relations were cool. Fortunately mutual respect developed in the following weeks, and Burke remained with Mitscher and the fast carriers until the last months of the war. A brilliant career lay ahead of Burke. He was appointed CNO in 1955, while still only a rear admiral, and served for six years. Another development was the presence of the newly promoted Rear Adm. J. J. ("Jocko") Clark aboard *Hornet* in TG 58.2. Clark was there on what the Navy called a "makee-learn" basis; the experienced former CO of *Yorktown* was required to learn by shadowing Rear Adm. Montgomery.[11]

The very long track of TF 58 lay south of Kusaie, Ponape, Truk, and Woleai in the eastern and central Carolines—rather than north of those places, which had been the route with the Marianas raid in February. Robert Winston, CO of AG 31 aboard CVL *Cabot*, later described this as "running the gauntlet"; New Guinea formed the southern side of the gauntlet. Winston also recalled the weather conditions. "The air was clear as crystal, the sky was cloudless, and the sea was glassy. On our aerial patrols we could easily spot the other task groups when they were twenty or thirty miles away."[12]

The Oplan for DESECRATE put an emphasis on surprise, but the excellent weather made this unlikely. The main part of Task Force 58 was sighted by a Japanese patrol plane from Truk as early as midday on 26 March. At this point the American ships were only about a fifth of the way from Majuro to their objective. This early sighting led Admiral Spruance to bring forward K-Day, the planned beginning of the strikes, by two days, from 1 April to 30 March. This meant missing the opportunity to make use of the first aerial photos of Palau from a planned long-range recon mission. On the same day Spruance's ships refueled and merged with Reeves' TG 58.1.

In the late evenings of 28 and 29 March, now north of New Guinea, TF 58 came under long-range attack by small groups of Betty medium bombers from the Peleliu air base at Palau or from bases in the Marianas to the north. These did not cause any damage to the American armada, and several were shot down.[13]

Thursday the 30th was now designated K-Day. The American carrier strikes began with a large fighter sweep in the morning. This was followed by the launching of deckload strikes by attack planes later in the day against targets around Palau, in what was now called the "Mitscher shampoo."

No major enemy warships were caught at Palau, but for the Combined Fleet the escape was narrower than at Truk in February. At Truk, the last heavy units had left for safety nearly a week before the American strike. At Palau, heavy surface ships based there—the super-battleship *Musashi*, and five heavy cruisers—only departed at 1530 on 29 March, fifteen hours before the American attack planes arrived with their bombs, torpedoes, and mines. Even then, the retreating ships immediately came under threat. *Musashi* had barely cleared the western channel when, at 1744, she was hit by a torpedo fired from submarine *Tunny*. The damage was relatively minor, but the battleship had to proceed to Japan for repairs.[14]

Admiral Koga Mineichi, the C-in-C of the Combined Fleet, had had his headquarters in Palau since 29 February; for three weeks, battle-ship *Musashi* was moored in Palau's Koror harbor. Koga was aboard, developing campaign plans with his staff. He now hoped to achieve a decisive victory over the Americans in a battle for the defense of the western Carolines and the Marianas.[15] On the afternoon of Tuesday (28 March), once the information became available that a major American operation was underway, Koga had moved ashore from *Musashi* with sixty-eight members of his staff. He evidently believed that if a battle were to take place it would be necessary to conduct it from a headquarters ashore, with better facilities for conducting an engagement involving both land-based air groups and warships.[16]

When it came, Mitscher's attack on the Thursday, 30 March, was another resounding success. This was true despite the absence of major warship targets. Numerous attacks were made on merchant ships, as well as facilities on land. The latter included the air base on Peleliu Island, where thirteen medium bombers and twenty-three single-engined planes were claimed destroyed on the ground.[17] This was, however, considerably less than losses inflicted on the Truk airfields.

On the following day, Friday, 31 March, planes from TG 58.2 and 58.3 (*Bunker Hill*, *Hornet*, *Lexington*, and *Yorktown*, as well as four CVLs) continued their attacks on Palau. Reeves' TG 58.1 (*Enterprise* and two CVLs) moved on to attack Yap, 240 miles northeast of Palau, and roughly a third of the way to Guam.

The Americans kept command of the air over Palau. This was true even though, unlike what had happened at Kwajalein and Truk, the Japanese were able to fly in reinforcements. These planes had arrived on Thursday evening after an 840-mile flight from Saipan and took part in air battles on the Friday. Lt John Gray, from VF-5 of *Yorktown*, recalled the enemy planes which were encountered in the big air battles of the second day: "They were bright and shiny, as though they had come right out of the factory. We were over Palau a little over an hour chasing them around. The hardest part of the fight was to beat some other Hellcat to getting a Zero." According to American reports, thirty-five airborne enemy planes were encountered on the 30th, of which twenty-two were shot down; on the 31st, sixty were encountered, and fifty-three claimed shot down.[18]

American combat losses were considerable, by the standards of early 1944: eleven fighters, nine dive bombers, and five torpedo planes. In addition, eighteen aircraft were operational (accidental) losses. Many of the crews of downed planes were rescued, but personnel killed or missing numbered thirteen pilots and thirteen aircrewmen.[19] Another casualty, on the first day of air strikes, was Rear Adm. Ginder, commander of TG 58.3, who suffered a nervous collapse on the flag bridge of *Yorktown*; he would be relieved of his duties and replaced by J. J. Clark when TG 58.3 returned to Majuro. Unlike the Gilbert and Truk operations, the Japanese failed to inflict any damage on the attacking task force, despite a small number of sorties by Judy dive bombers and Betty medium bombers.

Damage to Japanese merchant shipping was heavy, comparable to that of the better-known February 1944 Truk strike. Six tankers were sunk, as well as four cargo-ship types of between 11,000 and 4,000 tons, nine smaller ocean-going cargo ships, and some coastal vessels. Warships sunk were an old destroyer (*Wakatake*) and a 9,000-ton repair ship (*Akashi*), as well as a smaller repair ship and an 8,600-ton aircraft ferry. In total, five small Japanese warships and thirty-one naval auxiliaries and merchant ships were destroyed, for a total of 130,000 tons.[20]

In a new tactic for the U.S. Navy, magnetic mines were dropped by parachute on the passages into the harbor entrances. The mine-laying was carried by specially trained TBF Avenger crews just after dawn on 30 and 31 March. The operation had a dual objective. It would trap enemy ships in local waters, where they could be destroyed by other planes. And delayed-action mines would prevent ships from bringing reinforcements and supplies to Palau in the coming days and weeks.[21]

The Palau raid did not catch any major enemy warships in port, but in another and indirect way it did greatly disrupt the activities of the Combined Fleet. It led to the accidental death of Admiral Koga and many of his senior staff officers. As already noted, Koga had come ashore from *Musashi* with his staff on Tuesday afternoon (28 March). On Thursday evening (the 30th), fearing that the day's U.S. Navy air raids on Palau were preparations for an invasion, Koga decided that he and key staff members should immediately move west to the safety of the port city of Davao in the southern Philippines. Three giant Kawanishi H8K flying boats (with the Allied codename "Emily") were summoned from Saipan to effect the transfer. They arrived at Palau on Friday evening (31 March). Two of the Emilys picked up their passengers and flew off into the night.

The three-hour flight west to Davao was not an especially long one, only 535 miles, but the flying boat with Koga and a number of his staff officers aboard disappeared. It evidently crashed in a severe tropical storm. The event bore an eerie resemblance to the death of Admiral Yamamoto the year before, although that event had been the result of a planned interception, rather than a flying accident.[22] The second Emily, carrying chief of staff Fukudome, with fourteen more Combined Fleet staff officers, also did not make it to Davao. Diverted north to Manila, the flying boat ran short of fuel and crash-landed in the sea off the island of Cebu in the central Philippines. Vice Adm. Ugaki Matome, commander of the 1st Battleship Division, noted Koga's disappearance and the apparent death of Fukudome in his diary entry of 2 April: "What rotten luck at a critical time like this! It looks like God is testing the Imperial Navy."[23] In fact, Fukudome was for some days in the hands of American-led Filipino guerrillas on Cebu, before being rescued by the local Japanese garrison. Important documents about Japanese counterattack planning, the so-called "Z Operations," remained in the hands of the guerrillas. Their importance was recognized, and they were transferred by submarine from the occupied Philippines to Australia and translated.

On the American side, intelligence staff following Japanese radio traffic did note that after 3 April they had been unable to ascertain the location of the "C-in-C, Combined Fleet." This development was connected with an intercepted report which mentioned the search for an aircraft that had disappeared while flying from Palau to Davao. Moreover, it was learned that orders were currently being issued to elements of the Combined Fleet from a different headquarters, that of the C-in-C of the Central Pacific Area Fleet (Admiral Nagumo).[24] The Japanese did not announce Koga's death until 5 May; at this time they also made public the appointment of Admiral Toyoda Soemu as the new C-in-C of the Combined Fleet.

The big attack on Palau, and the sideshow at Yap, had been completed. Mitscher took TF 58, now with all three task groups operating together, and launched a final strike in their expedition to the western Carolines. This took place on 1 April, and the target was Woleai Atoll. Strategically positioned halfway between Palau and Truk, Woleai had a new airfield and a reinforced garrison. Five of the attacking planes were lost, although one pilot was rescued from the lagoon. This was to be the only carrier raid against Woleai, although from the middle of April 1944 onwards the place would be sporadically raided by AAF long-range bombers. It was isolated for over a year except for a few supply submarines.[25]

After the Woleai strike, Task Force 58's five-day voyage home to Majuro was completed without incident; part of the time it was protected by a storm front. On 6 April the Central Pacific Force, still commanded by Admiral Spruance, returned to Majuro.

DESECRATE, the Palau operation at the end of March, with the strikes against Yap and Woleai, was less dramatic than February's operations against the Marshalls, Truk, and the Marianas. The contrast was due in part to the feebleness of Japanese counterattacks and the growing confidence of the Americans. Nevertheless, these strikes in the western Carolines showed off again the "seven-league boots" of the fast carriers. As we will see, they drew Japanese attention toward the south—and away from the actual American objective of the Marianas. Most important, perhaps, they continued the rout of the Imperial Navy. The death of Admiral Koga after eleven months in command was an unintended result, but the event greatly shook the Combined Fleet. Even more important, the bases of the Japanese fleet were now pushed far to the west, and it was now even less able to intervene quickly in the Carolines, the Marianas, or New Guinea. (From mid-May 1944 the main base would be at Tawi Tawi in the southern Philippines, which was 850 miles west of Palau.) Far away in Singapore, Ugaki assessed the situation in his diary entry of 30 March.

An enemy task force appeared at ninety miles south of Palau and they have been repeating attacks since this morning . . . But what makes me mad is the insolent attitude of doing whatever they like and completely disregarding us. If we don't crush the whole lot of them and stop their spearhead at this stage there will be no end to their reckless onslaughts with serious effects on the future.[26]

INTELLIGENCE: FRUPAC AND JICPOA

The Combined Fleet documents captured with Rear Adm. Fukudome's briefcase at Cebu certainly represented a remarkable intelligence coup. Overall, however, less unexpected and more methodical intelligence-gathering efforts were of greater importance. The U.S. Navy fought the Central Pacific campaigns with the advantage of a great deal of intelligence about Japanese organization and deployments gathered from radio intelligence, air and submarine reconnaissance, captured documents and maps, and even prisoners of war.

Much has been written about the development in the U.S. Navy of radio intelligence (abbreviated in 1944 as "RI") and also known as "comint" (communications intelligence) or "Ultra." This was true especially in connection with the surprise attack on Pearl Harbor and the Battles of the Coral Sea and Midway.[27]

The Imperial Navy had a number of cipher systems and updated them at semi-regular intervals. The general-purpose code, which the U.S. Navy knew as JN-25, developed through a bewildering series of versions.[28] Despite this, for most of the war Allied codebreaking teams at Pearl Harbor and Washington, and also in Australia and Ceylon, were able to gain valuable material from decryption. As important, the Japanese military continued to believe that their code systems were unbreakable.[29] Although decryption ("codebreaking") is often seen as the main achievement of RI, highly valuable aspects of this intelligence did not require actually reading encrypted messages. RI also included traffic analysis ("TA"), which involved learning what ships and shore stations used particular radio call signs. Related to this, direction finding ("DF") established by triangulation the presence and approximate location of ships, planes, or bases that were transmitting, and even their level of activity.

From the point of view of American intelligence, 1944 was quite different from 1942. At the beginning of the Pacific War, RI was the main source from which Allied forces gained information about the organization and movements of Japanese forces. Famously, the American victory at Midway in June 1942 was enabled by RI. Much of the time this depended on traffic analysis and direction finding rather than decryption. There were also weeks and months when changes in Japanese codebooks or additive books meant that access to RI became more limited. An example, discussed in the Introduction, was at the time of the Battle of Santa Cruz, where two American task forces were deployed against a much superior Japanese carrier force. In addition, "real time" information was generally limited, because at the operational and tactical level Japanese warships were rigorous in observing radio silence.

The difference between 1942 and 1944 was partly the difference between defensive and offensive situations. In addition, American intelligence resources became so much greater than ever before, including the number of trained personnel (notably newly trained Japanese linguists) and technical developments actually involved in intelligence gathering and analysis. The Mandate had long been a mystery, but "objective intelligence" (information about islands to be invaded) became easier once the advancing Americans knew what potential objectives there would be. Paradoxically, one challenge for U.S. intelligence in the later stages in the Pacific War, including the first half of 1944, was that the Japanese no longer had the initiative. It was difficult to predict what specific *counter-measures* they would attempt; the Midway victory, in contrast, was possible because the Americans learned through RI about Japanese *intentions*.

As we have seen, RI was important in the decision to concentrate the February 1944 attack in the Marshalls on Kwajalein, and to add Majuro and Eniwetok as early objectives. It also gave some indication of the weakness of the Japanese fleet at Truk and elsewhere. In 1942–3, "Ultra," intelligence derived from RI, was used in attempts to organize submarine attacks on major warships, some of which were successful. The Allies also were able to read, from early 1943, the Japanese four-digit merchant shipping code (JN-42). Information made available included midday reports of the location of a convoy or individual ship, and it was vital to the submarine war against Japanese commerce and supply. Especially important was the interdiction of the flow of Army reinforcements to New Guinea and the Central Pacific islands in 1944.

Another element of RI was the assignment of a small number of linguist specialists to major commands such as Task Force 58 and some of its task groups. Notable were the small Radio Intelligence Units (RIUs), which consisted of an officer and four enlisted men. Initially the RIUs were a secure means of channeling Ultra intelligence to flag officers at sea, but they also played a direct role in air defense, monitoring enemy aircraft encountered. For example, they could ascertain whether friendly forces had been spotted and reported.[30]

Other intelligence sources besides RI became important in 1943 and 1944. Photo reconnaissance was not a capability that the U.S. Navy had developed extensively before the war, and to some extent the Army and its "Air Corps" were ahead.[31] Under pre-war agreements, the Navy had not been allowed to operate land-based long-range patrol aircraft. (This was one of the reasons for the Pearl Harbor disaster.) In wartime, long-range photographic reconnaissance aircraft, mainly the land-based four-engined B-24/PB4Y Liberator, were finally made available to the Navy. They were capable of flying at longer ranges than flying boats, and were less weather-dependent. The Liberators had a search radius of 1,100 miles. They operated from quickly constructed island bases with long runways. Bases captured in the Gilberts and the northern Solomons (especially Bougainville) made possible reconnaissance flights over the Marshalls and the Carolines. These were especially effective at observing enemy bases and ports from high altitude, and photographing ships in port and island fortifications. The important flight of Marine Liberators over Truk in early February 1944 has already been mentioned. Other recon planes overflew Palau from New Guinea before the March 1944 DESECRATE raid. Later, the capture of island air bases in the western Marshalls (Eniwetok), and in the Admiralties allowed flights even deeper into the enemy Pacific, over the Carolines and even Wake. On the other hand, the situation was different from that in the war in Europe; until the very end of 1944 Allied reconnaissance planes were not able to overfly the enemy homeland and could not obtain a comprehensive picture of Japanese capabilities.

Carrier aircraft were also now important for photo recon missions over island objectives. In 1944 the fast carriers put camera-equipped Hellcats and Avengers in range of objectives that even the land-based Liberators could not reach. They took low-level "oblique" photos in missions too dangerous for unescorted four-engined planes. The most remarkable example was the TF 58 raid on the Marianas in February 1944, which was essentially an intelligence-gathering expedition.

American submarines provided an exceptionally valuable source of information. They had a very long-range intelligence capability, both at the strategic and operational levels.[32] More and more boats became available in later 1943 and 1944. They could operate even beyond the range of the big land-based American patrol planes, not to mention those operating from aircraft carriers. They even provided some "objective" intelligence (periscope photographs) against distant Japanese-held islands. Indeed, they could operate off mainland Japan. Tactically, submarines also provided timely and highly valuable intelligence about

movement of Japanese warships. This would be of the utmost importance in the Battle of the Philippine Sea in June 1944.

As the Allied advance rolled forward, more and more information
about the enemy became available. Intelligence was found on captured
islands. Sources of information included POWs, although in 1943
there were few of these. (Rear Adm. Fukudome had been, potentially,
an extreme case.) Even when nearly all of a defending garrison was
killed in the fighting, large amounts of documentary evidence were
found, maps, codebooks, and equipment (including repairable aircraft).
Information was also found from accessible enemy warships, beached
or sunk in shallow water. An especially important prize in 1944,
captured in a vessel off Kwajalein Island, was a treasure trove of seventy
detailed, red-edged harbor and coastal charts of other Japanese positions, not yet captured.

Gathering information from a range of sources was only one aspect
of intelligence; another was developing experienced centers for analysis
and—not to be forgotten—for secure distribution of intelligence
information.

It was important that in the first months of the Pacific War Admiral
Nimitz developed confidence in the value and reliability of RI and his
own intelligence staff on Hawaii, especially Cdr Edwin Layton, the
Fleet Intelligence Officer, and Cdr Joseph Rochefort, the head of the
codebreaking center, Station HYPO. Rochefort, despite having helped
win the Battle of Midway, was removed in the autumn of 1942 as a
result of bureaucratic disputes with the parent RI organization in
Washington, Op-20-G. However, the codebreaking unit in Hawaii
continued to play an important role in signals intelligence under Capt.
W. B. Goggins, and veteran codebreakers like Thomas H. Dyer were
still involved. Cdr Layton, moreover, remained in post on the CincPac
staff, and Nimitz found invaluable his ability to interpret and commu-
nicate intelligence, especially from RI.

More broadly, to coordinate all sources of intelligence, a CIC
had set up in June 1941, which in the late summer of 1942 became
the Intelligence Center, Pacific Ocean Area (ICPOA) incorporating
Rochefort's HYPO as a section. By the early autumn of 1943, on the eve
of the Gilberts landings in the Central Pacific, it was clear that large

number of amphibious, aviation, and logistic elements from the U.S. Army and the Army Air Force would be involved, as well as the Navy and the Marines. In September 1943, ICPOA now became JICPOA, the *Joint* Intelligence Center, Pacific Ocean Areas. Admiral Nimitz's intelligence center was now housed in a large new building at Makalapa above Pearl Harbor and led by a Japanese-speaking Army colonel, Joseph Twitty. Capt. Goggins' RI section of ICPOA was detached and kept under the Navy as the Fleet Radio Unit Pacific (FRUPac), but it was located in an adjacent building to JICPOA, and the teams worked closely together. Intelligence staff at Pearl Harbor grew from a handful of officers and enlisted personnel in December 1941, to 4,500 at its peak.[33]

These developments in the collection and analysis of intelligence were directly relevant to the operations of TF 58 in the spring and summer of 1944. They allowed American commanders to have a good knowledge of the capabilities and location of the Japanese Navy, including its air formations.[34] In February 1944 it was known that much of the Combined Fleet was based in the Singapore area and that Japanese Army units were being transferred in convoys from China to reinforce Saipan and Truk in the Central Pacific. In March RI revealed that a new command called the First Mobile Fleet was expected to be concentrated in the southern Philippines by May.[35] As already mentioned, Admiral Nimitz had an accurate assessment of local enemy naval strength at Palau at the time of the DESECRATE operation. By the beginning of April intelligence about the movement of enemy fleet oilers indicated that a major anchorage was being developed in the extreme southwest of the Philippines; this was at Tawi Tawi Island in the Sulu Archipelago. The main elements of the Combined Fleet, including the big carriers, would actually move there from Singapore in mid-May. On 17 May, evidently following the RI lead, submarine *Bonefish* reconnoitered the Tawi Tawi anchorage and reported the presence of heavy ships.[36]

An intelligence summary in the planning documents of TF 58, dated 16 May 1944, included an accurate statement of Japanese strength. It noted that "[f]or the first time in more than 18 months the enemy has a large carrier force in fighting condition." Enemy strength was given as five battleships, three heavy carriers, two auxiliary carriers, five light carriers, twelve heavy cruisers, four light cruisers, and thirty-two destroyers. There were also estimated to be 353 planes in the southern Marianas.[37] On 29 May 1944 JICPOA would provide an "Estimate of Enemy Distribution and Intentions," naming enemy ships in the area of the Philippines and the former Netherlands East Indies. These included six battleships (including the giant *Yamato* and *Musashi*), three heavy carriers (including the new *Taihō*), one large auxiliary carrier, four light carriers, twelve heavy cruisers, two new and three old light cruisers, and thirty-three destroyers.[38] The movement of Japanese air flotillas and naval air groups could also be tracked. The information available to TF 58 at the start of the Marianas operation in mid-June gave even more detailed locations.[39]

Moving somewhat ahead in our narrative, details of the American intelligence effort are evident in plans for the amphibious invasion of the Marianas (which took place in mid-June). The intelligence annex to Spruance's Operation Plan, drafted in mid-May, listed the sources of information about the enemy that had been used: (a) "Estimate of Enemy Strength (ULTRA)," (b) CincPac daily bulletins to task force and task group commanders, (c) Pacific Fleet Intelligence Bulletins, (d) JICPOA bulletins on enemy bases, (e) JICPOA-printed Air Target Maps, and (f) JICPOA-built models of objectives.[40] This was a good example of how information was assembled and distributed about objectives deep within the Japanese defensive perimeter. Although Guam had been an American possession, access to the Japanese islands in the Marianas (notably Saipan and Tinian) had been limited in the interwar period, and there had been none at all for two years after Pearl Harbor. The intelligence effort really began with photographs taken by planes of TF 58 during the raid at the end of February 1944. The first high-altitude recon flights by land-based four-engined patrol planes over Saipan and adjacent Tinian took place on 18 April; a flight over Guam took place on the 27th, and another over Saipan and Tinian on 29 May. Meanwhile, the submarine *Greenling* took a large number of excellent photographs of the coast of Saipan through its periscope between 2 and 29 April, from which panoramic views were created.[41]

This brings us back to 1 April 1944, Cebu, and Rear Adm. Fukudome. The historian Milan Vego suggested that from the point of view of intelligence "[t]he biggest success was the reading of the Combined Fleet's actual plan to react [sic] to the Allied advances across the Central Pacific."[42] This was indeed a remarkable development, but its singular importance should not be exaggerated. The word "reading" suggests decryption, but the "Z" Operations documents literally fell from the sky into Allied hands on 3 April with the flying boat crash off Cebu. Only translation was required. And the documents were not an "actual plan" but a general outline of tactical doctrine.

As we will see, Spruance and Mitscher would not receive the translated text for some time. It had—understandably—taken over a month to extract the captured documents from the center of the occupied Philippines, aboard an American submarine. There was another delay— albeit shorter—involved in translating the material after it arrived in northern Australia. Mitscher's copy had to be dropped onto *Lexington* by a Liberator patrol bomber after he had already left Majuro in early June for the Saipan invasion.[43]

The actual importance of the "Z" Operations material for decisions made by Admiral Spruance in June will be discussed more fully in Chapter 8. For the moment, however, it should be noted that the information was by then two months out of date, and that a new Japanese Combined Fleet C-in-C was in post. The documents captured with Fukudome were just a general statement of doctrine ("fighting instructions") rather than a detailed plan of specific operations.[44] This was not comparable to the detailed information available before the Battle of Midway in June 1942, when codebreakers provided Admiral Nimitz with information about the planned Japanese objective, as well as details of the forward elements of the enemy fleet that would be taking part. And, as will be shown in Chapter 8, at the time of the Saipan landing in June 1944 Nimitz and Spruance actually thought that it was *unlikely* that the Combined Fleet would come out to fight, given the unfavorable balance of forces, the distance of Saipan from Japanese bases, and the small number of fleet oilers still available to the Japanese.

Because Ultra was largely secret until the 1970s, many earlier accounts of the U.S. effort in the Pacific, including that of Samuel Eliot Morison, are incomplete.[45] Later accounts arguably err in the opposite direction. One historian of U.S. Navy intelligence in the Pacific has argued that "intelligence played a pivotal role in paving the way for the triumph of the U.S. Navy."[46] Even now, much of what has been written about codebreaking deals only with the months leading up to Midway, which were unique. In that period of the war the numerical superiority of Japanese naval forces meant that early warning of their intended operations was of critical importance. Intelligence *was* also pivotally important later, especially in MacArthur's leapfrog advance west along the coast of New Guinea and in the submarine campaign. It was significant, too, in the Marshalls operation. But for the main sea/air campaign, including the advance from the Marshalls to the Marianas and especially the operations of TF 58, the key element was not codebreaking or intelligence. Victory, indeed accelerated victory, was made possible by the overwhelming strength and speed of the fast-carrier force and by Japanese weaknesses—the faulty island strategy and the low level of war production. If the U.S. had not been able to decrypt *any* Japanese communications at all in 1944 the outcome of the Central Pacific campaign would still have been an American victory, and one that would not have taken much longer.[47]

CHAPTER 6

TF 58

The Final Raids, April and May 1944

AIR STRIKES ON NEW GUINEA AND TRUK

On 6 April 1944 Task Force 58 returned to Majuro after the Palau raid. The period of respite in the anchorage would be short. Only a week later, on the 13th, most of the fleet set off for another series of long-range air strikes south of the Carolines, although this time commanded by Vice Adm. Mitscher alone. Like the Palau attacks in late March, the object was partly to assist General MacArthur's advance along the north coast of New Guinea.

MacArthur, as already mentioned, had lost the strategic argument. His SWPA would not be the central element of the whole Pacific campaign, with Nimitz's ships and planes reduced to a secondary, supporting role. A compromise was reached in Washington, under which there would be dual offensive, but with the greater emphasis on the Central Pacific.

Part of the compromise was that the fast-carrier force would participate in MacArthur's "jump" to the Humboldt Bay area of northern New Guinea, which was known to the planners as Hollandia, from a local village.[1] The amphibious operation, codenamed RECKLESS, was a most important one. Two U.S. Army divisions would be transported from western New Guinea (via Manus Island). Landing on beaches near Hollandia they would cut the supply lines of the Japanese Army fighting 400 miles to the east.[2]

1a. *Hornet* under attack during the Battle of Santa Cruz

Carrier *Hornet* of Task Force 61 (TF 61) under attack during the Battle of Santa Cruz on 26 October 1942. She was the newest carrier in the U.S. Navy and sank that night; over 100 members of her crew were killed.

1b. *Enterprise* at the Battle of Santa Cruz

After *Hornet* was damaged all the aircraft returning from attacks on the Japanese fleet had to land on *Enterprise*. The ship survived the battle, but she required extensive repairs. She would go on to play a prominent part in the 1944 Central Pacific campaign.

2a. American commanders

Vice Adm. Raymond Spruance (center) and Admiral Chester Nimitz (right) on Kwajalein Atoll. Nimitz commanded the Pacific Fleet (as CincPac); Spruance was his subordinate as commander of the Central Pacific Force (later redesignated as the Fifth Fleet). Task Force 58 was part of Spruance's command.

2b. Flagship *Indianapolis*

The heavy cruiser *Indianapolis* was Vice Adm. Spruance's seagoing headquarters. *Indianapolis* was typical of the 10,000 ton, 8-inch gun cruisers built under the terms of the Washington Treaty.

3a. Rear Admiral Charles Pownall
Pownall was the first commander of the fast carrier force TF 50. Regarded as too cautious for a task force commander, he was transferred to other posts in December 1943.

3b. Vice Admiral Marc ("Pete") Mitscher
Mitscher was one of the Navy's first aviators, qualifying in 1916. He took over the fast carrier force, Task Force 58, in January 1944. He is shown here in a typical pose: sitting in a chair on his flag bridge watching air operations, wearing his trademark lobsterman's hat.

4a. The first new "fast carrier"

This photograph shows the launch of carrier *Essex* (CV-9) at Newport News shipyard in Virginia in July 1942. Seven ships of this class reached the Pacific by June 1944.

4b. *Lexington* in Boston Harbor

The carrier lies in the icy waters of Boston Harbor on 17 February 1943, commissioning date *Lexington* was the third of the "Essex" class. She was built at Bethlehem Steel's Fore River shipyard at Quincy, Massachusetts, and joined the Pacific Fleet in August 1943.

5a. Cruiser conversion (I)
Commissioned in June 1942, *Cleveland* was the lead ship of a very large class. A number of these light cruisers escorted the fast carriers. Some twenty-nine vessels in the program were actually built as cruisers, and nine more were completed as "Independence" class light carriers (CVLs).

5b. Cruiser conversion (II)
Princeton was the second of nine "Independence" class light carriers. Unlike the "Essex" class, the CVLs were not part of the June 1940 Two-Ocean Navy Act; they were an improvisation, supported by President Roosevelt himself.

6a. *Essex*: shakedown cruise
The carrier cruises off the Virginia coast in May 1943. Air Group 9 are assembled on her flight deck.

6b. *Independence* in San Francisco Bay
This photograph shows the small flight deck of the CVLs compared to the "Essex" class. It was taken while the ship was in San Francisco Bay in June 1943, en route to Pearl Harbor.

7a. The Panama Canal
The Canal was crucial to American naval strategy. This is a photograph of a carrier completed after the war, but she was an "Essex" class (USS *Philippine Sea*). The very tight fit in the Gatun Locks is evident.

7b. Fast battleships
Indiana (BB-58) and *Washington* (BB-56) at Majuro Atoll. Eight new battleships had entered service by the spring of 1944. They never fought the expected "Pacific Jutland," but they provided valuable anti-aircraft (AA) defense for TF 58.

8a. Fleet oiler
Guadalupe refuels carrier *Lexington* and a destroyer. Fast fleet oilers were an essential element of the operations of TF 58.

8b. Underway replenishment
Light carrier *Langley* and a destroyer refuel from a fleet oiler. The "fleet train" enabled TF 58 and other formations to operate at very long distances from their permanent bases.

9a. Radar array on carrier *Lexington*

Radar and radio communication were central to the conduct of the sea/air war in Pacific. Radar was especially valuable in air defense, allowing fighters to intercept enemy patrol planes and attack incoming strikes at a safe distance from the task force.

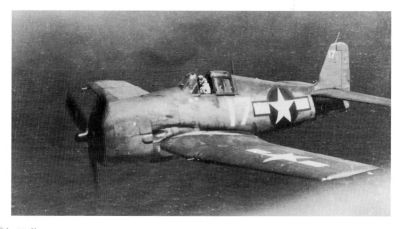

9b. Hellcat

The Grumman F6F Hellcat was the most important naval aircraft of the Pacific War. First flown in July 1942, and successfully rushed into service in the middle of 1943, it enabled the U.S. Navy to gain air supremacy. The Hellcat was also used as a fighter-bomber, attacking airfields and other ground targets.

10a. Hellcats landing on *Enterprise*
This photograph gives a good view of the Hellcat's folding wings and its twin-row radial engine the Pratt and Whitney R-2800 Double Wasp. This was the largest aircraft engine extant, producing an incomparable 2,100 hp.

10b. Dauntless dive bombers over Eniwetok
The Douglas SBD Dauntless was the most important U.S. Navy carrier dive bomber in the first two years of the Pacific War, especially in the Battle of Midway. By 1944 the larger SB2C Helldiver began to replace it.

1a. Grumman TBF Avenger
Introduced in the summer of 1942, the TBF served in large numbers throughout the Pacific War. The TBM was a later version produced by General Motors.

1b. Curtiss SB2C Helldiver
These planes are from Yorktown. The Helldiver entered service after a prolonged development period, and the initial production models had many faults. It entered service during the November 1943 raid on Rabaul.

12a. Helldiver production line
Some 7,000 Helldivers were built. The main production line was at a new plant in Columbus, Ohio. The Navy and Marines had 1,714 aircraft in 1941 and 22,116 in 1944.

12b. NAS Miami
This air station in Florida was only one of a large number of training schools. The number of U.S. Navy pilots increased from 4,112 in 1941 to 37,942 in 1944. The Japanese had much smaller training schemes; they were unable to replace carrier aircrew lost in action.

3a. Carrier launch

TBM Avenger bombers prepare to take off from light carrier *Monterey*. Three Flight Deck Officers (FDOs) wearing yellow shirts coach the pilots as they prepare to roll down the flight deck and take off.

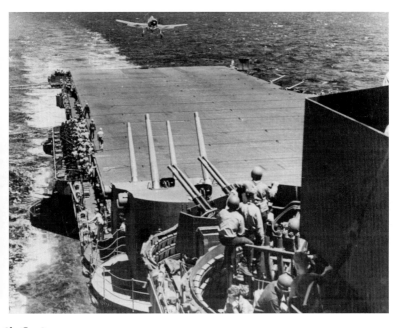

3b. Carrier recovery

A Hellcat fighter lands aboard *Lexington* and is about to snare one of ten landing cables. AA armament is clearly shown: in the foreground a 40-mm quad mount, in front of that two gun houses for 5-in/38 guns, and beyond, to the left, a gallery with 20-mm guns.

14a. Engaging the tailhook
A Hellcat snares an arrester cable on light carrier *Cowpens*. The deck crew shelter in the gallery beyond the flight deck. The antenna of the SK air search radar sticks up between the two pair of uptakes.

14b. Flight deck elevator
This is the rear elevator of *Enterprise* (CV-6), used to transfer planes from the hangar deck to the flight deck. The jeep on the port side is used for towing aircraft. The 19,900-ton *Enterprise* (CV-6) was commissioned in May 1938, and she was the only pre-war carrier to serve throughout the Central Pacific campaign of 1944.

5a. Hangar deck

Activity in the *Yorktown* hangar deck. Technical ratings were indispensable for maintaining engines, ordnance, and electronic equipment. In the background, amidships, part of the crew watch a movie.

5b. Ordnance man

The flight deck of *Essex* during the raid on Marcus Island in May 1944. The carrier in the background is the new *Wasp*.

16a. Loading a torpedo on a TBM Avenger
A TBM Avenger and an F6F Hellcat are prepared on *Wasp*. Torpedoes were the most effective weapon for sinking ships, but torpedo attacks were dangerous for aircraft attempting them.

16b. Flight deck emergency
Medical corpsmen and plane handlers remove casualties from a TBF damaged in air combat. One member of the three-man crew was killed, and another injured. The pilot had just made a one-wheel landing on carrier *Saratoga* with no flaps, ailerons, or radio.

7a. The first raids

arrier *Essex* en route to raid Marcus Island in September 1943; she had first arrived at Pearl arbor in May. Task Force 15, commanded by Rear Adm. Charles Pownall, also included *orktown* and CVL *Princeton*.

17b. Kwajalein: Operation FLINTLOCK
The Central Pacific campaign began with the assault on the Marshall Islands. This photograph shows the TF 58 strike on the Japanese air base at Roi Island on 29 January 1944; Roi lies in the northern part of Kwajalein Atoll.

18a. A wrecked Zero fighter
U.S. Marines pose in front of a damaged plane on Roi airfield. The first six months of the Centr
Pacific campaign were essentially about the "neutralization" of Japanese island air bases.

18b. Carrier strike on Eniwetok Atoll
The airfield on Engebi Island in Eniwetok Atoll under attack by TF 58 planes in February 194
Four wrecked medium bombers are visible. Captured quickly, the atoll soon became an America
forward base.

9a. Truk 1943: super-battleships *Yamato* and *Musashi*

In 1942–43 Truk Atoll became the main Combined Fleet base. The Japanese placed great hopes in *Yamato* and *Musashi*, which displaced 62,300 tons and mounted nine 18.1 guns. The major warships were withdrawn from Truk after the enemy established bases in the Marshalls in early February 1944.

9b. Carrier attack on Truk

Operation HAILSTONE, the first raid by TF 58 on Truk, took place on 17–18 February 1944, to cover the invasion of Eniwetok. The main Japanese warships had been withdrawn in previous weeks, but a large number of merchant ships and Japanese Navy planes remained and were destroyed.

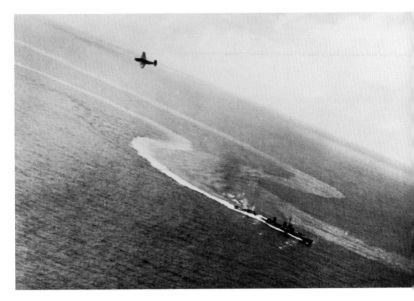

20a. Truk raid: Japanese destroyer under attack
During the first strike on Truk in February 1944, the old Japanese destroyer *Akikaze* maneuve
under attack by TBFs from *Intrepid*. *Akikaze* survived this attack but was sunk the followir
November.

20b. Eten Island burning
To the left the airfield on Eten Island in the Truk Atoll burns. As many as 200 aircraft we
destroyed on the ground in the first Truk raid, many of them under repair or recently delivere

21a. Saipan: February 1944
After the Truk attack part of TF 58 continued 600 miles to the west to reconnoiter the Mariana Islands and attack enemy airfields there. Altogether about 100 planes were destroyed on the ground. The raid took place four months before the invasion of Saipan.

21b. Task Force 58 at Majuro Atoll
Majuro Atoll was taken without fighting on 31 January 1943. It quickly replaced Pearl Harbor as the main base of TF 58. In the foreground (left) is a light carrier; on the right is the carrier *Enterprise*. Behind her lie four "Essex" class. To the left are three fast battleships.

22a. Shore leave on Majuro
In May 1944 sailors relax at the fleet recreation area on an island in Majuro Atoll. TF 58 was now operating at sea for long periods, with few trips back to major bases.

22b. Palau, March 1944
Operation DESECRATE was mounted by TF 58 on 30 and 31 March against Palau in the Caroline Islands. Large numbers of merchant ships were destroyed in the raid.

23a. *Enterprise* **at Palau**
TBF Avengers and SBD Dauntless dive bombers circle TG 58.1 after taking off to mount air strikes against Palau.

23b. Admiral Koga Mineichi
Koga and many of the Combined Fleet staff were killed in air crashes on the night of 1/2 April while evacuating Palau. Koga had followed Admiral Yamamoto Isoroku as C-in-C of the Combined Fleet in April 1943. He developed the "Z" Operations plan for the defense of the Central Pacific.

24a. *Langley* fighter pilots after the second Truk strike
After air attacks on New Guinea in late April 1944, TF 58 mounted a second strike on Truk. These pilots are from VF-32 aboard CVL *Langley*.

24b. "Jill" torpedo plane off Truk
A "Jill" torpedo bomber approaching CVL *Monterey* through heavy AA fire, during the second raid on the Japanese base. The plane was shot down and did not cause any damage.

25a. Saipan Island
Saipan in the Marianas in May 1944 shortly before the American invasion, with Aslito airfield in the center. At the top of the photograph is Tinian Island, invaded six weeks after Saipan.

25b. D-Day on Saipan
On 15 June 1944, the first day of Operation FORAGER, Marines of the first invasion wave hug the beach and prepare to move inland. Vice Adm. Spruance's objectives during the Battle of the Philippine Sea on 19–20 June were to protect and support the landing operation rather than to destroy the Japanese fleet.

26a. Vice Admiral Ozawa Jisaburō
Ozawa commanded the Japanese First Mobile Fleet, which sortied from the Philippines to contest the invasion of the Saipan. The admiral was not an aviation specialist, but he succeeded in launching an "outranging" air attack against TF 58 on 19 June.

26b. A light carrier under Japanese air attack
A Japanese carrier plane is shot down over TG 58.3 as it attacks either *Princeton* or *San Jacinto* during the Battle of the Philippine Sea on 19 June 1944.

27a. Near miss

A bomb dropped by a "Judy" dive bomber explodes next to carrier *Bunker Hill* (CV-17) in TG 58.2. This was probably during Raid II of the Battle of Philippine Sea.

27b. *Bunker Hill* under attack

Another photograph of the near miss on *Bunker Hill* during Raid II on 19 June. Above the bow of the carrier a bomber falls, its tail shot off by AA fire. None of the TF 58 carriers suffered serious damage from air attacks.

28a. Air battle in the Philippine Sea

A Hellcat in position for takeoff from *Yorktown* on 19 June 1944. The Flight Deck Officer (FDO) clears the plane to take off; behind him a man holds up a chalk board with last-minute flight and target information.

28b. Contrails

The crew of cruiser *Birmingham* watch the high-altitude battle over TG 58.3 on 19 June. Much of the air fighting actually occurred well to the west of TF 58, where the main interception took place.

29a. The Marianas "Turkey Shoot"
Lt Alex Vraciu on the flight deck of *Lexington* (CV-16), after intercepting the incoming Japanese strikes on 19 June 1944. Vraciu destroyed six Japanese "Judy" dive bombers. Altogether, the enemy lost about 330 carrier aircraft on 19 June. American losses were only thirty planes.

29b. Submarine *Albacore*
Submarines played a decisive role in the Battle of the Philippine Sea. On the morning of 19 June *Albacore* hit the Japanese carrier *Taihō* with one torpedo; she was destroyed in an internal explosion six hours later. Meanwhile *Cavalla* had torpedoed and sunk heavy carrier *Shōkaku*.

30. "Mission into darkness"

The Japanese fleet was located only on the afternoon of 20 June. A relatively small strike arrived over the Japanese fleet shortly before sunset and had limited success. The return trip was made in darkness; about eighty planes were lost after running out of fuel or in landing crashes.

31a. Carrier *Zuikaku* under air attack
Zuikaku was hit by one dive bomber, and the ship was not badly damaged. Only one Japanese ship was sunk in the air attack on 20 July, the auxiliary carrier *Hiyō*.

31b. Japanese "Van" Force under attack
None of the ships in the "Van" Force were seriously damaged. Japanese defensive fire was ineffective; only two American planes seem to have been shot down by AA guns on 20 June.

32. "Get the carriers"

Aircrew unwind in the ready room of Monterey, having just made successful night landings after the attack on the Japanese fleet. In the center is Lt Ronald P. ("Rip") Gift, who led a division of four bomb-carrying TBM Avengers.

MacArthur commanded substantial naval forces of his own in the form of Vice Adm. Kinkaid's Seventh Fleet, but in March 1943 this consisted of a relatively small force of cruisers and destroyers, amphibious landing ships, and transports. The area of the RECKLESS landing was distant from the airfields of MacArthur's own Fifth Air Force in eastern New Guinea, and appeared to be beyond the effective range of AAF bombers and their escort fighters. At the planning stage it seemed that only the fast carriers and heavy ships of the Central Pacific Force could protect the invasion force from a sortie of Japanese heavy ships; the dangerous events at Savo Island in 1942 and Empress Augusta Bay in 1943 were fresh in the memory of the Allied planners.[3] Meanwhile, three newly reinforced Japanese Army "airdromes" had been laid out inland from Hollandia. From all this came the expected need for carriers from the Central Pacific to support the landings and knock out the Japanese air bases.

Admiral Nimitz had flown to Brisbane in Australia for talks with MacArthur on 23 March 1944. Remarkably, this was the first ever face-to-face meeting between the commanders of the two American theaters of the war against Japan. In any event the admiral agreed to commit Task Force 58, but with two pre-conditions. First, that the carriers would remain off the RECKLESS beaches for only two days after the landings. And, in addition, that their absolute priority would be the battle with the Japanese Navy—should it come out to fight.

TF 77, the slow invasion convoy for RECKLESS, departed from Papua (eastern New Guinea) on 17 April. Four days earlier, on 13 April, the fast carriers had left Majuro.[4] Following Nimitz's conditions, the primary task assigned to Mitscher and TF 58 was to destroy or contain attempts by the Japanese fleet to interfere. The secondary task was to neutralize enemy airfields at Hollandia, and near Wakde, 120 miles to the west of Hollandia.

Admiral Spruance did not take part. He transferred his flag as commander of the Central Pacific Force from *New Jersey* to heavy cruiser *Indianapolis* at Majuro and departed on 10 April for Pearl Harbor. There, he and his staff would work ashore on the planning for Operation FORAGER, the momentous invasion of the Marianas; Admiral Nimitz issued his Oplan 3-44 for FORAGER on 23 April. Spruance then took a brief period of home leave with his family in California.[5] Spruance's command, the Central Pacific Force, would be officially redesignated as the "Fifth Fleet" on 26 April, although this title had already been in some use before that date.[6]

Mitscher and Arleigh Burke, his chief of staff, had come to enjoy Nimitz's full confidence. Mitscher kept his flag in *Lexington*, still part of TG 58.3, with *Langley* and *Princeton*, but now joined by *Enterprise*. Rear Adm. Reeves flew his flag in *Enterprise* as task group commander. TG 58.1 was now commanded by Rear Adm. J. J. ("Jocko") Clark, who would be the most colorful and best-known of the Pacific carrier task group commanders. He was a hard-driving but generally popular ship commander who had brought the new *Yorktown* into service; he habitually wore a locomotive engineer's cap. Much would be made of Clark's warlike Cherokee roots. CO of Rear Adm. Pownall's flagship during the December 1943 raid on Kwajalein, he openly criticized his superior officer's excessive caution. As a task group commander he would constantly seek action against the Japanese.[7] Clark now flew his flag in the new *Hornet*, which was accompanied by three CVLs—*Bataan*, *Belleau Wood*, and *Cowpens*. Rear Adm. Montgomery commanded TG 58.2, as he had in the March raid on Palau. He was still aboard *Bunker Hill*, along with CVLs *Monterey* and *Cabot*, but now with *Yorktown* rather than *Hornet* in his task group. Altogether Mitscher had five heavy carriers and seven CVLs under his command.[8] The total air strength on the fast carriers was higher than the month before, about 680 aircraft, including 370 fighters and 310 attack planes. As in March, a very large contingent of heavy ships and escorts took part in TF 58. Clark's TG 58.1 was accompanied by five light cruisers and eighteen destroyers. Battleships *Iowa* and *New Jersey* were with Reeves' TG 58.2, along with six heavy cruisers and seventeen destroyers. Four other fast battleships— *Alabama*, *Massachusetts*, *North Carolina*, and *South Dakota*—were with Montgomery's TG 58.3, as well as three heavy cruisers, and fifteen destroyers. The fleet train was vital to this long-range operation involving a very large number of ships. The Support Group (TG 50.7) was made up of twelve fleet oilers escorted by five destroyers.

TF 58 followed much the same route from Majuro that had been used during the Palau raid in March. The approach movement was kept as far away as possible from Japanese airfields. After a week at sea, and now steaming north of the Admiralties (roughly on the line of the equator), the carriers refueled from the Support Group; this was on 19 April. On the same day a Hellcat from *Princeton* shot down a patrolling Betty.

The carrier air attacks on New Guinea began two days later, with pre-invasion strikes against Hollandia and Wakde Island on Friday, 21 April (D-1). The attacks continued on D-Day itself, 22 April, and for several days afterward. As it turned out, a week after Nimitz's visit to Brisbane in late March, MacArthur's Fifth Air Force had been able to mount a series of long-range air raids on the Japanese air base complex near Hollandia. The attacks began with a devastating successful first raid on 30 March—the same time as Operation DESECRATE against Palau—and continued through the middle of April. The AAF air campaign effectively destroyed the force of several hundred Japanese planes (mainly from the Army) that had been assembled. When TF 58 launched its pre-invasion air strikes at Hollandia and Wakde two weeks later, they met very little opposition from Japanese forces in the air or on the ground—there turned out to be few enemy combat troops present in this rear area.

Clark's TG 58.1 hit "airdromes" on Wakde Island and on nearby Sawar on the New Guinea coast; also attacked were installations at Sarmi, near Sawar. Only light AA fire was encountered. On the night of the 21st, Clark sent cruisers and destroyers close inshore to conduct an artillery bombardment. After refueling at Manus from TG 50.17, Clark made a rendezvous with TG 58.2 and TF 58.3, and then launched final strikes against Wakde, Sawar, and Sarmi on 24 April. Meanwhile, Montgomery's TG 58.2 and Reeves's TG 58.3 struck the airfield complex southwest of Humboldt Bay, inland behind the Cyclops Mountains. TG 58.2 withdrew to the north on the 23rd to refuel. As mentioned, the fields had already been wrecked by AAF raids over the previous three weeks and few intact aircraft were found on the ground or encountered in the air.[9]

As in earlier amphibious operations since the Gilberts, TF 58 operated jointly with escort carriers. In RECKLESS these were under the overall command of Rear Adm. Daniel Barbey's amphibious force. Task

Force 78, eight CVEs, operated aircraft over Hollandia and Aitape, as well as providing CAP, and ASP for the amphibious force.[10]

MacArthur's amphibious force, TF 77 under Barbey, mounted the main amphibious landing at two points near Hollandia and at Aitape (100 miles to the east of Hollandia).[11] D-Day was on 22 April, the day after the air strikes began. Few Japanese combat troops were deployed in the area, and the second-line troops that were there had been caught by surprise. Many of them fled into the rough territory of the interior. AAF fighter planes began to operate from the captured Aitape airfield two days after the landing. Ground operations in the Hollandia-Aitape area were largely over by 4 May.

Planes from TF 58 were very active in the first three or four days, despite the lack of enemy air strength. Overall, they flew about 2,100 combat sorties and dropped 750 tons of bombs. Ten TF 58 aircraft were lost in combat, mostly from AA fire. No concerted enemy air attack was mounted against either TF 58 or the invasion force. Overall it was now clear that the participation of the fast carriers of TF 58 had been unnecessary for suppressing Japanese air power, supporting the landings, or consolidating the Allied position.

Despite weak Japanese resistance, RECKLESS was a military operation of real importance. The advance of U.S. forces along the long northern coast of New Guinea was greatly accelerated. MacArthur was now thrusting forward toward what were, for Japan, the vital objectives of the southern Philippines and the Netherlands East Indies. Meanwhile, the Japanese divisions east of Hollandia and Aitape, some 50,000 men of the Eighteenth Army, were trapped hundreds of miles behind Allied lines.

In addition, the operations of the American forces, including the commitment of the fast-carrier force to the Palau raid in March and the Wakde-Hollandia strikes in late April, had a powerful impact on the Japanese high command and its strategy. As Rear Adm. Ted Sherman later put it: "When our carrier task force appeared off Hollandia, they mistakenly assumed that we were committed to that line of approach only and failed to realize that the main blow would come from the Central Pacific."[12]

During the voyage back to Majuro, TF 58 mounted a second attack on Truk; this was on Saturday and Sunday, 29–30 April.[13] Mitscher issued an operation plan from *Lexington* on Thursday, 27 April. It is not clear whether the initiative for this remarkable addition to the New Guinea sortie came from Nimitz or Mitscher, but both would have been involved in the final approval (Spruance was on leave in California).[14] The date, 29 April, was special to the Japanese as the birthday of the Emperor, but the step was logical enough for other reasons. Munitions were still available after the Wakde-Hollandia air strikes, and the route back to Majuro passed not far south of Truk. The decision to hit the "Gibraltar of the Pacific" again was also testimony to the flexibility of American planning and a growing perception of Japanese weakness. Once again, the fleet train gave the carriers and their escorts great flexibility, and refueling operations took place on 25 April.

The first attack on Truk, in February 1944, had been launched with some feeling of apprehension. Two months later the estimation of Japanese strength had been greatly reduced. Indeed, since the middle of March the big atoll had come under repeated long-range attack by four-engined AAF B-24 Liberator bombers staged through Bougainville and Eniwetok. Flying in at night, or at high altitude, the unescorted bombers normally met only limited resistance from Japanese fighters or AA fire.

For the April carrier raid on Truk the three task groups were each assigned a particular section of the atoll. Morning sweeps by about eighty fighters were followed by staggered raids of attack planes. Some resistance was expected, despite the damage inflicted by the carriers in February and by the heavy-bomber raids which followed. The intelligence assessment was that as many as 100 planes were based at Truk and some 400 reinforcements might be flown in from nearby islands in the Carolines and from the Marianas.

Despite cloudy weather, the Hellcats engaged about forty enemy planes and claimed to destroy most of them. At about 0800 on the 29th the Japanese did assemble a counterattack of a large number of fighters (twenty to forty-five) escorting eight fast new Jill torpedo bombers. Cloudy weather made it difficult to direct fighters of the CAP into visual distance. At least four of the torpedo planes were claimed shot down near Montgomery's TG 58.2, but not before they had penetrated the outer screen of the task group. The planes attacking *Yorktown* and

CVL *Monterey* had completed apparently successful runs and constituted a "distinct threat." Nevertheless, the Jills were smothered in defensive fire and did not succeed in launching torpedoes, probably because their pilots had been killed.[15] Later on a Judy dive bomber attempted an attack on *Lexington*, but did not achieve a hit.

Japanese post-war sources reported that twenty-five of their fighters were shot down at Truk during the April raid, out of fifty-four that took to the air.[16] U.S. Navy losses were heavy, relative to other operations. Some twenty-six planes were from enemy action (mainly AA fire) and there were another nine operational losses. Fortunately rescue operations were successful, and over twenty pilots and crewmen were picked up by submarines and battleship or cruiser floatplanes, some of them from Truk lagoon itself. On the second day (30 April), no enemy fighters were encountered over the atoll. About 2,200 sorties were flown against land targets, a fifth by Hellcat fighter-bombers. A total of nearly 750 tons of bombs were dropped. There were few ships in the lagoon, and only a number of very small coastal vessels were sunk.

The last—and little-known—episode in the TF 58 operation took place on 30 April and 1 May. This was the artillery bombardment of two targets in the central and eastern Carolines. Clark's TG 58.1 provided air cover for the two groups of heavy surface ships. These missions had been added as objectives on 27 April, when the decision was made to attack Truk again.[17] Satawan, in the Mortlock island group, was just southeast of Truk and had a new airfield. Ponape (now Pohnpei) in the east Carolines had been used as a staging point for a successful air raid on Roi in Kwajalein Atoll in February. Both could provide staging bases for Japanese bomber operations against the Marshalls, or against the route over which American forces would pass from the Marshalls toward the Marianas. (Both places had also been subjected to strikes by squadrons of AAF B-24s.)

Satawan was bombarded on 30 April by nine heavy cruisers, including the brand-new *Baltimore*, *Boston*, and *Canberra*. The bombardment group was commanded by Rear Adm. Jesse Oldendorf, later well known for his role in the Battle of Surigao Strait in October. The 1 May bombardment of Ponape, 275 miles east of Satawan, was on a bigger scale. *Iowa*, *New Jersey*, *Alabama*, *Massachusetts*, *North Carolina*, and *South Dakota* took part. This was the first time six of the new fast battleships, commissioned between 1940 and 1943, had operated together in an independent operation. In pre-war plans, in the European theater, or in 1942, such an assembly of fast battleships would have been a major event. In the context of 1944 in the Pacific it was insignificant, worth hardly more than a footnote. As the CincPac report put it, "The exercise was of value not only because of the damage caused to the enemy, but also from a morale and training standpoint. The ships involved had had little opportunity to fire their guns in spite of many months at sea."[18]

The main elements of Task Force 58 returned to base on 4 May. The expedition of Task Force 58 that began on April 13 had continued even longer than the previous one. It lasted twenty-one days, from leaving Majuro to returning; the Palau strike in March had lasted only thirteen days. It was notable, above all, for the feeble reaction of the enemy.

AIR STRIKES ON MARCUS AND WAKE

On the American side, most of May was spent preparing for Operation FORAGER, the invasion of the Marianas. There was also a rapid advance by the forces of General MacArthur west along the coast of New Guinea. In addition, however, elements of TF 58 carried out raids against Wake and Marcus, in the empty northern part of the Central Pacific.[19]

Wake Atoll is well known. It was the American possession where a small Marine garrison conducted a heroic but doomed defense against a Japanese attack in December 1941. The failure to relieve the Wake garrison was one of the early humiliations of the U.S. Navy after Pearl Harbor—before the arrival of Admiral Nimitz. The atoll is made up of three small islands, which form the thick rim of a shallow lagoon. The Japanese Navy developed a base from the landing strip laid out by the Americans before the war. In 1944 a substantial garrison was in place. Marcus Island, a pre-Mandate Japanese territory, was known to them as Minamitorishima. A triangular island a little more than a mile on each side, it was surrounded by a coral reef. Most of the land was taken up by two runways, begun in 1935. In 1944 the garrison numbered several thousand men. Without port facilities or adequate land area, neither Wake nor Marcus was of much military value except as a small air base and radar station, although for the Japanese Marcus did cover the approaches to Tokyo from the distant southeast. (Marcus is 970 miles from Tokyo; Wake is much further out, at 1,750 miles.) Both places are isolated dots in the ocean with a tiny area and vulnerable to attack. Both are among the most isolated places in the Pacific, and they are also 770 miles from one another. Part of the Japanese outer crust, there was nothing between them and Hawaii or (after February 1944) Majuro; they were thus highly vulnerable.

Halsey had raided Wake with *Enterprise* in February 1942, and a second raid had been carried out in October 1943 by Montgomery, with no fewer than six carriers. As for Marcus, the *Enterprise* force also raided it in March 1942 (after Wake). In addition, at the very beginning of the Central Pacific offensive, in August 1943 Marcus was attacked by Pownall with *Essex*, *Yorktown*, and CVL *Independence*. For both Wake and Marcus, May 1944 would be their third visit by carriers of the U.S. Navy.

The force assigned to raid Marcus and Wake was designated as Task Group 58.6. It sortied from Majuro on 15 May. The purpose of the strikes was to "reduce [the] effectiveness of MARCUS and WAKE by destruction of aircraft, installations and surface craft at or in the vicinity of the two objectives."[20] A second stated objective was the provision of operational experience to new units, especially air groups. Both of these factors had also been important in earlier strikes, in 1942 and 1943. Although not explicitly mentioned, a third purpose was probably to divert the attention of the Japanese. Raiding Wake and Marcus suggested that a strike on mainland Japan might be attempted, and this would slow the movement of Japanese aircraft to the Central Pacific and away from Japan.

Rear Adm. Montgomery commanded TG 58.6, which was made up of three carriers, five cruisers (including the first "Baltimore" class—*Baltimore*, *Boston*, and *Canberra*) as well as twelve destroyers. The admiral's flagship was *Essex*, back from her refit in San Francisco and now repainted in the mid-war black, blue, and haze-gray dazzle scheme. She carried the new Air Group 15, under the soon-to-be-famous Cdr

David McCampbell. New to the Pacific was the "Essex" class *Wasp* (CV-18), commissioned in November 1943 and commanded by Capt. Clifton Sprague.[21] *Wasp*'s planes formed AG 14. Another new arrival was *San Jacinto*, commissioned in the same month as *Wasp* (and, like *Essex*, dazzle-painted); she was the last of the "Independence" class CVLs to enter service. On board *San Jacinto* was AG 51. The total strength of the three carriers was about 105 fighters and 105 attack planes.

On 18 May, three days out of Majuro, the task group refueled from fleet oilers *Schuylkill* and *Saranac*. On the same date a special Search Unit was detached to make a sweep of 370 miles around the north of Marcus. It was composed of *San Jacinto*, AA cruiser *San Diego*, and four destroyers. Their task was to look for picket boats, but they only encountered and attacked one sampan.[22]

The other two carriers reached a point 110 miles southeast of Marcus before launching their strikes. These began on the morning of Friday, 19 May, and lasted for two days. Results were described as "comparatively meagre," due to poor weather, heavy Japanese AA fire, and inexperienced aircrew. Sixty-nine planes (a fifth of the attack forces) were actually hit by AA fire. Some 373 sorties were flown, and 150 tons of bombs were dropped. Two fighters were lost, and two attack planes. There was no aerial opposition, although a Betty "snooper" was shot down in the early afternoon of the 19th.

The attack on Wake was carried out three days later, on 23 May, after the whole force had refueled from fleet oilers on the 22nd. This attack was confined to one day but involved all three carriers; *San Jacinto* mainly provided CAP and ASP. The scale of the attack and the results achieved were similar to those at Marcus. Some 354 sorties were flown, and 148 tons of bombs dropped. Two planes were lost, one in an accident.

A few weeks later, on the eve of the invasion of Saipan, Capt. Ofstie of *Essex* gave war correspondent Morris Markey his impressions of AG 15, only a handful of whose flyers had been in combat before: "We wanted them to drop some bombs on installations, get a taste of anti-aircraft fire." Instead, they threw themselves into the attack: "[T]hey thought they were winning the war there and then! They went absolutely all out. Some of them got killed and half their planes were ripped apart when they flopped in on the deck . . . Marcus and Wake weren't worth all that. They damned near left me out there without any Air Group at all." "My God!" he recalled, "I had to give them a hell of a talking to."[23]

In his monthly report to Admiral King, Admiral Nimitz pointed out that during the period February, March, and April 1944 most losses in carrier operations had come from anti-aircraft fire. A total of 131 planes had been lost. Thirteen (10 percent) had been shot down by enemy aircraft, sixty-eight (52 percent) by AA fire, and fifty (38 percent) were lost in accidents. Even if a plane was not lost, ground fire could cause serious damage; for each plane shot down by AA, between eight and twelve more were damaged. Nimitz noted that tactics needed to be developed to knock out enemy "flak" at an early stage of the attack.[24]

Montgomery's TG 58.6 returned safely to Majuro on 26 May, as the rest of TF 58 prepared for their departure to the Marianas. The expedition of TG 58.6 probably prevented or limited the use of Wake and Marcus as patrol-plane bases during the Marianas operation three weeks later. At this time a large amount of shipping would be sailing south of Marcus and Wake, proceeding from Eniwetok, Kwajalein, and Majuro toward the Marianas. It had also been a valuable training exercise for the new U.S. air groups. And it does seem to have been taken seriously by the Japanese. The raid on Marcus on 19 May, coupled with a very high level of American radio traffic, led the Combined Fleet headquarters, early on 20 May, to raise the level of alert for the naval operation that was frantically being planned to achieve decisive victory over the Americans—the "A" Operation (A-go).[25]

CHAPTER 7

APPROACHING THE MARIANAS
1–15 June 1944

OPERATION FORAGER

Allied forces landed in Normandy (Operation NEPTUNE) on 6 June 1944; the first wave of seaborne troops left English ports on 5 June. This was, of course, one of the most notable episodes in the Second World War. But these were also days of intense American military activity in the Central Pacific. On the same day that the Normandy troops embarked, the fast carriers of Task Force 58 sailed from Majuro in the Marshall Islands. They were the spearhead of Operation FORAGER, the invasion of the Marianas. An amphibious assault on Saipan, planned for 15 June, would be followed by landings on Tinian and Guam.[1]

FORAGER was in some ways a more ambitious operation than NEPTUNE. Roughly the same number of American ground-force divisions (three in Normandy, two on Saipan) were involved in the *initial* assault, but the distances were much greater. The Pacific assault troops and their supplies had to be transported up to 3,400 miles, compared to 90 miles in the Channel. Rather than a two-day cross-Channel crossing, the trans-Pacific movement of assault shipping began a month before the Saipan landings, with forces assembled from all over the American-held Pacific.[2] The number of American warships involved in the Normandy landings (excluding transports and landing ships) would also be very much less than those involved in the Marianas.

The historian Samuel Eliot Morison witnessed the departure: "A sortie from a coral lagoon is as handsome a naval spectacle as one can find anywhere . . ." Task Force 58 began its voyage from Majuro in the late morning of 6 June ELD, led by Rear Adm. William K. Harrill's TG 58.4, with carriers *Essex, Langley*, and *Cowpens*. At noon, Reeves' TG 58.3 followed. Destroyers and seven fast battleships came out first, then *Enterprise* and, 1,000 yards behind her, *Lexington*, Vice Adm. Mitscher's flagship. CVLs *Princeton* and *San Jacinto* followed in line astern.[3] Clark's TG 58.1 came shortly afterward, with *Hornet, Yorktown, Belleau Wood*, and *Bataan*. Bringing up the rear, in the early afternoon, was Montgomery's TG 58.2, with *Bunker Hill, Wasp, Cabot*, and *Monterey*. This was the most powerful naval force ever assembled.

Admiral Spruance had actually departed—from Pearl Harbor— several days earlier, as commander of the Fifth Fleet. Flying his flag in the newly dazzle-painted *Indianapolis*, he sailed on 26 May (WLD). He went first to Kwajalein and Eniwetok to confer with the leaders of the amphibious groups, including Vice Adm. Turner, before joining TG 58.3 at sea on 9 June, two days before the first air strikes on the Marianas.

Table 7.1. Operation FORAGER: Planned Deployments

Force	Planned objective	Commander	Land forces	Planned op. start	Approach movement
TF 58	—	Mitscher	—	11 June	From Majuro
TF 52	Saipan	Turner	2nd, 4th Div. (USMC)	15 June	From Hawaii via Eniwetok
TF 53	Guam	Conolly	III AC (USMC)	18 June	From Guadalcanal via Kwajalein

Note: USMC is U.S. Marine Corps. III AC is III Amphibious Corps, made up of 3rd Marine Div. and 1st Provisional Marine Bde, plus artillery. The Army's 27th Division was the general reserve for Saipan and Guam; it would actually be landed on Saipan, beginning on the night of 16/17 June. Eniwetok and Kwajalein are in the Marshall Islands. It was planned to take Tinian, adjacent to Saipan, in later landings by forces of TF 52. The planned invasion of Guam would be postponed for over five weeks, until 21 July.

Task Force 58 was the covering force. The amphibious force itself was divided into two parts. The Northern Attack Force (TF 52) was tasked to put two Marine divisions ashore on Saipan and (later) nearby Tinian. The Southern Attack Force (TF 53) was originally intended, nearly simultaneously, to land another Marine division and a Marine provisional brigade on Guam. As originally conceived, FORAGER was not unlike GALVANIC and FLINTLOCK, the simultaneous amphibious attacks on Tarawa and Makin in the Gilberts (November 1943) and on Roi-Namur and Kwajalein in the Marshalls (February 1944).[4]

As distinct from the fast carriers of TF 58, the amphibious elements of FORAGER were designated as TF 51, the "Joint Expeditionary Force." It was "Joint" because forces from the U.S. Army, U.S. Marine Corps, and U.S. Navy took part.[5] In overall command was Vice Adm. Richmond Kelly Turner in the command ship *Rocky Mount* (AGC-3). The Northern Attack Force was also commanded by Turner; it was designated as TF 52. The Southern Attack Force was TF 53, under Rear Adm. Richard Conolly in *Appalachian* (AGC-1).

Turner's Northern Attack Force comprised two transport groups. The ships of Group ABLE (TG 52.3) carried the 2nd Marine Division; Group BAKER (TG 52.4) carried the 4th Marine Division. Each group was made up of three transport "divisions" (TransDivs); a TransDiv comprised half a dozen big transport ships.[6] The transports, which were carrying assault troops (rather than cargo/supplies), had about 1,000–1,500 men aboard—usually a battalion landing team.

Two "tractor groups" moved separately from the Northern Force transport groups, because they were made up of slow, 12-knot Landing Ship Tanks (LSTs). The designation "tractor group" came from the vehicles carried by these vessels, which were amphibious tractors, or "amtracs"; these were officially designated as LVTs (Landing Vehicles, Tracked). The LSTs embarked the initial waves of assault troops from the two Marine divisions, who would board the LVTs in their tank decks and launch through their bow doors to "swim" to the beaches.

The movement plan of the approaching task forces was exceptionally complicated, given differences of speed, the great distances involved, the widely scattered starting points, and the different planned landing times.[7] The slowest vessels, and those furthest from the objective, departed first. In the Northern Attack Force these were the fifty LSTs of the Tractor Flotilla; they had left Hawaii for Eniwetok on 14 May WLD. The main elements of the ships and troops that would carry out the invasion of Saipan (the Northern Attack Force) had left the Hawaiian Islands on 29 May WLD, also bound for the American advanced base at Eniwetok in the Marshalls. They reached Eniwetok on 8 June ELD, and then departed for Saipan on the 11th. This was the same day that the Hellcat fighter-bombers of TF 58 began their preliminary air attacks on the Marianas, 950 miles to the west.

Meanwhile, far away in the South Pacific, the amphibious forces intended for the invasion of Guam (Conolly's Southern Attack Force, TF 53), had also departed from Guadalcanal. The island, famous for the 1942 battle, was now a big American base. The course of the Southern Attack Force was even longer than that of the Northern Attack Force, and more indirect. It skirted enemy bases in the Carolines by running 1,000 miles northeast to Kwajalein Atoll in the Marshalls, and then turning sharply to the northwest, in the direction of the Marianas. The LST Tractor Flotilla of the Southern Attack Force left Guadalcanal first, on 31 May ELD. The main body of transports, with flagship *Appalachian*, departed on 4 June; they arrived at their forward base at Kwajalein on 8 June, and left for the Marianas on the 12th. TF 53 reached a holding area east of Guam on the 17th. There the Marine units on board awaited orders to execute the assault on Guam, set for three days after the Saipan landing.

Leaving aside the ships carrying the invasion troops and the fast carriers of TF 58, a very powerful force of warships was dispatched to escort the vulnerable invasion convoys and to provide gunfire support for the planned landings on Saipan and Guam. The most prominent element was the battleships and cruisers. They were, again, to provide the heavy artillery to suppress the Japanese island defenses, and help American ground forces once they had gone ashore. The scale and training of the offshore artillery fire had increased rapidly since Tarawa.

Two fire support groups had been organized, broken down originally into seven "units." Fire Support Group One (TG 52.17) was commanded by Rear Adm. Jesse Oldendorf. Formally it was assigned to the Northern Support Group. It consisted of four of the older battleships: *Tennessee*, *California*, *Maryland*, and *Colorado*, all Pearl Harbor survivors. Unlike the fast battleships, they had trained in the Hawaiian Islands in the delivery of gunfire support. Heavy cruiser *Louisville* and new light cruisers *Birmingham*, *Montpelier*, and *Cleveland* were also in Group One; in the overall plan *Indianapolis*, Spruance's flagship, was included as well. The 5-in/38 batteries of the destroyers were also valuable for close-in artillery support, and Oldendorf had fourteen of these ships.

Fire Support Group Two (TG 52.10) initially was part of the Southern (Guam) Attack Force, although it also came from Hawaii, rather than Guadalcanal. Rear Adm. W. L. Ainsworth was in command. It was made up of the old battleships *Pennsylvania*, *Idaho*, and *New Mexico*, heavy cruisers *Minneapolis*, *San Francisco*, *Wichita*, and *New Orleans*, as well as light cruisers *Honolulu* and *St. Louis*.[8] Nine destroyers were also included.

As significant as the battleships and cruisers were the escort carriers (CVEs). They were smaller and slower than the heavy carriers and CVLs of TF 58. They were also more vulnerable; *Liscome Bay* had been sunk off Makin in November 1943. Nevertheless, they were invaluable for carrying out CAP and ASP for the convoys as they approached the Marianas, and they would also provide air support for the invading troops. TG 52.14 was Carrier Support Group One, under Rear Adm. G. F. Bogan. It was made up of four "Casablanca" class CVEs: *Fanshaw Bay*, *Midway*, *White Plains*, and *Kalinin Bay*, together carrying 100 fighters and attack planes. Five destroyers provided an escort. Carrier Support Group Two (TG 52.22) was commanded by Rear Adm. H. B. Sallada and was originally intended to support the landing on Guam. It included carriers *Kitkun Bay* and *Gambier Bay*, with forty-eight aircraft. The group's escort comprised three destroyers. Two more CVEs were with the TG 50.17, the Fueling Group: these ships, "Bogue" class *Copahee* and *Breton*, carried replacement aircraft for the front-line carriers.[9]

None of this massive movement, especially the spearhead role of the fast carriers, can be understood without logistics. Again, the fleet train and replenishment at sea were crucial. The fleet oilers were organized in the Fueling Group, TF 50.17, commanded by Capt. Edward Paré. It was made up of eight tanker "Units"; each consisted of two or three fleet oilers, escorted by three or four destroyers or destroyer escorts.[10] Over a dozen areas were designated where tankers could refuel fighting ships, before and during the battle for the Marianas.

DISTRACTION IN THE SOUTH

Although the story of the campaign in June 1944 is told here from the American point of view, the Japanese strategic priorities on the eve of FORAGER need to be taken into account.

In the background was the extraordinarily unrealistic Japanese plan to lure the enemy fleet and its expeditionary force into the western Carolines, around Palau or Yap, and to win a decisive victory there.[11] The battle would be won by a combination of the carriers and surface ships of the Combined Fleet, alongside the land-based naval aircraft of the First Air Fleet. Planning began in the Koga era, in the autumn of 1943, when the "Z" Operations were drafted to deal with a range of possible Allied threats to the Japanese defensive perimeter. It continued with the "A" Operation (*A-go*) plan of early May and with deployments made at the end of that month. The strategic corridor between the Carolines and New Guinea was regarded as especially important. This was based on strategic geography and hoped-for limitations of American strength. There was also a degree of wishful thinking, based on the relatively favorable geographical position of Japanese naval forces in this theater compared to the Marianas.[12]

From the end of March and the TF 58 raid on Palau and Yap (28–30 March 1944), the Japanese command had been increasingly preoccupied with the threat to the east–west strategic corridor. Each Allied hammer blow here was followed by another. First came the loss of the Admiralty Islands (late February and early March 1944), and the abandonment by the Japanese Army of eastern New Guinea. Then came the raid on Palau and Yap at the end of March, with Admiral Koga's fears of an invasion of Palau, and after that his tragic disappearance and death (1 April). Three weeks later, on 22 April, came Operation RECK-LESS against Hollandia, supported by the most powerful element of the Americans, the fast carriers.

Acting leadership of the Combined Fleet had been taken for four critical weeks after 1 April by the commander of the Southwest Area Fleet, Admiral Takasu Shirō. With his headquarters at Surabaya on Java, Takasu was understandably concerned with the Allied threat from western New Guinea to his own strategic area—rather than to the Central Pacific.[13] Admiral Toyoda took over as C-in-C of the Combined Fleet on 3 May but he, also, was especially concerned with the southern area.

Admiral Takagi, the inexperienced new commander of the submarine force (6th Fleet), reacted to American operations in the south by deploying from Saipan a covering force of medium-sized "RO" type submarines. From mid-May 1944 a patrol line (the "NA" Line) stretched from the Admiralty Islands north to Truk. Japanese messages decrypted by FRUPac provided accurate information on the position of each boat in the patrol line. The American destroyer escort *England* (DE-635), operating with several other units in a "hunter-killer" group, succeeded in sinking five of them between 23 May and 30/31 May. The level of American anti-submarine activity was another factor suggesting to the Japanese fleet command that important naval operations would be taking place in the western Carolines. After the destruction of the NA line, most of the Japanese submarines were pulled back to cover what was believed to be the Mindanao-Biak-Palau strategic triangle. As a result they were well out of place to deal with the American fleet that advanced to Saipan some 1,800 miles to the northeast; they only began to change their position on 13 June 1944, two days after the first FORAGER air strikes.[14]

Meanwhile, after his successes around Hollandia in April, MacArthur's forces had "leapfrogged" again on 17 May 1944 to land an Army regiment on Wakde Island. Situated on the north coast of New Guinea, Wakde was 100 miles west of Hollandia. A new Japanese airstrip was captured and quickly developed for the use of American patrol planes and heavy bombers.

An even more alarming (for the Japanese) leap occurred ten days later on 27 May, five weeks after RECKLESS. This was the landing on Biak of a U.S. Army division, transported from Humboldt Bay. Biak was a forty-mile-long island, opposite the very western tip of New

Guinea, the so-called "Parrot's Beak." It was strategically vital for both sides, as it could be the jumping-off point for American operations west against the Netherlands Indies and north against Mindanao in the Philippines. The threat was existential; the oil of the Netherlands Indies was essential to the Japanese war effort, and the Philippines were on the route to the Japanese mainland. American control of Biak also confirmed the isolation of nearly all the Japanese Army forces in New Guinea. As one of the senior Japanese commanders, Admiral Ugaki Matome, put it in his diary at this time: "Biak Island is the most critical crossroad of the war."

> [T]he enemy's steady advance . . . is most painful to us. Many air strips can be built on Biak island and then it will be very hard for us to maintain airstrips on the western end of New Guinea. Palau will also be within this striking range, so movements of the [Japanese] task force east of Mindanao will be impossible. Finally, Operation "A" will be made impracticable.[15]

The Japanese Army had built an airfield complex on Biak as the base for an air flotilla; an infantry regiment was also deployed there. But it was a large island and the garrison was—again—taken by surprise. The American landing itself met little resistance at first. However, rough terrain, long American supply lines, and defending infantry of good quality suggested that Biak could be held if it were supported and reinforced. The commitment of a Japanese counter-landing at Biak with a "decoy force" might also bring American forces west to a point where they could be attacked. There were strong parallels here with the set-up of the 1942 Midway battle, although the roles of invader and counter-invader had now been reversed.[16]

At the very beginning of June the Japanese Navy flew about 190 shore-based naval aircraft in from the Marianas and Palau to support Biak. Their new base would at Sorong on the western tip of the New Guinea mainland (opposite Biak) and on Halmahera Island in the northeastern part of Netherlands Indies. They were never able to make the return flight to the Marianas, partly because many of the aircrew came down with malaria.[17]

At the same time, Japanese troops from the southern Philippines were loaded aboard destroyers at the beginning of June, intended for Biak and for a repetition of Guadalcanal's "Tokyo Express." This was known as Operation KON. The first attempts were turned back by a force of Allied cruisers and destroyers, but Admiral Toyoda then ordered in a very powerful force of surface ships, including the super-battleships *Yamato* and *Musashi*, two heavy cruisers, and a new light cruiser. They were commanded by Vice Adm. Ugaki, and their destination was Batjan (Bacan) in the Netherlands Indies, near Halmahera and only 200 miles west of Biak. The ships of the large KON force left Tawi Tawi in the southern Philippines on the afternoon of 10 June ELD. They arrived at Batjan two days later, but by then news of the air attacks on Saipan, 1,400 miles to the northeast, had arrived. Biak was forgotten, and on 13 June Ugaki departed Batjan for the north, never to return.[18]

SUBMARINE FORCE, PACIFIC FLEET

This book is primarily about Task Force 58, and especially about the fast carriers. However, understanding the American naval victory in the Central Pacific requires a short introduction to the operations of American submarines. The Submarine Force, Pacific Fleet, was commanded from February 1943 by Rear Adm. Charles Lockwood as ComSubPac.[19] The top leadership of the U.S. Navy had a strong interest in underwater warfare. Admiral King and Admiral Nimitz had both served in the submarine force between the wars. When Nimitz raised his flag as CincPac in December 1941 he did so aboard submarine *Grayling* at the Pearl Harbor submarine base.

The United States built a considerable number of small submarines during and after World War I and a handful of larger boats in the 1920s. When construction resumed in the later 1930s, the Navy concentrated on a standard design. Nearly all the "fleet submarines" displaced about 1,500 tons, were 300–310 feet long, and had a wartime crew of about eighty men. Powered by four diesel engines providing a total of about 5,500 hp, they were capable of a maximum of 20 knots on the surface. Range was 11,000 miles at 10 knots, a cruising speed that allowed patrols of six to eight weeks. They were armed with eight to ten torpedo tubes and a 3-in/50 or 4-in/50 deck gun. In the summer of 1942, the first submarines were equipped with the new SJ search radar, and by the end of 1943 all boats had received these radars.

American submarines had only limited success against Japanese warships or merchant ships in the first two years of the Pacific War. This was partly due to the limited number of submarines and torpe- does. Also important were the shortcomings of their Mk XIV torpe- does—strictly speaking, the shortcomings of their contact and magnetic detonators ("exploders") and their depth-keeping mechanism. This was one of the worst technical failures of the U.S. armed forces in World War II. Only after September 1943 did fully effective submarine torpe- does—and submarines—become available.

Both the Japanese and the Americans designed submarines that could operate over long ranges in the Pacific and which were fast enough to support the battle fleet. They were much larger than the more numerous German U-boats, most of which displaced only 750 tons. The Japanese produced a relatively small number of large boats in different classes, while the Americans concentrated on a standard large "fleet boat" design. The U.S. Navy built about forty boats just before the war in four classes, nearly all at the private Electric Boat Co. in New London, Connecticut, or the Portsmouth Navy Yard in southern Maine. These pre-war designs developed into the wartime "Gato" (SS-212) class of seventy-seven boats (mostly built at the same two shipyards). The lead unit (*Gato*) was commissioned on the last day of 1941. The "Balao" (SS-285) sub-class came next, with the lead boat being commissioned in February 1943; 119 boats in this group were completed; but many did not reach the fleet before June 1944.[20]

By the beginning of 1944, the submarine force in the Pacific had reached 100 boats, of which about eighty were under Nimitz and Lockwood; these were based at Pearl Harbor, with advanced bases at Midway and Majuro. The remainder operated under the Seventh Fleet from bases in eastern and western Australia near Brisbane and Fremantle.

This is not the place to discuss the commerce-raiding operations of the U.S. Navy's submarine force. They were, however, highly important in obtaining supremacy at sea in 1944, when they had achieved an increasingly effective blockade of Japan. As Admiral Spruance would later put it, the distant blockade "tightened as we pushed forward, until finally the economic life of the Empire was almost completely throttled. It would be difficult to overestimate the part that our submarines played in bringing about the defeat of Japan." Admiral Halsey rated submarines as the most important instrument in the winning of the Pacific War.[21] In its pre-war policy, the United States had foresworn unrestricted submarine warfare, including attacks on merchant ships without warning; the U.S. had entered World War I ostensibly in reaction to the unrestricted U-boat attacks of Imperial Germany. The considerable force of large long-range submarines, which had been built up in the 1930s, was primarily intended to support the battle fleet and attack enemy warships. Immediately after Pearl Harbor, however, the Navy removed all restrictions. By late 1943, thanks to better torpedoes and the ability to intercept radio signals about shipping movements, the submarine force was achieving remarkable results both against Japanese merchant shipping and against enemy warships.[22]

American submarines also took part in combat operations in the Central Pacific, both directly and indirectly. By late 1943 and 1944, aided by very good RI, Lockwood's boats were able to limit the reinforcement and resupply of enemy island garrisons, including Saipan and Guam, as the Japanese Army belatedly attempted to transfer troops from China. At the same time the submarines inhibited the movement of the Combined Fleet by sinking tankers and limiting the shipment of fuel oil and aviation gasoline to the Japanese mainland.

The submarines were also involved in sea/air operations in a more immediate way. In their "lifeguard" role they rescued aircrew that came down in the sea after being hit by ground fire or attacked by enemy fighters. (Floatplanes from battleships and cruisers also carried out lifeguard missions, sometimes under enemy ground fire.) Lifeguards were important for the morale of attacking aircrew, who had no illusions about the shark-ridden ocean, barren Pacific islands, or the treatment they might receive from the Japanese. The new *Skate* carried out the first submarine lifeguard mission during the Wake raid in October 1943. At times under air attack, the boat picked up six members of aircrew, including the commander of the *Lexington* air group. A total of 117 aircrew would be rescued by submarines in the course of the Pacific War.[23]

The American submarines also reconnoitered island objectives. As mentioned before, *Greenling* played a vital role in the preparation of the Marianas operation, when she spent her ninth war patrol in March 1944 reconnoitering Saipan, Tinian, and Guam. They also helped locate the enemy fleet units at long range, both in their new bases and in real time as operations took place. On 15 May 1944, *Bonefish* had confirmed RI assessments of the concentration of the Japanese carrier force at Tawi Tawi in the southwestern Philippines.[24]

The final important element to consider here was the use of fleet submarines for attacking and sinking enemy warships. In 1942 it had been hoped to achieve important success with this mission, using intelligence gained from RI (Ultra), and setting up ambush positions off Truk, Rabaul, the Bungo Channel, and Tokyo Bay—the last two of which were known as "Empire waters." For various reasons this campaign had little success. The number of submarines was limited, fast-moving warships were inherently hard to intercept, and the torpedoes were faulty. As for general fleet engagements like the Coral Sea and Midway (or Santa Cruz), submarines were slow-moving, especially when forced to proceed submerged, and difficult to maneuver into unexpected positions. A major American deployment during the Battle of Midway in 1942 achieved no successful attacks, and in the course of the whole year of 1942 only two major Japanese warships (both cruisers) were sunk. The following year was little better. *Trigger* damaged the big auxiliary carrier *Hiyō* off the Yokosuka naval base near Tokyo in June 1943, but she failed to sink that ship, after multiple failures of her torpedoes. It was this incident that led Rear Adm. Lockwood finally to abandon the troubled magnetic detonator. A similar failed attack in July by *Tinosa*, against a huge whaling factory ship, led to the redesign of the contact detonator. The problem of torpedoes running too deep had been detected and largely resolved in 1942. Still, it was only in September 1943, twenty-two months into the war, that all the faults in the Mk XIV submarine torpedo were finally remedied.

During 1943 the number of American submarines rapidly expanded. Stationed at choke points, like the entrance to the Inland Sea, or off Japanese mid-Pacific naval bases like Kavieng, Truk, Palau, and Tawi Tawi, they began to have successes against enemy warships. Boats based in Hawaii and later in Fremantle in western Australia had growing success against merchant shipping. In December 1943, *Sailfish* succeeding in sinking the 18,000-ton escort carrier *Chuyō* as she approached Yokosuka. This was the first submarine destruction of a large Japanese warship since November 1942. On Christmas Day 1943, *Skate* damaged super-battleship *Yamato* north of Truk. In February 1944, *Skate* struck again off Truk, sinking new light cruiser *Agano* (as TF 58 approached Truk from the east). In late March 1944, *Tunny* damaged super-battleship *Musashi* as she departed from Palau. An important campaign against Japanese destroyers, prioritized by Admiral King himself, was also remarkably successful.

The Americans now had the strategic initiative in the island-hopping campaign. Nimitz and Lockwood knew in advance where and when to deploy the Submarine Force for combined-arms operations. Between 12 and 22 June 1944, twenty-nine American submarines—nearly a third of the entire force—would form a vast perimeter around the FORAGER objective. Five were in the Bonins, watching the approach routes from the Japanese mainland. Three were southeast of Formosa, covering the northwest. Five were west of the Marianas. Five were in the southern Philippine Sea, from the central Philippines to the east, including one patrolling the San Bernardino Strait. Three were southeast of Mindanao in the southern Philippines. Five were around Tawi Tawi in the southwestern Philippines, where the advanced base for the Combined Fleet had been established. One was covering the main exit from the central Philippines into the Philippine Sea, the Surigao Strait. Two were in the Luzon area.[25]

The Japanese submarine force needs mentioning only in the sense that—along with land-based aircraft—it woefully failed to fulfil its mission.[26] It is not generally realized that the Japanese conventional submarine force (and not just six midget submarines) had been assigned a major role in the December 1941 Pearl Harbor attack, but it achieved almost nothing. Although concentrated for the Midway operation in June 1942, the submarines again largely failed in their mass reconnaissance and attack role (although the crippled *Yorktown* was finished off by *I-168*). Only a limited number of submarines had been in operation at the start of the war, and from the end of 1942 many would be tied down supplying encircled and starving island garrisons. Meanwhile, the air attacks on Kwajalein and Truk in February 1944 sank two important submarine depot ships and greatly dislocated the Pacific submarine force.

The submarines would have a belated and limited role in the battle of the Marianas, being caught by surprise when the American air raids and shore bombardment began on 11–13 June. Ironically, the headquarters of the whole Japanese submarine force—Sixth Fleet—had been moved to Garapan on Saipan on 7 June. On 13 June there was a belated change, as submarines were ordered to redeploy to cover the Marianas. As it turned out, they had no success in locating U.S. naval units, let alone successfully attacking them. Ten of the twenty-six Japanese boats ordered to take part in the defense of the Marianas were lost. They would not even be able to fulfil orders to evacuate the staff of the submarine command from Saipan (after the 19–20 June battle). The commander of the 7th Submarine Flotilla at Truk attempted coordination of submarine action, without success.[27]

CHAPTER 8

TF 58 AND THE BATTLE OF THE PHILIPPINE SEA (1)

Invasion and Air Battle

COUNTDOWN TO BATTLE

Sunday, 11 June. Task Force 58 began one of the decisive battles of the Pacific War in the afternoon of 11 June 1944. D-Day for the landing of two Marine divisions on Saipan Island in the Marianas, Operation FORAGER, was scheduled for four days in the future. This Sunday was D-4.[1]

As with the previous Central Pacific operations, the first step was to secure air superiority. The Marianas run from north to south, and the four task groups of TF 58 were positioned at intervals in a line 200–225 miles east of the line of islands. From there some 225 Hellcat fighter-bombers mounted a sweep against Saipan and the other islands in the southern Marianas, including Tinian and Guam. They changed their previous routine by attacking in the afternoon (under Plan "JOHNNY"), rather than just after dawn. The damage to Japanese planes and airfield facilities was heavy. The air strikes would be repeated on 12 June, this time with attack planes. By then, however, and for the following two days, the enemy would not be capable of significant air activity.[2]

Mitscher's fast carriers had achieved surprise. They sortied from Majuro in the Marshall Islands on 6 June. Operating as a united force of four task groups, they followed a course northwest and then west, and kept as far as possible from potential Japanese air-patrol bases. Carrier strikes in the preceding months and repeated B-24 raids from the Marshalls and the Admiralties had greatly reduced the ability of these places—even Truk—to mount regular air patrols.

Even as the first air strikes took place, neither side had a clear idea of how the situation would develop. The Japanese did not know whether the attacks of 11–12 June were just another hit-and-run raid like the one in February 1944, with the real offensive to come—as they hoped—further south, near Palau and Biak. The Americans, for their part, had been aware since mid-May that the enemy fleet had been concentrated at Tawi Tawi in the southwestern Philippines, but they did not know if the Japanese carriers, battleships, and cruisers would come out to fight when the Marianas were invaded.

The operations plan prepared in TF 58 by Vice Adm. Mitscher and his chief of staff, Arleigh Burke, suggested a considerable threat: "The fact that major units of his fleet are less than sixty hours cruising time from the Marianas, and that nine of his carriers are ready for action . . . presents the enemy with the most favorable opportunity for fleet action that he has had for many months."[3] However the "prevailing opinion" in the American naval command was that the Japanese fleet would not risk battle for the Marianas.[4] This was the conclusion reached by Admirals King and Nimitz when they conferred in San Francisco on 5–6 May.[5] The Americans now had a great superiority in warships and aircraft, and the Japanese would have to fight at a long distance from their bases with only a limited number of fleet oilers. Past experience had also shown the Japanese that their airfields ashore could be quickly neutralized, and could not be counted on to support the defending fleet. By the end of May the American command had learned that the captured "Z" Operation Order Ops No. 73 (issued by Adm. Koga in early March) had noted that "[f]or the time being . . . Carrier Nucleus forces will not be used unless conditions are especially favorable" and that fuel shortages were presenting major difficulties in concentrating forces.[6]

Monday, 12 June. With the situation still uncertain, Spruance accepted the risk of dividing TF 58 into two separate components, a deployment which was part of his original 14 May Operation Plan (Oplan No. Cen. 10-44).[7] One element was made up of Montgomery's TG 58.2 and Reeves' TG 58.3. They were led by Mitscher into a position west of the Marianas on Monday night. The two task groups passed side by side into the Philippine Sea through the forty-five-mile passage north of Saipan, between Marpi Point and islet of Farallon de Medinilla. The force comprised *Bunker Hill*, *Enterprise*, *Lexington*, *Wasp*, and four CVLs, as well as the seven fast battleships.

The second element was made up two task groups which were detached to the north to hit the Bonin Islands. This was made up of Clark's TG 58.1 and Harrill's TG 58.4, with *Essex*, *Hornet*, *Yorktown*, and three CVLs. On 11 and 12 June TG 58.1 had been operating furthest south, conducting strikes against Guam and Rota Island. Now Clark ran up the east side of the Marianas, linked up with Harrill's TG 58.4, and then proceeded north to the Bonins, refueling from a fleet oiler group on the way. Their task would now be to block the movement of reinforcement aircraft to the Central Pacific from the Japanese mainland, an eventuality referred to in the captured "Z" Operations documents. This movement was seen as a great threat to the Saipan (and Guam) landings, even if the enemy carrier fleet did not sortie. The ferry route for Japanese Navy air reinforcements was through the airfields on the (then) little-known island of Iwo Jima, located in the Bonins. American air strikes were originally planned to be carried out over two days, 16 and 17 June.[8]

While the two U.S. Navy task groups moved to cut off the air threat from the north, other aircraft were interdicting the Japanese air bases around the Marianas, at Truk, Palau, Yap, and Woleai. This was the task of the four-engined AAF and Navy bombers commanded by of Vice Adm. John Hoover. They operated from Eniwetok in the Marshalls and Los Negros in the Admiralty Islands. In the week before FORAGER B-24s were attacking Truk on a nearly daily basis, with raids of two or three dozen unescorted bombers.[9]

Tuesday, 13 June. The invasion of Saipan was still two days away. Two carrier task groups were now operating west of Saipan, and at dawn the seven fast battleships were detached to carry out a long-range bombardment of the island; Spruance accompanied them aboard *Indianapolis*. Despite firing 2,500 16-inch shells, as well as 12,500 5-inch shells from their secondary batteries, the battleships had little effect on the Japanese defenses. They fired from a long range (10,000 to

16,000 yards) to keep clear of enemy coastal guns and the six-mile shoal area on the west side of Saipan, and their training in this use of their heavy artillery in shore bombardment had been limited.

This bombardment was mainly important because it finally alerted the Japanese naval command to what was happening. These events in the Marianas were more than just a hit-and-run raid. Offshore shelling meant that a critical part of the Empire was under threat of invasion.

By the evening, vital information had been received about Japanese movements from Tawi Tawi, located 1,700 miles from Saipan. Submarine *Redfin* was able to send a signal that Japanese ships had sortied from the anchorage there, headed north. Her CO, Lt Cdr Marshall Austin, reported the passage that morning of two groups of ships, the second of which was "the main body of the Jap fleet." It had been too dangerous for *Redfin* to surface immediately, but at 2000/13 Austin sent his message. *Redfin* had been as close as 4,500 yards (about 2 miles) from the enemy ships. Unlike some later submarine sightings, considerable detail was provided: six carriers, four battleships, five heavy cruisers, a light cruiser, and two destroyers.[10]

Wednesday, 14 June. On D-1, four older battleships of the American Fire Support Group arrived west of Saipan, following the same route around the north point of Saipan as the fast carriers and fast battleships. Better trained and equipped for amphibious support than the fast battleships, and firing at closer range, they began a more effective preparatory bombardment of Saipan and nearby Tinian. Since Tarawa, thorough gunfire support from the heavy artillery of warships had been identified as vital to the success of any major landing operation.

Meanwhile, news of the Japanese movement from Tawi Tawi led CincPac and ComSubPac hastily to revise the position of the submarines in the Philippine Sea area. One of these boats was *Cavalla*, which had been proceeding to replace *Flying Fish* on watch near the San Bernardino Strait in the central Philippines. Lt Cdr Herman Kossler was her CO. In the evening Kossler received the order to move east to a possible interception position out in the Philippine Sea. In addition, *Finback*, *Bang*, *Stingray*, and *Albacore*, which had been on lifeguard duty off the Marianas, were ordered to form a patrol "square" in the

Philippine Sea, 60 miles on each side, of four submarines. Each was to patrol for 30 miles around a fixed point in the corner of the square. *Albacore*, commanded by Lt Cdr James Blanchard, reached her new position (the southwest corner) in the early morning of Thursday. *Cavalla* and *Albacore* would have a vital role in the coming battle.[11]

Thursday, 15 June. This was D-Day for Saipan. At 0843, on the fourth day after the air strikes began, two Marine divisions began to land on the southwest coast of the island, near Charan Kanoa. This was south of Garapan, the main town. Within twenty minutes, 8,000 marines had come ashore, riding in 700 amphibious tractors (LVTs).[12]

Pre-invasion hopes for a quick victory were quickly dispelled. Of course, it was to be expected that Saipan was not going to be like the February invasions of Kwajalein and Eniwetok, where the Japanese defenses had had no depth. Kwajalein had been only 1.2 square miles in area, Saipan covered 45 square miles (making it about the size of Jersey in the Channel Islands, and twice the size of Manhattan Island). Marines on the beachhead came under heavy artillery fire and were unable to move as far inland as the "O-1" line—a low ridge—which had been planned as the initial objective. In addition, the strength of Japanese ground forces had been seriously underestimated by American intelligence. This was partly due to the difficulty in obtaining information, and partly because of the recent reinforcement of the island's garrison.[13]

Fortunately for the Americans, the Japanese also underestimated their enemy. The orders of the Japanese commander, General Saitō Yoshitsugu, to "destroy the enemy, during the night, at the water's edge," could not be fulfilled. A poorly organized evening counterattack by the Japanese from Garapan was stopped, broken up by naval artillery. Bodies of some 700 Japanese soldiers were left on the battlefield.

The Americans were ashore, but the advance inland, held up by rough terrain and skillful and stubborn enemy resistance, was slower than expected. Meanwhile, a strong groundswell from the Philippine Sea made more difficult the landing of supplies and reinforcement. American losses had been considerable: 2,000 U.S. casualties on D-Day, counting killed and wounded.

On the positive side, the big Japanese airfields on Saipan and nearby Tinian had been put out of action. They had been damaged by air attacks and then by naval bombardment, and on Saipan the Marines would take one of them, at Aslito, on D+2. The same was true on nearby Tinian, although that island was not invaded by ground troops until 24 July. The only working airfields in the Marianas were now the two on Guam, and even they had suffered serious damage in the American carrier raids.

Expectations that the Japanese fleet would not sortie to oppose the invasion also turned out to be unfounded, although the enemy ships were still at least two or three days away. During D-Day on Saipan, CincPac was presented with an intelligence assessment of the movements and intentions of the enemy. The movement reported by *Redfin*, and high-level signal traffic intercepted (but not decrypted) on the afternoon of 13 June, suggested that the "enemy had reached a decision and Opords [operation orders] were being issued in regard to surface action against BLUE [i.e. U.S.] force in Marianas." This assessment had been prepared by Cdr Edwin Layton, the Fleet Intelligence Officer. It was also informed by a knowledge of the decisive-battle concept of Admiral Koga's March 1944 "Z" Plans, which had recently been captured in the Philippines.[14]

Cdr Layton attempted to calculate the movements of what he thought were three Japanese naval forces. He concluded that by 0930 on 17 June ELD (at the earliest) these forces could have come together at a point (16°N, 140°E) about 350 miles west or northwest of Saipan. This was at the center of a ring of bases suitable for Japanese patrol flights.[15] Layton also made two significant points about enemy carrier strikes. The first was that they might stress "surprise from the flank." The second was that attack strikes might be launched from extreme range, with the planes landing on airfields in the Marianas, rather than returning to their ships; this is what has been translated from the Japanese language as "outranging" tactics. Both these possibilities were at least partly based on the Japanese discussion of tactics in the captured "Z" Operations documents.[16]

Events were now moving ahead rapidly. Layton's analysis was modified by news of another sighting, which (evidently) reached Admiral Spruance on Thursday evening. Toward the end of the afternoon (1622/15), submarine *Flying Fish*, stationed off the San Bernardino

Strait in the central Philippines, had sighted the passage of a "large task force" steaming at high speed eastward into the Philippine Sea. Her CO, Lt Cdr Robert Risser, looking through his periscope at a range of no nearer than 22,000 yards (12 miles), could not provide full details. He described what he saw as a "large task force" and estimated its strength as three carriers and three battleships, as well as several cruisers and destroyers; the only vessel identified was the battleship *Nagato*.[17]

Meanwhile, the two American task groups that had been sent north to the Bonins were approaching their objective. Having reached a point 600 miles north of Saipan, they turned back toward their target at about noon on Thursday. "Jocko" Clark, an officer always given to showing initiative, had increased speed to launch an early strike of 200 planes from his TG 58.1 in the afternoon. The weather was bad—cloudy with frequent rain squalls. Two dozen enemy planes were claimed destroyed in the air and on the ground, but there were also American losses from AA fire, and rough seas caused landing accidents.[18]

At dusk on D-Day and 600 miles to the south, planes of Kakuta's First Air Fleet were able to mount their first strikes against American ships off Saipan. The attacks came from bases in the Marianas and other places in the Central Pacific. A small formation of single-engined Kate torpedo planes attacked a group of four escort carriers operating 30 miles east of Saipan. Four of them were claimed shot down by the FM-2 Wildcat fighters of the CAP. A fifth launched a torpedo at CVE *Fanshaw Bay*, but it missed.[19]

Shortly afterward two of Mitscher's fast-carrier groups came under attack. They were about 40 miles out to sea on the far side of Saipan, supporting the troops ashore and protecting the landing fleet from Japanese air and submarine attacks. Some of the attacking enemy planes had been sent from distant Yap, but the main strike seems to have come from Guam. The Japanese air bases there had been attacked for three days, but they were now able to send off a handful of Judy dive bombers and ten new Yokosuka P1Y/Frances medium bombers carrying torpedoes; some Zero fighters were available for escort.[20] Aircraft flying at 20,000 feet distracted the American CAP, and the ten bombers came in at low level out of the darkness, evading two radar-equipped F4U-2N Corsair night fighters.

The main target was Task Group 58.3 with *Enterprise* and *Lexington*, as well as CVLs *Princeton* and *San Jacinto*. The screen included five fast battleships, three light cruisers, and thirteen destroyers. Senior U.S. commanders were aboard these ships—Mitscher (in *Lexington*) and Vice Adm. Willis Lee (in battleship *Washington*), as well as task group commander Reeves (in *Enterprise*).[21] As many as five torpedoes were launched against *Lexington*, but the skillful ship handling of Capt. Ernest Litsch enabled the big carrier to "comb" the torpedoes. *Enterprise* also came under torpedo attack.[22]

Mitscher and his staff watched the attack from the flag bridge of *Lexington*. "Fine thing," the admiral apparently stated, "they send a Frances after me."[23] Few Japanese planes were involved, and the task force suffered no damage, but in some respects this was the most dangerous moment for Task Force 58 in the whole Marianas battle. In earlier operations *Independence* and *Intrepid* had been badly damaged in similar attacks, and in October 1944 CVL *Princeton* would be sunk after a hit from a single dive bomber.

Friday, 16 June. Aside from the fighting on Saipan, Admiral Spruance was most concerned on Friday with the position and intention of the carriers and other ships of the enemy "fleet strike force." Japanese ships might well be in range as soon as the following day.

Early in the morning (0400/16), Spruance received belated news of another sighting by a submarine. On the evening of the previous day, *Seahorse*, en route to take up her station off the Surigao Strait and with Lt Cdr Slade Cutter in command, had encountered six large ships and two smaller ones steaming at high speed on a course to the northeast. They were too far away for Cutter to get details of the ships, and they were steaming too fast for *Seahorse* to pursue. (In fact, this force included super-battleships *Yamato* and *Musashi*.) Cutter had attempted to report his sighting at 1945/15, but this was delayed by Japanese radio jamming. The location of the contact (9°30N, 128°49E) was some 200 miles east of Mindanao, so these ships were even nearer to the Marianas than the force sighted in the San Bernardino Strait by *Flying Fish*. The *Seahorse* sighting reinforced the view held by Spruance and others that the Japanese might be operating in several tactical groups, with the intention of carrying out a flanking maneuver.[24]

That Friday morning, Admiral Spruance traveled from *Indianapolis* to the headquarters ship *Rocky Mount* off the Saipan beachhead to consult with Vice Adm. Kelly Turner and Lt Gen. Holland Smith. Turner was commander of the Joint Expeditionary Force, and Smith was Marine commander of V Amphibious Corps. *Rocky Mount* (AGC-3) mounted extensive communications equipment; built on a fast cargo-liner hull, she had entered service in January 1944. The three men made a number of decisions that morning, in light of the unexpectedly heavy fighting on Saipan and the new intelligence about the movements of Japanese fleet units. Most important, they agreed to put off the planned landing by the Southern Attack Force. W-Day on Guam had been scheduled for 18 June, only three days after D-Day on Saipan. The 27th Division of the U.S. Army, in reserve for Saipan or Guam, was to be put ashore as soon as possible on Saipan, where it would join forces with the Marines. The first regimental combat team (RCT) and the divisional artillery were brought ashore during Friday night (16/17 June). This meant accepting a lengthy delay for Guam, where American troops would only land on 21 July.

It was also agreed that, despite the Japanese naval threat, the unloading of troops and supplies would continue until the evening of the following day (17 June). At that point most ships of the transport forces would be moved temporarily to a safer holding area in waters 200–300 miles east of the Marianas. Turner had reported to Spruance that operations were not going as well as expected, and that he did not support withdrawal of the entire transport force. Spruance, for his part, promised Turner that he would "try to keep the Japs off your neck."[25] As the commanders conferred, the Marines ashore had consolidated their position. The small gap between the 2nd and 4th Marine Divisions was closed, but little forward progress was made, even to the O-1 line.

Spruance also decided that a large number of warships were to be transferred from the fire support operations off the Charan Kanoa beachhead to reinforce the screen of TF 58. These comprised five heavy cruisers, three light cruisers and twenty-one destroyers. The whole task force was to assemble at a point 180 miles due west of Tinian in two days' time, by 1800 on 18 June.[26] Meanwhile, the seven older battleships of the bombardment force were to prepare to deploy 25 miles west of Saipan.[27]

By midday on Friday, Clark and Harrill began their return course to the south. The weather was still bad, but they were able to launch a second attack against Iwo, which caught the Japanese with no fighters in the air and destroyed a number of enemy planes on the ground.[28] Overall, however, the Bonins strikes were probably not the most important factor in slowing down the flow of Japanese aircraft from Japan through Iwo; near-typhoon weather had a greater effect.[29]

Saturday, 17 June. The Japanese Army's main effort came at 0330 on the 17th. It involved something not seen earlier in atoll battles: a large-scale tank attack supported by infantry. The operation was directed against the northern half of the beachhead, held by the 2nd Marine Division. It came a day too late, as the Marines were now well dug in. Warships offshore provided constant star shells to illuminate the battlefield. The Japanese tanks were not well coordinated, and they were quickly knocked out. By 0700 the battle was over; the attackers had again been driven off with heavy losses.

During the same pre-dawn hours (At 0545/17) ComSubPac received a report from Lt Cdr Kossler in *Cavalla* that he had sighted and attacked (unsuccessfully) a group of two tankers and several escorts. (The location was 13°30N, 130°40E.) Contact was then lost, but Kossler was ordered to follow the trail of the tanker group, in the hope that it would lead to the Japanese fleet.[30]

In the morning the carriers of the two task groups operating west of Saipan, TG 58.2 and TG 58.3, launched search planes to the west. The Japanese were still too far away to be located. Another search was made in the afternoon. Again, no enemy ships were found, but at least Japanese carrier scout planes were encountered flying in from the opposite direction, a positive indication of a distant presence.

Late in afternoon, at 1741/17, *Indianapolis*, with Vice Adm. Spruance aboard, caught up with Reeves' Task Group 58.3 out in the Philippine Sea. At 1415, as his flagship hurried forward, Spruance had transmitted a general statement of his intentions:

> Battle Plan. Our air will first knock out enemy carriers, then will attack enemy battleships and cruisers to slow or disable them. Task Group 57.8 [i.e. Lee's battleships] will destroy enemy fleet either by

fleet action if the enemy elects to fight or by sinking slowed or crippled ships if enemy retreats.[31]

Unusually, Spruance drafted this wording himself, rather than relying on Carl Moore, his chief of staff.[32] The "plan" was not inconsistent with a proposal made by Mitscher earlier that day. This had been to steam west through the night of 17/18 June to put the Task Force in a position to mount a dawn strike on the advancing Japanese carriers. (However, at this moment TF 58 was still at half strength, with only two of the four task groups, TG 58.2 and TG 58.3—*Bunker Hill*, *Enterprise*, *Lexington*, *Wasp*, and four CVLs. Clark and Harrill were still on their way back from the Bonins with TG 58.1 and TG 58.4.)

After sending the "Battle Plan," Spruance signaled to Mitscher and Lee that he (Spruance) was in overall control but would leave details to them: "Desire you proceed at your discretion selecting dispositions and movements best calculated to meet the enemy under most advantageous conditions. I shall issue general directives when necessary and leave details to you . . ."[33]

At some point on this Saturday Mitscher suggested that the battleships with their escorts be immediately detached from the two southern carrier task groups and deployed in a separate force. This would avoid confused movements during the expected battle, and Spruance accepted the proposal. The battleship force would take position to the west of the carriers, and be available for offensive or defensive purposes—spearhead or screen. The change took place in the afternoon, and the new element was designated TG 58.7. In addition to the seven fast battleships, the new task group included four heavy cruisers, as well as a screen of thirteen destroyers. Lee was in command, flying his flag in *Washington*.

On Saipan, the American situation was improving. By the end of the day the whole of the 27th Division of the Army had been brought ashore, bringing the number of American troops on the island to 50,000. The local Japanese Army commander now gave up the planned aim of destroying the invasion on the beaches. He began to withdraw his troops north to better defensive ground, or southeast to the Nafutan peninsula, beyond the airfield.

To the east of Saipan, and some distance from TF 58, the Japanese were mounting small-scale attacks by their land-based fighters and bombers. In the evening, at 1750, five Jill torpedo planes, apparently from Truk, attacked a convoy of sixteen LSTs (landing ships). This was Tractor Group 3, standing east of Saipan and waiting for the scheduled invasion of Guam. The enemy planes missed the escorting destroyer *Stembel*, but one succeeded in putting a torpedo into the small landing ship/gunboat *LCI(G)*-468, which eventually sank, with fifteen of her crew killed.

An hour and a half later, other planes attacked escort carriers on station northeast of Saipan. The Japanese were on their way home to Yap Island after flying over the invasion beaches. *Gambier Bay* and *Coral Sea* escaped with near misses but *Fanshaw Bay*, the flagship of Bogan's Carrier Support Group One (TG 52.14), was damaged. One of five attacking planes, evidently a Zero fighter-bomber, hit the after part of the flight deck with two small bombs. One of them penetrated to the hangar deck, causing extensive damage; eleven crewmen were killed. *Fanshaw Bay* was forced to return to Eniwetok and then Pearl Harbor for a month of repairs.[34]

Sunday, 18 June. Spruance kept to his normal routine on Saturday evening and went to bed at 2100, having ordered Mitscher to turn TF 58 back to the east at midnight. He was woken in the early hours of Sunday (0345/18) to deal with a second signal from *Cavalla*. Kossler's message about the Japanese tanker force had arrived on the previous morning. Now he reported major enemy combat units, "fifteen or more large combatant ships." They were at a point about halfway across the Philippine Sea (12°23N, 132°20E) and proceeding northeast at high speed. This was a definite report of a large force of Japanese warships headed toward Saipan, but it was important that the force reported by *Cavalla* amounted to only about a third of the ships known to be available to the enemy.[35] Spruance would later recall that the apparent composition of this force strengthened his own view that there was more than one Japanese force, and that a flanking attack was a real danger:

It appeared from the *Cavalla* reports, however, that the entire enemy force was not concentrated in one disposition; that if the force sighted by *Cavalla* was the same as that sighted by *Flying Fish* in San Bernardino Strait [at 1622/15], a speed of less than 10 knots had been made good; and that the position of the *Cavalla* contact indicated a possible approach to the Marianas by this task group via the southern flank.[36]

Aboard *Lexington*, Lee, Mitscher, and Burke had made a different calculation. They suggested positioning the task forces as far as possible to the west, in order to launch a strike on the afternoon of the current day, 18 June. The two components of TF 58 were due to rendezvous (position 15°N, 143°E) at noon, as Clark's TG 58.1 and Harrill's TG 58.4 returned from the Bonins. Assuming that the whole enemy force was near the ships sighted by *Cavalla*, and assuming their rate of advance continued, then an American air strike in the late afternoon could be attempted—along with a thrust by surface units during the night of 18/19 June.[37]

During Sunday morning Mitscher exchanged messages with Vice Adm. Lee, commander of the battleship force. Mitscher queried whether Lee wanted a surface battle on Sunday night (18/19 June): "Do you seek night engagement? It may be we can make air contact this afternoon [18 June], and attack tonight. Otherwise we should retire eastward tonight." Mitscher was probably influenced here by his chief of staff, Arleigh Burke, who was a prominent surface-fleet advocate. To the surprise of Mitscher and his staff (and apparently to Spruance), Lee replied in the negative: "Do not, repeat not, believe we should seek night engagement. Possible advantages of radar more than offset by difficulties of communications and lack of training in fleet tactics at night. Would press pursuit of damaged or fleeing enemy however at any time." Lee was essentially arguing that his battle line, with its superior numbers, would be sure of success in a daylight action but that darkness would increase the unnecessary element of risk.[38]

These conversations between Spruance, Mitscher, Burke, and Lee were significant but, as we know from hindsight, academic. The Japanese admiral was keeping to the west, well out of range of American scout planes and bombers. He was preparing for an "outranging" attack, using shuttle tactics.[39] As a result, there was no likelihood of a sighting by American scout planes on 18 June, and even less chance of a battle with American surface ships during the night that followed (18/19 June). But Spruance's attitude to the *Cavalla* report did indicate caution on his part, something that was reinforced before noon when he made a crucial second signal to Mitscher and Lee regarding the tactics to be adopted once TF 58 was reunited:

> Task Force 58 must cover Saipan and our forces involved in that operation. I still feel that main enemy attack will come from westward but it might be diverted to come in from southwestward. Diversionary attacks may come in from either flank or reinforcement might come in from Empire [i.e. mainland Japan]. Consider that we can best cover Saipan by advancing to the westward during daylight and retiring to eastward at night so as to reduce possibility of enemy passing us during darkness . . . Consider seeking night [surface] action [on 18/19 June] undesirable initially in view of our strength in all types, but earliest possible strike on enemy carriers is necessary.[40]

This was quite different from the "battle plan" of the preceding afternoon (1415/17).

Spruance's attitude at this crucial point was based on a number of considerations. The classic "flanking attack" had been the Battle of Midway, a close analogy to FORAGER (although with the *Japanese* attempting the invasion). An undetected flanking force (partly led by Spruance himself) had achieved a decisive American victory; four Japanese carriers were destroyed and the invasion of Midway had to be abandoned. As the admiral later recalled, "The Japanese often operated with well separated forces, as at Midway and in the South Pacific previously and as they did later at Leyte Gulf."[41] Furthermore, as mentioned earlier, the recent intelligence briefing from Cdr Layton, based at least partly on the captured "Z" Operations documents, had identified a flanking attack as a current danger. Finally, the various U.S. submarine sightings could be interpreted to suggest that more than one enemy force was approaching.

In any event, Mitscher followed Spruance's instructions. TF 58 steamed WSW during Sunday afternoon and evening until 2030, as darkness fell on 18 June. In the course of this movement the Task Force was (again) located by scout planes from the Japanese carriers.[42] At 2030, as planned, Spruance altered his course to the east, back toward Saipan. Recon planes from his own carriers had still not flown far enough west to sight the Japanese fleet.

Japanese land-based planes were also active in the early evening. At 1630/18, three fleet oilers of Unit 1, fueling destroyers 40 miles southeast of Saipan, came under attack from a handful of Zero fighter-bombers, evidently from Yap or Palau. *Neshanic* and *Saugatuck* suffered minor damage, which was made good by ServRon 10 at Eniwetok. *Saranac*, however, had eventually to retire to California for two months of repairs; eight of her crew had been killed. This was the first attack on any of these invaluable ships in the Central Pacific campaign.[43]

Late on Sunday evening (18 June), contradictory information became available to Spruance and Mitscher about Japanese force movements. On the one hand there was a message relating to submarine *Stingray*, which suggested that this boat had attempted to report the location of a Japanese force about 210 miles southwest of TF 58 and 390 miles from Saipan.[44] But CincPac had also reported from Hawaii that a Japanese force (of unknown identity) had broken radio silence at 2020/18, and that the DF "fix" indicated a position 330 miles west of Task Force 58.[45]

Mitscher and Spruance differed in their interpretation of this information. Mitscher, aboard *Lexington*, based his assessment on the new DF fix. At 2335/18, he suggested by VHF voice radio (TBS) to Spruance that TF 58 reverse course to sail due west. This would enable the carriers to be in the best position to launch an early strike (based on the DF position) at daybreak of Monday: "Propose coming to course 270 degrees [i.e. due west] at 0130[/19] in order to commence treatment [sic] at 0500[/19]. Advise." In his post-battle report Mitscher would claim that if TF 58 had reversed its course at 0130/19, and if the enemy fleet had maintained its course and speed, this would have resulted "in our force attaining the ideal striking distance of 200 to 150 miles at 0500" on the morning of the 19th.[46]

Monday, 19 June. Spruance did not concur, although after midnight he spent half an hour discussing Mitscher's proposal with his staff. At

0038/19 he told the commander of TF 58 that he had made up his mind:

> Change proposed in your TBS message does not appear advisable. Believe indication given by *Stingray* more accurate than that contained in [CincPac dispatch from Hawaii]. If that is so continuation as at present [i.e. withdrawing to east] seems preferable. End run by other fast ones remains a possibility and must not be overlooked.[47]

Spruance's fear of an "end run"—the possible flanking attack—had now emerged as the key consideration. The Fifth Fleet war diary would later stress this element. "The possibility existed that the enemy fleet might be divided with a portion of it involving carriers coming around one of our flanks . . . [S]uch a flank attack could inflict heavy damage on our amphibious forces at Saipan."[48]

Mitscher's hunch was right; Spruance's was wrong. Neither man was ignoring convincing evidence. But the opportunity that, in reality, would probably have led to an attempted offensive strike by TF 58 against the Japanese carriers on 19 June, had been missed. Off Saipan, as the sun rose to the east, Task Force 58 was finally set for a unique *defensive* battle, rather than a carrier-versus-carrier duel.

MONDAY, 19 JUNE: AN OLD TIME TURKEY SHOOT

The greatest air battle fought by Task Force 58 had finally begun.[49] The American carriers launched search patrols to the west before dawn on Monday, 19 June. The position of the enemy force (or forces) was still not known. Meanwhile, the enemy fleet had launched a large number of long-range scout planes, several of which sighted the American task groups.

Vice Adm. Mitscher, aboard *Lexington*, began the day looking over the huge fleet that had been assembled around him; since dawn it had been moving again to the southwest. Sitting in his swivel chair on the wing of the carrier's bridge, he had a brief conversation with J. R. Eyerman, who was posted aboard the flagship as a photographer for *Life* magazine. "Are you excited?" he quietly asked Eyerman, who very much was, but just replied "I guess so." "Well, *I'm* excited" was Mitscher's comment.[50]

TF 58 was now operating as a single fleet, but dispersed into five groups, covering an expanse of ocean measuring 40 miles across. TG 58.3 (*Enterprise, Lexington*, two CVLs) was in the center of the whole task force. Spruance and Mitscher were located here, Mitscher aboard *Lexington* and Spruance aboard *Indianapolis*. To the north of TG.58.3 steamed Harrill's TG 58.4 (*Essex* and two CVLs). To the east, in the direction of Saipan and Tinian, was Clark's TG 58.1 (*Hornet, Yorktown*, two CVLs). To the south was TG 58.2 (*Bunker Hill, Wasp*, two CVLs).[51] The centers of all three carrier task groups were about 12 miles from the Spruance's flagship—within visual signaling distance.

Some 15 miles to the west of TG 58.3 was TG 58.7. This comprised a ring of big-gun ships under Lee, formed around *Indiana* and with *Washington* in the lead. Two destroyers, *Yarnall* and *Stockham*, were even further to the west. They steamed 20 miles beyond the rest of TG 58.7, acting as radar pickets for the whole task force. TG 58.7 had a triple role: as a fast-battleship striking force, as a defensive screen against enemy surface ships, and as an AA battery (and lure) to attract and destroy enemy planes approaching from the west.

Spruance and Mitscher had good intelligence about the overall strength and capabilities of the Japanese fleet. On the morning of 19 June, however, they still had no knowledge of its disposition, or even whether part of it would attempt a flanking attack. The American commanders did understand that the enemy might try to mount their air strikes at very long range, to stay clear of counterstrikes from a much stronger U.S. Navy carrier force. The Japanese could take advantage of the longer range of their carrier attack planes; they could also use shuttle attacks, landing on bases in the Marianas.

In fact, the Japanese *had* divided their fleet (at 2100/18), but rather than making a flanking attack they formed into two groups advancing on the same axis, separated by about 100 miles. The leading group (the "Van" Force) was closest to the American fleet. The second, following, group was made up of two carrier forces ("A" Force and the "B" Force). The Van Force included three light carriers equipped mainly with Zero fighter-bombers. Their mission was to strike first, at relatively short range, and knock out the flight decks of the American carriers. They would clear the way for dive bombers and torpedo planes from the "A" and "B" forces, which would mount shuttle attacks.[52]

Following Admiral Spruance's decision of the previous night, TF 58 had continued withdrawing to the east until just before dawn. Faced into the prevailing wind, the carriers had been able to launch search patrols and a "CAP strike" (a fighter sweep) over Guam. Then, at 0620, Mitscher changed course to the southwest to get nearer a potential enemy fleet; this movement was punctuated by two turns into the prevailing wind to launch aircraft. A final prolonged turn ESE into the wind was made at 1023. This would allow the constant launch and recovery of hundreds of Hellcat fighter planes.

Raid I. For TF 58, the main action of the day began with a radar report at 1000 hours. A large group of aircraft were approaching directly from the west toward TG 58.7. This would later be known to the Americans as "Raid I."[53] The attackers were flying high, at about 18,000 feet, and contrails made them clearly visible. There were approximately sixty aircraft.

The bulk of this air attack group consisted of about forty single-seat Zeros operating as a "special" force of fighter-bombers.[54] They were flying the 1941 version of the Zero (Mitsubishi A6M2), with a 250-kg (550-lb) bomb slung under the fuselage. These "special" fighter-bombers could neither dogfight effectively nor sink large enemy armored warships. The intention was that they would disable the enemy carriers by putting their vulnerable flight decks out of action—repeating what the American dive bombers had achieved at Midway in 1942. With this, the fighter-bombers would allow other Japanese aircraft to gain air superiority for the later stages of the decisive battle.[55] Only eight Jill torpedo bombers took part, and their role was navigation and coordination. The fighter escort for the "special" force numbered only fourteen planes, although they were a newer model of the Zero fighter (A6M5) and were not weighed down by a bomb. The escort planes were apparently flown by the more experienced pilots.[56]

Raid I had been located by American radar. The "first large 'bogey' of the day" was reported by battleship *Indiana*, bearing 265 degrees, distance 125 miles, height 24,000 feet and above. Fighters already in the air over TF 58 were vectored toward it. The Japanese strike leader was pausing to set up a coordinated attack of the type that had worked so well against the old *Hornet* at Santa Cruz in 1942. In 1944, however, the delay was fatal. The main characteristic of this air battle and the ones that followed it that day—unlike Santa Cruz—was that the raiding formations were intercepted by the CAP 60 miles or more away from their intended targets. This was a result of the Japanese delay in forming up and of highly effective American radar and fighter direction.

Although TF 58 had a total of 466 fighters, they came in to attack in small formations. The first group of two divisions of Hellcats descended on the Zero fighter-bombers at 1036. They were from the new VF-15 fighter squadron, attached to *Essex* in TG 58.1. The pilots claimed to have destroyed twenty Japanese aircraft with no loss to themselves. Elements of six other U.S. Navy squadrons joined the attack over the next few minutes, with a total of about fifty Hellcats. Few Americans were lost, but among them was Lt Cdr Ernest W. Wood, the CO of the *Princeton* air group (AG 27).

Pressing on, the pilots of the surviving Zero fighter-bombers attempted to attack the first warships they came upon. These were not the carriers that they had been tasked to disable, but the battleships and cruisers of Lee's TG 58.7. This was an extremely powerful surface fleet. It included seven fast battleships, all of which had entered service since 1940. They each had powerful AA batteries, including twenty 5-inch guns, and between forty-eight and eighty 40-mm guns in quad mounts. Also in Lee's battle formation were heavy cruisers *Wichita*, *San Francisco*, *Minneapolis*, and *New Orleans*, which also now mounted powerful AA batteries. The screen also included sixteen destroyers.

At 1049, about ten minutes after the air battle began, a Zero hit the main deck of battleship *South Dakota* with a bomb, blowing a sizeable hole in it, and killing twenty-seven of the crew. Nevertheless, aside from the loss of one quad 40-mm mount, the battleship remained fully operational, and this would be the worst damage suffered by any American vessel that day.[57] In the confusion, destroyer *Hudson*, steaming alongside *South Dakota*, was hit by friendly AA fire and lost two men serving a port 40-mm mount. Zero fighter-bombers achieved near misses on cruisers *Wichita* and *Minneapolis*, but no casualties were suffered.

Raid I had proved a very costly failure. None of the attacking aircraft had reached their intended targets. Indeed, it is possible that none of these planes actually sighted any of the four carrier task groups steaming ahead of the battleships. The "special attack" Zero fighter-bombers suffered extreme losses; only thirteen of the forty-five launched made it back to their carriers.

After the war, Ted Sherman explained the outcome of the air battles of 19 and 20 June 1944 with simple bluntness. "The principal reason for this Japanese defeat was the amazing ineptitude of their poorly trained aviators, and by contrast, the superb fighting efficiency of ours . . . By contrast, the Japanese airmen in this battle were mere novices."[58] The veteran carrier admiral was known for his strong and frank views, but the inadequate training and inexperience of Japanese naval aviators at this stage of the war was without doubt a major factor (and American fighter pilots were indeed well trained). To be sure, some able and experienced Japanese Navy flyers took part in the battle, and even "novices" displayed tragic courage. But most of the attacking planes of the First Mobile Fleet were flown by inexperienced young men who were insufficiently trained and had not been in combat before. Cdr Okumiya Masatake, the air officer of CarDiv 2 for the previous two years, later recalled, "Within two and a half years after the war's start, our training standards and aircrew proficiency had deteriorated to a point where the men stood little chance of survival against the enemy. The marked loss in minimal qualifications underscored dramatically the fact that our personnel preparations for this war had never been adequate."[59] Pilots and crews had few flying hours, and squadrons had had little time to train together or to gain experience in formation flying. The last month had been especially difficult, as Tawi Tawi did not have an airfield for training, and the carriers were rarely able to leave the anchorage to exercise their air groups, due to the danger of American submarines. The fighter-bomber pilots of Raid I, flying from the light carriers of the Van Force, were particularly unprepared.[60] They could do little else but fly in close cruising formation, navigated to near their targets by pathfinders. The escort could help herd them to their destruction, but did little to protect them; of the escort Zeros (A6M5s) in Raid I, eight out of fourteen made it back to their carriers.[61]

Special blame must be assigned to Japanese planners for their choice of tactics, knowing as they did the untrained quality of their personnel. Cdr Okumiya recalled after the war that "at no time did I feel that our air-group leaders possessed the minimum capabilities required for combat leadership." They were younger men, with less command experience.[62] As an aviator, Okumiya also had a low opinion of the experience of the overall commanders of the First Mobile Fleet:

> Vice-Admiral Ozawa, his chief of staff, and his entire senior, operations, and air staffs [sic] had never participated in a battle against enemy aircraft-carriers. Moreover, with the exception of two air staff officers, Vice-Admiral Ozawa and his supporting staffs knew little about the problems of air-groups. They had only the barest knowledge of aviation problems ... I could not help but feel, prior to the battle, that we suffered from a severe handicap in leadership.[63]

Japanese aircrew were inadequately trained, and they were also flying inferior aircraft. The Zero fighters and the Kate and Val attack planes had been effective in the glory days of 1941–42, but now they were well outclassed and outnumbered by the new generation of American fighters. Basically, Japanese planes had always been lightly built and poorly protected, lacking features like self-sealing fuel tanks, but now this really mattered; they were vulnerable to the heavy .50-cal. machine guns of the Hellcats. All the Zeros were slower than the Hellcats; the A6M2s burdened with bombs were at a special disadvantage.

Jill torpedo bombers operated as pathfinders in Raid I. They were new and fast, and they fared much better, with six out of eight returning.[64]

In all, forty-two Raid I planes were lost. Deaths among the Japanese air leaders were extremely high—eight out of nine squadron (*chutai*) commanders. The American pilots claimed 105 enemy planes destroyed from Raid I, but this was a substantial exaggeration. Assuming (low) losses to AA and perhaps some operational (accidental) losses, the actual number destroyed in air-to-air combat must have been "only" in the high thirties. On the American side, four pilots were lost.[65]

The American fighter control system performed very effectively. As Nimitz later reported, "fighter direction and communications met the test, and throughout the day directed interception with clockwork regularity providing enough fighters to meet each raid and placing them almost always with initial altitude advantage." Overall distribution of interceptor forces was handled from *Lexington*, while local direction was usually handled by the flagship of each of the four carrier task groups.[66]

Raid II. Only ten minutes elapsed after the end of the first raid before another wave of attackers was picked up on the American radar. The time was now 1107. This attack would later to be known as Raid II. Its composition was different from the first. It was much larger and potentially much more dangerous, with eighty modern attack planes and nearly fifty escorting Zeros. As in Raid I, the Japanese attack-force leader made the mistake of pausing to coordinate his strike, circling for fifteen minutes to the west of TG 58.7. The planes were flying high, at 19,000–20,000 feet and in a stack 1,500 feet deep.[67]

Raid II was first engaged from about 40 miles west of Task Force 58. The first fighters to intercept were, again, part of VF-15 from *Essex*. They were led by Cdr David McCampbell, CO of the *Essex* air group (AG 15). McCampbell was thirty-four, an advanced age for a fighter pilot in this era. He made a series of runs through the Japanese formation and later claimed five Judys destroyed. McCampbell would also claim two Zeros over Guam in a second sortie that afternoon. His eventual total of thirty-four Japanese planes shot down in the course of the war would make him the U.S. Navy's leading ace. He was also awarded the Congressional Medal of Honor, the highest American military decoration. The citation for the medal covered his actions both in the Philippine Sea and at Leyte Gulf (in October 1944). A second pilot, who engaged the Japanese formation a few minutes later, was Lt (jg) Alexander Vraciu from *Lexington*'s fighter squadron, VF-16. Eight years younger than McCampbell, Vraciu was already one of the Navy's most successful fighter pilots. He claimed six Judys in the morning interception of Raid II. There is a memorable photograph of an elated Vraciu after his return to *Lexington* that afternoon, holding up six fingers. Mitscher himself came down from the flag bridge to the flight deck to congratulate him.[68]

The Japanese lack of training at aircrew and squadron level was evident here, as in Raid 1. Individual survivors broke though the CAP, but there were few examples of coordinated strikes. Torpedo planes attacked *South Dakota*, *Alabama*, *Indiana*, and *Iowa*, but they achieved no hits, and in any event the battleships were not supposed to be their main targets. At 1157 Jills and Judys actually reached TG 58.3 (*Lexington*, *Enterprise*, *San Jacinto*, *Princeton*), which was in the center of the whole task force. A Judy approaching in a shallow dive dropped a bomb on *Enterprise*, but missed her by a good margin. Admiral Spruance watched the distant air action from the open forecastle of *Indianapolis*, despite the sounding of the general-quarters alarm. The admiral eventually retired to the cruiser's flag bridge. He sat in a chair and read quietly, leaving the tactical conduct of the battle to Mitscher, aboard *Lexington*.[69] Some Japanese planes did come close, but the flagship was only one of five cruisers in TG 58.3; one of the attacking planes was shot down.

To the south, Montgomery's TG 58.2 (*Bunker Hill*, *Wasp*, *Cabot*, *Monterey*) was also the object of small-scale attacks. A Judy dropped a bomb off the port beam of *Wasp*. The midships deck-edge elevator was put out of action, but otherwise the ship was operational. One sailor was killed by a bomb fragment and three more were injured. *Bunker Hill* was attacked by two Judys. One of them dropped a bomb (and crashed) just off the deck-edge elevator, disabling it. Small fires were started. Two men aboard the ship were killed, and seventy-two wounded.

As with Raid I, the Japanese loss figures are inexact. About ninety of the Japanese planes that took part in Raid II failed to return to their carriers or to land on bases in the Marianas (mostly on Guam). Probably seventy or eighty were shot down by the Hellcats of the TF 58 CAP, the balance lost due to AA fire or operational causes.[70] It seems to have been at this time that one of the fighter pilots of VF-16 made a comment in the fighter squadron ready room aboard *Lexington*, "Hell, this is like an old time turkey shoot [down home]." It was an expression his squadron commander, Lt Cdr Paul Buie, passed on to his superiors, and to posterity.[71]

Raid III. The action of Raid II in the area over TF 58 came to an end just after noon, at about 1215. Ten minutes later, the radar of Harrill's TG 58.4 (*Essex*, *Langley*, *Cowpens*), on the north flank of the task force, detected yet another large inbound "bogey," 110 miles away and located to the northwest. This was later known as Raid III, and it consisted of about fifty enemy planes. Only about twenty of these, mostly fighters and fighter-bombers, actually approached TF 58. The other thirty returned to their carriers having—surprisingly—failed to find the huge American task force, which had been under direct attack since 1045.[72]

The planes of Raid III at least avoided being shot up by their own ships over the Van Force or flying over the American battleships of TG 58.7. A few attackers from the Raid III force did get through to TG 58.4. One fighter-bomber dropped a bomb some distance from *Essex*; there was no damage to any American ship and no casualties. Defending fighters went into attack over half an hour later, at 1301. Compared to the first two attack groups, Japanese air losses in Raid III, as a fraction of the attacking force, were lower: seven out of the twenty aircraft that actually attacked.[73]

Raid IV. At about 1320 American radar picked up a final concentration of enemy planes, this time to the south. A second radar report was made at 1405. This was later known as Raid IV.[74] The Japanese attack unit had been attempting to follow up an inaccurate sighting, one located about 120 miles SSW of the actual position of TF 58.[75] Most of the Raid IV force were unable to find the American fleet. Some of the planes, eighteen from *Zuikaku*, turned back to the west and toward their mother ship.[76] The bulk of the attack unit flew on to the east as an "outranging" shuttle flight, intending to land on Guam, which lay about 50 miles to the southwest.

The small group of about sixteen planes of the Raid IV force that were able to locate TF 58 slipped in at medium altitude—12,000 feet—under the CAP, and reached Montgomery's TG 58.2 (*Bunker Hill, Wasp, Cabot, Monterey*), located on the southern flank of the task force. Due to American communications problems, a radar sighting made at 1320 was not confirmed as hostile for nearly an hour, at 1413. Fighters from CVL *Monterey* sighted the small group of oncoming attackers at 1420, but they were 13,000 feet above them, and could not quickly intercept. A small group of fighters from *Wasp* was able to engage and shoot down three of the attackers, but by this time the enemy had reached the ships of the task group. They came in on shallow dives from about 6,000 feet.

A Judy, one of a group of eight or nine dive bombers, was destroyed as it attempted to drop its bomb on *Wasp*. This big carrier, slightly damaged during Raid II, suffered three near misses by bombs, and an incendiary (phosphorus) bomb which exploded overhead. Five crewmen aboard *Wasp* were injured by shrapnel. *Bunker Hill*, in the same task group, also had some near misses but suffered little damage. A parked Hellcat rolled overboard as a result of the carrier's violent evasive maneuvers; the plane captain ("crew chief") was in the cockpit but was later rescued from the sea.[77]

The rump of Raid IV was the fifty planes that had not turned back to their own carriers, and which had not succeeded in attacking TG 58.2. This group suffered heavy losses as they attempted to land on bases in the Marianas, mostly Guam No. 1 airfield (Orote). The majority were Zeros and obsolete Val dive bombers; the latter had fixed undercarriage and a maximum speed of 230 knots.[78] The leader of VF-25, from *Cowpens*, spotted them: "Forty enemy planes circling Orote Field at angels three (3,000 feet), with wheels down." The situation was confused by the arrival, at about the same time, of thirteen Zeros, completing a long flight from Truk.[79]

About forty Hellcats from six fighter squadrons were vectored in to intercept. In a series of dogfights lasting from 1510 to 1645, they shot down thirty enemy planes altogether, and inflicted unrepairable damage on nineteen more. Among the first to get involved were three divisions of VF-15 from *Essex* led by Cdr McCampbell, who destroyed two of the enemy.

The last air fighting on 19 June came shortly before dusk, when a formation of Zeros arriving from another base surprised *Essex* Hellcats over Guam. The Japanese succeeded in shooting down two of the American fighters, including the CO of VF-15 (*Essex*), Lt Cdr Charles Brewer. Brewer had led the fighters that mounted the first attack on Raid I, eight hours earlier. He and the other pilot were killed.

Admiral Nimitz stressed the scale of Japanese threat in his report to King in Washington: "The air attack which continued throughout the

19th involved the largest number of planes ever sent against an opposing fleet."[80] Constant air battles had been fought on the edges of the Task Force. A mere handful of enemy planes had reached TG 58.3, in the center of the task force, and TG 58.1, to the east. Only a few Jill torpedo bombers reached a position from which they could launch their deadly weapons; no hits were achieved. The Zero fighter-bombers and Judys, both with small bomb loads, had attacked in shallow dives, and in small numbers. Withering AA had prevented them from putting out of operation any warship of the U.S. Navy, large or small. No American carrier had been hit by anything other than shrapnel. One American battleship had been struck by a bomb and suffered minor damage. No cruisers or destroyers had been hit, despite some near misses.

On the other hand, the American carriers had failed even to *find* any part of the Japanese fleet, let alone mount attacks on it. TF 58 had spent most of the day steaming on an easterly course, away from the enemy fleet, as Mitscher's ships launched and recovered fighters. By the early afternoon lookouts aboard the carriers had actually sighted Rota and Guam islands on the horizon to the east, only about 40 miles away.

At 1630, two hours after the last small attack by elements of Raid IV on TG 58.2 and four hours after the end of the main Japanese attack (Raid II), Spruance communicated his intentions to Mitscher:

> Desire to attack enemy tomorrow if we know his position with sufficient accuracy. If our patrol planes give us required information tonight no carrier searches should be necessary. If not, we must continue searches tomorrow to ensure adequate protection for Saipan. Point OPTION should be advanced to westward as much as air operations permit.[81]

Yet, for all Spruance knew, the Japanese carrier force might have shot its bolt and was now beating a hasty retreat to bases in the Philippines or Japan. The Japanese admiral's tactic of staying out of range and using the longer range of his aircraft had, to that extent, worked.

Nevertheless, the damage to the Japanese Navy's carrier squadrons had been terrific and irreversible. In the evening of 19 June in his signal to Nimitz, Spruance claimed at least 300 enemy planes destroyed. The post-war calculation of S. E. Morison was that the Japanese lost 330 of the 430 carrier planes that had been available in the First Mobile Fleet on the morning of 19 June, plus sixteen of forty-three floatplanes. Against that, American air losses on 19 April had been thirty aircraft with twenty-seven pilots and aircrewmen.[82]

According to an American newspaperman aboard *Lexington*, the commander of TF 58 was still looking ahead. "Like everyone else, Admiral Mitscher must have been bursting with pride at the score our fliers rolled up during that long, exhilarating, wearying, spectacular day. Yet that night he offered only one quiet comment, 'Well, we took the first trick, didn't we?' "[83] The battle was, perhaps, not yet over.

CHAPTER 9

TF 58 AND THE BATTLE OF THE PHILIPPINE SEA (2)

Submarines and the American Air Strike

SUBMARINE OPERATIONS, 19 JUNE

During Monday, 19 June, the great air battle over Task Force 58 in the Philippine Sea had been fought and won. Different, and equally dramatic, events had taken place further west.

As already mentioned, Vice Adm. Lockwood (ComSubPac) had positioned a large number of his submarines on the eastern approaches to the Philippine Sea and around the Marianas. At 0850 on the morning of the 19th, *Albacore* made a periscope sighting of an enemy carrier force; an attack with torpedoes began twenty minutes later.[1]

Albacore was a veteran submarine, commissioned in June 1942 and on her ninth war patrol. She was a big "Gato" class boat of 1,550 tons, with ten torpedo tubes. Her third wartime CO, Lt Cdr James Blanchard, had taken over in December 1943. Blanchard had come to periscope depth again at 0910 and found himself within 9,600 yards of a Japanese carrier group, which was heading southeast, at high speed. Visibility was only fair, with low cloud and a hazy horizon. Blanchard could see two big carriers, two heavy cruisers, and at least six destroyers. He let the first flattop go by in order have a better shot at the second one, which he identified as a "Shōkaku" class. Six torpedoes were fired, at a final range of 1,400 yards. The TDC torpedo-launch computer had failed, so Blanchard had to fire his spread by only his "seaman's eye."

At 0911, submerged and "going deep," he recorded: "Heard and felt explosion, definitely not a depth charge. Time of run correct for a hit with no. 6 torpedo." *Albacore* was immediately counterattacked by three destroyers, and Blanchard had to take his boat down to safer depth. "Evasive tactics may be summed up in a few words. Deep and silent, fish-tailing to keep attackers astern . . . After quiet periods, three attempts to reach periscope depth were frustrated by charges dropped in our vicinity." The depth charge attack lasted several hours, as the big ships of the enemy battle force sped off to the southeast. *Albacore* was not able to surface until 1400.

At 1218—three hours later—while Blanchard and *Albacore* were still keeping "deep and silent," a second submarine, 60 miles away to the southeast, also engaged Japanese ships.[2] Like *Albacore*, *Cavalla* was a "Gato" class, but she had been commissioned much more recently, in February 1944; this was her first war patrol. She reached Pearl Harbor on 14 May 1944, only weeks before the Philippine Sea battle. Lt Cdr Herman Kossler, the CO, was a Pacific submarine combat veteran, but his crew were new, and they had continued their training in Hawaiian waters. *Cavalla* departed from Pearl Harbor for the western Pacific on 31 May.

As described in the preceding chapter, Kossler had reported the sighting of two Japanese fleet oilers on 17 June, and a larger force of warships on the following night. The ships were moving at high speed, and in both cases *Cavalla* had not been able to keep up with them. However, shortly after noon on the following day, 19 June, airplanes were observed through the submarine's periscope, circling to the WNW, and the JP hydrophone detected surface ships on the same bearing. Kossler headed that way, and thirteen minutes later, at 1152, he took the boat to periscope depth.

> When I raised my periscope at this time the picture was too good to be true. I could see four ships, a large Carrier with two Cruisers ahead on the port bow and a Destroyer about 1,000 yards on the starboard beam. The Carrier was later identified as Shokaku Class and Cruisers as Atago Class.[3]

At 1218 Kossler began his attack, firing a spread of six torpedoes. The first was heard to hit the target after fifty seconds, and the second and third at eight-second intervals after that. The submarine then came under heavy depth-charge attack from the escorting destroyers, but eventually this ceased. At 1508, three hours after the torpedoes had been fired, the results of the attack became evident through the submarine's hydrophones: "Four distinct explosions were heard in the direction of the attack, these were not depth charges or bombs, as their rumbling continued for many seconds." Late in the evening, Kossler was finally able to surface and, at 2225/19, radio a report of his successful attack to ComSubPac.

Albacore and *Cavalla* had attacked the same group of Japanese ships, the "A" Force of the First Mobile Fleet, commanded by Vice Adm. Ozawa Jisaburō. The two groups of Ozawa's fleet had come together in the middle of the Philippine Sea in the early evening of Friday, 16 June. Steaming to the east and then to back to the west, the ships of the fleet refueled from an oiler group through much of Friday and Saturday. Early on Saturday afternoon (17th) they all turned to the northeast. Shortly afterward (1957/17), in the evening darkness, *Cavalla* made her distant radar sighting of "fifteen or more large combatant ships." The Japanese run to the northeast ended on Sunday afternoon with a turn in a generally southern direction. This run continued until the evening (2100/18) when, as part of the Ozawa's attack plan, the First Mobile Fleet split into two main elements. The Van Group under Vice Adm. Kurita (battleships, cruisers, and three small carriers) steamed east and then northeast, toward the Americans. The carrier "main body" (the "A" Force and the "B" Force, each with three carriers) continued to the south until 0300 on Monday, when it, too, changed course to the northeast, before turning to the southeast at 0807/19.

Ozawa was overall commander of the First Mobile Fleet, but he also directly commanded the "A" Force. This included all three of the surviving Japanese heavy carriers. Imperial Japan only ever put seven such ships into operational service, and four of them had been lost at Midway. The best of the pre-war ships, the 26,100-ton sister ships *Shōkaku* and *Zuikaku*, had had the good fortune to miss the June 1942 battle. They would be the most active of the Japanese flattops, taking part in the Pearl Harbor attack, the raid on Ceylon, and the battles of the Coral Sea, Eastern Solomons, and Santa Cruz. *Taihō*, in contrast, was a brand-new ship, completed in March 1944. She was the best carrier the Japanese ever built, and not surprisingly, Ozawa selected her to be his new flagship. She was some 780 feet in length and displaced 30,250 tons. Powered by four steam turbines delivering 160,000 shp, *Taihō* was slightly larger and faster than an "Essex" class. Unlike the American ships, she had an armored flight deck. Fifty-three operational aircraft were carried on two hangar decks. The three carriers of the "A" Force were escorted by battleship *Nagato*, cruisers *Haguro*, *Myōkō*, and *Yahagi*, and seven destroyers.

When *Albacore* sighted the "A" Force at 0850/19, the three carriers were heading southeast and were just completing the launch of their deckload strikes against the American fleet (known now as Raid II).[4] The submarine fired a spread of six torpedoes, beginning at 0910, and one hit *Taihō* (misidentified as a "Shōkaku" class) forward, on her starboard side, about a minute later. In the judgement of the admiral and Capt. Tomozō, the hit did not affect the flagship's capability to steam on at high speed along with *Shōkaku* and *Zuikaku*. The only immediate internal damage appeared to be to *Taihō*'s forward elevator. Located above the point of torpedo impact, the heavy armored elevator platform had dropped and was jammed partway open. However, air operations could be continued when emergency wooden decking was fitted.

The three carriers of the "A" Force continued rapidly to the southeast. At 1120–1130 *Zuikaku* had begun launching a small attack strike of ten Zero fighter-bombers and four Jill torpedo planes (part of Raid IV), as well as a CAP of four Zero fighters.[5] Three hours after *Albacore*'s attack, "A" Force was 60 miles further to the southeast and still steaming at high speed. At 1152 the Japanese ships ran into *Cavalla*, which fired her spread of six torpedoes at 1218. The "Shōkaku class ship" on which Kossler recorded hits with three or four torpedoes was, in fact, *Shōkaku* herself.

Not surprisingly, the multiple torpedo hits on *Shōkaku* had a more immediate effect than the single one on *Taihō*.[6] *Shōkaku* had been hit by three or four torpedoes forward and amidships on the starboard side. Fires were started on ruptured aviation fuel lines. Boiler rooms on the starboard side began to flood, affecting power and speed. *Shōkaku* fell out of formation and soon lay dead in the water. At 1310 an event on the hangar deck, probably an exploding bomb, set off a gasoline vapor build-up and a series of fires and explosions, which could not be contained. The crews of nearby ships could soon see flames emerging above the deck. Loss of power prevented the pumps from working effectively. At 1430, two hours after the torpedo hits, the crew were ordered to assemble on the flight deck and prepare to abandon ship.

Shōkaku sank suddenly by the bow, as water poured into her forward elevator well. Her four screws were visible as the stern rose, and she sank at 1501. Other ships picked up the survivors; there were only 570 of them. It seems that a very high proportion of the crew were lost—1,272 officers and men.[7]

Having left the crippled carrier behind, the surviving ships sped ahead at 20 knots. *Taihō* was still leading the "A" Force, despite her torpedo damage. She even carried out some air operations, presumably launching and recovering CAP, as well as launching the ten Jills that took part in Raid IV. Nevertheless, the big carrier was in trouble. Vapor had built up from leaking aviation fuel lines and storage tanks in the depths of her hull. Because *Taihō* had two enclosed hangar decks, it was very hard to dissipate the fuel vapor.

At about 1530 Ozawa reversed the course of both "A" Force and "B" Force. They began a run to the northwest, still on close parallel courses.[8] At about the time of this turn, at 1532, more than six hours after the original torpedo hit, *Taihō* was rocked by a massive internal explosion. Vapor from aviation gas, probably concentrated in the area of the forward elevator well, was the main cause. The stiff armored flight deck directed the force of the explosion downward, although it was buckled and cracked in places. Auxiliary machinery for pumps failed. The ship came to a halt and began to settle. The crew were ordered to abandon ship. At about 1600, Ozawa boarded destroyer *Wakatsuki*, with the Emperor's portrait; at 1706 he would transfer from the destroyer to heavy cruiser *Haguro*.[9]

Taihō stayed afloat for an hour and a half after the admiral's departure. She sank, on an even keel, at 1728; this was eight hours after she been torpedoed and two hours after the internal explosion.[10]

There are several explanations for the extraordinary twin disasters that befell Ozawa's carriers on the morning of 19 June. First of all, it must be said that the Japanese were extremely unlucky. Admiral Ozawa may well have assumed that a force operating at high speed and in the open ocean would face relatively low risk from submarine attack. Two American submarines found themselves presented with the possibility of a clear torpedo shot. The carriers had been launching aircraft and presumably steering a straight course. Another striking misfortune was that just one torpedo could cause such devastation to a large and modern ship like *Taihō*.

Underlying what happened (and as discussed in Chapter 7) was the development of the U.S. Navy's submarine force, with a large number of radar-equipped submarines, with experienced, aggressive commanders and crews, as well as effective torpedoes and torpedo fire-control systems. The Philippine Sea battle is often seen as a triumph of carrier aviation but it was actually very much a "combined arms" battle (to use the appropriate technical term), with the submarine playing a crucial role in both reconnaissance and attack.

A second factor involved the shortcomings of the Japanese Navy. The carrier force was poorly escorted, and individual ships had fatal design flaws. The "A" Force had a screen of only seven destroyers, considerably fewer than the escort that was normally deployed around a comparable American task group. The radar, sonar, and anti-submarine weapons and tactics of the destroyers were inferior to those of their American counterparts. The "A" Force destroyers were probably tasked primarily with protecting the carriers from air attack. As for anti-submarine air patrols from the carriers they were, at least on 19 June, inadequate and possibly completely absent; aircraft were being used to locate the American carrier fleet and then to take part in a mass air strike against it.[11] Despite attempts to reduce the general vulnerability of their carriers—after losing four of them at Midway—the design and damage-control systems of Japanese warships proved still not fit for purpose. In addition, the unrefined fuel oil that powered the engines of the carrier was especially volatile—although the initial and ultimately fatal explosions seem to have involved gasoline vapor.

Albacore and *Cavalla* had just carried out the most successful submarine attack of World War II. Looking at events from the point of view of naval history, they transformed the Philippine Sea action from a successful defensive air battle into a decisive naval victory. However, the successful attack had no effect on decisions made by the American naval command on Monday, 19 June, and only a marginal effect on the course of events on the following day. The American command knew that the enemy had lost over 300 planes; they did not know that the Japanese had lost two of their three heavy carriers.

Admiral Spruance only learned of the attack by *Cavalla* in the middle of Monday night (19/20 June). The submarine surfaced after sunset; at 2224/19 Kossler reported three hits on a "Shōkaku" class carrier, as well as explosions and deep rumbling in the aftermath. Spruance, as we will see, would shortly afterward urge Mitscher to send out his carrier planes to hunt the damaged carrier and any ships attempting to support her. As regards *Taihō*, neither Spruance, Mitscher, nor Lockwood seems to have been informed by Blanchard of the 0850/19 sighting of the carrier force by *Albacore*, or of the submarine's attack on *Taihō* twenty minutes later. And, because eight hours and many miles passed between the torpedo attack and the explosion aboard the carrier, Blanchard himself can have had no idea that the ship he attacked had been sunk, and neither could CincPac or ComSubPac.[12]

On the following day (20 June), American carrier planes would attack the First Mobile Fleet. They only came into contact with one big carrier, but even that could not justify a firm conclusion about the absence of one or two Japanese heavy carriers. The air attacks were made at the end of the day, the weather was cloudy in the target area, and the enemy fleet was widely spread out. It seems to have been only in the middle of August 1944, by the time he endorsed Kossler's war patrol report, that ComSubPac had concluded there was "sufficient evidence" that *Cavalla* had sunk a "Shōkaku" class.[13] As for *Albacore* and her carrier, it was apparently not until late in 1944 that a POW interrogation revealed the loss of *Taihō* in the Philippine Sea battle.[14] Most of the *Albacore*'s crew never learned what had happened, because the boat was sunk on her next patrol, off Hokkaido in November; she was lost with all hands.

The submarine attacks fundamentally reduced the capability of the Japanese. *Shōkaku* and *Taihō* could never be replaced. For the rest of the war the Japanese had to fight with only one operational heavy carrier.

More immediately, over the vital next twenty-four hours, the sinking of the flagship *Taihō* affected the ability of Ozawa to command his fleet. Aboard a cruiser (*Haguro*) with inadequate radio and information facilities, he was unable to control the situation and missed the opportunity to pull the surviving elements of the First Mobile Fleet out of the battle area without further loss.

MISSION BEYOND DARKNESS, 20 JUNE

The main strike by the air groups of TF 58 was launched in the late afternoon of Tuesday, 20 June. It arrived over the enemy fleet as the sun was setting, and it was recovered under chaotic conditions in the black of night. It has aptly been called "the mission beyond darkness."[15]

The aim of Japanese "outranging" tactics had been to allow a weaker carrier fleet to engage a stronger one with as little risk as possible. On 17–19 June Ozawa had been careful to stay beyond the reach of American search planes and attack strikes. Having expended his own air groups and lost two of his three big carriers to American submarine attacks, he might have been expected to withdraw to the Philippines or Japan, preserving his surviving carrier force. But that is not what he did.

After the harrowing escape from the inferno aboard *Taihō*, the Japanese admiral had eventually been able to transfer his flag to *Haguro* in the early evening of Monday, 19 June. But even in the relative safety of the heavy cruiser the admiral had only limited knowledge of the situation. His staff had brought the Emperor's portrait from *Taihō*, but not the special codebook required to decipher the most important signals from Combined Fleet headquarters in Japan.[16] Meanwhile, Ozawa did not know how much damage had been inflicted on the American fleet by his carrier air squadrons and by the land-based planes of Kakuta's First Air Fleet. He did not know the full extent of Japanese aircraft losses, or how badly the shuttle bombing arrangements had worked. Some of the attacking planes did successfully land on Guam or one of the other islands, and Ozawa could have (incorrectly) expected that their number was large. In addition, he still had seven undamaged carriers and a completely undamaged and powerful fleet of heavy surface ships, including super-battleships *Yamato* and *Musashi*.

Even had Ozawa known more, an unreadiness to admit defeat would
have kept his ships near the battle area. If the loss of the Marianas
meant the loss of the war, then an all-out but risky continuation of the
battle was justified. The landings on Saipan were still at a critical stage,
and a Japanese garrison of unprecedented strength might be on the
point of driving the invaders into the sea. But whatever the Japanese
admiral decided, his ships had to refuel. The fleet continued to steam
to the northwest in order to rendezvous with the fleet oilers of his
Supply Force.

The following morning, 20 June, Vice Adm. Kurita of the Van Force
forwarded new sighting reports from his scout planes to *Haguro*. It
turned out that, far from being wiped out, the American fleet was still
active and approaching striking range. Kurita evidently urged a retirement to Japan, but Ozawa rejected this.[17] At 1202 *Haguro* caught up
with undamaged carrier *Zuikaku* and the admiral transferred his flag.
There he was able to obtain a better idea of the situation regarding
losses on the previous day and the very limited number of attack planes
still available in the First Mobile Fleet. But by then the rendezvous with
the fleet oilers of the two Supply Forces had been set, and it was not far
enough to the west.[18]

How close the Japanese fleet had been to safety became clear when
the eventual enemy attack did occur, at dusk on the 20th and at the
very edge of the American range. Had the First Mobile Fleet been
another 100 miles further west, its surviving ships would probably have
escaped altogether.

On the American side the decisions on the 20th were easier than on
the day before. The danger of a Japanese carrier air attack had been much
reduced by the enemy's losses of the previous day. The major problem
now was that the Japanese fleet might already be on its way back to base
in Japan or the Philippines. Nevertheless, at 0800/20, Mitscher received
a dispatch from Spruance, in which a major element was the news from
Cavalla about the successful attack on a big Japanese carrier:

> Damaged *Zuikaku* [sic] may still be afloat. If so believe she will
> be most likely headed northwest. Desire to push our forces today
> as far to westward as possible. If no contact with enemy fleet

results, consider it indication that fleet is withdrawing and further pursuit after today will be unprofitable. If you concur, retire tonight [20/21 June] toward Saipan . . . *Zuikaku* [sic] must be sunk if we can reach her.[19]

Mitscher had been heading west all through the night of 19/20 June and the following morning, with three of his four fast-carrier task groups. The pursuit force was made up of *Bunker Hill*, *Enterprise*, *Hornet*, *Lexington*, *Wasp*, and *Yorktown*, as well as five CVLs. The three carrier task groups were deployed in line abreast. Reeves' TG 58.3 was still located in the center; Mitscher rode in *Lexington* as the TF 58 flagship, and Spruance was aboard *Indianapolis*. Clark's TF 58.1 steamed about 30 miles to the north and Montgomery's TG 58.2 about 30 miles to the south. Fifty miles ahead of TG 58.3, to the west, were the battleships of Lee's TG 58.7.

Harrill's Task Group 58.4 (*Essex* and *Langley*) was left behind to refuel, and then to continue suppression of enemy air bases on Guam. The admiral had raised his flag in *Essex* only in April 1944, and he had proved to be excessively cautious and indecisive during the Bonins raid, without the traits required to command a fast-carrier task group. He came down with appendicitis aboard his flagship shortly after the Philippine Sea battle, and was consigned to a stateside administrative post after his recovery.[20]

Mitscher sent out a search from TF 58 at 0530/20, the first of a number that day. The limited range of most of the carrier search planes (325 miles) was such that it took ten hours before the Japanese fleet was located. Lt Robert S. Nelson had flown from *Enterprise* in a TBM Avenger with one Hellcat as escort. He sent an "Enemy sighted" report at 1540, giving the position, course, and speed of the enemy fleet, as well its disposition. The initial position reported was inaccurate (60 miles too far east), but subsequent reports from Nelson corrected this and provided more information[21] Above all, it was clear that a large part of the Japanese fleet had been sighted, and not just one crippled straggler.

In response, the launch of the long-awaited and long-discussed air attack against the Japanese fleet began at about 1620.[22] It was not an all-out operation. The heavy carriers each put up a "deckload" strike, which amounted to rather less than half the aircraft complement of each ship. Total attack planes committed were seventy-seven dive bombers (SB2C Helldivers and SBD Dauntlesses) and fifty-four TBF/TBM Avengers. Only twenty-one of the Avengers were carrying torpedoes, the rest each carried four 500-lb GP (general-purpose) bombs in their weapons bay. The Dauntless and Helldiver element was only about 40 percent of the total number of dive bombers available in the three task groups, and the Avenger element only a third of the total. Also involved were eighty-five Hellcats, about a quarter of the fighters available; many of them were carrying bombs.[23]

Mitscher had originally ordered his carriers to prepare and dispatch a second deckload strike that afternoon, and he informed Spruance to this effect. However, the commander of TF 58 changed his mind when it was realized that the initial sighting had been incorrect, and the Japanese fleet was 60 miles further out than expected; Spruance was informed that the second strike would be launched the following morning. From hindsight it would have been wiser to have recalled the first strike once it was discovered that the distances involved were so great. Even without that factor the late-afternoon launch meant that the returning planes would have to fly home in the darkness as they searched for their carriers and attempted to land. Many of the pilots had not been qualified for nighttime carrier landing.

In any event, the air strike reached the area of the Japanese carrier fleet at about 1830, after a flight of about two hours. Sunset was only forty-five minutes away. The Japanese fleet was scattered into four groups, with each element some distance from the others. From the point of view of the attackers, the target warships were divided into a northern group, a central group, and a southern group.[24] The central group was 15 to 20 miles southwest of the northern group, and the southern group was about 10 miles south of the central group. A separate fleet oiler group was about 90 miles to the east, actually nearer the American fleet.

The Japanese carrier attack squadrons had been shredded in the Monday's "Turkey Shoot," but over sixty defending Zero fighters were

Table 9.1. Elements of the Japanese First Mobile Fleet Attacked on 20 June 1944

Relative position	Japanese designation	Carriers	Other major ships
Northern group	"A" Force/CarDiv 1	*Zuikaku*	*Haguro, Myōkō, Yahagi*
Central group	"B" Force/CarDiv 2	*Hiyō, Junyō, Ryūhō*	*Nagato, Mogami*
Southern group	Van Force/CarDiv3	*Chiyoda*	*Haruna, Kongō, Chōkai, Maya*
Oiler group	Supply Force	—	—

Note: The southern group was the only element of the Van Force (CarDiv 3) that was attacked by planes of TF 58. There were two other elements of the Van Force, slightly further north, that never came under attack: CVL *Chitose* (with *Musashi*, and cruisers *Atago* and *Takao*), and CVL *Zuihō* (with *Yamato*, and cruisers *Chikuma, Kumano, Suzuya,* and *Tone*).

aloft over the main fleet. They seem to have been flown by the more experienced and able surviving pilots, and their performance was better than the day before. Unlike the Americans on Monday, they were not able to intercept the attacking enemy planes on the distant approaches to their target, destroying attack plane units or breaking up their formations. Air fighting took place over or near the target fleet. Much of it involved Helldivers and Avengers which had already completed their attacks and were flying eastward to rendezvous points for the homeward flight. The Japanese had radar, but they did not have a fighter direction system comparable to that of the U.S. Navy. The Japanese claimed that their CAP destroyed forty American planes; in reality the Americans lost only six Hellcats, five Helldivers, and one Avenger to enemy fighters. About eighty Hellcats were in action over the three Japanese warship groups, although some of them were carrying out fighter-bomber attacks.[25]

Japanese AA fire looked impressive, creating as it did clouds of smoke in different colors. Long-range DP guns, used for barrage fire, were the 5-in/40 and 3.9-in/40 in single or twin mounts; these were not as good as the ubiquitous American 5-in/38, and fewer of them were mounted on each type of ship. There was no Japanese proximity fuse. Heavy ships were fitted with central AA directors, but most destroyers were not. The 25-mm short-range gun (a license-built French Hotchkiss), in single, twin, or triple mounts, was fitted in large numbers. Like the comparable U.S. Navy 20-mm, however, it lacked sufficient range or power to destroy attack planes before they had launched their weapons. There was no weapon comparable to the U.S. Navy's medium-range 40-mm. The main armament of the big ships was also used to create a long-range barrage against torpedo planes; this was spectacular but ineffective.[26]

On 20 June, the Japanese AA guns were remarkably unsuccessful. They destroyed very few of the attacking planes, although they may have made it dangerous for the American flyers to press home their attacks. In an extreme case of over-claiming, the Japanese would maintain that seventy American planes were destroyed by the gunfire of their ships. In fact, only two or three seem to have been lost.[27]

The setting sun and limited fuel available meant that the attack could not be carefully planned and coordinated, either by the strike group as a whole or by individual squadrons. Pilots and crewmen had frequently been in action against static targets like island airstrips and other installations, but they had little experience dealing with rapidly maneuvering warships. Although this first deckload strike contained over 200 planes, it was engaging targets spread out over a wide area. There was no overall strike leader.[28] Nevertheless, the aviators of TF 58 did succeed in attacking most elements of the enemy fleet.

Two of the American attacks took place at virtually the same time, about 1830, although some distance apart. One of these lasted for ten minutes and was directed against a group of ships to the south. The attack force, led by Cdr Ralph Shifley, flew toward the first carrier they sighted, which was accompanied by two battleships. The first attackers were from three of the TG 58.2 carriers, *Bunker Hill* and CVLs *Monterey* and *Cabot*.[29] Two divisions of *Bunker Hill* Helldivers pushed over from 12,000 feet to drop their bombs at 2,000 feet. The captain of the carrier under attack skillfully maneuvered his ship to avoid all

Table 9.2. TF 58 Air Strikes on the Japanese First Mobile Fleet, 20 June 1944

Task Group	Ship	Air Group	Aircraft	Main target
TG 58.1	*Hornet* (F)	AG 2	34	northern group ("A" Force); central group ("B" Force)
	Yorktown	AG 1	35	northern group ("A" Force); central group ("B" Force)
	Bataan	AG 50	10	northern group ("A" Force)
TG 58.2	*Bunker Hill* (F)	AG 8	34	southern group (Van Force)
	Wasp	AG 14	35	fleet oiler group (Support Force)
	Cabot	AG 31	4	southern group (Van Force)
	Monterey	AG 28	4	southern group (Van Force)
TG 58.3	*Enterprise* (F)	AG 10	28	central group ("B" Force)
	Lexington	AG 16	27	central group ("B" Force)
	Belleau Wood	AG 24	10	central group ("B" Force)
	San Jacinto	AG 51	2	northern group ("A" Force)

Note: AG 27 from CVL *Princeton* (TG 58.3) did not take part in the 20 June air strike. TG 58.4 had remained near Guam. "Aircraft" is the number of fighters and attack planes that actually reached the Japanese fleet, i.e. excluding 12 planes that aborted after takeoff.

Source: Dickson, *Philippine Sea*, p. 246.

the bombs. Unable to see the carrier clearly through the smoke, some of the attackers dropped their loads on a battleship and a heavy cruiser in her escort, causing minor damage to the latter.[30] A group of bomb-carrying TBM Avengers from *Monterey* and *Cabot* arrived a few minutes later. Eight of them came down in a shallow diving ("glide-bombing") attack. It seems one hit on the carrier was made by these planes, on the after part of the flight deck. Thinking this target had suffered mortal damage, the last of the Avengers dropped their bombs on one of the battleships. This killed fifteen men but caused only minor local damage.[31] A final attack came from the south, in the form of eight torpedo-carrying Avengers from *Bunker Hill*. The main target was the carrier; five torpedoes were dropped but none hit the rapidly moving vessel.

With that, the attack on the southern group came to an end. Minor damage had been inflicted by hits or near misses on three ships (carrier *Chiyoda*, battleship *Haruna*, and heavy cruiser *Maya*); their mobility and combat-readiness were not seriously affected. No American planes were lost to AA fire, but during their withdrawal the TG 58.2 strike group were "bounced" by Zeros, which shot down two of the Helldivers.

The second group of ships to be attacked (also at about 1830) was located 30 or 35 miles to the north. The strike leader, Cdr Jackson Arnold, CO of the *Hornet* air group, chose this group because it contained a big carrier.[32] The attack came from the three carriers of Clark's TG 58.1—*Yorktown*, *Hornet*, and CVL *Bataan*—and it was on a larger scale than the one against the southern group.[33] The Helldivers from *Hornet* attacked first, in two groups, followed by a Helldiver squadron from *Yorktown*. The big carrier was hit by a 1000-lb bomb on the starboard side of the flight deck, behind the island. This caused some damage on the carrier's hangar deck, where fires broke out, but they were quickly brought under control. The Japanese also recorded six near misses on this ship by dive bombers. A simultaneous attack by six bomb-carrying *Hornet* Avengers was followed by ten Hellcats from *Bataan*. Some of these attackers went after the escorting cruisers, but they did not succeed in hitting any of them. Altogether, the attack on the northern group by planes from TG 58.1 achieved one hit on the big carrier and six near misses, for the loss of three of their own planes shot down by Japanese fighters.[34]

The attack on the central group of the Japanese fleet developed at about 1845, a few minutes later than the strikes on the southern and northern groups. The delay was apparently due to the slower speed of the Dauntless aircraft that were part of this strike force.[35] It was also more complicated, involving multiple carrier targets and attackers for different air groups.

In the middle of this central group were three carriers, two of them big sister ships. Surrounding them were two heavy ships and a ring of ten destroyers. The attack was actually begun by bomb-carrying Hellcats from *Hornet* in TG 58.1, led by Cdr Arnold himself, and it was joined by other fighters from *Yorktown*. Next were eight Avengers from *Yorktown*, five carrying torpedoes and three carrying bombs. During a torpedo attack at low altitude, two were shot down by Japanese AA fire. It was, seemingly, some of these aircraft that achieved two early hits on one of the carriers: a bomb grazed the ship's foremast and blew up over the bridge, injuring her CO and killing many of the bridge personnel.[36]

Next to arrive over the central group—and ultimately the most successful attackers—was a division of three or four torpedo-carrying Avengers from *Belleau Wood*. A torpedo hit the carrier on her starboard quarter, reportedly at 1845, reducing her speed. Half an hour later, as dusk fell, a secondary explosion occurred. The Japanese account credited this to a submarine torpedo, but it must have been the induced result of the first aircraft torpedo hit. With fires burning out of control, most of the carrier's crew were taken off by the accompanying destroyers. She rolled over and sank at 2032.[37]

Meanwhile, a group of late-arriving attack planes from *Lexington*'s AG 16, under Lt Cdr Ralph Weymouth, attempted to attack other ships in the central group from the west. They came under determined attack by enemy fighters and lost an Avenger and an escorting Hellcat. Pushing over with the other SBD Dauntless dive bombers from 11,500 feet at 1904, Weymouth aimed for another Japanese carrier in the central group. Following closely behind was a glide-bombing attack by five bomb-carrying Avengers from *Lexington* and two from *San Jacinto*. In the course of the action against this second carrier, two bombs hit and badly damaged her funnel and killed dozens of the personnel on the superstructure.[38] There were also six near misses. The attack planes were met by enemy fighters as they flew out at low altitude toward their rendezvous point for the trip home; one SBD was downed by a Zero.

Meanwhile, at about 1900, the central group was strafed by eight Hellcats from *Enterprise*, led by the AG 10 commander, Cdr William R. ("Killer") Kane. They were supporting six Dauntless dive bombers from *Enterprise* that were apparently targeting the third carrier in this group. Toward the end of the attack on the central group, at about 1915, five bomb-carrying Avengers from *Enterprise* came down in a glide attack against the same carrier. They dropped their bombs fairly high and apparently only achieved near misses.[39]

Overall the air attack on the three groups of combat warships in the First Mobile Fleet had only limited effect (and, after darkness fell, the cost in American aircraft was going to reach a record high). In the end, the auxiliary carrier in the central group (*Hiyō*) was the only ship sunk. No other combat warship in the Mobile Fleet suffered really serious damage.[40]

Forty miles back to the east a fourth and separate attack was mounted against the supply groups, which consisted of six fleet oilers and six destroyers. This was carried out by fighters and attack planes from *Wasp*, which had split off from the rest of the TG 58.2 strike force (planes from *Bunker Hill*, *Monterey*, and *Cabot* went on to engage the southern group of the main warship force). On their initial approach, the *Wasp* planes had bypassed the oiler force and flown on 40 miles to the south in search of carriers. Finding none, and now running short of fuel, they came back to the supply ships. The time of the attack seems to have been just after 1900. Two oilers were so badly damaged that the Japanese had to sink them.[41]

For Task Force 58 and the U.S. Navy the most difficult and costly part of the Battle of the Philippine Sea now began—at the very end.[42] It was after sunset when the last attacking planes broke off. The distance home was 250–300 miles. Flying at low speed to save fuel and navigating through the darkness, the journey took two and a half hours. Vice Adm. Mitscher and the task group commanders decided to light up the fleet to allow returning planes to home in on their carriers. This had a degree of risk from enemy submarines, as did the use of destroyers for the recovery of ditched aircrew rather than anti-submarine patrols. Lt Cdr Robert Winston, aboard CVL *Cabot* in Task Group 58.3, recorded his impressions:

> Then an amazing, incredible thing happened. Our blacked-out ships began to turn on their lights—red truck lights on the outer screen, bright flashing lights to identify the individual carriers, glow-lights to outline the flight decks, vertical searchlight beams and star-shells to mark our position for those still too far out to see us—friend and foe alike. We stood open-mouthed on the

deck for a moment . . . at the sheer audacity of asking the Japs to come and get us, then a spontaneous cheer went up. To Hell with the Japs around us! Let them come in if they dared. Japs or no Japs, the Navy was taking case of its own; *our* pilots were not expendable![43]

The lights could not prevent confusion and chaos. As already mentioned, many pilots had not had experience in night landings. Even when they could find the carriers there were problems getting into the crowded landing circuits. Discipline was weakened as desperate pilots competed to get aboard before their fuel ran out. A considerable number of planes crashed on landing. By "fouling" the flight deck they blocked the landing of other planes, which were then forced to ditch in the sea. A number of leaders were very angry about what had happened. Weymouth, CO of *Lexington*'s VB-16, climbed up the ladder to the flag bridge and complained to Mitscher: "God damn it, sir! We can fly at night, but we've got to practice like hell!"[44]

Despite the famous story of the landing lights, the bare statistics do indicate that the "mission into darkness" turned out to be an operation with deep flaws. Table 9.3 lists aircraft losses on the return flight, where the overall loss rate was nearly 40 percent. *Wasp* and *Bunker Hill* each launched twelve Helldivers, and in both cases only one plane returned safely. The lower loss rate from TG 58.3 relates to the fact that all dive bombers involved were SBD-5 Dauntlesses rather than SB2C-3 Helldivers.

Fortunately, the loss of life by American aircrew was low, despite the conditions and the number of aircraft involved. A total of sixteen pilots and thirty-three aircrew (gunners and radiomen) were killed, as well as two officers and four enlisted men in the flight deck crews. Fifty-one pilots and fifty crewmen were picked up on the night of 20/21 June, mostly by warships, after their planes had ditched. A further thirty-three pilots and twenty-six crewmen were rescued by warships and seaplanes in the following days, as U.S. ships cruised forward along the track of the return flight.[45]

The "mission into darkness" is best remembered for the decision to turn on the landing lights. Although, thankfully, losses of aircrew were

Table 9.3. TF 58 Operational Losses, 20 June 1944

	Returning aircraft	Operational losses	% lost
F6F Hellcat	91	23	25%
SBD Dauntless	24	4	17%
SB2C Helldiver	47	34	72%
TBF/TBM Avenger	45	18	40%
Total	207	79	38%
TG 58.1 (Clark)	79	34	43%
TG 58.2 (Montgomery)	73	32	44%
TG 58.3 (Reeves)	55	13	24%
Total	207	79	38%

Note: The loss percentage column is the proportion of *returning* aircraft. "Operational" losses are non-combat losses (ditching, crashing into the sea, and deck accidents) while returning to TF 58. "Returning aircraft" excludes planes that turned back (aborted) en route to the Japanese fleet and those lost due to enemy action during the attack itself. Harrill's TG 58.4 did not take part in the attack on 20 June.

Source: Y'Blood, *Red Sun*, pp. 230–1; Dickson, *Philippine Sea*, p. 246.

relatively low, in other respects the wisdom and success of the 20 June air strike can be questioned, certainly compared to what had happened on the previous day. The loss of nearly eighty planes on the return flight to TF 58 made this the most costly single strike mission attempted by the U.S. Navy. Despite misjudgments by the Japanese admiral and traumatic losses of ships and aircraft on the preceding day, the First Mobile Fleet was able to escape with the loss of one auxiliary carrier. This did not make the two-day battle of the Philippines anything less than a decisive American victory, but it was certainly also an incomplete and more costly one.

THE OUTCOME OF THE NAVAL BATTLE

At 1900 on 20 June, in the middle of the air attack by over 200 American planes on all four elements of the Mobile Fleet, Vice Adm. Ozawa, aboard *Zuikaku* would actually order a surface thrust by his surface ships to the east. It was only at 2046 that Ozawa finally received a signal from Admiral Toyoda's Combined Fleet headquarters in Japan, instructing him to break off the battle when possible.[46] On the afternoon of the 22nd, the whole fleet was ordered to Nakagusuku Bay (known as "Buckner Bay" during the 1945 battle) on the south end of Okinawa, where it arrived the following day. On the American side there were still thoughts of a successful pursuit on the morning of 21 June. American planes briefly made contact with the enemy fleet during the morning, but then it was decided that the Japanese were out of range and could not be caught.

In reaching conclusions about the Philippine Sea battle we can start with the Japanese perspective. Vice Adm. Kakuta and Vice Adm. Takagi paid, on the spot, with their lives, for the failure of the First Air Fleet and the submarines of the Sixth Fleet, respectively. Neither Admiral Toyoda, C-in-C of the Combined Fleet, nor Vice Adm. Ozawa, commander of the First Mobile Fleet, were officially blamed for the failure of Operation "A." Both remained in post; both would go on to lose another battle four months later—at Leyte Gulf.

Ozawa's battle report, dated 5 September 1944, was largely factual, although it included one odd formulation: "In all, it is certain that 4 or 5 [U.S.] aircraft carriers and 1 battleship were sunk or damaged, and it is not possible to assert that others did not blow up and sink." The number of American planes shot down in the naval battle was estimated at a total of 160.[47] In reality, no major American warship had been sunk or seriously damaged, and U.S. Navy losses in air-to-air combat had been about twenty-five planes.

A more rational and comprehensive Japanese analysis was made of why the "A" Operation had failed to bring about decisive victory, despite commitment of nearly all the resources of the Combined Fleet.[48] Relating to Ozawa's First Mobile Fleet, five points were enumerated: (1) The enemy attacked the Marianas sooner than expected; (2) Koga, who had prepared the basic plan (i.e. the "Z" Operation), had died and been replaced by Toyoda; (3) Training of air units was insufficient, and especially of carrier-based units;[49] (4) Surface units were insufficiently trained because of a shortage of supply ships and a lack of suitable anchorages;

(5) On the first day of the decisive battle, the First Mobile Fleet "committed the blunder of planning a long-range [i.e. outranging] attack." This last point was developed in another post-war analysis. "The gravest concern in this operation was that the pilots of the mobile force lacked sufficient training. The fact that such a long range attack . . . was planned in spite of this handicap meant assigning a mission far too great for the limited capability of the pilots, and this factor led to the failure of the operation."[50] Interestingly, neither of these reports directly commented on misleading reports by Vice Adm. Kakuta about the capabilities and successes of his First Air Fleet.[51] Another point not made in these reports, but made elsewhere on the Japanese side, was that the delay in deploying the First Mobile Fleet had been an important factor.[52]

As regards the land-based First Air Fleet, the Japanese analysis of Operation "A" stated that it had lost half of its aircraft in the response to the landing on Biak (which had taken place on 27 May). Planes and crews were lost in the transfer to the Netherlands Indies and the western Carolines, and then in attempts to return to the main battle area of the "A" Operation. It was also noted that heavy losses were suffered as a result of American air attacks on air bases in the Marianas, Carolines, and Bonins. As a result, only about 20 percent of the 1,644 planes (i.e. about 340 planes) in the First Air Fleet actually participated in the "A" Operation. Elsewhere in the report it was stated that "The reason for the failure and near self-destruction of the [First Air Fleet] was the tactical shortcomings of the command, the inadequate training of crew members and the lack of base facilities in the Mariana and Caroline Areas (either in time or material) [sic]."[53]

All of that was relevant and accurate, but fundamental points must be added in explaining the Philippine Sea defeat. The first was that the U.S. Navy had a great quantitative and qualitative superiority in aircraft and ships. The second was that the leaders of the Japanese Navy had based their strategy on a decisive battle that would defeat a major amphibious landing. As laid out in the captured "Z" Operations order, "The Combined Fleet . . . will bring to bear the combined maximum strength of all our forces to meet and destroy the enemy, and to maintain our hold on vital areas." This expectation was completely unrealistic in 1944.[54]

On the American side, of course, there was less cause for dissatisfaction. In his overall report to Admiral King in Washington, Nimitz stated that the outcome of the amphibious operation for the capture of Saipan had been "gratifyingly successful."[55] In terms of the naval battle, it is certainly the case that the air defense of TF 58 on 19 June—the "Turkey Shoot"—had been an outstanding success. The same can be said for deployment and performance of Lockwood's submarines, although that was underrated at the time and later. What might also be stressed here is that the Philippine Sea was for the U.S. forces a "combined-arms" battle. It involved an amphibious landing on an unprecedented scale for the Pacific theater. It involved carriers and carrier aircraft (above all, from TF 58), as well as land-based aviation. It involved a powerful submarine force. Last of all, it involved a powerful U.S. Navy surface force—battleships and cruisers—at least at the planning stage.[56]

On the other hand, the decision to launch the "mission beyond darkness" on 20 June, which required a nighttime recovery and led to the loss of nearly eighty planes, can certainly be questioned. Another general weakness revealed was the short range (325 miles) of American carrier-based scout planes, which made it impossible for any of them to actually sight the enemy fleet before the second afternoon of the battle.[57]

The biggest controversy about the Battle of the Philippine Sea related to Spruance's orders on the night of Sunday, 18/19 June. Mitscher wanted to advance to the west and get within range to attack the Japanese carriers. Spruance wanted to stay close to the Marianas to avoid an "end run" or a "flanking attack." Spruance's critics believed that TF 58 could have achieved a decisive victory along the lines of Midway, destroying the Japanese carrier fleet so that it could never challenge American forces again; such a victory might even have been a sufficient shock to bring the Japanese government to the peace table.

Spruance defended his orders in his Fifth Fleet "initial report," dated 13 July. "It was of the highest importance that our troops and transport forces on and in the vicinity of Saipan be protected and a circling movement by enemy fast forces be guarded against."[58]

American intelligence about Japanese intentions was based partly on the captured "Z" Operations documents. These indicated that attacks on the amphibious transport forces were a high priority for the enemy. The "fighting instructions" laid out a series of scenarios in which the target to be attacked was either a carrier task force or a "transport convoy." It was stated that "[T]he main objectives of the enemy's forces which must be destroyed are his transport convoys." This meant that "[i]f the enemy carriers and a transport convoy appear at the same time aim the full attack at the transport convoy" and "[i]f the enemy is accompanied by an occupation force, the greater part of our air strength would be directed to annihilating its transports and only sufficient attention would be paid to the carriers so to limit and hamper their use of airplanes." The sequencing of the attack was also laid out: "If the enemy has an occupation force as well as a task force, the normally recognized procedure would be to strike heavily at a large number of carriers in a dusk or night attack and then direct the main attack the following morning against the [transport] convoy."[59]

In his own report, dated 11 September 1944, three months after the battle, Mitscher made a strong case for the course of action that he had suggested late on 18 June. In particular he queried the threat of an "end run." This query was based partly on the availability of other U.S. Navy forces that would provide close cover for Saipan, including the escort carriers, old battleships, cruisers, and destroyers. More important, he noted,

> Even the slight possibility of damage to our landing forces could be avoided if the [U.S.] Fast Carrier Task Forces [sic] did not go more than 300 miles from the Marianas ... for we could attack a [Japanese] diversionary force as easily from a position 300 miles west (downwind) of the Marianas as we could from the near vicinity of Saipan.[60]

When Mitscher laid out the overall consequences of the action, including the air strike on 20 June, he included a strongly implied criticism: "The enemy had escaped. He had been badly hurt by one aggressive carrier air strike, *at the one time he was within range* [my emphasis]. His fleet was not sunk."[61]

Spruance's "endorsement" of Mitscher's report dismissed the proposal that he (Spruance) should have done something different on the morning of 19 June: "The opinion expressed in the narrative that the covering force should have proceeded earlier to the westward [on 19 June] in search of the approaching Japanese forces *is not concurred with* [my emphasis]." He also referred back to his own initial report of 13 July.[62]

Admiral Nimitz's opinion on this controversy was important. During the battle itself, according to Nimitz's biographer, the admiral refused to go against Spruance's decisions. Vice Adm. John Towers (Deputy CincPac) wanted Nimitz to order Spruance to move to the west to shorten the range and reduce the advantage the enemy gained through shuttle bombing; Nimitz refused to send such an order on the grounds that this would be an unwarranted intrusion in the decisions of his fleet commander.[63]

Later on CincPac came down very much on the side of Spruance, notably in his overall report on the Marianas battle. Writing to King, he stressed the extremely positive results: "The operation quickly evoked reaction from the major portion of the Japanese Fleet, which risked itself in an action against our covering forces. As a result the Japanese Fleet suffered a severe defeat, and only circumstances most fortunate for it, prevented a major disaster to its forces."[64] Above all, he thoroughly approved Spruance's caution:

[F]or our fleet to go very far to the west while the enemy fleet was still unlocated and intact meant jeopardising the task for which our combatant fleet and carriers were out there, namely the protection of our Expeditionary Forces and the landing on Saipan,

This basic fact cannot be ignored or minimized. There is no objective exposed more temptingly to attack than an amphibious expedition, particularly in its early critical stages . . . It comprises a vast number of transports and other types which are deficient in speed, compartmentation, and anti-aircraft fire as compared to combatant vessels . . . As an even greater factor of vulnerability, this shipping objective is definitely pinned down in location . . .

Thus, to have kept his carriers beyond our air range and made an "end around" run from the northwest or southwest with part or all of his carrier air groups, striking our shipping in the vicinity of Saipan without interference from the air forces of Task Force 58, would have netted the Japanese far more than did their actual attack on Task Force 58. It might not have prevented our occupation of the Marianas eventually, but it would certainly have slowed it up and caused a considerable disruption of all our plans throughout the Pacific Areas. It might have aroused outcry in the press and among the public at home, since anything in the nature of being surprised or outwitted or of failing to protect what we should protect against seems more blameworthy than losses in a regular engagement. To guard against any such possibilities, Task Force 58 had to be not only merely within easy two-way flight range of Saipan, but close enough to intercept any attack, since the further west our carriers lay, the more chance had the enemy of evading them and striking the shipping unloading at Saipan.[65]

As Admiral Nimitz put it, "Hindsight is notably cleverer than fore-sight."[66] Nevertheless, it is worth considering what would have happened if Spruance had accepted Mitscher's proposal, and reversed the direction of Task Force 58 at 0130 on 19 June. The task force would have had to release several deckload strikes of attack aircraft against an enemy force on the morning of the 19th. The precise location of the elements of that force might well not have been not known at first. At the same time the Japanese had a good idea of the location of the task groups of TF 58, based on their air searches. The American fighter force would have been divided between escorting attack strikes and providing CAP cover over the task groups. American carrier operations would have been complicated by the need to launch and recover large waves of strike aircraft, while also trying to launch and recover CAP planes. In addition the details of the actual air attack on the Japanese fleet in the late afternoon of 20 June suggest that an attack on 19 June might not have been an overwhelming success, especially if interceptors from *Taihō* and *Shōkaku* had been available.

In any event, the Battle of the Philippine Sea was certainly an American victory, if not as complete as Midway. As Nimitz reported, "The exchange of carrier based air attacks on 19 and 20 June was an outstanding, perhaps epochal, event in naval warfare to date." It would also be the last of a remarkable series of carrier-versus-carrier battles fought in World War II.[67]

AFTERMATH IN THE MARIANAS

Spruance and Mitscher may not have wiped out the entire Japanese fleet, but thanks to the air battle and submarine attack on 19 June it had been mortally wounded. In addition they had protected the Saipan landing force, prevented any further intervention by Japanese air and sea forces from outside the Marianas, and isolated Tinian and Guam, vital strategic islands that would be in American hands within eight weeks.

On the second day of the sea/air battle, 20 June (D+5 of FORAGER), the three American divisions ashore on Saipan completed their drive to gain control of most of the flat southern part of the island.[68] They then pivoted around to begin a steady advance north, where the strategically located high point of Topotchau was taken on the 27th. The following Sunday (2 July) the main town, Garapan on the west coast, fell to the Marines. Japanese Army units, cut off from their supplies, were now squeezed into the northwestern part of the island. In the end, on the night of 6/7 July (Friday), Lt Gen. Saitō ordered a final mass attack (what the Americans called a "Banzai charge"). This was the largest such onslaught that would take place in the whole Pacific War, and it was a failure. Two days later, on the 8th, Saipan was declared "secure," after a three-week ground battle. On 17 July, Admiral Nimitz from Hawaii and Admiral King from Washington flew in to inspect the battlefield.

The fall of Saipan also wiped out the headquarters of the Japanese Central Pacific Area Fleet, formerly located at Garapan. Its commander, Nagumo Chūichi, committed suicide on the evening of 6 July. Spruance later reported this development in a letter home:

One thing that has appealed to me most in this operation was the end of the Saipan commander, Vice Admiral Nagumo. He is the gentleman who commanded the Jap Fleet on December 7th, 1941 and again at Midway. After Midway he went ashore to Sasebo [sic] and then came here in May. Three strikes and out.[69]

The headquarters of the Sixth Fleet, the Japanese submarine command, had also been at Garapan. On 24 June, Combined Fleet headquarters had ordered that Vice Adm. Takagi and his staff be rescued. The giant submarine *I-10* set out to take off the Sixth Fleet staff, but she was unable to break through American anti-submarine patrols and was sunk 100 miles east of Saipan on 4 July. Takagi died, marooned on Saipan, apparently on the 8th.[70]

The fall of Saipan had a profound political effect in Tokyo, which was also indicative of the importance of TF 58 and the Battle of the Philippine Sea.[71] The losses of ships and aircraft in the naval battle could to some extent be concealed, but not the resultant fall of strategic Saipan. Nevertheless, in Japan the news was held back for nearly two weeks, until 19 July. General Tōjō Hideki, who had accumulated so much power since becoming prime minister in October 1941, was finally forced to resign on 21 July, along with his entire cabinet (including Navy Minister Shimada). Tōjō had lost the approval of the Emperor and the elder statesmen (*jushin*) who advised him. This was to be the most striking political development in the Japanese government before the August 1945 surrender.

The American interrogation teams working in occupied Japan after the war concluded that these events had been of the greatest importance: "Almost unanimously, informed Japanese considered Saipan as the decisive battle of the war and its loss as ending all hope of a Japanese victory."[72] One prominent example was Admiral Nagano, former Chief of the Naval General Staff. After the war, under American interrogation, he was asked at what point, in his personal opinion, the turning point had been reached. Nagano replied: "When we lost Saipan, 'Hell is on us.'"[73]

The loss of Tinian and Guam followed, inevitably, after the defeat of Saipan. Tinian lay only 3 miles south of Saipan.[74] With flatter terrain than Saipan, and an area roughly two-thirds the size, Tinian also had a smaller Japanese garrison (a brigade of 8,000 men). On 24 July, the 2nd and 4th Marine divisions crossed over to Tinian in a "shore-to-shore" operation. The Americans landed on an unexpected beach. Admiral

Spruance, who approved the attack plan, later concluded that the capture of Tinian was "the most brilliantly conceived and executed amphibious operation of the War."[75] In less than a week the island was declared secured. Only 290 American troops were lost in the battle.

The final stage in the Marianas campaign was the invasion of Guam.[76] The former American possession was 30 miles long, and more than four times the area of Saipan. W-Day finally came on 21 July, five weeks later than originally planned. The original Marine landing force earmarked for Guam had been committed to Saipan, as had the overall reserve force consisting of an Army division. The training of a second Army force, the new 77th Infantry Division, and its transport from the Hawaiian Islands, had taken some time to complete.

The Orote peninsula was a key position on Guam. Jutting out to the west of the island, it commanded Apra Harbor (to the north) and contained the main Japanese airfield. The Americans landed north and south of Orote to trap the enemy there. This followed a record thirteen-day bombardment by U.S. Navy ships, the longest "shoot" in the Pacific War. Fighting on the beaches was heavy, and in the north the 3rd Marine Division was hemmed in, with high ground in front of it. (This was the last island battle where the Japanese attempted to destroy the invaders at the landing area.) The main Japanese counterattack—delayed—came on the night of 25/26 July. There was a coordinated general assault against the northern beachhead, and to the south an attempt to break the blockade of Orote. Both of these attacks failed. The Marines then advanced west into the peninsula. By 29 July the airfield had been taken, and a ceremony was held in the nearby ruins of the old U.S. Marine barracks, in the presence of Admiral Spruance. At 1530 the American flag was raised again over Guam.

The forces from the northern and southern American beachheads had joined hands on 28 July. They then moved inland to defeat the Japanese forces, which were now scattered over the wooded northern part of the island. Guam No. 2 (Tiyan) airfield, from which the air attack against TF 58 off Saipan on 15 June had been launched, was overrun on the morning of 2 August. Probably not by chance this was also the recorded date of the death of Vice Adm. Kakuta, commander of the First Air Fleet, and his chief of staff, Capt. Miwa Kazuo.

Guam was declared secure on 10 August. This was the day Admiral Nimitz arrived on the island. General Obata was killed in fighting on the morning of the 11th; the commander of the Thirty-First Army died at his command post near Mount Mataguac, 17 miles northeast of Apra Harbor. There were some 10,000 Japanese stragglers ("enemy remnants") at large on the big island, but organized resistance was over.[77]

The hopes that the Imperial Army could hold the islands—or make their capture unacceptably costly for the Americans—even with a lack of local naval power, turned out to be unfounded. Total Japanese losses on the three islands were 50,000 men, core forces comprising thirty infantry battalions in two Army divisions and the two Army independent brigades, as well as a naval Base Force.

For the Americans the land battle for the Marianas cost some 4,600 men killed, mostly marines. Losses were higher than expected,[78] and higher than for other Central Pacific battles at Kwajalein, Eniwetok, and Makin, and even at Tarawa. On the other hand, much larger forces were involved, on both sides, over a much larger area. The main fighting lasted for six or seven weeks, rather than two or three days, as had been the case on the Pacific atolls.[79]

The capture of the Marianas was decisive for the outcome of the Pacific War. Under Nimitz's formal command, as C-in-C of the POA, huge air bases for the B-29 "very heavy bomber" (VHB) were developed in the Marianas—one on Saipan, two on Tinian, and two on Guam. Each base could accommodate a "wing" of B-29s (each wing contained several groups). The first B-29 landed on Isley Field (a greatly enlarged Aslito airfield) on Saipan in October 1944.[80] The first (high-altitude) B-29 raid on Tokyo took place in November. B-29s from Tinian carried out the atomic-bomb attacks on Hiroshima and Nagasaki in August 1945.

On 26 August 1944, Task Force 58 ceased to exist. Two weeks had passed since the end of organized Japanese resistance in the Marianas. The Fifth Fleet was redesignated as the Third Fleet; Task Force 58 became Task Force 38. Raymond Spruance and his Fifth Fleet staff handed over their responsibilities to Bill Halsey. As Halsey described the change, "Instead of using the stagecoach system of keeping the drivers and changing the horses, we changed the drivers and kept the horses. It was hard on the horses, but it was effective."[81]

There were significant differences between the two organizations. Spruance's fleet had included a large amphibious force, as well as Task Force 58. Halsey's main force was now essentially just the fast carriers of Task Force 38. Mitscher's role was to some extent redundant, although he remained under Halsey as commander of TF 38 until 30 October 1944, when Vice Adm. John McCain took over. In any event, the Task Force 58 designation would be revived when Spruance returned to replace Halsey in command of a revived Fifth Fleet on 26 January 1945; Mitscher came back to Task Force 58 at the same time, replacing McCain. But that is another story.

CHAPTER 10

SUPREMACY AT SEA

ENDING THE PACIFIC WAR

Under Admiral Bill Halsey the newly activated Third Fleet, and the redesignated Task Force 38, took part in a series of battles in the Western Pacific. In late 1944 the most important of these was the amphibious invasion of the Philippines, which led in October to the Battle of Leyte Gulf.

That battle and the June 1944 Battle of the Philippine Sea have been compared more than once. Leyte Gulf is better known; it was the larger battle and saw more destruction of Japanese warships and higher American losses. On the other hand, the enemy carrier striking force—ships, planes, trained aircrew—had been effectively shattered four months earlier, on 19–20 June. In addition, the Marianas turned out to be of greater strategic importance as an objective than the Philippines. Saipan and Tinian had greater political weight for the Tokyo government, and they provided (with Guam) a base for the long-range bombing of the Japanese cities.

The situation in the Philippines was confused by a flawed command structure. The Marianas battle was certainly better run, despite the escape of part of the enemy fleet.[1] Spruance had had overall control of both Vice Adm. Turner's amphibious landing on Saipan (mainly a Marine operation) and the covering operation of Mitscher's TF 58. The Leyte invasion was largely an Army operation, with Kinkaid and the

Seventh Fleet in charge of planning the amphibious element and its immediate naval support. Halsey and his Third Fleet only provided a naval covering force, mainly in the form of the fast carriers of TF 38.

Halsey, eager for a decisive battle, was lured away by a Japanese decoy fleet approaching from the north. Believing Spruance's excessive caution had led him to a miss a vital opportunity in the Philippine Sea, Halsey had prevailed on Admiral Nimitz to insert a key sentence in his orders: "In case opportunities for destruction of [a] major portion of the enemy fleet is offered or can be created, such destruction becomes the primary task."[2] Poor communications between Halsey and Kinkaid allowed the Japanese to slip a large battleship-cruiser force in between them (in exactly the kind of "end run" that Spruance had warned against in June 1944). Mitscher was still present, commanding TF 38, but Halsey, as commander of Third Fleet, made all the (mistaken) decisions. Mitscher did not question Halsey's actions, just as he had not immediately countered Spruance's cautious orders off Saipan in June. Only the great disparity of strength between the two fleets and the overall impracticality of the Japanese plan made possible the ultimate American victory.

However they are compared, the Central Pacific fighting and the liberation of the Philippines, both in 1944, had more in common with one another than either campaign had with earlier fighting in 1942, or with the final battles close to Japan in 1945. In 1942 the Japanese held the initiative for most of the year and operations were conducted by their "first team."[3] Even the counterattacks of the Japanese fleet around Guadalcanal came near success—exemplified by the battle of Santa Cruz. The U.S. was still fighting with its pre-war Navy. Despite a sensational victory at Midway, Nimitz's battle fleet was weaker at the end of 1942 than it had been at the beginning. Losses of ships were high, and the number of U.S. Navy personnel killed in action in that year was 8,900.[4]

In 1944 it was the U.S. forces that were on the offensive, and the Japanese that were attempting to hold a defensive perimeter. In the Marianas the Japanese Navy deployed warships and land-based planes to fight what its admirals hoped would be a decisive battle against a carrier fleet covering a major amphibious operation. In the Philippines the objective was the American amphibious force itself, not the destruction of Halsey's carrier fleet. In both cases the Japanese land-based air groups were located at a relatively small number of forward airfields, even in the occupied Philippines. It was possible for Mitscher's fast carriers to "smother" them (Spruance's description) and put them out of action in a fairly short period of time. Other operations blocked Japanese air reinforcement routes, what Spruance called "air pipe lines," through Formosa and the Bonin Islands. The few surviving planes that approached the perimeter of the task force from carriers and land bases were repelled by radar-controlled fighters and heavy AA fire.[5]

What made the difference in 1944 was the rapidly growing strength of the U.S. Navy in new warships, and new aircraft. Another central feature was low losses. The potential for loss was still there, with the sinking of the first new fast carrier in the form of CVL *Princeton*, attacked by a single land-based Judy dive bomber in October 1944 (and in 1945 the loss of the unescorted cruiser *Indianapolis*, sunk by a submarine in July).[6] But losses in 1944 were only 5,500 men, and as the number of U.S. naval personnel in the Pacific was now so great this represented a much lower proportion of the whole.[7]

In turn, what happened in the near approaches to Japan in 1945 was very different from 1944. Admiral Spruance returned to his command post (relieving Halsey) in February 1945, and the reactivated Fifth Fleet took part in the invasions of Iwo Jima and Okinawa and carrier air strikes against the Japanese mainland. Allied strength was greater than ever before. By August 1945, when the war ended, no fewer than ten additional "Essex" class carriers had joined the seven that had been with the fleet in the critical first half of 1944.[8] They were joined by four recently built British "armored" fleet carriers. Meanwhile, Japanese surface naval units were largely unable to take part. The grotesque exception was the "death run" of the super-battleship *Yamato* toward Okinawa in April 1945. In the spring and summer, the surviving ships of the Combined Fleet were picked off in their home ports by carrier air strikes.

The dominant new feature of air warfare was the kamikaze, what the Americans called the "suicide" attack, now carried out on an operational scale.[9] In addition to bizarre tactics, however, the enemy was now able to operate from a large number of air bases in the Japanese mainland; there was no pipeline of reinforcements that could be interdicted. They had a much larger force than they had used in the Central Pacific or the Philippines in 1944. The enemy suicide crews were often poorly trained and organized, and they were usually flying obsolete planes, but their dispersed raids gave some ability to flood the air defenses of the Americans and to achieve precision hits. One-way missions also gave the kamikazes greater range, albeit at a high cost in pilots and aircraft.

The number of U.S. Navy personnel killed in action in the last seven months of the war against Japan was nearly twice that of the twelve months of 1944; losses in 1945 were 9,600 personnel. In the battle after the invasion of Okinawa, some 3,800 American naval personnel were killed, many of them in the thirteen destroyers sunk by kamikazes.[10] Vice Adm. Mitscher himself was caught up in the deadly fighting. *Bunker Hill*, his flagship in TF 58, was hit by two bomb-carrying kamikazes off Okinawa on 11 May 1945. Nearly 400 of the ship's crew were killed. Mitscher was not wounded but he, Arleigh Burke, and other survivors of the TF 58 staff had to transfer to *Enterprise*. Three days later, *Enterprise* in turn was a hit by another suicide plane. Fortunately, loss of life was much smaller, but Mitscher was forced to move from the damaged carrier to *Randolph* (a new "Essex" class).[11]

The kamikazes were a desperate expedient, but despite causing heavy losses of U.S. personnel and inflicting heavy damage to some carriers and their screening destroyers, they did not sink any conventional armored warships. In the words of the British historian H. P. Willmott, "Allied sailors who fought in order to live were more than a match for airmen who died in order to fight."[12]

The U.S. Navy, led by the fast carriers, had achieved naval supremacy. Whether the war could have been won by naval blockade is unknown; also impossible to predict is the course and outcome of an invasion. The Japanese finally surrendered after atomic bombs were dropped on two of their cities, and after the Soviet Union entered the war. But sea power was surely the core of the struggle. As Spruance later put it, speaking in London in 1946, "[I]n the Pacific the vast extent of that ocean and the fact that Japan was defeated without our having to land a single soldier on her shores should leave the role of sea power clear to all."[13] The surrender document was signed on the veranda deck of the new battleship *Missouri* in Tokyo Bay on 2 September. General MacArthur presided. Admirals Nimitz and Halsey were present. Raymond Spruance was in Manila working on plans for the occupation of Japan, and Pete Mitscher was already back in Washington.

POST-WAR

In 1945 things changed, including the leadership of the U.S. Navy. It was a new political era in Washington after the death of President Roosevelt in April 1945 and his replacement by Harry Truman. Roosevelt had been a great friend of the Navy, Truman less so. It was the end of the Old Navy too. Fleet Admiral King, now aged sixty-six, stepped down as C-in-C of the U.S. Navy and CNO in December 1945; Truman would later describe him as a "crusty martinet" with whom he had "difficulties."[14] In any event, King suffered a serious stroke in 1947 and died in 1956.

King's replacement was Fleet Admiral Nimitz, who served for two years, although neither Truman nor Secretary of the Navy Forrestal had been keen on another powerful professional along the lines of King.[15] Although he had worked ashore in headquarters at Pearl Harbor and Guam, Nimitz as CincPac had surely been one of naval history's greatest commanders, responsible in no small measure for the American triumph over the Japanese. Admiral Spruance briefly, in November 1945, moved up to the CincPac post, replacing Nimitz when the latter moved to Washington. In February 1946, as he turned sixty, he was appointed to the post he really wanted, returning to Newport, Rhode Island, as President of the Naval War College.

The five-star rank of "Fleet Admiral" had been established before the end of the war, in December 1944, when Admirals Leahy, King, and Nimitz were promoted. Halsey was awarded this rank a year later, in December 1945.[16] Before he returned to American waters in October 1945, Halsey had requested that he be put on the retired list, in order to open the higher commands to younger officers. Spruance did not receive the same rank as his old friend, although Nimitz urged his (Spruance's) promotion. According to legislation there could be only four Fleet Admirals. Spruance later stated his own view, put forward with typical grace: "So far as my getting five star rank is concerned, if I could have had it along with Bill Halsey, that would have been fine; but, if I had received it instead of Bill Halsey, I would have been very unhappy over it."[17]

Whether Halsey or Spruance was a better commander overall is a point worthy of discussion, although Halsey has played only a minor role in this book. Various factors explain Halsey's promotion to the rank of fleet admiral, including his popularity with the American public. *The Quiet Warrior*, the title of Buell's biography of Spruance, contrasts the subject of his work with the "unquiet" Halsey, who relished publicity in a way that Spruance definitely did not. A better justification for Halsey was that he had held high (and highly visible) command posts throughout the war. He led some of the carrier raids of early 1942. Above all, he took over and won the South Pacific campaign in 1942–43 (despite the early defeat at Santa Cruz). In the second half of 1944 and early 1945, as commander of the Third Fleet, he oversaw the strikes of Task Force 38 across the western Pacific. On the other hand, "The Bull"—as the press nicknamed him—made mistakes. In addition to the serious miscalculation and confusion at Leyte Gulf, he was formally judged responsible for losses suffered by his Third Fleet in typhoons during December 1944 and June 1945.

The commander of the Fifth Fleet was very different. As his biographer Thomas Buell put it, "Spruance remained almost unknown to the American public at war's end. He was shy and reticent and avoided publicity." The naval historian Arthur Marder described him as "a highly respected but in no way charismatic admiral."[18] Spruance was also not an impressive public speaker. However, he was intelligent, and had a masterful understanding of a naval strategy and operations. He was efficient and worked better with his staff (notably Capt. Carl Moore) and subordinates than did Halsey. King's assessment of Spruance, when comparing him with Halsey for fleet-admiral promotion, was: "As to brains, the best man in every way."[19]

In November 1946 Spruance addressed the Royal United Services Institute (RUSI) in London. His host introduced him as "an officer, so rarely found, who has studied his profession on the high academic plane and, at the same time, has proved himself to be one of the greatest sea commanders of our time." Spruance was—perhaps inevitably—a "battleship" admiral, but he adapted to profound changes in naval technology. In his RUSI lecture he identified "the net increase in strength of our carrier air force" as one of three things essential for victory in the Pacific:

> With the large number of carriers which began to become available in the Summer of 1943, we were able to have a real strategic air force—one which had great strength and great mobility. Its strength became so great that, not only could it overwhelm Japanese island outposts, but eventually, supported by the guns of the fast battleships, cruiser and destroyers, it was able to go repeatedly to the coasts of Japan itself.

But Spruance also noted that the "carrier air force" would not have been successful without two other elements: improvement of amphibious capability and "capacity to give the logistic support to maintain our Fleet at ever increasing distances."[20] From his years in the War College he undoubtedly understood the importance of decisive battles, but he was also a master of base-building and logistics.

At an operational/tactical level, Spruance's relationship with Mitscher was probably healthier than that of Halsey, after TF 58 became TF 38. Spruance gave Mitscher his head after Kwajalein and only assumed "tactical command" at critical moments. Halsey put Mitscher (and later Vice Adm. John McCain) in a clearly subordinate role. Historians criticize Spruance for only one decision, holding back TF 58 to cover Saipan on 18 June 1944, rather than putting Mitscher in a position to attack the Japanese carrier force. That decision has been discussed at length in the previous chapter; if it was a mistake, it was compensated by results—the near annihilation of Japanese carrier air groups, the sinking of two out of three big Japanese carriers, and the successful development of the land battle on Saipan. This was achieved by sensible tactics and an element of good luck.

Admiral Spruance left the Navy after his stint at the War College, but in 1952–55 he served as ambassador to the newly independent

Philippines. After that followed a long retirement at Pebble Beach on the Monterey Peninsula. Nimitz had arranged that he, Spruance, and Kelly Turner would be buried in Golden Gate National Cemetery at San Bruno, overlooking San Francisco Bay, along with Charles Lockwood, the commander of the Submarine Force. Turner passed away first, in 1961, Nimitz himself—following a stroke—in 1966, and Lockwood in 1967. Spruance was the last; he died in December 1969 after suffering the consequences of arteriosclerosis. These were the four victors of the Pacific War. None of them were aviators.

Mitscher's post-war path was somewhat different. The admiral with the wizened face and the lobsterman's hat gave the impression of being a taciturn man of action. He claimed that he had learned what he needed to know while serving in the fleet and in naval aviation and directing their operations, without needing the theoretical (and battleship-centered) training of the War College. Actually, Mitscher was only fifty-eight when the war ended, and he had had plentiful experience in Washington. A favorite of Secretary of the Navy Forrestal, he was appointed Deputy Chief of Naval Operations for Air—DCNO (Air)— in June 1945, under King and then Nimitz.[21] On 11 August 1945, when the surrender was imminent, Mitscher issued a press release boasting that "carrier supremacy defeated Japan." He admitted that winning the "Battle of the Pacific" had been done as part of as "air-surface-ground team." On the other hand, and anticipating a bureaucratic storm that was about to break out with full force in Washington, he noted that "[t]his could not have been done by a separate air force, exclusively based ashore, or by one not under direct Navy control."[22] The conflict in the Navy, between the "battleship admirals" and the aviators, was about to become one between the Navy and an independent Air Force.

In any event, Mitscher then went to sea again in March 1946 with the Eighth Fleet, which was the carrier striking force of the Atlantic Fleet. In September 1946 he became C-in-C of the whole Atlantic Fleet (CincLant). Unfortunately his health now declined, after a diagnosis of chronic appendicitis. In January 1947 he suffered a heart attack and was told he would not be returned to active duty. He died of heart failure on 3 February at the Naval Hospital at Norfolk, Virginia.

Mitscher had been, without doubt, the most successful of the air admirals.[23] (Vice Adm. John McCain, Mitscher's rival as fast-carrier task force commander, enjoyed an even shorter life after VJ-Day. He attended the surrender ceremony aboard *Missouri* on 2 September 1945, but died in California four days later; the cause of death was a heart attack brought on by extreme exhaustion.)

The size of the Navy declined rapidly. From 3,406,000 personnel in 1945, the total fell to 530,000 in 1947. The numbers would surge during the Korean and Vietnam wars, but in fiscal year 2022 there were 346,000 personnel on active duty, about the same as that during the 1941 build-up.[24] As the officers and enlisted personnel of the fleet departed, the number of vessels in service shrank. Newer ships were "mothballed," older ones were scrapped, beginning with those built before the war. At the same time a number of the new ships under construction were scrapped on the building ways or put immediately into reserve. Of the very large number of "Essex" class carriers, all those that had taken part in the war were laid up in reserve, mostly in 1947. When the Korean War broke out in June 1950, only four, all completed post-war, were in active service.[25]

Among those ships scrapped, albeit in the late 1950s, was the veteran *Enterprise*. This took place despite a campaign (involving Halsey) to preserve the carrier as a museum and memorial in Washington. (Moving forward in time, a remarkable number of the ships involved in the Central Pacific campaign *were* eventually preserved as museum ships. These include carriers *Hornet*, *Intrepid*, *Lexington*, and *Yorktown*, fast battleships *Alabama*, *Iowa*, *Massachusetts*, *New Jersey*, and *North Carolina*, and a number of smaller vessels.[26])

The development of the U.S. Navy, and especially the carrier force, went through a peculiar and turbulent period at the end of the 1940s, which was a time of international tension and (in America) economic recession. Factors involved included debates about U.S. nuclear weapons and a reduction in the overall defense budget. President Truman's political attempts to rationalize expenditure and to reduce pervasive inter-service rivalry had the short-term effect of worsening the latter. The National Security Act (July 1947) provided for a stronger, more formal Joint Chiefs of Staff (JSC) structure, established a Secretary of Defense at Cabinet level, and created a U.S. Air Force (USAF), independent of the Army.[27]

James Forrestal, the first Secretary of Defense, was a friend of the Navy; he had served as Undersecretary and then Secretary of the Navy during the war. Forrestal struggled to make the new system work and then fell out politically with the President. He was removed in March 1949 after Truman won the 1948 election; Forrestal's replacement in the Cabinet was Louis A. Johnson, a political supporter of Truman. Secretary Johnson supported the new USAF and its strategic bombing strategy, and questioned the utility of conventional forces in the atomic era. Forrestal, ousted from office, exhausted and suffering from depression, committed suicide two months later.

As it happened, one of the most significant issues of the time was carrier procurement. In April 1949, Secretary Johnson had abruptly terminated construction of the super-carrier *United States* (CVA-58), which had just been laid down at Newport News. The 66,000-ton ship was specifically designed to launch strategic nuclear strikes against land targets. The decision, and the way it had been handled, led the Secretary of the Navy to resign. Strong dissatisfaction developed in the U.S. Navy leadership over the carrier decision, and over Johnson's funding of a USAF strategic bomber, the Convair B-36. Polemical stories circulated about the ambition of the USAF to take over all aviation matters in the armed forces and the aspiration of Army to take over the functions of the Marine Corps. Six months after the carrier cancellation, what *Time* magazine labeled as "The Revolt of the Admirals" broke out, in connection with Congressional hearings held in October 1949.[28] A number of senior officers spoke or had statements presented, including Admirals King, Nimitz, Halsey, Spruance, and Kinkaid. They defended the Navy, criticized the USAF strategy based on atomic bombing, and resisted the extremes of military unification. Admiral Louis Denfeld, CNO after Nimitz, was removed for his outspoken statements at the hearings, which opposed the decisions of Secretary of Defense Johnson and the chairman of the Joint Chiefs of Staff (Gen. Omar Bradley of the U.S. Army).[29]

Although the debate left scars, from the Navy's point of view some of the basic issues were soon resolved. Fast-developing external events were important: growing tension with Russia in Europe, the first testing of a Soviet nuclear device (August 1949), and the final victory of the Chinese Communists (October 1949). A new defense policy was taking shape, based on conventional as well as nuclear forces, and embodied in the secret policy document NSC-68 (April 1950). This won presidential support in June 1950 with the outbreak of the Korean War, and the turn toward *militarized* containment quickly followed. Korea demonstrated the continuing value of conventional forces in Cold War conflict; aircraft carriers supported ground troops, and a decisively successful amphibious operation was mounted at Inchon. Future conflict would evidently involve non-nuclear confrontation with the Russians and the Chinese on the oceanic periphery of Eurasia, in the Atlantic, the Mediterranean, and the western Pacific.

The Navy had already been brought back into the fold. Denfeld was replaced in October 1949, but by a naval aviator who had the confidence of both Truman and most of the admirals. This was Forrest Sherman, who had been recommended to Truman by Fleet Admiral Nimitz. Sherman had been CO of *Wasp* (CV-7) in 1942, and after that deputy chief of staff in the Pacific to Vice Adm. Towers (as ComAirPac) and then to Nimitz (from November 1943). Admirals Radford and Burke had been involved in the 1949 "revolt" and the resistance to comprehensive service unification, but after President Eisenhower was inaugurated in 1953 they held very senior posts. Radford, an aviator who had commanded carrier task groups in the Pacific under Spruance and Halsey, became chairman of the Joint Chiefs of Staff for four years after August 1953. Arleigh Burke, Mitscher's chief of staff during 1944–45 in the fast-carrier task force, became the CNO in August 1955 and served for two terms.[30]

EIGHTY YEARS OF NAVAL SUPREMACY

It was in the first half of 1944 that the U.S. Navy advanced across the Central Pacific and decisively defeated the main force of the Japanese Combined Fleet. Less obvious at the time, this was also when the United States overtook Britain as the supreme sea power. As Arthur Marder put it: "War . . . taught Britain and Japan the limits to their power. However abundantly displayed, bravery was never enough."[31] In the first six months of 1944, Task Force 58 had shown itself to be much the most powerful naval battle force in the world, defeating Japan and overtaking Britain. Three-quarters of a century later, the United States still retained naval supremacy.

The Battle of Trafalgar in 1805 resulted in the decisive defeat of a Franco-Spanish battle fleet. As the British naval historian N. M. Rodger has put it: "At the end of the [Trafalgar] campaign Britain had an unchallenged command of the sea, in quantity and quality, material and psychological over all her actual or potential enemies, which she had never known before."[32] The same thing could be said about the United States after the Central Pacific campaign of 1944, and the decisive Battle of the Philippine Sea.

The United States had only begun to develop a significant ocean-going battle fleet in the 1890s. When the First World War began in August 1914 the Royal Navy had on hand twenty-two dreadnought battleships and nine battle cruisers. The U.S. Navy consisted of only ten dreadnoughts (and no battle cruisers). In the 1922 Washington Treaty Britain accepted parity with the United States in capital ships to avoid an expensive building "race," but when World War II began Britain's maritime resources were still superior. The Royal Navy possessed a more balanced fleet, and the British overseas empire was huge, providing a global base system; the British "merchant navy" was the world's largest, and the shipbuilding industry was diminished but still a world leader.

When war came, Britain began to buckle under the challenge, but nevertheless the Royal Navy played a central part in the war effort. Despite the unexpected defeat of France in 1940, the Royal Navy was able—at high cost in ships and men—to deal with the German and Italian Navies and develop a system of global Imperial support. The entry of the Soviet Union and the United States into the war and the distraction of German forces made it possible to maintain effective sea control. The Royal Navy dominated the North Atlantic, defeating the German U-boat fleet. It developed "combined" (amphibious) operations and carried out successful landings in North Africa, Sicily, and southern Italy. But it would probably be fair to say that NEPTUNE, the

Normandy landing in June 1944, would be the last great effort of the Royal Navy. What it could not do was extend successful naval operations to Southeast Asia and the Pacific. Stephen Roskill, the official historian of the wartime Royal Navy, wrote about how the British were "trying to fight a five-ocean war with, at best, a two ocean Navy."[33]

Meanwhile, American warship construction accelerated rapidly, especially with the Two-Ocean Navy Act of June 1940. The U.S. Navy achieved overwhelming numerical superiority three or four years later. By the first half of 1944, eight modern battleships had been completed, compared to four surviving modern ships for the Royal Navy. Important above all was the presence of nine heavy carriers and nine light carriers (compared to only five modern carriers for the Royal Navy).[34] And naval power was no longer just warships. Especially important, in contrast with Britain, were advances in American naval aviation. This involved the development of a new type of navy in the form of the fast-carrier task force, supported by a well-equipped fleet train. For a number of reasons the British were unable to deploy anything comparable until the very end of the Pacific War.[35] The British Pacific Fleet of 1945 was a significant force operating off Okinawa and Japan, but it was essentially just one task group, compared to four or five American ones at sea in the same area.

The Royal Navy enjoyed residual strength for some decades as the second largest navy. By the 1970s, however, the naval build-up of the Soviet Union had overtaken it. As the late Eric Grove put it, the post-war decades saw "Britain's political and naval decision makers grappling with the intractable problems of too many commitments chasing too few resources."[36] By 1949, total British naval personnel were 144,000, about a third that of the (reduced) U.S. Navy; the current strength is about 30,000, less than a tenth.[37] Ironically, the Royal Navy ended up from the early 1970s being responsible for the most powerful strategic element of the British armed forces, in the form of a handful of nuclear-powered submarines (SSBNs) with Polaris and Trident ballistic missiles. Nevertheless, this deterrent force had been bought partly at the cost of conventional sea power.

As for the United States Navy, it remained the most powerful in the world. In addition to the ten "Essex" class that entered service between

July 1944 and August 1945, a further seven vessels were completed immediately *after* the war, bringing the overall total constructed to twenty-four. A very large number of cruisers, destroyers, and other surface vessels were also available, either on active service or in reserve.[38]

After the beginning of the Korean War the U.S. Navy began construction of four 61,000-ton carriers. The lead ship, significantly, was named *Forrestal* (CVA-59) in memory of the ill-fated Secretary of Defense. Laid down at Newport News in July 1952, three years after the canceled *United States*, she was commissioned in 1955. Meanwhile, a program had begun to modernize the wartime "Essex" class. In the mid-1950s, many of these were fitted with angled decks and steam catapults, enabling them to operate the larger and faster jets of the era.[39] Some would operate in the Gulf of Tonkin during the Vietnam War. The "Forrestal" class were followed by four similar "Kitty Hawk" class, commissioned in 1961–67. Meanwhile, a new *Enterprise* (CVA(N)-65), the first nuclear-powered super-carrier, was commissioned in 1961; she was a giant ship of 71,000 tons. *Enterprise* was followed over three decades by a class of ten 74,000-ton nuclear-powered "Nimitz" class super-carriers (CVN-68 to CVN-77), commissioned between 1975 and 2009; CVN-70 was named *Carl Vinson*, after the influential Congressman behind the Two-Ocean Navy Act of 1940. The first ship of a successor class, *Gerald R. Ford* (CVN-78), was laid down in 2009 and commissioned in 2017.[40]

The Navy's overall role did change and develop in the Cold War. Especially important, from the early 1960s, was a large new fleet of nuclear-powered ballistic-missile submarines (SSBNs), which operated as part of the nuclear deterrent force. Nevertheless, the super-carriers and their air groups remain a key means for the projection of the global power of the United States (and the military "containment" of Russia and China). The carriers were deployed supporting overseas operations or acting to deter Communist aggression in Europe or Asia; they could also protect maritime lines of communication.

What the U.S. Navy did *not* have to do was to fight—or even plan for—a "symmetrical" war against an enemy with a carrier fleet, as they had had to in 1942–44. The age of sailing ships and the "line of battle" lasted at least three centuries, the age of the armored steamship for about ninety years. The "era" of carrier-versus-carrier war lasted less than three years, from 1942 to 1944. The age of the decisive fleet battle between fleets had passed. In 1943–45, after they lost their brief carrier superiority at Midway, the Japanese attempted to counter the American carrier task forces with land-based aviation. Similar circumstances led their Cold War successors to attempt the same strategy, although technology had moved ahead. The main likely opponent, the USSR, developed an "anti-carrier" force, which used guided missiles carried by long-range bombers, surface ships, and submarines. Something similar underlay Chinese preparations.[41]

The post-war super-carriers became, from the 1950s, key symbols and instruments of American naval supremacy and "force projection." The carrier groups are still at the center of fleets that form a global system of power. The Sixth Fleet projects American power in the Mediterranean. The Seventh Fleet does the same in the western Pacific, as does the Second Fleet in the Atlantic. Most recently, since 1995, another naval force has exercised American power in the Indian Ocean, as part of Central Command. Designated the Fifth Fleet, it revives the force commanded by Admiral Raymond Spruance in the Central Pacific that, with Mitscher's Task Force 58 as its spearhead, had such a decisive impact fifty years earlier.[42]

THE FAST CARRIERS OF TF 58
JANUARY TO JUNE 1944

	Hull number	Builder	Laid down	Cmsn	Arrived Pearl H.	Air Group 1/44	Notes
Saratoga	CV-3	NYSB	9/20	11/27	pre-war	AG 12	Only present in Marshalls
Enterprise	CV-6	NN	7/34	5/38	pre-war	AG 10	
Essex	CV-9	NN	4/41	12/42	31/5/43	AG 9	Refitted San Francisco 3–4/44 AG 15 in 5/44
Independence	CVL-22	NYSB	4/41	1/43	20/7/43	AG 22	Dam. 11/43, under rep. to 7/44
Yorktown	CV-10	NN	12/41	4/43	24/7/43	AG 5	AG 1 in 3/44
Lexington	CV-16	BQ	7/41	2/43	9/8/43	AG 16	Dam. 12/43, under rep. to 3/44
Belleau Wood	CVL-24	NYSB	8/41	12/42	9/8/43	AG 4	
Princeton	CVL-23	NYSB	6/41	10/42	9/8/43	AG 23	
Cowpens	CVL-25	NYSB	11/41	1/43	19/9/43	AG 25	
Bunker Hill	CV-17	BQ	9/41	5/43	2/10/43	AG 17	AG 8 in 3/44
Monterey	CVL-26	NYSB	12/41	2/43	9/10/43	AG 28	
Cabot	CVL-28	NYSB	3/42	4/43	2/12/43	AG 31	
Langley	CVL-27	NYSB	4/42	8/43	25/12/43	AG 27	

Intrepid	CV-11	NN	12/41	8/43	10/1/44	AG 6	Dam. 2/44, under rep. to 6/44
Hornet	CV-12	NN	8/42	11/43	4/3/44	AG 2	
Bataan	CVL-29	NYSB	8/42	8/43	22/3/44	AG 50	
Wasp	CV-18	BQ	3/42	11/43	4/4/44	AG 14	
San Jacinto	CVL-30	NYSB	10/42	11/43	19/4/44	AG 51	

Carriers are listed in order of their first arrival at Pearl Harbor. CV = heavy carrier, CVL = light carrier. All CVs are "Essex" class except CV-3 and CV-6; all CVLs are "Independence" class. Shipyard abbreviations: BQ = Bethlehem Shipbuilding, Quincy MA (Fore River); NN = Newport News (Virginia); NYSB = New York Shipbuilding Corp. (Camden NJ).

Before December 1941, aircraft carriers were named after American historic battles (all on land) or after American historic warships. *Langley* (CVL-27) was an exception. She was named after the first American carrier (CV-1), which had been converted into a seaplane carrier (AV-3) and was sunk in February 1942; CV-1, in turn, had been named after aviation pioneer Samuel Langley.

THE OTHER SIDE OF THE OCEAN
Japanese Forces and Strategy

This book is the story of American operations, told from the viewpoint of the U.S. Navy in 1944. It tries to avoid relying too much on hindsight, i.e. on what was learned afterward about Japanese forces and strategy. This perspective also has the advantage of keeping a complex story simpler and shorter. In some respects it is also closer to "reality." Decisions and events are generally assessed on the basis of what American commanders actually knew *at the time* about the enemy's forces and strategy. Details of Japanese forces and actions have been provided in the notes. This information is not necessary for the basic narrative, but it gives the reader the option to follow developments in more specific detail. What follows here is a brief view of the situation, as a whole, from the Japanese side.[1]

The Allied Potsdam Declaration in July 1945 accurately described Japan as being "controlled by those self-willed militaristic advisers whose unintelligent ['and irrational'] calculations have brought the Empire of Japan to the threshold of annihilation."[2] Historians of today still—again accurately—assess the Japanese government as dysfunctional, with no clear political center, and with a military establishment both unchecked and deeply divided within itself (between the Army and Navy). An overall command structure did exist in the form of the Imperial General Headquarters (IGHQ), but the two armed services functioned independently within it.

The Japanese Empire had been fighting a full-scale war of aggression in China since June 1937. In 1941 the country's leaders made the "calculation," an "unintelligent" one indeed, to resolve the conflict by attacking Britain and the United States. They were also taking advantage of the successes of Nazi Germany in Europe, which had mortally wounded those European states with colonial holdings in Southeast Asia. The hope was that the conquests and operations of Germany (now allied with Italy) would at least preoccupy the Americans, British, and Russians. The Japanese core strategy at this point was to take over resource areas in Southeast Asia, as well as to establish military strongpoints there and in the Pacific. The "calculation" was that this vast regional advance would combine an essential resource base with an unassailable military position. Outside powers would eventually have to accept the regional supremacy of the Japanese Empire in Asia, even if those powers survived (or even won) the war with Germany.

In the first months of the "Pacific" war, stunning victories were achieved, both by the Army and the Navy. The "Hawaiian Operation," a daring carrier raid on Pearl Harbor, crippled the American fleet. Meanwhile, torpedo bombers based on land in Indochina sank the main units of the Royal Navy in Southeast Asia. In the winter of 1941–42, the Imperial Army and Navy worked successfully together in what was called the "Southern Operation." Malaya, the Philippines, Burma, and the Netherlands Indies were overrun, with weak and unprepared British, Dutch, and American forces overwhelmed.

For the Japanese, less territorial change of strategic importance occurred in the Central Pacific. The island Mandate, which the Japanese had held for twenty years in the Marshalls and the Carolines, remained the main defensive rampart. This front line in the Central Pacific was made even more secure by the capture of pre-war American positions behind it—the Philippines, Guam, and Wake. In the South Pacific the perimeter was extended by the capture, from the British Empire, of Rabaul and the Solomon and Gilbert islands. The Japanese Army only committed small elements to this Pacific advance, and the generals remained for a number of months concerned with other things: the ongoing war in China, consolidating new conquests in Southeast Asia (Burma), and preparing for a possible war with the Soviet Union.

The Japanese war leaders underestimated the martial spirit and the skill of their enemies. They had a tendency to exaggerate their own

successes and to conceal or minimize their own failures. As one perceptive British historian of the Pacific War put it, "All armed services of all
nations overstate their own effectiveness, but with the Japanese forces
this approached an art form that was increasingly divorced from reality."[3]

The administration of the Imperial Japanese Navy was conducted by the
Navy Ministry led by a Navy Minister (never a civilian) and the Naval
General Staff (NGS), both located in Tokyo. The main operational
force, directly subordinate to the Emperor, was the Combined Fleet
(*Rengō Kantai*). From 1939 to April 1943, Admiral Yamamoto Isoroku
served as C-in-C of the Combined Fleet. He was replaced by Admiral
Koga Mineichi from May 1943 to March 1944, and then by Admiral
Toyoda Soemu from the start of May 1944 to the end of the war.

The Combined Fleet was organized in numbered fleets.[4] The First
Fleet was originally the main battleship force, made up in 1941 of eight
vessels; *Yamato* and *Musashi*, two 65,000-ton super-battleships with
18-inch guns, were added in 1942. In 1942–43 most of the battleships
were kept in reserve, ready for a decisive battle with their U.S. counterparts. They remained in the Inland Sea of mainland Japan, except for
their distant support of the Midway/Aleutians expedition. The Second
Fleet contained at the start of the war the powerful force of eighteen
heavy cruisers, although some fast battleships (modernized battle
cruisers) were attached to it. This fleet was commanded from August
1943 by Vice Adm. Kurita Takeo. The carrier task force, which delivered the attack on Pearl Harbor, was originally known as the Mobile
Force (*Kidō Butai*) and was commanded by Vice Adm. Nagumo
Chūichi. From June 1942 (after Midway) this force was redesignated as
the Third Fleet. In November 1942, after the Battle of Santa Cruz, Vice
Adm. Ozawa Jisaburō replaced Nagumo as commander. On 1 March
1944, in the aftermath of the American Truk raid, the Second Fleet
(Kurita) and the Third Fleet (Ozawa) were brought together as the First
Mobile Fleet (*Dai-Ichi Kidō Kantai*) under Ozawa's overall command.
The First Fleet, which had become largely a training command, was
disbanded. The submarine force, the Sixth Fleet, was also subordinate
to the Combined Fleet. Vice Adm. Takagi Takeo took over command
of the Sixth Fleet in June 1943.

The First Air Fleet (*Dai-ichi Kōkū Kantai*) was a new command, originally (until March 1944) distinct from the Combined Fleet. It was created in July 1943, after the death of Yamamoto, and was intended to develop and operate the Navy's planned force of land-based fighters, attack planes, and medium bombers from a network of new bases.[5] The First Air Fleet was commanded by Vice Adm. Kakuta Kakuji. Commander Fuchida Mitsuo, leader of the Pearl Harbor air attack, was air officer on Kakuta's staff.[6]

A fundamental miscalculation in the Imperial Navy was that the enemy would be defeated not by attrition but by victory in a decisive battle.[7] This mindset had a complex basis, which included the writings of the American naval writer Alfred Thayer Mahan and the experience of the Russo-Japanese War. Also relevant was an awareness of a Japanese industrial and demographic inferiority that made victory in a war of attrition uncertain.

For the Japanese Navy, the all-out offensive was followed from the early summer of 1942 by much less successful sallies beyond the rampart of the Mandate, in what was termed the "second phase" of the Pacific War. These showed the limits of Japan's strength. The operation against Midway and the Aleutians in June was intended to lure the American fleet to destruction by the entire force of the Combined Fleet. In reality, the expedition resulted in a very major Japanese defeat in which four carriers were sunk, although the battleship fleet survived intact. Guadalcanal in the Solomon Islands was a second strategic setback. Taken by the Japanese in May 1942, the division-strength American counter-invasion there in August 1942 achieved surprise. The war leaders in Tokyo had understood that the Allies would attempt counter-offensives, but they expected that these would begin at the earliest in 1943.

In the spring of 1943, the IGHQ recognized that the war effort had entered a defensive phase. Admiral Yamamoto tried to head off American advances further north from Guadalcanal and Papua (New Guinea) toward Rabaul. His main weapon was now land-based naval air power (including carrier aircraft operating from land bases). Losses were suffered by both sides, but Japan could not win such a war of attrition against an industrially stronger opponent. Meanwhile, Allied advances continued, and the admiral was killed in the fighting.

Admiral Koga would command the Combined Fleet for eleven months after Yamamoto's death in April 1943. A year younger than his predecessor, Koga had been Vice Chief of the Naval General Staff in 1937–38, commander of the Second Fleet in 1939–41, and commander of the China Area Fleet from September 1941. Unlike Yamamoto he had no aviation experience. Rear Adm. Fukudome Shigeru worked with Koga both in the Naval General Staff and as his chief of staff in the Combined Fleet. In his post-war interrogation, Fukudome assessed his superior:

> Admiral Koga was conservative and cool, particularly when compared with Yamamoto who was an extremely colorful officer. However, Admiral Koga settled things in a logical manner. From the very beginning, he insisted on the one decisive action, first with ships, and later with shore-based planes. Under the circumstances, this strategy seemed to be the only logical one. As a Commander-in-Chief of a great fleet, he was not up to Yamamoto's standard . . . Koga was quite strong willed. Koga was very frank when alone with me, and remarked on occasion that Admiral Yamamoto died at exactly the right time and he envied him that fact.[8]

Koga attempted to develop an effective defensive strategy. Former senior Japanese naval commanders, in a post-war outline of Koga's intentions, aptly summed up his "strategic concept of establishing zones in the strategic perimeter areas in which to intercept and fight the enemy advance under the support of land-based aircraft." The initial version in the autumn of 1943 envisaged "interception areas" ranging from the Kuriles to Singapore. Each interception area would be developed in depth with a "key advance base" and three "zones of defense." For example, the "Inner South Seas area" had as its "key advance base" Truk; the "third zone of defense" was the Marianas and Carolines, the "second zone of defense" was Eniwetok, Kusaie (Kosrae), and Ponape (Pohnpei), and the "first zone of defense" comprised the Marshalls and the Gilberts, as well Nauru and Ocean islands. Airfields were to be established about 300 miles apart.[9]

The mechanism for decisive-battle concept under Koga were the so-called "Z" and "Y" operations. These were laid out in six Combined Fleet directives issued in August and September 1943. The "Z" operations concerned operations in the Pacific, where nine "interception zones" were demarcated.[10] Koga actually attempted to put these plans into practice, moving his big ships around the Pacific with the aim of catching the American fleet. Initially he hoped to engage the enemy fleet in the Aleutians (after the Allied landing at Attu in May 1943). In September and October 1943 he twice sent major elements of the fleet east from Truk to the Japanese forward anchorage at Eniwetok Atoll to confront expected threats (which did not immediately materialize).[11]

The strategy of the Imperial Navy and its Combined Fleet in 1943–44 has to be seen in the context of the overall strategy of the Empire, which was developed by the Imperial General Headquarters. The first attempt at a general reassessment came in September 1943. This followed setbacks in the South Pacific, but more important for the Japanese planners was the overall global situation. The defeat and surrender of Italy had re-opened the strategic Mediterranean-Suez-Indian Ocean route for Allied shipping. At the same time, the German retreat in Russia suggested that the outlook for the war in Europe was no longer as favorable for the Axis as it had seemed in 1941 or 1942.

An "Absolute National Defense Sphere" was agreed by the IGHQ and then approved at an Imperial Conference on 30 September 1943. The "strategic main line of resistance" took in the Kurile Islands (north of Japan), the Carolines (with Truk), western New Guinea, and the Banda Sea (between New Guinea and Celebes/Sulawesi in the Netherlands Indies). Bases would be built up and forces assembled by the Army and Navy within the Defense Sphere to prepare the eventual Japanese counterattack. The Army now began sending troops from China and Manchukuo (facing the Soviet Union) to supplement the limited detachments of naval infantry already stationed on the islands of the Central Pacific. The area *east* of the "main line of resistance" would now include the Marshalls, the northern Solomons, Rabaul and eastern New Guinea, and it was to be held as long as possible. In reality, however, the leaders of the two services were loath to pull back from embattled forward positions. The Army General Staff hoped to defend eastern

New Guinea, and the Navy did not want to give up Rabaul, because its loss would threaten the approaches to Truk and the Marshalls.[12]

Koga's unexpected death in May 1944, and the lack of major naval warship actions during his short tenure, have obscured his significant place in the Pacific War.[13] Like his predecessor Yamamoto, he was eager for a decisive battle with the American fleet. He insisted on staying with the fleet at Truk rather than commanding it from a stationary head-quarters in the rear (like Admiral Nimitz, or later, Admiral Toyoda). As well as the surviving Japanese carriers, whose potency had been demon-strated at Santa Cruz in October 1942, Koga still had a powerful surface fleet with the two new super-battleships, as well as the force of heavy cruisers.

Despite Koga's aspirations for a decisive battle, the Combined Fleet would be inactive during the invasion of the Gilberts and the Marshalls in November 1943 and February 1944. The explanation for this lies with events in the northern Solomons and at Rabaul. Information had become available at the end of October 1943 about the forthcoming invasion of the Japanese-held island of Bougainville (in the northern Solomons). To counter this, Koga committed the bulk of Admiral Kurita's Second Fleet (nine out of the twelve heavy cruisers still in service). Two of these cruisers were already in the Rabaul area, but seven more left Truk for Rabaul on 3 November. In the event the movement was detected by American RI, and heavy air raids were mounted on Rabaul. The cruiser force was sufficiently damaged that the planned counter-invasion at Bougainville had to be abandoned. Even more detrimental was Koga's decision to send fighters and attack planes from his carriers (still at Truk) to Rabaul (Operation RO). They were caught up in the air defense of Rabaul and battles over Bougainville. Few returned to the carriers. As Fukudome later put it: "The almost complete loss of carrier planes was a mortal blow to the fleet since it would require six months for replacement, and it was felt that it would take until May or June of 1944 to complete that replacement." As a result of the reduc-tion of their air groups, the big carriers were withdrawn from Truk shortly afterward and never returned.[14]

Meanwhile, and as already mentioned, the Imperial Navy had begun to develop the strong land-based First Air Fleet to supplement the carriers and big-gun ships of the Combined Fleet. John Prados described the First Air Fleet as "a homogeneous combat unit of air groups that had flown and trained together for the stated purpose of winning the Decisive Battle."[15] The headquarters of the new formation was created in June 1943, under Vice Adm. Kakuta. The high level of importance attached to the air fleet was indicated by the involvement of the Emperor himself in its foundation ceremonies. Kakuta's initial task was to assemble and train in mainland Japan Naval Air Groups (NAGs) of fighters, attack planes, and medium bombers. He also commenced an ambitious program of air base construction, primarily in the Philippines and the Central Pacific. Unfortunately for the Japanese, the speed of the American advance did not allow time to construct sufficient airfields, obtain enough modern planes, or train aircrew to the required standard. As noted in Chapter 4, the first NAGs of the Air Fleet were prematurely thrown into action, now under Combined Fleet command, when TF 58 raided the Marianas in February 1944.[16]

The government in wartime Tokyo had given very high priority to aircraft production. Although heavy aircraft losses had been suffered in 1942 and 1943, Japanese factories were not yet under air attack, and in fact September 1944 would be the peak month for aircraft production for the Army and Navy. In fiscal year 1943 (April 1943 to March 1944) production of naval fighter planes more than doubled, compared to the previous year. Some 3,864 were built, mostly improved versions of the Mitsubishi Zero. Production of naval attack planes (now mostly new Judy and Jill types) nearly quadrupled to 1,820. The production of medium bombers in the Navy only increased by a small amount, 774 compared to 674 in FY42, although the new Yokosuka P1Y/Frances, a superior type, was now entering service.[17]

Events in the winter of 1943/44, the neutralization and isolation of Rabaul by the Americans and the sudden loss of the Gilberts and the Marshalls, were significant setbacks for Japan. Nevertheless, all three areas were east of the Absolute National Defense Sphere laid out in September 1943. A more profound shock, throughout the Japanese military establishment, was the raids on Truk in late February 1944 by U.S. Navy carriers and long-range AAF bombers, and the abandonment of that place as a central base for the battle fleet. Immediately

Table AII.1. Japanese Naval Air Strength, 1943–44

	April 1943 March 1944			April 1944 March 1945		
	On hand 1 April 1943	Produced	Expended	On hand 1 April 1944	Produced	Expended
Fighters	883	3,864	2,843	1,854	5,074	4,151
Attack planes	10	1,820	1,191	639	2,415	2,150
Medium bombers	486	774	969	291	1,661	1,436

Source: USSBS, *Interrogation/*2, pp. 373–4.

after the first Truk carrier raid, Gen. Tōjō Hideki further centralized his power. Already Prime Minister and War [Army] Minister—among several other posts—he was now made Chief of the Army General Staff. Meanwhile, Admiral Shimada Shigetarō, Tōjō's Navy Minister since November 1941, was appointed to the additional post of Chief of the Naval General Staff. Shimada replaced Admiral Nagano, who had led the NGS since April 1941. The Army now increased the movement of its troops—but not its aircraft—from China and Manchukuo to the Central Pacific. A new Thirty-First Army was created in mid-February 1944 to defend Truk and the Marianas.[18]

At the same time, Admiral Koga took steps to respond to the defeat in the Marshalls and to the abandonment of Truk as a base for heavy surface ships. After taking part in top-level planning meetings in Tokyo, Koga incorporated a modified version of the "Z" operations into Combined Fleet Order No. 73 (8 March 1944).[19] As already mentioned, the "Z" operations documents were not a detailed plan of attack, but rather a set of general "fighting instructions," what the U.S. Navy called "tactical orders and doctrine."

Order No. 73 provided a doctrine for counter-measures to Allied advances by Japanese surface ships, land-based aircraft, and submarines. The main sequence of operations was described:

(1) Long-range reconnaissance and raids to gain intelligence and annihilate enemy forces.

(2) Concentration of forces to bring to bear the maximum strength.

(3) Use of planes, submarines and patrol boats to find and assess advancing enemy forces at an early stage and then to maintain constant contact.

(4) Engagement and defeat of enemy carriers and transports.

(5) Destruction of remaining enemy landing forces as far as possible out to sea, but in any event to destroy "at the water's edge" such enemy landing forces as might get through.[20]

Task "4" merits quotation in full:

> To meet the enemy Fleet Occupation force [sic], and to seek out and destroy enemy airplane carriers with the major portion of our air strength, to ensure control of the air before directing our main attack against transport convoys. (Under certain circumstances enemy transport convoys may be attacked and destroyed first.) Coordinating our plans with the aforesaid air attack, to strike suddenly with our surface forces, and annihilate enemy transports or the enemy fleet.

As with the August–September 1943 version, the "Z" Operations, Order No. 73 laid out "areas of operations" for "Z" operations, wherever the enemy attack might come, from the Kurile Islands to New Guinea.[21]

The Combined Fleet air staff also drafted on 11 March 1944 "A Study of the Main Features of Decisive Air Operations in the Central Pacific."[22] Again, this was not a specific plan, but an outline of responses to different contingencies for two types of enemy force: (1) a carrier group, and (2) an "occupation force." Smaller aircraft (fighters and single-engined attack planes) were to move to airfields near the enemy objective; for example, if the enemy threatened the Marianas the planes should move there from Truk or Woleai (Mereyon). Large aircraft (medium bombers) would operate from their original bases. This document also stressed the decisive importance of accurate air reconnaissance.

As recounted in Chapter 5, Admiral Koga died in an air accident in the Philippines on 1 April 1944, three weeks after these documents were produced. Admiral Toyoda became acting C-in-C of the Combined Fleet on 4 April, even as the fruitless search for Koga continued. Toyoda was officially appointed to the post on 3 May; this was four weeks before the Biak landing and six weeks before the invasion of Saipan.[23]

The change of command at the top did not lead to any fundamental alteration of Combined Fleet fighting instructions or strategy, although Koga's "Z" operation now essentially became Toyoda's "A" Operation, or *A-go*. Three secret orders were issued just before the public announcement of Toyoda's appointment. One was an IGHQ directive No. 373, dated 3 May 1944.[24] It was addressed to Toyoda and signed by the new Chief of the NGS, Shimada. The task of the Combined Fleet, the directive stated, was to win a decisive battle in the Central Pacific. Toyoda's forces were to be prepared by the end of May, avoiding action until then. The First Mobile Fleet would be based in the southern Philippines, the First Air Fleet would be based in the Central Pacific, the Philippines, and the former Netherland Indies (termed "the area north of Australia"). Cooperation with the Army was stressed, and also the role of aviation: "Priority will be given to preparations for air operations."

The second order was issued by Toyoda on the day of his appointment (3 May). This was Combined Fleet Order No. 76, for the "A" Operation.[25] In Order No. 76, stress was placed on what were called "raiding" operations, "by which a great diminution of enemy strength is expected"; "raiding" presumably meant attrition operations by land-based aircraft and submarines. This would be followed by a decisive battle.

> The greater part of the Base Air Force [the operational designation of the First Air Fleet] and the full Strength of the Task Force [i.e. the First Mobile Fleet] will be concentrated in the battle area. The enemy will be lured into this area and a decisive battle with full strength will be opened at a favorable opportunity. The enemy task force will be attacked and destroyed for the most part in a day assault.

The use of "outranging" tactics was important: "Stress will be laid on day air attacks with large forces operating beyond the range of enemy carrier-type planes."

The third message, dated 3 May (dispatch 041213), was from Toyoda to all his commanding officers.[26] He noted that the general strategic situation was one in which "the enemy [has] recovered his fighting strength and, taking advantage of our supply difficulties, [has] moved over to a full-scale counterattack." He then made a rather contradictory statement: "[A]n unprecedented opportunity exists for deciding who shall be victorious and who defeated. *This autumn* we will make this great task our responsibility [my emphasis]."[27]

In fact, the "opening" of the "A" Operation was communicated on 20 May.[28] This message came before the invasion of Biak on 27 May and may relate to the state of readiness of the First Mobile Fleet, which had assembled at Tawi Tawi in the southwestern Philippines just before this date. The order "Prepare for *A-Go*, Decisive Operations" was issued at 1727 on 13 June.[29] At 0717 on 15 June the "A" Decisive Operation was ordered activated.[30] As Admiral Ozawa reported in his post-battle analysis (dated November 1944): "The Task Force [First Mobile Fleet] decided to destroy in daytime the regular [sic] carrier group in accordance with Combined Fleet Operations Plans. This was to be followed up with an all-out attack aimed at the annihilation of the enemy."[31]

An early post-war Japanese analysis summed up the situation on the eve of the Battle of the Philippine Sea: "Anticipating that Operation 'A,' which employed the entire surface and air strength of the Imperial Navy Combined Fleet, would be the final decisive surface battle of this war, the preparations for the operation were carried out with the maximum effort and full use of the nation's resources."[32]

ENDNOTES

INTRODUCTION: FOURTEEN MONTHS EARLIER

1. Basic sources for the Battle of Santa Cruz: CominCh, Secret Information Bulletin No. 3; CincPac, WD, 10/42; CincPac, "Operations of Carrier Task Forces" [19/1/43]; CincPac, "Solomon Islands Campaign, Battle of Santa Cruz" [6/1/43]; CTF 16, WD, 10/42; CTF 17, WD, 10/42; NHHC, ONI Combat Narrative "Santa Cruz" [1943].

   A good, published history devoted to Santa Cruz is Hammel, *Carrier Strike*, supplemented by Stille, *Santa Cruz*. The battle is detailed in broader works: Frank, *Guadalcanal*, pp. 368–403; Lundstrom, *First Team/2*, pp. 323–459; Mor/5, pp. 199–224; Prados, *Combined Fleet*, pp. 379–87; Prados, *Islands*, pp. 126–59; Stafford, *Big E*, pp. 170–211. Okumiya/Horikoshi, *Zero*, pp. 207–24, is an account co-written by a surviving Japanese participant, Cdr Okumiya Masatake. On the American side, see also Ewing, *Reaper Leader*, pp. 123–44.

2. Noel Busch, "Task Force 58," *Life*, 17 July 1944, p. 80.

3. The Japanese search was made by carrier planes from their main element, the Mobile Force (*Kidō Butai*), commanded by Vice Adm. Nagumo Chūichi. This comprised large carriers *Shōkaku* and *Zuikaku*, light carrier *Zuihō*, a heavy cruiser, and eight destroyers.

4. As would be expected, the identity of the specific vessels under attack was not known to the American flyers. The light carrier damaged was 11,400-ton *Zuihō*; she carried 27 planes.

5. Wheeler, *Kinkaid*, p. 276.

6. The Allies assigned their own names to Japanese aircraft. This was partly because of a lack of information and partly because of the complexity of the designation system used by the Imperial Japanese Navy (IJN). To maintain the American perspective of the time, and for the sake of simplicity, these codenames will also be used in this book. The "Kate" was the Nakajima B5N (Type 97) carrier "attack bomber," the "Val" was the Aichi D3A (Type 99) dive bomber. The attack planes consisted of twenty Kates from heavy carrier *Shōkaku* and twenty-one Vals from heavy carrier *Zuikaku*. The Japanese fighters were the famous Mitsubishi A6M

(Type 00). It had the Allied codename "Zeke" but was generally known as the "Zero," and that name will be used here.

7. Beaver, *Sailor*, pp. 182–3.

8. Frank, *Guadalcanal*, p. 386.

9. The ship hit by the dive bombers was the 29,800-ton *Shōkaku*, although her identity was not known to the Americans at that time.

10. Beaver, *Sailor*, pp. 183–4; Frank, *Guadalcanal*, pp. 390–91. *Enterprise* was hit by Val dive bombers from the *Shōkaku* second wave; this had comprised 20 Vals, launched at 0810. The second wave of Kate torpedo planes came from *Zuikaku*.

11. Frank, *Guadalcanal*, p. 393. This fourth vessel was the 24,100-ton auxiliary carrier *Junyō*, which had an air group of 44 planes. A newly converted ocean liner, she was operating with Vice Adm. Kondō's Advance Force.

12. The undamaged carrier in the main force was the 29,800-ton *Zuikaku*; her air group had originally comprised 63 planes. The carrier which joined her was *Junyō*.

13. CTF 17, WD, 10/42, p. 20.

14. Beaver, *Sailor*, p. 185; Kernan, *Crossing*, p. 74.

15. The Kate was from a second *Junyō* attack. The Vals were from a third strike of five attack planes launched by *Zuikaku* at about 1300.

16. NHHC, ONI Combat Narrative "Santa Cruz," p. 68; Prados, *Combined Fleet*, p. 387; Okumiya/Horikoshi, *Zero*, p. 207.

17. Frank, *Guadalcanal*, p. 373. The auxiliary carrier *Hiyō* had been operating with sister ship *Junyō*. She missed the battle because she suffered a mechanical breakdown on 22 October and had to return to the Truk base for repairs.

18. Parker, *Priceless Advantage*, p. 69; Prados, *Combined Fleet*, pp. 380–3; Prados, *Islands*, pp. 123–5; Blair, *Silent Victory*, pp. 337–40, 918, 920.

19. Potter, *Halsey*, p. 164. See also Prados, *Combined Fleet*, p. 383.

20. In a report to Nimitz immediately after the battle (31 October), Halsey said that he had intended for Kinkaid *not* to proceed north of the Santa Cruz Islands if Japanese carriers had come down from Truk (Lundstrom, *First Team/2*, pp. 337–8, 353).

21. Lundstrom, *First Team/2*, p. 355; Lundstrom, *Black Shoe Admiral*, p. 494. However, Lundstrom *does* also describe the result of the battle as an "Allied strategic victory" because of Japanese losses of irreplaceable aircrew (*Black Shoe Admiral*, p. 492).

22. Reynolds, *Towers*, p. 409; Wheeler, *Kinkaid*, pp. 281–94. Despite mistakes made at Santa Cruz, Halsey and Kinkaid redeemed themselves in later campaigns. In the autumn of 1944 they held the U.S. Navy's two main combat commands in the Pacific, respectively the Third and Seventh Fleets.

23. In the early summer of 1944, Nagumo commanded the Fourth Area Fleet in the Marianas, and Kakuta the land-based First Air Fleet. Kusaka was chief of staff to the C-in-C of the Combined Fleet (Admiral Toyoda Soemu).

24. Frank, *Guadalcanal*, p. 402. The first Japanese strike actually involved three carriers, as fighters from light carrier *Zuihō* took part.

25. Boslaugh, "Radar," ch. 8; Friedman, *Fighters*, pp. 121–2, 407n35. The FDO on *Enterprise* was Cdr John H. Griffin, temporarily assigned to Kinkaid's staff; he was normally in charge of the Pacific Fleet Radar Center in Hawaii (and later returned to that duty). Griffin later produced a valuable detailed critique of the radar problems on 26 October 1942 (Lundstrom, *First Team/2*, pp. 458–9).

26. CTF 17, WD, 10/42, p. 97.

27. Losses suffered by marines and soldiers fighting on the ground were higher, especially on Saipan and Guam.

28. Mor/8, p. 258.

29. Books about logistics exist, but remain outside the mainstream: Wildenberg, *Gray Steel*; Carter, *Beans, Bullets*.

30. The best single source on amphibious warfare in the Pacific remains Isely/Crowl, *Marines*.

31. The fullest account of the U.S. submarine campaign is still Blair, *Silent Victory*.

1. THE ORIGINS OF TASK FORCE 58

1. Miller, *Orange*, pp. 186–202.

2. In these months the surviving pre-war U.S. carriers were no longer in the Central Pacific. *Saratoga* was with Halsey in the South Pacific, and *Enterprise* was refitting at the Puget Sound Navy Yard in Bremerton, Washington, after damage suffered at Santa Cruz.

3. Rear Adm. Ted Sherman's TG 50.4 (*Saratoga*, CVL *Princeton*), formed the "Relief Carrier Group." Its initial task was to knock out facilities on Nauru Island west of the Gilberts, through which air raids by Japanese Betty long-range medium bombers could be staged.

4. Carter, *Beans, Bullets*, pp. 97–8; Wildenberg, *Gray Steel*, p. 180.

5. Several factors explained Japanese naval inactivity during GALVANIC. The U.S. fleet had achieved surprise, and overwhelmed the Japanese garrison quickly. Moreover, many of the Combined Fleet's carrier planes had been flown off to support Rabaul. Carrier strength at Truk consisted of only three ships: heavy carriers *Shōkaku* and *Zuikaku*, and light carrier *Zuihō*, now without most of their aircraft. Auxiliary carrier *Hiyō* and light carrier *Ryūhō* were in Japanese home waters. Auxiliary carrier *Junyō* was under repair in Japan after a submarine attack on 5 November.

6. For details see CTF 50, "Post-GALVANIC Operations." Pownall commanded only part of Spruance's carrier fleet. The carriers of TG 50.4, *Saratoga* and *Princeton*, were returning to Pearl Harbor and then to West Coast ports to refit. Meanwhile, *Bunker Hill* and *Monterey* were supporting a task group of six fast battleships which bombarded Nauru Island on 8 December.

7. CTF 50, "Post-GALVANIC Operations"; Hata/Izawa, *Naval Aces*, pp. 52, 166–7, 387, 430; Mor/7, pp. 192–3; Reynolds, *Fast Carriers*, p. 107, citing Clark, *Carrier Admiral*, pp. 138–40.

8. *Life*, 17 January 1944, pp. 22–3. The Jill was operating with NAG 581 (Chambers, *Nakajima*, pp. 80–81). (NAG is an abbreviation of "Naval Air Group," in Japanese, *Kōkūtai*). CTF 50, "Report of Enemy Air Attacks [night 4–5/12/43]." Morison, following American reports, maintained that thirty to fifty Japanese planes were involved in these night strikes on 4/5 December (Mor/7, p. 195). A more recent source by a Japanese historian stated that the main Betty attack force coming from the Marshalls was nine aircraft from Maloelap-based NAG 752 and eight from NAG 753, staging through Roi (Tagaya, *Rikko Units*, p. 81). It is possible that additional single-engined attack planes from NAG 581 were also operating in the area during these night attacks.

9. See also Coletta, *Mitscher*, pp. 186–8. The historian Clark G. Reynolds, an expert on the carrier war, was critical of Pownall in a number of books written over forty

years: His most damning comment—surely unfair—was: "Pleasant, affable, too polite to wield authority shore or afloat; apparent distaste for combat, perhaps due to Quaker origins." (*Fast Carriers*, p. xxi).

10. Coletta, *Mitscher*, pp. 186–8; Reynolds, *Fast Carriers*, p. 122; Reynolds, *Towers*, pp. 426, 450, 452; Buell, *Quiet Warrior*, pp. 237, 252. In his general history of U.S. Navy operations S. E. Morison mentioned Pownall's departure without explanatory comment (Mor/7, p. 208). In late January and February Pownall served as Spruance's aviation advisor during the Marshalls invasion. After that he would replace Towers for a few months as ComAirPac, before going home in July 1944 to head the Naval Air Training Command.

11. After leaving *Enterprise* in early 1941, Pownall had been "Commander, Patrol Plane Squadrons" (gaining flag rank) and then "Commander, Fleet Air, West Coast," in San Diego.

12. Two good biographies have been written: Forrestel, *Spruance* (1966), and Buell, *Quiet Warrior* (1974/1987). Capt. Emmet P. Forrestel (not to be confused with James Forrestal) was operations officer on Spruance's staff.

13. Buell, *Quiet Warrior*. The Lundstrom quotation comes from his Introduction to the second (1987) edition of Buell (p. vii). Lundstrom also noted that the character of Mr Spock in *Star Trek* could have been patterned on Spruance. (Presumably Captain Kirk could have been patterned on Bill Halsey.)

14. The date of the change of designation to Fifth Fleet is somewhat unclear. The "official" date seems to have been 26 April 1944 (ComFifthFlt, WD, 4/44, p. 8; Cressman, *Chronology*; Mor/8, p. 28). Contemporary documents use the term Central Pacific Force until then, with Spruance as ComCenPacFor (only later was he ComFifthFlt). Thomas Buell's explanation was that Central Pacific Force referred to Spruance's overall command, which included Army and AAF elements; the Fifth Fleet was the naval element of the Central Pacific Force, of which Spruance was also commander (Buell, *Quiet Warrior*, p. 188n). The PAC-10 manual issued in June 1943 stated that the Fifth Fleet consisted of naval units under the control of the Commander, Central Pacific Force (NA, PAC-10, p. I-1).

15. Buell, *Quiet Warrior*, pp. 133–6.

16. Buell, *Quiet Warrior*, p. 135 Hughes, *Halsey*, p. 173.

17. Buell, *Quiet Warrior*, p. 154.

18. Valor/Browning, /Fletcher, /Spruance. The DSM of the U.S. Navy was awarded to senior officers for outstanding performance. Browning's citation was actually the most fulsome, stating that "[h]is judicious planning and brilliant execution was largely responsible for the rout of the enemy Japanese fleet." Unfortunately, Browning's later career would be less highly praised.

19. On Spruance's very close relationship with Nimitz as his chief of staff see Potter, *Nimitz*, pp. 228–9.

20. Buell, *Quiet Warrior*, p. 100.

21. A biography by Theodore Taylor came out quite soon after the war, in 1954 (Taylor, *Mitscher*); Mitscher had died in 1947, at the age of sixty. A fuller biography is Coletta, *Mitscher* (1997).

22. Waite, "Airway," p. 20; Coletta, *Mitscher*, p. 189.

23. Buell, *Quiet Warrior*, pp. 164–5; Coletta, *Mitscher*, pp 119–52; Lundstrom, *Black Shoe Admiral*, pp. 245–8, 303; Buell, *Quiet Warrior*, pp. 164–5. For a full discussion of this episode see Symonds, "Mitscher."

24. Taylor, *Mitscher*, p. 139.

25. Taylor, *Mitscher*, p. 145.

26. Mitscher may have suffered two minor heart attacks during his time on Guadalcanal, but they did not become part of his medical record (Taylor, *Mitscher*, p. 160). He would die of a heart attack four years later.

27. Valor/Mitscher.

28. Task Forces were ad hoc tactical formations. "Carrier Divisions" (CarDivs) were administrative organizations, including several fleet carriers.

29. The Mitschers did not have any children. Frances passed away thirty-five years after her husband, in 1982. In 1971 she recorded for the Naval Institute an account of her life with her husband.

30. Taylor, *Mitscher*, pp. 84, 86.

31. The essential guide is Furer, *Administration*.

32. Love, *Chiefs*, pp. 137–80; Buell, *Master*; King/Whitehill, *Fleet Admiral*. See also King's "Philosophy of Command" in Furer, *Administration*, pp. 943–5. A valuable 1982 account of informal press briefings held by King with journalists is Perry, *Dear Bart*.

33. Perry, *Dear Bart*, p. 78.

34. On Admiral Leahy see O'Brien, *Second Most Powerful Man*.

35. Trent Hone suggests that relations between King and Nimitz improved after their first conference, in San Francisco in April 1942: "Although not documented in the record, Nimitz almost certainly confronted King about his tendency to micromanage operations and interfere with commanders at sea" (Hone, *Mastering*, p. 67).

36. Layton, *Secrets*, p. 89. Potter, *Nimitz*, is a solid biography written in 1976. A new archive-based work stressing Nimitz's wartime administrative abilities and structures is Hone, *Mastering*.

37. For the CincPac HQ building (Facility 250) and other wartime structures, see HABS, "Makalapa Support Facilities."

38. Layton's role is discussed further in Chapter 5.

39. Reynolds, *Towers*, p. 558.

40. Hone, *Mastering*, pp. 186–93.

41. NA, PAC-10, p. v; Hone, *Learning*, pp. 256–60. PAC-10 became the basis of USF-10, a Navy-wide manual (CARL, USF-10, "Current and Tactical Orders and Doctrine, U.S. Fleet"). A related November 1944 document was FTP 143(A) (NHHC, "War Instructions United States Fleet 1944").

42. Trent Hone discusses this at length, using the modern concept of a "distributed network" (Hone, *Learning*, 250–99).

43. Buell, *Quiet Warrior*, pp. 189–93.

44. Moore was replaced as Spruance's chief of staff by Rear Adm. Arthur C. Davis, a former CO of *Enterprise*, who had been Adm. King's operations officer in Washington.

45. Buell, *Quiet Warrior*, p. 189.

46. As the in-house history of CincPac/CincPOA *Command History* observed, "Admiral Spruance . . . frequently emphasized his desire to remain wholly a Task Force Commander, without area responsibilities. Thus the Central Pacific campaign was planned by CincPac's own staff and carried out chiefly by Admiral Spruance" (CincPac/CincPOA *Command History* p. 85, cited in Hone, *Mastering*, p. 190).

47. Of course, aviation personnel were extremely important; they are dealt with separately in Chapter 3. Material for this outline of fleet personnel in general: King, *Reports*/1–3; Furer, *Administration*; *Building the Navy's Bases*; NHHC, "US Navy Personnel Strength," and NHHC, "US Navy Personnel [in WWII]." Davidson, *Unsinkable Fleet*, pp. 119–40, provides an analysis of personnel policy in 1943–44.

48. For comparison, the 2021 strength of the U.S. Navy was about 340,000 personnel, with about 100,000 more in the Ready Reserve.

49. Furer, *Administration*, p. 279.

50. Fisher, *Sustaining*, pp. 96–105, 210; Mundy, *Code Girls*.

51. "Enlisted training," as well as the rating system (with pay grades) is explained in *Bluejackets' Manual 1944*, pp. 68–84.

52. Jernigan, *Tin Can Man*, pp. 24, 26.

53. Mason, *Battleship Sailor*, p. 169.

54. A good description of working up a new crew on carrier *Yorktown* (CV-10) in early 1943 is given in Reynolds, *Warpath*, pp. 173–210.

55. Jernigan, *Tin Can Man*, p. 45.

56. An example of an individual who did not immediately receive a USN commission was David McCampbell (USNA '33), future CO of AG 15 aboard *Essex* and the most successful USN fighter pilot of the Pacific War. He was invited to rejoin the regular navy as an ensign in 1934 (Russell, *McCampbell*, pp. 13–15).

57. The Naval Reserve became the "Navy" Reserve in the 1960s.

58. Leach, *Now Hear This*, pp. 7–8, 14–24. For a colorful fictional account of the V-7 midshipman's course at Columbia University in New York, with the apt title of "Through the looking glass," see Wouk, *Caine Mutiny*.

59. The big V-12 College Training Program should also be mentioned here, although it was only authorized in July 1943 and came too late to have much effect on the Central Pacific campaign. It provided trainees with at least four terms (semesters) of college and entry to the USNR through the Reserve Midshipman Schools. Some 50,000 personnel took part in V-12 in the last two years of the war.

60. Roberts, *Intrepid*, p. 9. These figures are approximate, but the wartime complement was larger than the original specification, and numbers increased in the course of the war, with a larger air group and additional AA guns and electronic equipment.

61. For a good introduction to shipboard organization: *Bluejackets' Manual*, pp. 260–71.

2. FLINTLOCK: TF 58 AND THE INVASION OF THE MARSHALLS, JANUARY–FEBRUARY 1944

1. *Essex*, AR, Roi-Namur, p. 7. For published work on carrier operations: Celander, *How Carriers Fought*, pp. 22–37; Faltum, *Essex*, pp. 38–43; Herder, *Task Force Tactics*, pp. 31–4.

2. Fisher, *Sustaining*, p. 118–19.

3. Morison maintained that 83 Japanese planes were based at Roi-Namur and all were destroyed (Mor/7, p. 242), but that figure may be too high. The main Japanese fighter force operating from Roi in January 1944 was Naval Air Group (NAG) 281; it comprised about twenty-five planes (Hata/Izawa, *Naval Aces*, pp. 166–7, 388). Some eight Betty medium bombers were destroyed on the ground, and six more were destroyed that morning while trying to escape to

another base. These bombers were probably from NAG 752 (Tagaya, *Rikko Units*, pp. 81–2).

4. Hammel, *Aces* [John Dear].

5. Basic sources for naval operations supporting the invasion of Kwajalein: CincPac, RO POA, 1/44, 2/44; ComCenPacFor, WD, 1/44, 2–3/44; ComCenPacFor, RO, Marshalls; ComFifthPhibFor, RO/Marshalls; CTF 58, AR, 29/1/43–12/2/44 Marshalls; CTG 58.1, AR, 29/1/44; CTG 58.2, AR 29/1/44 Roi-Namur; CTG 58.3, RO, Roi-Namur; CTG 58.3, WD, 1/44, 2/44.

6. As mentioned in the Introduction, local dates are used throughout this book. The International Date Line lies between Hawaii and the Marshalls. The local date for D-Day in the Marshalls was 31 January (ELD, East Longitude Date), which corresponded to 30 January (West Longitude Date, WLD) in Hawaii.

7. Espiritu Santo (now Vanuatu) lies southeast of Guadalcanal, and about 1,300 miles south of Majuro. Two of the newly completed fast carriers, *Lexington* and *Independence*, were absent from FLINTLOCK, both under repair on the West Coast after being hit by aerial torpedoes.

8. Buell, *Quiet Warrior*, p. 232; Crowl/Love, *Seizure*, pp. 168–9; Dyer, *Amphibians/2*, p. 741; Forrestel, *Spruance*, p. 101; Shaw, *Central Pacific Drive*, pp. 121–2. This staff discussion is interesting in light of Rear Adm. Pownall's problematic air strike with TF 50 against Kwajalein only ten days earlier (see previous chapter).

9. Mor/7, pp. 343–51, provides a full order of battle. For details of the amphibious invasion of Kwajalein and Majuro: Crowl/Love, *Seizure*, pp. 166–332; Mor/7, pp. 225–81; Peattie, *Nan'yo*, pp. 267–8; Shaw, *Central Pacific Drive*, pp. 117–80.

10. Assault troops were ferried by landing craft from their big transport ships to nearby LSTs (tank landing ships) which carried the LVTs; the LSTs were organized as the "Tractor Group." Each LVT could carry up to 24 infantrymen with their equipment, which they took directly ashore.

11. Peattie, *Nan'yo*, pp. 267–8.

12. Mor/7, p. 278; Shaw, *Central Pacific Drive*, p. 180.

13. ComCenPacFor, WD, 1/44, p. 31; Polmar/Carpenter, *Submarines*, pp. 35–6, 44–45. Aside from improved American anti-submarine capability, the Japanese effort was hampered by poor decisions made by the inexperienced new commander of the submarine force (Sixth Fleet), Vice Adm. Takagi.

14. ComCenPacFor, WD, 1/44, pp. 31, 401–10. Trent Hone suggests that the intention was "to entice the Japanese to battle in the Central Pacific," concentrating if required a battle line of no fewer than fifteen battleships from the carrier task groups and the shore bombardment groups ("Surface Battle Doctrine," p. 80). This is more likely to have been a contingency plan for an unlikely contingency. The recent biography of Vice Adm. Willis Lee, overall commander of the U.S. battleship force, makes no reference to such an intention (Stillwell, *Battleship Commander*, pp. 195–7).

15. Wartime medium (40-mm) and light (20-mm) AA guns, foreign designs replacing outmoded U.S. ones, only reached the fleet during the war; they are covered in Chapter 3. Friedman, *Naval Anti-Aircraft Guns*, pp. 108–42, 223–79, deals with the important subject of AA guns and director systems.

16. The naval architecture firm Gibbs & Cox acted as consultants, although at that time they had no experience with warships. Overcoming the technical conservatism of the largest private shipbuilders, the Navy ordered more compact, more fuel-efficient turbines from "outsiders" like Westinghouse and General Electric.

In 1939 the high-pressure, high-temperature "steam condition" for the new generation of warships were set at 600 psi (pounds per square inch) pressure and 850°F (Fahrenheit). Standard machinery of this quality would be installed in all sizes of large combat warship in the U.S. Navy (Friedman, *U.S. Destroyers*, pp. 88–118; Gardiner, *Eclipse*, p. 12; Heinrich, *Warship Builders*, pp. 75–85).

17. Heinrich, *Warship Builders*, pp. 66–7; Gardiner, *Eclipse*, p. 13.

18. The newer ships which took part in the 1942 fighting were products of the 1938 Navy Act. These included carrier *Hornet* (CV-8), the new fast battleships *Washington* and *South Dakota*, and four "Atlanta" class AA cruisers. The destroyers involved in the battles of late 1942 were mostly pre-war, although a few new "Benson" and "Fletcher" classes took part.

19. Specialization was not comprehensive and some big yards (like Bethlehem Fore River) built all types of ship, especially in the later war years. On the other hand, Newport News was the main aircraft carrier yard, followed closely by Bethlehem Fore River. New York Shipbuilding in Camden, New Jersey, undertook a huge cruiser and light-carrier program, and other yards like Bath Iron Works in Maine and Federal Kearny in New York built a large number of destroyers. Even larger in scale, but rather different in terms of organization and technology, was the construction of transport ships and landing craft on green-field sites by new firms like Kaiser Shipbuilding.

20. Gardiner, *Conway's*, pp. 86–90. President Roosevelt was a strong supporter of the Navy. Nevertheless, he had not been enthusiastic about the immediate introduction of the bill which led to the Two-Ocean Navy Act. Mid-June was the beginning of the campaign season for the November 1940 elections (in which Roosevelt was considering running for an unprecedented third term). The President was concerned that the high expenditure demanded of taxpayers for the naval program might be used to gain political support by his Republican opponents, some of whom were isolationists. In the event, Vinson ignored the President's objection and introduced the bill, which passed through the House and Senate without opposition, and was signed into law by FDR (Cook, *Vinson*, pp. 150–3; Davidson, *Unsinkable Fleet*, p. 21).

21. As the most powerful and important warships of World War II, much has been written about the "Essex" class: Faltum, *Essex*; Friedman, *U.S. Aircraft Carrier*, pp. 134–58; Roberts, *Intrepid*; "Design Histories/Essex Class".

22. Hull numbers are used here, and elsewhere, as the original, planned name was sometimes changed during construction.

23. Friedman, *U.S. Aircraft Carrier*, pp. 134–8. Newport News completed *Essex* in twenty months; in contrast it had taken the yard twenty-eight months to build the old *Yorktown* (CV-5), and forty-six months to build *Enterprise*. Bethlehem Fore River actually completed *Lexington* in seventeen months; this can be compared with the forty-eight months the yard had needed to complete the old *Wasp* (CV-7), a small, 14,700-ton ship laid down in April 1936. *Taihō*, the Japanese equivalent to the "Essex" class, was laid down in July 1941 and took thirty-two months to complete. The British carrier *Indefatigable* was under construction for fifty-four months, and was only completed in May 1944.

24. Carriers that reached the Pacific in time for the Battle of the Philippine Sea are listed in Appendix 1. The last six "Essex" class ships of the August 1940 contract arrived *after* the battle (i.e. in the second half of 1944 or before August 1945). CV-13/*Franklin*, CV-14/*Ticonderoga*, and CV-15/*Randolph* were built at Newport

News. CV-19/*Hancock* was built at Fore River. CV-31/*Bon Homme Richard* was built at the New York Navy Yard, CV-36/*Antietam* at the Philadelphia Navy Yard, and CV-38/*Shangri-La* at the Norfolk Navy Yard. An eighth ship reached the fleet in wartime: CV-20/*Bennington*, also built at Newport News, had been ordered in December 1941.

On 7 August 1942, after American carrier losses at the Battles of the Coral Sea and Midway, a further ten "Essex" class were ordered (CV-31 to CV-40), and more smaller batches were ordered later in the war. None were completed in time for World War II. On the excesses of the late wartime warship-construction programs see Davidson, *Unsinkable Fleet*, pp. 141–59, and Heinrich, *Warship Builders*, pp. 119–21.

25. *Essex* had only one deck catapult, fitted shortly after her commissioning. Later ships of the class were equipped with two, more powerful (H-IVB) deck catapults.

26. The color scheme was initially quite drab. In 1943 and early 1944 the whole ship, including the flight deck surface, was painted in a dark shade of bluish gray (5-N, Navy Blue), which the U.S. Navy knew as Measure 21.

27. *Essex*, WD, 2/43, 3/43, 4/43, 5/43.

28. *Building the Navy's Bases*/2, pp. 23–31.

29. Faltum, *Intrepid*, pp. 7–8. Reynolds, *Warpath*, pp. 213–14, provides a colorful description of the passage of *Yorktown* through the canal in July 1943.

30. Clark Reynolds' biography of J. J. Clark, *Warpath*, pp. 172–239, provides a detailed description of the fitting out of *Yorktown*. See also Reynolds, *Fighting Lady*, pp. 4–31.

31. Faltum, *Independence*; Friedman, *U.S. Aircraft Carrier*, pp. 177–90; "Design Histories/*Independence*." The designation of the "Independence" class was later changed from CV to CVL, but the pennant numbers remained the same, i.e. CV-22 became CVL-22. The arrival of the CVLs in the Pacific is detailed in Appendix 1.

32. "Design Histories/*Independence*," p. 349. BuShips was formed in June 1940 after the merger of the Bureau of Construction and Repair and the Bureau of Engineering.

33. The two names divided by a slash are the original cruiser name (city), followed by the final CVL name (battle or famous ship).

34. Only nine "Independence" class were built, as they were essentially an emergency force. By 1944 half a dozen "Essex" class were in service, and many more were in the pipeline. Two larger light carriers, based on the "Baltimore" class heavy-cruiser hull, were completed, but only after the war.

35. The numerous "Casablanca" class were built as CVEs from the keel up in the Kaiser shipyards, but the design and materials used were similar to those for merchant ships.

36. *Independence*, WD, 2–3/43, 3/43, 4/43, 5/43, 6–7/43.

3. HAILSTONE: TF 58 RAIDS TRUK, FEBRUARY 1944

1. Mor/7, pp. 288–304; Peattie, *Nan'yo*, pp. 270–1. Shaw, *Central Pacific Drive*, pp. 181–216, covers ground operations on Eniwetok.

2. Mor/7, p. 304. These soldiers were from the Japanese Army's 1st Amphibious Brigade, commanded by Major Gen. Nishida Yoshima. They had arrived from Manchuria on 4 January 1944.

3. *Building the Navy's Bases*/2, pp. 324–6; Mor/7, p. 307; Pacific Wrecks/Eniwetok Atoll. A decade later, Eniwetok Atoll would be famous as the site for many nuclear tests. These included IVY MIKE, the first test of a hydrogen bomb, in November 1952; the epicenter of the blast was an islet situated only 2.5 miles west of Engebi. The more famous Bikini Atoll, where the first "public" A-bomb explosion (Operation CROSSROADS) took place in July 1946, also lies in the Marshalls, about 200 miles to the east of Eniwetok.

4. For background on Truk: Goldstein/Dillon, *Pacific War Papers*, pp. 63–5; Pacific Wrecks/Truk Islands; Peattie, *Nan'yo*; Stewart, *Ghost Fleet*. Histories of the Pacific War usually refer to the Truk raid as Operation HAILSTONE. However, contemporary operational documents of Spruance's Central Pacific Force describe it as part of Operation CATCHPOLE, the invasion of Eniwetok. The Truk raid had been assigned the codename HAILSTONE in the GRANITE I campaign plan of 15 January 1944. In that document, however, the raid was provisionally scheduled for 24 March, and was to coincide with the landing on Emirau, east of Rabaul. CATCHPOLE and Eniwetok had originally been scheduled to take place five weeks later, on 1 May (DTIC, GRANITE I).

5. Waite, "Airway," p. 20.

6. DTIC, GRANITE I, p. 14.

7. Basic sources for the Truk raid: CincPac, RO POA, 2/44 (Annex B, Section II "Truk Strike"); ComCenPacFor, WD, 2–3/1944; ComTaskFor 58, AR, 12–22 Feb. 1944. Secondary sources include Mor/7, pp. 315–32, 352–3; Stewart, *Ghost Fleet*.

8. Mor/7, pp. 352–3. Not all of TF 58 took part in the Truk strike. Ginder's TG 58.4—*Saratoga* and CVLs *Princeton* and *Langley*—remained behind in the Marshalls to support the invasion of Eniwetok; a number of escort carriers also supported the Eniwetok landing. CVL *Independence* was still under repair in the U.S.

9. Goldstein/Dillon, *Pacific War Papers*, pp. 63–5, 279–82; Hata/Izawa, *Naval Aces*, pp. 155–6, 430. Goldstein/Dillon, *Pacific War Papers*, p. 282. These figures, from Cdr Chihaya Masataka, are based on information provided by a member of the Fourth Fleet staff. (Chihaya later assisted the American historian Gordon Prange and edited the diary of Vice Adm. Ugaki Matome). Chihaya also wrote that 250 planes were "under repair" at Eten, and that on 15 February there were 82 operational aircraft at Truk bases (p. 279). Morison produced a similar account of about 265 Japanese planes destroyed on the ground in the initial strikes (Mor/7, p. 320).

Regarding air combat losses, Admiral Koga's chief of staff later stated that a new "combat corps" of fifty–sixty fighters was wiped out, although this might include some hit on the ground (USSBS, *Interrogation*/2 [Fukudome], p. 518). According to a later (1990) Japanese source (Hata/Izawa, *Naval Aces*), only thirty-six defensive sorties were flown, mostly by fighters of NAG 204; thirty-one fighters were lost in air-to-air combat. This source stated that fighter units on Truk included NAG 201 and NAG 204, and that Zero fighter-bombers made up part of NAG 501, a ground-attack group which had been evacuated from Rabaul (Hata/Izawa, *Naval Aces*, pp. 155–6, 173, 430); see also Chambers, *Yokosuka*, p. 22.

10. Mor/7, p. 319; Prados, *Combined Fleet*, pp. 513–14, 534–5.

11. The two surviving Japanese heavy carriers, *Shōkaku* and *Zuikaku*, had left Truk for the last time on 7 and 12 December 1943 respectively, having expended their air groups in the November RO operation defending Rabaul. The two large auxil-

iary carriers (*Hiyō* and *Junyō*) were under repair in Japan after submarine attacks. The five heavy ships that left Truk for Palau on 1 February 1944 were the old battleships *Nagato* and *Fusō*, and heavy cruisers *Kumano*, *Suzuya*, and *Tone* (CF/TROM/*Nagato*). When *Musashi* left Truk on 10 February she was apparently accompanied by light carriers *Chiyoda* and *Zuihō*, light cruiser *Ōyodo*, and five destroyers (CF/TROM/*Ōyodo*). The heavy cruisers departing for Palau, also on 10 February, were *Atago*, *Chōkai*, *Haguro*, and *Myōkō* (CF/TROM/*Atago*). They reached their destination on 13 February, and then moved on to Lingga Roads near Singapore, rejoining other fleet units there on 25 February.

The other super-battleship, *Yamato*, had been damaged by the American submarine *Skate* as she approached Truk from Japan on 25 December 1943; she limped home and would be under repair at Kure until April 1944.

12. Goldstein/Dillon, *Pacific War Papers* [Chihaya] p. 280. Chihaya stated that on 15 February (two days before the American raid) about fifty operational Zero fighters had been based on Eten, twenty-four Jill single-engined torpedo bombers on Param, and eight twin-engined Bettys on Moen.

13. Hata/Izawa, *Naval Aces*, pp. 155–6; Belote/Belote, *Titans*, p. 218; Goldstein/Dillon, *Pacific War Papers* [Chihaya], p. 281. Aircrew were apparently allowed liberty in Dublon Town on the evening of 16 February, and when the raid began the following morning many of them were caught across the narrow strait separating Eten from Dublon.

14. Hata/Izawa, *Naval Aces*, pp. 155–6; Belote/Belote, *Titans*, p. 218.

15. One source gives a figure of twenty-six Jills (Goldstein/Dillon, *Pacific War Papers* [Chihaya], p. 279). Another source gives a figure of twenty-six Jills in NAG 551 at Param, of which eighteen were destroyed on the ground; most of the remainder were destroyed in the air (Chambers, *Nakajima*, p. 80). A number of squadrons of attack planes and medium bombers were still in Japan being trained as part of the new First Air Fleet, and were not yet part of the Combined Fleet.

16. NHHC/*JANAC Report*, pp. 53–5; USSBS, *Interrogation*/2 [Fukudome], p. 518; CincPac, RO, 2/44, p. 120.

17. Lacroix/Wells, *Japanese Cruisers*, pp. 431, 596.

18. Lacroix/Wells, *Japanese Cruisers*, pp. 673–4; Buell, *Quiet Warrior*, pp. 253–4. Ted Sherman was later critical of Spruance's initiative: "[T]his expedition accomplished little and only complicated the attack by the carrier planes. We were ordered to maintain fighter cover over this group at all times, which involved a wasteful use of planes" (Sherman, *Combat Command*, p. 193).

19. Faltum, *Intrepid*, pp. 24–6. The plane which hit *Intrepid* was apparently a Betty of NAG 755, operating from Tinian in the Marianas (Tagaya, *Rikko Units*, p. 83). Tinian was located 600 miles to the northwest of Truk. Morison's version, less likely, was that the attacker was a radar-equipped Kate from Param Island in Truk Atoll (Mor/7, p. 321).

20. Mor/7, pp. 321–5.

21. Belote/Belote, *Titans*, p. 217; Mor/7, p. 330; Reynolds, *Fighting Lady*, p. 102.

22. Kawamura, *Emperor*, pp. 125–6; Peattie, *Nan'yo*, pp. 275–6; Prados, *Combined Fleet*, pp. 538, 567.

23. Stafford, *Big E*, p. 291.

24. On this, see especially Matloff, *Strategic Planning*/2, pp. 451–65. This was not a straightforward argument between the U.S. Army and the U.S. Navy. MacArthur

was only a theater commander. He was not infrequently in conflict with the Army Chief of Staff, General George Marshall, his contemporary, whose focus was largely on the campaigns in the Mediterranean and Northern Europe.

25. Nimitz's differences with King were evident at the Pacific Planning Conference, which took place at Pearl Harbor on 27–28 January 1944, on the eve of the Kwajalein attack. It was essentially a meeting between POA and SWPA, and the majority of senior officers present opposed the Marianas option. This was due to lack of harbor facilities in the Marianas, limited living space there for the garrison and other facilities, and doubts about effectiveness of a long-range bomber (B-29) campaign mounted from there against Japan (Buell, *Master*, pp. 440–2; Hone, *Mastering*, pp. 220–1; Matloff, *Strategic Planning/2*, pp. 455–6; Potter, *Nimitz*, pp. 279–84).

26. Morton, *Strategy*, pp. 668–9.

27. DTIC, GRANITE I, p. 7.

28. DTIC, GRANITE I, pp. 12, 14. Manus was occupied by forces of MacArthur's SWPA without significant Japanese resistance on 25 March 1944. It was built up as an important facility, used by the U.S. Navy and the British Royal Navy (in 1945), but it was not a major operational base for the Fifth Fleet or Task Force 58. The major base of the fast carriers (now TF 38) was moved from Majuro and Eniwetok to Ulithi in the western Carolines in October 1944.

   For various hydrographical reasons the lagoon at Kwajalein was regarded as less suitable as a major warship base than the lagoon at Majuro. The "fleet train" will be described more fully in Chapter 4.

29. Matloff, *Strategic Planning/2*, pp. 458–9. GRANITE II was issued on 3 June 1944. It envisaged a landing in the Marianas on 15 June, on Palau on 8 September, on Mindanao on 15 November, and on Formosa or Luzon on 15 February 1945 (DTIC, GRANITE II, p. 9). This too was also accelerated in late summer, with a decision to bypass Mindanao and go directly for the central Philippines (Leyte) in November 1944.

30. MacArthur's extremely successful campaign along the north coast of New Guinea, from the Huon Peninsula to Biak Island, and covering 1,000 miles in five months, is described in Chapter 7.

31. In mid-February, after the loss of Kwajalein, and just before the Truk raid, the C-in-C of Combined Fleet, Admiral Koga, traveled to Tokyo aboard the *Musashi*. He took part in the discussions of the high command about strategy. His view was that the Combined Fleet must make the western Carolines (Palau, Yap and Woleai) and the Marianas the last line of defense (USSBS, *Interrogation/2* [Fukudome], p. 517). He requested the concentration/deployment there of the Navy's land-based aircraft (the First Air Fleet). Meanwhile, he ordered the battleships and cruisers of the Second Fleet to redeploy to Palau, while the carriers of Vice Adm. Ozawa's Third Fleet (mostly now in Japan) were to assemble at distant Singapore in the west for training. It was anticipated that the strengthening of this position in the western Carolines would be completed by June 1944. For more details see Appendix II.

32. Evans/Grossnick, *Naval Aviation/2*, p. 207. Figures are for "aviators," but these figures apparently refer to pilots rather than all aircrew.

33. Buchanan, *Navy's Air War*, pp. 307–29; Lundstrom, *First Team/1* and *First Team/2*.

34. *Building the Navy's Bases*, pp. 227–60.

35. Boomhower, *Fighter Pilot*; NHHC/Modern Biographical Files/Vraciu.

36. Founded by President Roosevelt in late 1938, the CPTP was renamed the War Training Service (WTS) in 1942, and phased out in 1944. At their peak these programs involved 1,100 colleges and other educational institutions.

37. USS *Wolverine* was a large Great Lakes paddle steamer built in 1912. She had been hurriedly converted into a training carrier with a large flight deck to train flyers in waters safe from U-boat attack.

38. On World War II most air services operated fighters in loose groups of four ("finger four"), made up of two pairs. In the U.S. Navy this was a "division" and made up of two "sections." Each section had a leader who was followed and covered by a "wingman" flying in echelon.

39. Vraciu retired from the Navy in 1963 with the rank of commander. He passed away in 2015, at the age of ninety-six.

40. Buchanan, *Navy's Air War*, pp. 353–61; Fisher, *Sustaining*, p. 110. Stan Fisher notes that historians of U.S. naval aviation "have failed to recognize that skilled labor, or the maintenance of naval aircraft, played as critical of a [sic] role in the war as did the pilots and airplanes" (p. 27).

41. Hata/Izawa, *Naval Aces*, pp. 405–25; Lundstrom, *First Team*/1, pp. 454–7; Peattie, *Sunburst*; Tagaya, *Aviator*, pp. 4–21.

42. USSBS, *Interrogation*/2, pp. 373–4. See also my Appendix II. The figures for combat aircraft available, both for the Japanese and the Americans, include combat aircraft working up in new units away from the actual Pacific battles. Nevertheless, the balance of forces in forward areas was probably not dissimilar.

43. Friedman is a basic source on naval fighter planes and their tactics; for the U.S. experience see *Fighters*, especially pp. 93–9, 127–41, 410n62. Also valuable for its appraisal of Allied naval aircraft, including those of the USN, is Brown, *Wings*. The F6F had two major variants, the "dash-3" (F6F-3) was the first, superseded on the production line by the "dash-5" (F6F-5) in the spring of 1944.

44. American aircraft engine designations are based on cylinder displacement in cubic inches; the R-2800 displaced 2,804 cubic inches (46 liters). The "R" prefix stands for "radial." A suffix was added to indicate a modification. The F6F-3 was powered by an R-2800-10, the F4U-1 Corsair was powered by an R-2800-8, the 1945 Grumman F8F-1 Bearcat by an R-2800-34W, and the AAF P-47D Thunderbolt by an R-2800-59.

45. Gallons are U.S. gallons. 235 U.S. gals equals 195 (British) Imperial gals. A U.S. gallon equals 0.83 Imperial gals or 3.79 liters.

46. The XF6F-2, between the prototype F6F-1 and the production F6F-3, was powered by a turbocharged Wright R-2600. It did not enter series production.

47. On the question of the F4U versus the F6F, see especially Friedman, *Fighters*, pp. 136–8, 411nn69–74.

48. In contrast to this evaluation, VF-12 had already been formed to operate Corsairs from *Saratoga*. The F4U-1A deployed with VF-17 on *Bunker Hill* had apparently eliminated many of the original problems. One of the VF-17 pilots later recalled the VF-17 Corsairs were fully carrier-ready, and it was logistic factors that caused the replacement (Blackburn, *Jolly Rogers*, p. 83).

49. Ferguson, "One Thousand Planes"; Francillon, *Grumman Aircraft*, p. 47; Thruelsen, *Grumman Story*.

50. Friedman, *Attack Aircraft*, especially pp. 47–159.

51. Francillon, *Japanese Aircraft*, is the standard general source. Chambers, *Wings*, is a recent study of the Allied capture and evaluation of Japanese aircraft.

52. Halsey/Bryan, *Story*, p. 69; "bulldozers" for airfield construction came in fourth place. Background on naval radar: Boslaugh, "Radar"; Friedman, *Fighters* (especially pp. 117–26); Friedman, *Naval Radar*, pp. 81–5. A useful contemporary survey is NHHC, "US Radar: Operational Characteristics."

53. Boslaugh, "Radar," ch. 8.

54. A transponder used in IFF is an electronic device which responds in an identifiable way to a radar signal. The British-developed Mk III, adapted for use with VHF radar, was the standard Allied device in 1944.

55. Boslaugh, "Radar," chs. 8 and 14; Hone, *Learning*, pp. 208–49. The CIC was also a vital element for cruisers and destroyers engaged in night surface battles with similar Japanese forces in the central and northern Solomons. This made it possible to overcome the initial enemy advantage in night surface warfare.

56. Boslaugh, "Radar," ch. 11.

57. Friedman, *Naval Anti-Aircraft Guns* is the standard source. See also: Reilly, *Destroyers*, pp. 68–79; Roberts, *Intrepid*, pp. 9, 15–16, 83–9; Rowland/Boyd, *Bureau of Ordnance*, pp. 219–90, 390–432.

58. Chambers, *Yokosuka*, pp. 20, 22.

4. SEVEN-LEAGUE BOOTS: TF 58 RAIDS THE MARIANAS, FEBRUARY 1944

1. This apt metaphor was used in Ted Sherman's memoir (*Combat Command*, p. 197), and also by S. E. Morison (Mor/7, p. 107).

2. Primary sources for the February 1944 carrier raid on the Marianas: CincPac, RO, 2/44 (Annex B, Section IV. "Attack on Marianas"); ComCenPacFor, WD, 2–3/44; CTF 58, AR, Marianas Operation 21–2 Feb. 1944; CTG 58.2, AR, 21–3 Feb. 1944; CTG 58.3, WD, 2/44. See also: Coletta, *Mitscher*, pp. 198–202; Forrestel, *Spruance*, p. 117; Mor/8, pp. 154–5; Prados, *Combined Fleet*, pp. 545–7; Reynolds, *Fighting Lady*, pp. 102–8; Taylor, *Mitscher*, pp. 185–9.

3. Six of the TF 58 fast carriers involved in the invasion of the Marshalls did not take part in the Marianas strike. *Intrepid* had been damaged off Truk; she returned to Pearl Harbor, escorted by *Cabot*. *Enterprise* (with TG 58.1) was detached to Majuro; her air group carried out a strike, in passing, against Jaluit. *Saratoga* and CVLs *Princeton* and *Langley* (TG 58.4) were still supporting operations at Eniwetok. During the Truk raid *Yorktown* and *Belleau Wood* had been in TG 58.1. *Yorktown* now replaced *Intrepid* in TG 58.2; *Belleau Wood* replaced *Cabot*.

Three of the fast battleships did not take part. *New Jersey* returned to Kwajalein with Spruance aboard. *Washington* had collided with *Indiana* on 1 February during night refueling, and both vessels were under repair at Majuro. *Biloxi*, *Mobile*, *Oakland*, and *Santa Fe*, all light cruisers, accompanied TG 58.2; with TG 58.3 were *Baltimore*, *Minneapolis*, and *New Orleans*.

4. For background on the Marianas: Mor/8, pp. 149–53; Peattie, *Nan'yo*.

5. Japanese airfields in the Marianas: Aslito (Saipan No. 1), Marpi Point (Saipan No. 2), Charan Kanoa (Saipan No. 3), Ushi Point/North (Tinian No. 1), Gurguan Point (Tinian No. 2), Ushi Point/South (Tinian No. 3), Orote (Guam No. 1), Tiyan (Guam No. 2).

6. Taylor, *Mitscher*, p. 186; Coletta, *Mitscher*, p. 198. It is not clear whether this message was sent to Spruance, or just to the ships of TF 58.

7. Japanese air losses in attempts to attack TF 58 were certainly very heavy, but evidence is patchy. Morison, based on information provided by Capt. Ohmae

Toshikazu, stated that 74 Japanese planes took off from airfields in the Marianas. Some of these were attack planes and medium bombers hunting for the American fleet on the night of 22/23 February and the morning of the 23rd; others were defending fighters which took off on 23 February. According to these figures, sixty-seven planes did not return, and forty-seven of these were bombers (Mor/8, p. 155n). Jon Prados, a reliable American historian who also made use of Japanese sources, stated that on the night of 22/23 February some twenty-seven twin-engined torpedo-carrying bombers and nine recon planes from the First Air Fleet took off from air bases in the Marianas and none returned; the same thing, he maintained, happened with fifty-four dive bombers sent out on the morning of 23 February (Prados, *Combined Fleet*, pp. 546–7). However, the Americans did not claim anything like that number of aircraft shot down trying to reach the two task groups. It might be speculated that there was a very high number of "operational losses" (e.g. accidents) suffered by inexperienced crews in unfamiliar surroundings.

8. Morison incorrectly stated that the task groups launched their attacks from *west* of the island chain to take advantage of prevailing easterly winds (carriers normally launch aircraft into the wind) (Mor/8, pp. 154–5). This was not actually the case, and TF 58 launched its strike from well to the *east* of the islands. Morison seems to have been repeating a mistake made in Nimitz's report (CincPac, RO, 2/44, p. 44).

9. Hata/Izawa, *Naval Aces*, p. 430. This source states that thirty more aircraft (also presumably fighters) were destroyed on the ground.

10. Anti-shipping attacks were also planned, and some cargo ships were damaged west of Saipan. The attackers hoped to ambush the light carrier *Chitose*, which was expected to be delivering planes to Saipan from Japan. Presumably information about the ship's movements was based on RI. The ambush did not come about; *Chitose* departed Kagoshima in southern Japan on 20 February and arrived at Saipan three days after the American raid (CincPac, RO, 2/44, p. 132; CF/ TROM/*Chitose*).

11. Moore, *Spies*, pp. 99–105.

12. CTF 58, AR, Marianas Operation 21–2 Feb. 1944, pp. 2–3. Morison, based on post-war Japanese sources, stated that the Japanese lost eleven planes destroyed on the ground at Guam, twenty at Saipan, and seventy at Tinian. (Mor/8, p. 155n).

13. Great importance was attached to the new formation of the First Air Fleet, and the Emperor himself took part in its commissioning ceremonies. The HQ was at Kanoya in southeastern Kyushu. The first two air groups were NAG 261 (fighters) and NAG 761 (medium bombers) and these were apparently the force sent to the Marianas in February. Eight more shore-based air groups began formation within the air fleet in the months through January 1944, but for the most part these were not ready for operational service in February.

The "air officer" on Kakuta's staff was Cdr Fuchida Mitsuo, air leader of the 1941 Pearl Harbor raid. Fuchida was highly critical of the premature deployment of the air fleet and the decision not to bring the surviving elements back to Japan after 23 February. A valuable source on this is his biography (Prange/Goldstein/ Dillon, *God's Samurai*, chs. 12 and 14). Air group commanders of the First Air Fleet were selected from among the most experienced and capable aviation officers. The training of aircrew, however, left much to be desired, and experienced ground staff were also lacking. The plan was to equip the First Air Fleet with the latest aircraft, but production was slower than expected; construction of island air bases was also delayed.

U.S. Intelligence first detected the designation First Air Fleet through RI in October 1943, but it was not until February 1944 that its central operational role became clear (Prados, *Combined Fleet*, pp. 543–5).

14. The First Air Fleet aircraft, which arrived in the Marianas from Japan in mid-February, were mostly single-engined attack planes and twin-engined medium bombers; movement of single-seat fighters was held up by bad weather. According to the post-war interrogation of Rear Adm. Fukudome, chief of staff of the Combined Fleet at the time, about 100 aircraft had been rushed to the Marianas. Of these, eighteen were Zero fighters and the rest were attack planes, medium bombers, or reconnaissance planes; half were lost (USSBS, *Interrogation/*2 [Fukudome], p. 519).

Air strength in the Marianas had been small before the arrival of these reinforcements. It seems that on 25 January 1944 only thirty fighters were based on Saipan (NAG 201) and eighteen medium bombers on Tinian (NAG 755); no combat planes were based on Guam or Rota (USSBS, *CPW*, p. 201). Some of these aircraft seem to have been sent away to reinforce Truk after the costly air battle there on 17 February (Hata/Izawa, *Naval Aces*, p. 108). Another Japanese source, prepared immediately after the war, detailed Japanese availability on 20 February as follows: thirty Zero fighters and ten Judy dive bombers on Saipan; forty Betty medium bombers and ten Irving (Nakajima J1N) night fighters on Tinian; five Tabby transport planes (license-built Douglas DC-3) on Guam (USSBS, *CPW*, p. 203). These figures may include some of the first new arrivals from the First Air Fleet.

15. USSBS, *CPW*, p. 203.

16. Potter, *Nimitz*, pp. 288–9; Reynolds, *Fast Carriers*, p. 141.

17. Sources on bases and logistics: Ballantine, *Naval Logistics*; *Building the Navy's Bases*; Carter, *Beans, Bullets*; Fisher, *Sustaining*; Furer, *Administration*, pp. 691–736; Mor/7, pp. 100–13; Mor/8, pp. 341–50.

18. Ballantine, *Naval Logistics*, pp. 245–6; Spruance, "Victory," p. 545.

19. Ballantine, *Naval Logistics*, pp. 30–4, 246–7. Miller, *Orange*, discusses advanced mobile fleet bases (pp. 36, 75–6, 147–9, 210–11, 338, 351–2).

20. Ballantine, *Naval Logistics*, p. 134.

21. Ballantine, *Naval Logistics*, p. 153n. On the other hand, a good deal of construction material had been sent to Central Pacific, in preparation for the future campaign there.

22. Ballantine, *Naval Logistics*, p. 134.

23. Carter, *Beans, Bullets*, pp. 91–3; *Building the Navy's Bases/*2; Mor/7, pp. 78, 106, 341. The C3 was a standard fast cargo ship class; the hull and machinery were adapted for use as naval auxiliaries, attack transports, and even escort carriers.

24. Carter, *Beans, Bullets*, p. 136; Mor/8, p. 420; Spruance, "Victory," p. 547.

25. Two more ServRons would be established in 1944 and 1945. ServRon 12, set up in March 1944, was envisaged as a "harbor stretcher." Its task involved clearing obstacles and dredging anchorages and ports to increase the capacity of newly occupied atolls and islands. It would be especially important in developing the harbor at Guam after July 1944. ServRon 6 was created in January 1945, forward of ServRon 10. It was given the task of supplying fuel, food, and ammunition at sea to the advanced units of the battle fleet at Iwo Jima and Okinawa and off the Japanese mainland. As Admiral Spruance later stressed, "The problem of how to transfer the heaviest bombs and shells at sea was solved, and the ships involved were equipped with the necessary gear" (Spruance, "Victory," p. 552).

26. The original intention had been to use Seeadler Harbor at Manus Island as the main fleet base; Manus was in the Admiralty Islands, west of Rabaul. Although Manus was developed and used to base tankers during the Palau raid in March–April 1944, it was not used as the main U.S. Navy fleet base. The forward base of the British Pacific Fleet would be located at Manus in 1945.

27. Fisher, *Sustaining*, pp. 139–41, 153–6. Larger-scale centralized maintenance depots, Aviation Repair and Overhaul Units (AROUs) were deployed into the Pacific in 1944. By late 1944 and 1945 the emphasis was more on replacement rather than personnel-demanding repair, as so many new planes were being manufactured.

28. The best sources on fleet oilers are Wildenberg, *Gray Steel*, and Carter, *Beans, Bullets*.

29. One barrel (bbl) is equivalent to 42 (U.S.) gallons, or 159 liters. A U.S. gallon (3.8 liters) is smaller than the "imperial" gallon used in the United Kingdom (4.5 liters). The fuel oil was not, of course, carried aboard oilers in physical barrels but in the main cargo tanks. *Cimarron* was built with twenty-four of these.

30. Wildenberg, *Gray Steel*, pp. 276–84.

31. Fuquea, "Advantage Japan."

32. Mor/7, pp. 107–8.

33. Faltum, *Essex*, pp. 158–9; "Design Histories/Essex Class," p. 342; HyperWar/ USN, "War Service Fuel Consumption . . ." (FTP 218), p. 173.

34. HyperWar/USN, "War Service Fuel Consumption," pp. 260–1.

35. Carter, *Beans, Bullets*, pp. 143–4. "Guadalupe" is the correct spelling. The ship was named after the Guadalupe River in Texas, not the better-known French Caribbean possession of Guadeloupe.

36. Carter, *Beans, Bullets*, pp. ix, 12.

5. DESECRATE: TF 58 RAIDS PALAU, 30–31 MARCH 1944

1. Primary sources for the March 1944 carrier raid on Palau: CincPac, RO, 3/44, pp. 34–43 (Annex A, Section II "Palau Operation"); ComCenPacFor, WD, 3/44; CTF 58, AR, Palau Air Strikes 3/44; CTG 58.3, AR, Palau 30–31/3/44. See also: Buell, *Dauntless Helldivers*, pp. 220–4; Buell, *Quiet Warrior*, pp. 269–73; Coletta, *Mitscher*, 198–202; Forrestel, *Spruance*, p. 117; Mor/8, pp. 27–34; Peattie, *Nan'yo*, pp. 170–80; Prados, *Combined Fleet*, pp. 547–51; Reynolds, *Fighting Lady*, pp. 113–19; Smith, *Approach*, pp. 457–9, 461–3, 573–5; Stafford, *Big E*, pp. 349–57; Taylor, *Mitscher*, pp. 185–9.

2. Following a common convention, the name "Palau" will be used for the Palau Islands. These were a sub-group of the Caroline Islands. After World War II the Carolines became part of a U.N. Trust Territory administered by the U.S. When the Federated States of Micronesia (centered on Chuuk/Truk) was created as an independent country in 1979 it included Yap, but not Palau, which became an independent republic.

3. Although U.S. forces did not take the main islands, there would be a long and bloody battle (from September 1944) to take Peleliu (25 miles south of Koror) and its air base; there was also fighting on nearby Angaur. The U.S. Navy would also eventually use the Kossol Passage as an emergency base.

4. CincPac, RO, 3/44, p. 36.

5. CincPac, RO, 3/44, p. 36.

6. The Major Action Plan is included in ComCenPacFor, WD, 3/44, pp. 143–50 (Annex E).

7. Five of the fast carriers did not take part in DESECRATE. *Essex* was refitting at Hunters Point, San Francisco. *Intrepid* and *Independence* were still under repair at the same shipyard. The new *Wasp* had reached the Pacific but was still working up; she would arrive at Pearl Harbor (from San Diego) only on 4 April. The older *Saratoga* had been dispatched to operate with the British Eastern Fleet in the Indian Ocean.

8. CincPac, RO, 3/44, pp. 35–6; ComCenPacFor, WD, 3/44, pp. 154–5;

9. Blair, *Silent Victory*, p. 574.

10. Potter, *Burke*, pp. 119–23; Taylor, *Mitscher*, pp. 189–98.

11. Reynolds, *Warpath*, pp. 321–8.

12. Winston, *Fighting Squadron*, p. 103.

13. Tagaya, *Rikko Units*, pp. 84, 86. CTF 58, AR, AA Action off Palau 29–30/3/44.

14. CF/TROM/*Musashi*; Blair, *Silent Victory*, pp. 574–5. The force that left Palau on 29 March comprised *Musashi*, heavy cruisers *Atago*, *Chōkai*, *Haguro*, *Myōkō*, and *Takao* (CF/TROM/*Atago*, *Musashi*, *Takao*). The intention had evidently been that the ships should stand by, northwest of Palau, in the hope of carrying out a surface action (Prados, *Combined Fleet*, p. 548). The cruisers eventually proceeded to Lingga Roads near Singapore, by way of Davao in the southern Philippines.

   Musashi arrived at Kure in Japan on the morning of 3 April. Repair and refit work was completed by 1 May (CF/TROM/*Musashi*). Cruisers *Atago*, *Chōkai*, *Haguro*, *Myōkō*, and *Takao* proceeded to Davao in the southern Philippines. At the end the first week of April they moved on to Lingga Roads near Singapore (Lacroix/Wells, *Japanese Cruisers*, p. 337; CF/TROM/*Atago*).

15. Admiral Koga, it will be recalled, had departed Truk for Japan (also aboard *Musashi*) on 10 February, just before the Truk raid. On arrival he took part in strategic planning conferences in Tokyo. When he returned to the Central Pacific on 29 February he began to implement plans for a decisive battle.

   Rear Adm. Fukudome Shigeru was his chief of staff. Fukudome stated during U.S. interrogation after the war that when Koga reached Palau "he announced his decision to hold [the western Carolines/Marianas] line until death . . . [T]he decision of the Imperial General Headquarters was that it must absolutely be held; and Admiral Koga's feeling was that should that line be lost, there would be no further chance for Japan." The use of both shore-based naval air groups and the carrier fleet was stressed. Koga planned to set up two alternative headquarters ashore; these would come into use, depending on the direction of the Allied advance. One would be at Davao in the southern Philippines, the other at Saipan in the Marianas. "Whichever the direction," Fukudome emphasized, Koga "was determined to make his last stand and consequently to die at either Saipan or Davao in defending this line" (USSBS, *Interrogation*/2 [Koga], p. 519).

16. Fukudome recalled Koga's view that his HQ should now be located ashore rather than on a ship. This was after "a decision to change from a decisive naval [i.e. carrier] engagement to an engagement in which land-based air forces would constitute the main strength, but with the fleet units cooperating as fully as possible" (USSBS, *Interrogation*/2 [Koga], p. 519). Had Koga gone to sea aboard *Musashi* he would have had to observe radio silence.

17. CTF 58, AR, Palau 3/44–4/44, p. 2.

18. Astor, *Wings*, p. 242; CincPac, RO, 3/44, p. 39. American claims for Japanese planes shot down were overstated, but they do indicate that air-to-air combat was on a larger scale on 31 March than on the previous day. Japanese figures state that forty-nine fighters were lost at Palau on 30–31 March (Hata/Izawa, *Naval Aces*, p. 430). Zero fighters of NAG 201 had been based on the Peleliu airfield since mid-March, but out of twenty fighters that took off on the 30th, nine failed to return, two made crash landings and the other nine were severely damaged.

   Some fifty-seven Zero fighters of NAG 261 and NAG 263 flew in from Saipan on the evening of 30 March and fought in larger air battles over Palau on the following day. Nearly all of them were destroyed in the air (Hata/Izawa, *Naval Aces*, pp. 109, 168–9, 178, 430). A Judy dive-bomber air group (NAG 523) also flew in from Saipan on the 30th; en route it attempted unsuccessfully to find the American task force. Meanwhile, Betty medium bombers of NAG 751 and NAG 761 were based at Peleliu, NAG 755 operated from Marianas and at Truk, and the "Yokosuka" NAG from Tinian (Tagaya, *Rikko Units*, pp. 84–5).

19. CTF 58, AR Palau, 30/3/44 to 1/4/44, p. 1; Belote/Belote, *Titans*, p. 227.

20. *JANAC Report*, pp. 56–7; Rohwer/Hümmelchen, *Chronology*, p. 267.

21. CTF 58, AR, Mining of Palau, 30–31/3/44.

22. Such tragedies were not unique to the Imperial Navy. Lt Gen. Frank Harmon and his chief of staff, Brig. Gen. James Anderson, disappeared on a flight from Kwajalein to Johnston Island, en route to Hawaii, in February 1945. Harmon was commander of the USAAF in the Pacific Ocean Area. In January 1943, Rear Adm. Robert English, Commander, Submarine Force, Pacific Fleet (ComSubPac), died in a plane crash in California, while flying from Hawaii with senior staff members.

23. Ugaki, *Fading Victory*, p. 345. Bradsher, "Z Plan," outlines the circumstances. (The third Emily flying boat departed somewhat later and arrived safely to Davao.)

24. Vego, *Major Operations*, p. 196.

25. In what Mark Peattie described as "the torment of Woleai," the garrison would literally starve. "Of all the tales of privation and suffering ... none is more appalling than that of the seven-thousand-man garrison of Woleai Atoll." When the island surrendered in September 1945, only 1,600 survivors remained (Peattie, *Nan'yo*, pp. 305–7).

26. Ugaki, *Fading Victory*, pp. 342–3.

27. Secondary sources on wartime naval intelligence include: Blair, *Silent Victory*; Budiansky, *Battle of Wits*; Ford, *Elusive Enemy*; Lewin, *Other Ultra*; Moore, *Spies*; Spector, *Listening*. The most important is Prados, *Combined Fleet*. Well-known memoirs include Layton, *Secrets* and Captain W. J. Holmes, *Double-Edged*.

   Strictly speaking, "Ultra" is a classification of intelligence, in this case intelligence obtained from decryption of intercepted radio messages (Holmes, *Double-Edged*, p. 23).

28. A unique outline of the evolution of JN-25, with its various "additives," is an internet source: Sinclair, "JN-25 Fact Sheet" (http://sysengr.engr.arizona.edu/OLLI/codebreaking/Sinclair.html).

29. Prados, *Combined Fleet*, p. iii.

30. Spector, *Listening*, pp. 76–129.

31. Stanley, *Photo Intelligence*, pp. 100–6. A significant weakness on the U.S. Navy side was the lack of dedicated long-range search planes operating from carriers (and cruiser catapults). In this category, at least, Japanese capability was superior.

32. U.S. Navy submarine operations are outlined further in Chapter 7.
33. Furer, *Administration*, p. 120.
34. Vego, *Major Operations*, pp. 193–207, provides a good summary.
35. Vego, *Major Operations*, p. 194; Prados, *Combined Fleet*, p. 568.
36. *Bonefish*, RWP/4, pp. 35–6, 42; Blair, *Silent Victory*, p. 625; Vego, *Major Operations*, p. 195.
37. CTF 58, RO Marianas, 6/44, pp. 123–31. This is CTF 58, Oplan 7-44 (24/5/44), Annex E. Intelligence Summary (16/5/44).
38. Vego, *Major Operations*, p. 201. A second auxiliary carrier, *Junyō*, although actually present, was apparently not listed in the Estimate.
39. CTF 58, RO Marianas, 6/44, pp. 35–8. The is the Narrative Report for 17–21/6/44 (Section II, "Possible Enemy Courses of Action").
40. ComFifthFlt, WD, 5/44, p. 105.
41. CincPac, RO 6/44, p. 71. See also Moore, *Spies*, pp. 99–115.
42. Vego, *Major Operations*, pp. 193, 200.
43. Prados, *Combined Fleet*, p. 551.
44. Vego, *Major Operations*, p. 201; Bradsher, "Z Plan"; Prados, *Combined Fleet*, pp. 550–1. S. E. Morison, writing in 1952, made no reference to Fukudome or the Cebu events and stated that the "Z" Operation documents were captured at Hollandia, New Guinea—where an amphibious landing took place on 22 April 1944 (Mor/8, pp. 173, 253n).

   Admiral Koga's Combined Fleet order "Ops. No. 73," dated 8 March 1944, was twenty-two pages in translation (MMAL, ATIS Translation No. 4, pp. 4–28). It was accompanied by "A Study of the Main Features of Decisive Air Operations in the Central Pacific," produced by the Combined Fleet "Air Staff" and dated 10 March 1944; this was nine pages in translation (MMAL, ATIS Translation No. 5, 26 May 1944, pp. 5–13).

   According to the historian John Prados, the "Z Plan" concept actually dated back to August 1943. Admiral Koga created nine "interception zones" for what he termed "Z operations [sic]" emphasizing carriers and land-based Navy aircraft (Prados, *Combined Fleet*, pp. 487–9). It would seem that the planning documents drafted eight months later, in March 1944, were an adaptation of the basic IJN operational concept to a new situation. This was one in which the Americans had seized the Gilberts and the Marshalls and had mounted—in February 1944—successful raids on Truk and the Marianas.

   Prados remarked that "it is astonishing that the Japanese do not seem to have paid much mind to the capture of the 'Z' Operation [sic] plans. It can only be conjectured that Japanese commanders considered the operational concept to be the only one practicable by that point in the war and therefore went ahead anyway." As Prados noted, the plan introduced by Koga's successor, Admiral Toyoda Soemu, as soon as he took command, was designated as the "A" Operation (*A-go*). In Prados's words, the "A" Operation was only a "slightly" modified version of the old "Z" Operation (p. 555). For further details see my Appendix II.
45. On Morison and codebreaking see Layton, *Secrets*, p. 500.
46. Ford, *Elusive Enemy*, p. 221
47. John Ferris, the eminent Canadian intelligence historian, suggested that the "victory in intelligence shaved a year and tens of thousands of Allied lives from the Pacific War" (Ferris, "Intelligence," p. 663). That may well be true, but in my view the "shaving" occurred in 1942 when an intelligence victory at Midway allowed

the beginning of a counter-offensive in the South Pacific six months earlier than might otherwise have happened. An American *defeat* at Midway, or an indecisive draw, would not have allowed the counter-offensive to begin until the middle of 1943. With reference to the Pacific War, the British historian Ronald Lewin argued that "in the major American strategic decisions taken during [the year beginning in April 1943] Ultra's role was not significant" (*Other Ultra*, pp. 191–2). This is a view with which I would concur.

6. TF 58: THE FINAL RAIDS, APRIL AND MAY 1944

1. Hollandia itself was a very small place. It is now grown into the substantial city of Jayapura in Indonesia, the capital of Papua.
2. Smith, *Approach*, pp. 11–205, and Craven/Cate, *Pacific/Guadalcanal*, pp. 575–614, still provide the best overall account; these are the official histories. The Japanese side is outlined in Hayashi, *Kōgun*, pp. 102–4.
3. The Japanese Navy had dispatched powerful cruiser forces to counter American landings at Guadalcanal in August 1942 and Bougainville in November 1943. The first sortie resulted in one of the worst USN defeats, at Savo Island, where four Allied heavy cruisers were sunk and the supply ships off Guadalcanal were forced to withdraw. The second sortie resulted in the Battle of Empress Augusta Bay; this time the Japanese were not successful, but they had mounted a serious threat. By the middle of April 1944, with the reduction of Rabaul, Truk, and Palau, the danger from the Japanese surface fleet would be considerably smaller.
4. Basic sources for the "Wakde-Hollandia" operation of TF 58: CincPac, RO, 5/44, pp. 24–8; CTF 58, AR, Hollandia 1–24/4/44. See also: Belote/Belote, *Titans*, pp. 228–30; Mor/8, pp. 34–40, 59–90, 403–6; Reynolds, *Fast Carriers*, p. 151–3; Reynolds, *Fighting Lady*, pp. 121–4; Reynolds, *Warpath*, pp. 334–5; Stafford, *Big E*, pp. 357–65.
5. The Spruance family had rented a house in Monrovia, a town in the San Gabriel Valley, east of Los Angeles. Spruance's daughter Margaret (born in 1919) had contracted tuberculosis and was recovering in a nearby sanitorium. As with his leave in December 1942, the admiral arrived at his home without any prior notice.

     Spruance was invited to speak to the local Rotary Club. He wanted to appear in civilian clothes, but his wife (also named Margaret) insisted on full uniform. A neighborhood boy idolized him, she told Spruance: "When you appear up there in your worn old clothes he'll think you're just another old man" (Buell, *Quiet Warrior*, pp. 175, 275–6).
6. ComFifthFlt, WD, 4/44, p. 8.
7. Clark was the only one of the carrier task group commanders to get a full-scale biography (Reynolds, *Warpath*), published in 2005. (Ted Sherman did produce memoirs (*Combat Command*)—in 1950—but there is little of interest in them.) The native American element in Clark's ancestry was limited (he was one thirty-second Cherokee), but he did grow up in the Cherokee Nation of Oklahoma. Clark Reynolds, J. J. Clark's biographer, and an outstanding historian of the Pacific War, was the nephew of Clark's wartime aide and flag lieutenant, "Bob" Reynolds.
8. Three of the completed "Essex" class did not take part in the Hollandia operation. *Essex* was now refitting in San Francisco, and *Intrepid* was still under repair. *Wasp*

had just joined the fleet and was undergoing her shakedown. Two of the nine "Independence" class CVLs were absent: *Independence* was still under repair, and *San Jacinto* had just joined the fleet and was working up.

9. These operations by TF 58 did not have a codename. Essentially they were part of RECKLESS. For clarity's sake they will be referred to as the Wakde-Hollandia operation.

10. TF 78 was made up of four large escort carriers of the "Sangamon" class (*Chenango*, *Sangamon*, *Santee*, and *Suwanee*) and four "Casablanca" class (*Coral Sea*, *Corregidor*, *Manila Bay*, and *Natoma Bay*); it was divided into two task groups. Air strength was about 210 planes. Rear Adm. Van Ragsdale was CTF.

11. The landings nearest Hollandia were at Humboldt Bay and at Tenahmerah Bay. A landing (codenamed Operation PERSECUTION) was also made on the same day at Aitape, east of Hollandia. Although Rear Adm. J. J. Clark's TF 58.1 launched air attacks against Wakde Island, Sawar, and Sarmi, west of Hollandia, on D-1, there would be no landing there at this time. The object of Clark's task group was to neutralize the airdromes and prevent Japanese aircraft from flying in from the west. Wakde Island would be invaded four weeks later, on 17 May 1944, and an AAF base capable of operating heavy bombers was built there.

12. Sherman, *Combat Command*, p. 198.

13. Basic sources for the second Truk raid: CincPac, RO, 4/44, pp. 15–20; CTF, 58 AR Truk, 4/44. See also Belote/Belote, *Titans*, pp. 230–1; Buell, *Dauntless Helldivers*, pp. 231–5; Mor/8, pp. 38–40; Reynolds, *Warpath*, p. 336; Stafford, *Big E*, pp. 365–70.

14. The Truk raid was evidently not under consideration when TF 58 set out from Majuro for Hollandia. From the point of view of Task Force 58 the two operations involved separate operational plans: Oplan 6-44 for the Hollandia attacks and Oplan 7-44 for the attacks on Truk and Ponape. Mitscher's biographer gave the admiral and his new chief of staff, Capt. Arleigh Burke, credit for the last-minute addition (Taylor, *Mitscher*, p. 205). Morison and Reynolds, however, state that the idea was originally from Nimitz and his staff (Mor/8, p. 38; Reynolds, *Fast Carriers*, p. 152); Nimitz's own report does not clarify the point (CincPac, RO, 4/44).

15. CincPac, RO, 4/44, p. 19; There is a series of spectacular photographs of the attack by one of the Jills in Reynolds, *Fighting Lady*, p. 128.

16. Hata/Izawa, *Naval Aces*, p. 430.

17. CincPac, RO, 4/44, p. 20–1, 5/44, p. 10; CTF 58, AR Truk, 4/44, pp. 19–20. See also Mor/8, pp. 40–1; Stillwell, *Battleship Commander*, pp. 205–6.

18. CincPac, RO, 5/44, p. 10.

19. Basic sources for the May 1944 raids on Marcus and Wake: CincPac, RO, 5/44, pp. 14–15. See also: Reynolds, *Fast Carriers*, p. 154; Russell, *McCampbell*, pp. 52–64. Surprisingly, Morison did not write about the May 1944 operations, beyond a sentence describing them (accurately) as "diversionary air raids" (Mor/8, p. 220).

20. CincPac, RO, 5/44, p. 14.

21. McCampbell ended the war as the leading ace of the U.S. Navy, credited with destroying 34 Japanese aircraft. AG 15 replaced the *Essex*'s original AG 9. Sprague would later achieve fame as the commander of Taffy 3, the unit of escort carriers that took the brunt of the Japanese naval attack during the Battle off Samar in the Philippines in October 1944.

22. A picket boat had sighted Halsey's carrier group at the time of the Tokyo raid in April 1942, forcing a premature launch of his B-25 AAF bombers.

23. Markey, *Well Done!*, pp. 33–4. Morris Markey was a well-known freelance journalist who had written for the *New Yorker*, *McCalls*, and other magazines; he was accredited as a war correspondent to the U.S. Navy in March 1943.

24. CincPac, RO 4/44, p. 18. Takeoff and landing accidents were not included in these loss figures. They also did not include the Marcus-Wake raids.

25. *JM*/90, p. 24. The "A" operation (*A-go*) plan is discussed in greater depth in Chapters 7 and 8, as well as Appendix II. This was a plan to bring about a decisive battle using warships and land-based aircraft, in the event of another American offensive. The location of that attack was still not determined, although the situation seemed clearer when a U.S. Army division landed on Biak Island—in western New Guinea, far away from Marcus—on 27 May. The raids on Marcus and Wake did not lead the Japanese to expect an invasion specifically in the Marianas.

7. APPROACHING THE MARIANAS, 1–15 JUNE 1944

1. Monday, 5 June WLD in the English Channel, the day the Normandy convoys departed from southern England, corresponded to Tuesday, 6 June ELD, when the fast carriers left Majuro. The Marshall Islands lay 7,400 miles away, on the western side of the International Date Line. A common misunderstanding is that NEPTUNE was the naval aspect of Operation OVERLORD. In reality, NEPTUNE was the codename used for the *initial* operations in Normandy.

2. On the other hand, NEPTUNE/OVERLORD was indeed the most ambitious and important maritime operation of World War II. More *Allied* divisions were involved in the landings on D-Day, 6 June (including two American airborne divisions); only half the ground and air forces involved on D-Day in Normandy were American, and only a minority of the warships (most warships were British; most of the transports and landing ships were American). A much larger ground-based air element was involved in NEPTUNE, operating from bases in Britain. (The only carrier element was three CVEs on anti-submarine patrol in the western English Channel.) The enemy coastal defenses in Normandy were stronger than those on Saipan, and the number of enemy divisions that would be deployed to counterattack was much larger. Above all, NEPTUNE was intended as an *initial* entry point. Through the Normandy beaches, "follow-on" forces, dozens of Allied divisions, would be landed in subsequent days and weeks; they would take rapid control of a "lodgment area" very much larger in size than Saipan, Tinian, and Guam.

3. Mor/8, p. 173; *Lexington*, WD, 6/44, p. 2.

4. Space does not allow full details of the FORAGER amphibious operations. For the background to FORAGER and approach see also Crowl, *Marianas*, pp. 33–52; Dyer, *Amphibians*, pp. 858–902; Isely/Crowl, *Marines*, pp. 510–18; Mor/8, pp. 149–85; Shaw, *Central Pacific Drive*, pp. 231–6.

5. ComFifthFlt, WD, 5/44, contains Oplan 10-44 dated 12 May 1944. For details of the order of battle see Mor/8, pp. 406–11. For Spruance's planned force composition as of 12 May 1944 see ComFifthFlt, WD, 5/44, pp. 9–25; the Fifth Fleet Movement Plan is on pp. 70–96.

6. The composition of the three TransDivs of the Northern Group was as follows: (1) TransDiv 18, which consisted of two APA, two AP, one AKA, and one LSD

(carrying tanks); (2) TransDiv 10, which consisted of four APA, one AKA, and two AK; (3) TD 28, which consisted of three APA, one AP, one AKA, and one LSD (Mor/8, p. 407). (APA = attack transport, AP = transport, AKA = attack cargo ship, AK = cargo ship, LSD = Landing Ship Dock.)

7. The Movement Plan for TF 58, part of its Oplan 7-44, is in CTF 58, RO, 11/6–10/8/44, pp. 109–16. For the movement of the amphibious force see ComFifthPhibFor, WD, 5/44 and 6/44.

8. *Idaho* and *New Mexico* had not been at Pearl Harbor in December 1941. *Pennsylvania* had been in drydock there and was not badly damaged.

9. "Casablanca" class CVEs *Manila Bay* and *Natoma Bay* were tasked to fly off Army P-47 Thunderbolt fighters to the captured island airfields. The two carriers did not leave Pearl Harbor until 5 June, but they arrived east of Saipan on 19 June.

10. ComFifthFlt, WD 5/44, pp. 136–40; Mor/8, p. 411.

11. *JM*/90, pp. 31–6 provides an outline of this version of the "A" Operation, based on post-war interrogations. See also Prange, *God's Samurai*, ch. 16. An early post-war account explained the terminology: "The term 'A-go Operation' was the code designation given to the Japanese invasion operations conducted at the onset of the Pacific War and now the term was again used for luck in memory of the success achieved in those initial stages" (*JM*/117, p. 21).

12. In his post-war interrogation, Admiral Koga's chief of staff, Rear Adm. Fukudome Shigeru, was asked, "What was the reason for the concentrated interest on the south; what was the reason for the belief that the American effort would come there?" In his reply Fukudome said that he, personally, had believed at the time that "there was no sound basis for that view" and that he had feared a "direct thrust" against the Marianas, given their vital strategic position and actual U.S. capability. The view of some officers that the initial threat would come from the south "was based more or less on wishful thinking"; they felt that the Allies would take what was for them "the easiest" objective and only after that "come north-ward [to the Marianas] step by step, each new step providing a new base for your next step"(USSBS, *Interrogation*/2 [Fukudome], p. 523).

   Fukudome's testimony may, of course, have been based on hindsight. It is also not clear whether the admiral had in mind discussions in the Combined Fleet staff under Admiral Koga when the "Z" Operations plans were drafted in March 1944 or about discussions in May and early June, after he had been rescued from Cebu.

   Aside from Fukudome's opinion, another attraction of the south was that it was much nearer than the Marianas to the new fleet base at Tawi Tawi in the southern Philippines. Because of a shortage of fleet oilers the operations of the Combined Fleet were severely limited. Palau and Biak were also surrounded by a ring of Japanese air bases, which could—in theory—provide support for any counter-invasion operation.

13. Takasu's command, set up in April 1942, took in naval forces in the Netherlands Indies, as well as the Philippines, Malaya, and Indochina. Earlier, from September 1941 to June 1942, Takasu had commanded the battleships of the First Fleet. He took over the SWAF from September 1942, and commanded it until June 1944; he was promoted to full admiral rank in March 1944. Takasu died of illness in Japan in September 1944.

14. CincPac, RO, 5/44, pp. 28–30, 33; Boyd/Akihiko, *Submarine Force*, pp. 140–3; Hashimoto, *Sunk*, p. 109; Polmar/Carpenter, *Submarines*, pp. 46–7; WWJ/4, pp. 105–11, 261–2. FRUPac determined the position of a number of enemy submarines, the U.S. Third Fleet dispatched a "hunter-killer" group of three

destroyer escorts (DEs), including *England*, from a base near Guadalcanal. Ships of the DE type had only recently arrived in the Pacific. They were equipped with effective radar and sonar, as well as the "Hedgehog" anti-submarine mortar; the forward-firing Hedgehog had been developed by the British in the Atlantic as a significant improvement on the conventional depth charge.

15. Ugaki, *Fading Victory*, p. 376 [27 May 1944]. Ugaki commanded Battleship Division 1 (*Sentai* 1), and had been Admiral Yamamoto's chief of staff in 1941–3. Operation "A" was, as we know, the Imperial Navy's counterattack plan, issued by Admiral Toyoda in May 1944, and developed from Admiral Koga's "Z Operations." *JM*/90, pp. 31–6 provides an outline of this version of the "A" Operation, based on post-war interrogations and reconstructions. See also Prange, *God's Samurai*, ch. 16.

16. *JM*/90, p. 40–41. There is no specific evidence that the Japanese Navy thought in these terms, but the parallels were striking. In June 1942 a numerically inferior American fleet was secretly deployed on the flank of a Japanese force advancing to occupy Midway. Supported by land-based aircraft from Midway, the Americans were able to win a decisive victory over the Japanese covering force, the carriers of the *Kidō Butai*.

17. The considerable number of Japanese planes flown south actually had little effect on the fighting around Biak.

18. CF/TROM/*Yamato*. U.S. Army troops fought on Biak until 22 June 1944, when organized Japanese resistance ended and the airfields became available for use by Allied planes.

19. Background sources: Blair, *Silent Victory*; Alden, *Fleet Submarine.*

20. None of the very similar "Tench" (SS-417) sub-class entered the fleet before late 1944.

21. Spruance, "Victory," p. 542; Halsey/Bryan, *Story*, p. 69. As already mentioned, for Halsey radar was rated second, planes third, and bulldozers fourth.

22. On the beginning of unrestricted submarine warfare see Holwitt, *Execute*. Spector, *Listening*, pp. 133–5, contains Vice Adm. Lockwood's summary of the value of RI for American submarine operations.

23. Blair, *Silent Victory*, pp. 521–2, 818.

24. Mor/8, p. 218. Six of the smaller Japanese carriers had come south to Tawi Tawi, departing Saeki in the Pescadores on 11 May. The best of the large carriers, *Shōkaku*, *Taihō*, and *Zuikaku*, had transferred from their training base at Lingga Roads near Singapore at the same time (CF/TROM/*Hiyō*, *Shōkaku*).

25. CincPac, RO, 6/44, pp. 126–8; See also Blair, *Silent Victory*, pp. 643–9; Mor/8, pp. 241–2; Zimmerman, "Forager."

26. Evans/Peattie, *Kaigun*, pp. 428–34, deals with the general shortcomings of the Japanese submarines and their pre-war doctrine.

27. On the ineffectiveness of the Japanese submarines in the Marianas battle: Boyd/ Akihiko, *Submarine Force*, pp. 134–57; Mor/8, pp. 229–31; Polmar/Carpenter, *Submarines*, pp. 47–8; Prados, *Combined Fleet*, pp. 563–5; *WWJ*/4, pp. 105–111, 261–2.

8. TF 58 AND THE BATTLE OF THE PHILIPPINE SEA (1):
INVASION AND AIR BATTLE

1. Basic sources for FORAGER naval operations: CincPac, RO, 6/44; ComFifthFlt, Initial Report/Marianas, p. 5; ComFifthFlt, WD, 5/44, 6/44; CTF 58, RO,

Marianas 11/6–10/8/44; CTG 58.1, RO, 6–27/6/44; CTG 58.3, RO, 6/6–6/7/44; CTG 58.4, RO, 6/6–6/7/44; *JM*/90 and *JM*/91. Published accounts are Belote/Belote, *Titans*, pp. 232–300; Dickson, *Philippine Sea*; Mor/8, pp. 149–321; Prados, *Combined Fleet*, p. 566–80; Reynolds, *Fast Carriers*, pp. 156–210; Tillman, *Clash*; Vego, *Major Operations*, pp. 167–301; Y'Blood, *Red Sun*.

2. CTF 58, RO, Marianas, pp. 30–4. Figures provided by Hata/Izawa indicate 122 Japanese sorties over the Marianas on 11 June; the loss of 22 fighters was admitted. No "major air battles" (i.e. air-to-air combat) over the Marianas are listed in the period 12–14 June, or during daylight on the 15th (*Naval Aces*, pp. 430–1).

3. CTF 58, RO, Marianas, p. 128. The TF 58 staff also assessed, however, that such an action would give the fast carriers a valuable opportunity to fight and win a decisive battle.

4. CTF 58, RO, Marianas, p. 36; Vego, *Major Operations*, p. 248.

5. Hone, *Mastering*, p. 238. See also Buell, *Quiet Warrior*, p. 280.

6. MMAL, ATIS Translation No. 4, pp. 13, 16. The "Z" Operations "fighting instructions" related to the situation expected by the Japanese in late March and April 1944, not necessarily in May and June. The Japanese "Main Features of Decisive Air Operations" study, translated at the same time, stated that the air groups of First Mobile Fleet carriers should be immediately flown off the carriers to operate from land bases at Palau and Yap (MMAL, ATIS Translation No. 5, p. 12).

7. ComFifthFlt, WD, 5/44, pp. 9–164. Oplan 10-44 was dated 12 May 1944.

8. CincPac, RO, 6/44, p. 56; ComFifthFlt, WD, 5/44, p. 30. Iwo Jima is actually in the Volcano Islands; Chichi Jima and Haha Jima are in the Bonin Islands. The Japanese know these two island groups together as the Ogasawara Islands. U.S. Navy sources usually referred to all the islands as the Bonins, and that convention is followed here. The captured "Z" operations documents gave an expected deployment ("if necessary") of 210 planes coming from Yokosuka in Japan by the end of May (MMAL, ATIS Translation No. 4, p. 18).

9. Craven/Cate, *Pacific/Guadalcanal*, p. 687.

10. The *Redfin* report was incomplete. The force actually comprised nine fleet carriers, three battleships, eight heavy cruisers, a light cruiser, and twenty-two destroyers. These were fleet carriers *Shōkaku*, *Taihō*, and *Zuikaku*, large auxiliary carriers *Hiyō* and *Junyō*, light carriers *Chitose*, *Chiyoda*, *Ryūhō*, and *Zuihō*, battleships *Kongō*, *Haruna*, and *Nagato*, heavy cruisers *Atago*, *Takao*, *Maya*, *Chokai*, *Mogami*, *Kumano*, *Chikuma*, and *Tone*, as well as light cruiser *Yahagi* (CF/TROM/*Shōkaku*, *Hiyō*, *Atago*); Dull, *IJN*, p. 310.

11. *Cavalla*, RWP/1 pp. 6–7; *Albacore*, RWP/9, p. 6; Zimmerman, "Forager," p. 84.

12. For the ground battle on Saipan: Alexander, *Storm Landings*, pp. 62–85; Crowl, *Marianas*, pp. 33–268; Hoffman, *Saipan*; Isely/Crowl, *Marines*, pp. 310–58; Peattie, *Nan'yo*, pp. 280–8; Shaw, *Central Pacific Drive*, pp. 231–356.

13. Moore, *Spies*, pp. 99–116.

14. Winton, *Ultra Pacific*, pp. 164–5; Prados, *Combined Fleet*, pp. 569–70. The *CincPac Bulletin* that included Layton's report was dated 14 June WLD, which was 15 June ELD in the Marianas.

A later assessment in the *CincPac Bulletin*, dated 16 June WLD and based on decryption, noted the following: "Cinc Combined Fleet [Admiral Toyoda] placed 'Able Operations' [A-GO] in effect at 13 1721 [1721 on 13 June ELD] with remark [that] these operations [were] to be decisive. CincPac [Nimitz HQ] estimates Able operations generally similar to Zebra operations ['Z' operations] translations of which [were] forwarded [to] fleet and type commanders [from Australia via CincPac]" (Winton, *Ultra Pacific*, pp. 164–5).

15. Layton had incorrectly assumed that the 2nd Carrier Division (CarDiv 2, carriers *Hiyō*, *Junyō*, and *Ryūhō*) was temporarily detached from the main First Mobile Fleet and was located at Davao in the Philippines. In this respect the *Redfin* sighting had been incomplete. Layton described the KON force from Batjan (*Yamato*, *Musashi*, and three cruisers) as the 1st Battleship Division (BatDiv 1) and suggested that it would join up with the two other groups within the Philippines.

His assessment was generally correct, but he anticipated a faster pace of advance by the Japanese than would actually occur. Rather than refueling and exiting though the Surigao Strait, as Layton suggested, Admiral Ozawa would take a different route. The First Mobile Fleet had been bound for Guimaras in the central Philippines, and once Ozawa realized (during 13 June) that a major American landing was underway in the Marianas, he decided to quickly refuel at Guimaras and then exit from the Philippines, en route for Saipan, through the San Bernardino Strait. This passage was 150 miles to the north of the Surigao Strait.

16. On "outranging" tactics, see the account by Nomura Minoru in Evans, *Japanese Navy*, p. 305. The translated "Z" Operations "Plan of Operations" twice referred to flanking attacks: [1] "The striking force of the carrier nucleus . . . will attack the enemy striking forces on the flank and annihilate them . . ."; [2] The Carrier Nucleus Force was to "manoeuvre to strike its enemy in the flanks" (MMAL, ATIS Translation No. 4, pp. 12, 14). It also referred to planes taking off from carriers and landing at bases, from which they could launch subsequent operations (MMAL, ATIS Translation No. 4, pp. 9, 21).

17. *Flying Fish*, RWP/10, pp. 48–9; Blair, *Silent Victory*, p. 650; Prados, *Combined Fleet*, p. 573. *Flying Fish* sighted the Japanese ships at 1622/15, and attempted to report this by radio at 1925/15. This was actually the whole force that had left Tawi Tawi on 13 June. There were evidently two sightings by coastwatchers as the Japanese fleet passed through the Surigao Strait on 15 June. These were passed on to Spruance by CincPac on 17 and 18 June ELD. One of these provided accurate details of enemy strength: nine carriers, three battleships, ten cruisers, and eleven destroyers (Winton, *Ultra Pacific*, p. 166).

18. CTG 58.1, RO, Marianas, pp. 8–9, 28–30; CTG 58.4, WD, 6/44, pp. 13–14. Reynolds, *Warpath*, pp. 346–41; Reynolds, *Fighting Lady*, pp. 143–7. One Japanese source gave a loss of sixteen defending fighters, out of thirty-seven that took part in the air battle over Iwo on 15 June (Hata/Izawa, *Naval Aces*, p. 431); an earlier source reported that twenty-eight of thirty-seven failed to return (*JM*/91, p. 17).

19. *Fanshaw Bay*, WD, 6/44, pp. 20–1. The escort carriers were in TG 52.14, commanded by Rear Adm. Gerald Bogan.

20. The Japanese bombers were led by Lt Cdr Egusa Takashige, who was killed in the attack. Egusa was one of the Imperial Navy's outstanding air leaders; he had commanded dive-bomber squadrons at Pearl Harbor, off Ceylon, and at Midway. In August 1943 he had been given command of NAG 521, the first formation to receive the new Frances medium bomber (Smith, *Fist*).

21. Spruance, aboard *Indianapolis*, would only rejoin TG 58.3 two days later, on the 17th.

22. CTG 58.3, RO, Marianas, pp. 8–9; *Lexington*, AR, 11–19/6/44, pp. 22–3.

23. Taylor, *Mitscher*, p. 215. According to one modern Japanese source, only 1 of 3 Judy dive bombers was shot down, and 8 of 10 Frances medium bombers (Hata/ Izawa, *Naval Aces*, p. 431).

24. *Seahorse*, RWP/4, p. 2; Blair, *Silent Victory*, p. 651. The *Seahorse* sighting was the KON force, returning from their abortive mission to Batjan near Biak. Making up the group were *Yamato* and *Musashi*, heavy cruisers *Haguro* and *Myōkō*, new light cruiser *Noshiro*, and four destroyers. They were not operating as a flanking group, but were actually heading for a rendezvous with the other elements of the First Mobile Fleet.

25. Buell, *Quiet Warrior*, pp. 284–5; Smith, *Coral*, pp. 154–6. For the retirement from Saipan of transports and support ships see ComFifthPhibFor, WD, 6/44, pp. 38–40.

26. The four task groups of TF 58 actually came together at 1200/18.

27. *Tennessee*, WD, 6/44, pp. 7–8; ComFifthFlt, Initial Report, Marianas, p. 3.

28. CTG 58.1, RO, Marianas, p. 7, 28–30; CTG 58.4, WD, 6/44, pp. 13–14; CTG 58.4, RO, Marianas/Bonins, p. 5. The American attack reports claimed 63 planes were destroyed on the ground at Iwo in the afternoon of the 16th.

29. Hata/Izawa, *Naval Aces*, p. 234. Milan Vego, professor at the U.S. Naval War College, considered the Bonin strikes a mistake. The aircraft involved would not be available to Mitscher to conduct search operations for the Japanese carriers to the west (*Major Operations*, p. 260).

30. *Cavalla*, RWP/1, pp. 6–7; Blair, *Silent Victory*, pp. 652–3. *Cavalla* had encountered Supply Force 2, with fleet oilers *Genyo Maru* and *Seiyo Maru*, escorted by two destroyers.

31. CincPac, RO, 6/44, p. 132; ComFifthFlt, Initial Report, Marianas, p. 5. This signal was presumably intended for motivation, rather than as a detailed war plan. Nevertheless, the stress on the battleships is remarkable.

32. Buell, *Quiet Warrior*, pp. 286–7.

33. CincPac, RO, 6/44, p. 132; ComFifthFlt, Initial Report, Marianas, p. 5; Forrestel, *Spruance*, p. 133.

34. *Fanshaw Bay*, RA, 17/6/19; Mor/8, p. 207.

35. *Cavalla* RWP/1, pp. 8–9; Blair, *Silent Victory*, p. 653. *Cavalla* had in fact come near the entire Japanese First Mobile Force, but only saw part of it. The initial contact had been made by radar at 1957/17. Kossler surfaced and made his first report at 2245/17. Spruance reported that this signal was received at 0321/18.

36. ComFifthFlt, Initial Report, Marianas, p. 6. "[A] speed of less than 10 knots *had been made good*," meant the average speed between two points, taking into account zigzagging, changes of course etc. Spruance's concern was evidently that part of the enemy task force was moving more rapidly, to get into a flanking position.

What had actually happened was that the whole First Mobile Fleet (operating together) had been refueling from late on the 16th until the afternoon of the 17th. Ozawa had actually reversed course (to the west) for a time while doing this, in order to stay out of range of American patrol planes.

37. Y'Blood, *Red Sun*, p. 82.

38. CTF 58, RO, Marianas, p. 46; Mor/8, 244; Stillwell, *Battleship Commander*, pp. 210–12; Taylor, *Mitscher*, p. 218. The historian Gerald Astor, apparently mistakenly, places this Mitscher-Lee exchange of the morning of 18 June much later, during the night of 18/19 June (*Wings*, p. 274).

Morison argued that the battleships had trained together and mastered their Mk 8 gunnery radar (Mor/8, pp. 244–5). The historian Trent Hone, however, noted that the battleships had been operating in several different task groups, and some of the heavy cruisers had been occupied with shore bombardment; as a result there had been little joint training. Hone also suggested that not preparing for night battle was an American mistake (Hone, "Surface Battle Doctrine," pp. 85, 94).

39. The First Mobile Force reversed course to the south at 1540/18.

40. ComFifthFlt, Initial Report, Marianas, p. 6–8; ComFifthFlt, WD, 6/44, p. 20.

41. Spruance, "Victory," p. 549. The Battle of Santa Cruz in the South Pacific in 1942 had also been a good example of the Japanese Navy operating with well-separated forces.

42. Japanese carrier scout planes located Mitscher's carrier task groups in mid-afternoon. Rear Adm. Obayashi Sueo of CarDiv 3 in the Van Force prepared a large strike and actually put some fighters and attack planes into the air. However, Ozawa ordered his fleet to turn to the west to lengthen the range, and Obayashi's strike was recalled (Dickson, *Philippine Sea*, p. 89; *JM*/90, pp. 51–2; Y'Blood, *Red Sun*, pp. 84–7). It is uncertain whether this partial strike could have produced a better outcome for the Japanese than the mass strikes that were mounted on the following day.

43. *Saranac*, AA AR, 18/6/44; Mor/8, pp. 207–8, 345–6, 411.

44. At about 2230/18 a signal from ComSubPac about submarine *Stingray* was read by Spruance's radio staff. This related to an earlier garbled transmission from the sub. It seemed to Spruance and his staff that the transmission might have been a sighting report that had been distorted by local Japanese jamming; this, in turn, implied the presence of enemy warships. *Stingray* had been in position in the southeast corner of the four-boat patrol "square." Spruance had an estimated location for *Stingray* (12°10N/139°00E). If in fact the transmission had been a sighting report, then Japanese warships might be only 210 miles WSW of the current position of Task Force 58. The original message from *Stingray* had been sent at 1955, roughly two and a half hours before the discussion aboard *Indianapolis*. In the time elapsed, the Japanese force could have moved 50 miles nearer Saipan.

In fact, the *Stingray* transmission had *not* been a sighting report. It had been garbled, not by enemy jamming but by a technical problem, an antenna wiring fire aboard the submarine (Y'Blood, *Red Sun*, pp. 93, 241n51; Zimmerman, "Forager," p. 86; *Stingray*, RWP/11, pp. 16–17).

45. Direction Finder (DF) fixes were made from distant shore stations, which determined the area of transmission by triangulation. The distances involved meant that the fix was not exact and could be within 100 miles of the actual position. In reality the fix on the 2020/18 transmission was quite accurate, within 40 miles of the enemy flagship (Mor/8, p. 251). At the time, the transmission was not decrypted, but it was later learned that the message had been a request from Ozawa to Kakuta, at the HQ of First Air Fleet on Saipan, requesting coordinated air strikes on the following day, 19 June. The DF fix indicated a position (13°00N/136°00E) roughly 330 miles WSW of the current (2245/18) position of Task Force 58.

46. CTF 58, RO, Marianas, pp. 48.

47. This is the version of the signal from Spruance contained in Mitscher's post-battle reports (CTF 58, RO, Marianas, p. 48). The wording given in Spruance's post-battle reports, pertaining to the same signal, is slightly different: "Change proposed does not appear advisable. Believe indication given by *Stingray* more accurate than that determined by direction-finder [i.e. DF]. If that is so continuation as at present seems preferable. End run by other [enemy] carrier groups

remains possibility and must not be overlooked." (ComFifthFlt, Initial Report, Marianas, p. 7).

48. ComFifthFlt, WD, 6/44, pp. 20–1.

49. Narratives specifically about air combat over TF 58 on 19 June: Belote/Belote, *Titans*, pp. 259–73; Dickson, *Philippine Sea*, pp. 105–34; Friedman, *Fighters*, pp. 124–7; Tillman, *Clash*. See also CincPac, RO, 6/44, pp. 133–140.

50. Taylor, *Mitscher*, pp. 225–6.

51. The frequently reprinted plan of the disposition of TF 58, following S. E. Morison, is not wholly accurate. It depicts TG 58.1, TG 58.3 and TG 58.2 in a straight line running from north to south, with TG 58.4 situated west of TG 58.1 (Mor/8, p. 259). As of 1010/19 the actual disposition of TF 58 was as follows: TG 58.1 was to the NNE of TG 58.3, rather than to the north of it; TG 58.4 was roughly to the WNW of TG 58.1, rather than to the west of it; and TG 58.2 was SSE of TG 58.3, rather than due south of it (Dickson, *Philippine Sea*, pp. 106–7, 114; Y'Blood, *Red Sun*, pp. 98, 106).

52. The First Mobile Fleet had been divided at 2100/18 into three task groups. The tactical designations were "A" (*Kō*) Force, "B" (*Otsu*) Force, and Van Force (*Zeian butai*).

The first Japanese carrier attack of 19 June, later known as "Raid I," was launched from the Van Force, the ships of which were under the overall command of Vice Adm. Kurita. Vice Adm. Ozawa was with "A" Force, aboard his flagship, the new fleet carrier *Taihō*. The "A" Force and "B" Force kept as far as possible from the Americans; they contained the main air striking power of the First Mobile Fleet, with a total of 6 carriers and 342 aircraft.

The Van Force contained the bulk of the Imperial Navy's big surface ships (battleships and heavy cruisers), including the super-battleships *Yamato* and *Musashi*. It was put in a position where it could go forward to finish off the American fleet with gunfire and torpedoes after successful Japanese air strikes from carriers and shore bases. The carrier element of the Van Force was made up of light carriers *Chitose*, *Chiyoda*, and *Zuihō*, which formed Carrier Division 3 ("CarDiv 3") under Rear Adm. Obayashi Sueo. The eighty-eight aircraft aboard the three carriers were designated as NAG 653, under Cdr Kimura Kunji.

53. The terms Raid I, II, III, and IV were not actually used as tactical designations by either side on the day itself. They were adopted in the post-battle American analysis, and by later historians. For the sake of simplifying a complex series of events, they will be used here in the main text.

Tactical raid numbers used by the American fighter director officers (FDOs) on 19 June were somewhat different. The Japanese also used other tactical designations. Raid I, for example, was evidently for the Japanese, "Carrier Division 3, 1st Attack Force" (CarDiv 3/Attack Force 1). This is based on the translation in *JM*/90, p. 51, and in *JM*/91, p. 27.

54. Raid I had been launched from the Van Force at about 0800. As launched, it consisted of forty-five A6M2/Zero fighter-bombers, sixteen newer A6M5/Zero fighters (as an escort) and eight Jill torpedo bombers. There were also two Kate torpedo bombers acting as pathfinders and communications aircraft (Tillman, *Clash*, p. 137; Y'Blood, *Red Sun*, 103).

The total aircraft strength of the three light carriers in the Van Force at the start of the battle had been forty-six A6M2/Zero, seventeen A6M5/Zero, eighteen

Kate, and nine Jill torpedo planes (Tillman, *Clash*, p. 310). Most of the Kates had been used for early-morning scouting flights. Because of the long takeoff run required by Judy dive bombers, they could not operate from Japanese light carriers (Okumiya/Horikoshi, *Zero*, p. 264).

55. On the "special" tactics see Okumiya/Horikoshi, *Zero*, pp. 264-5. Ugaki, *Fading Victory*, pp. 408-9, 421, exemplifies the high expectations of the naval leadership regarding the fighter-bomber units. Bomb-equipped Zeros would also be used for *one-way* "special" attacks in the last year of the war, beginning in October 1944; these were the infamous kamikazes.

56. The A6M5 (Model 52) version of the Mitsubishi Zero entered service in late 1943. It was slightly faster than the A6M2 and had better diving speed, but it was still generally inferior to the F6F-3 Hellcat (Francillon, *Japanese Aircraft*, pp. 371, 376-7).

57. NHHC, *DANFS/South Dakota*; *South Dakota*, WD, 7/44, p. 7.

58. Sherman, *Combat Command*, p. 211.

59. Okumiya/Horikoshi, *Zero*, pp. 263.

60. On the low level of training of NAG 653 pilots (even compared to the other carriers in the First Mobile Fleet) see Hata/Izawa, *Naval Aces*, p. 83.

61. Y'Blood, *Red Sun*, pp.102, 112; Hata/Izawa, *Naval Aces*, pp. 83-4. Evidently, none of the Raid I survivors flew on to Guam or Rota; they returned to their carriers. A contemporary Japanese assessment, regarding all four raids, was as follows: "[I]t seems that our airplane units were attacked by enemy fighters while in cruising formation, and practically all our planes were attacked and shot down before our fighter planes could protect them" (*JM*/90, p. 64).

62. Okumiya/Horikoshi, *Zero*, pp. 262-5.

63. Okumiya/Horikoshi, *Zero*, pp. 264. Surprisingly, Okumiya contrasted the poor expertise of the Japanese commanders with "Rear Admiral [sic] Spruance, the talented leader at Midway"; this was a view that would not necessarily have been fully shared with John Towers, Ted Sherman, and other Pacific Fleet "aviators."

64. Y'Blood, *Red Sun*, pp. 102, 112; Hata/Izawa, *Naval Aces*, pp. 83-4.

65. Tillman, *Clash*, p. 152; Y'Blood, *Red Sun*, p. 12.

66. CincPac, RO, 6/44, p. 134.

67. The need to reorganize (and delay) may have followed the accidental overflying of the Van Force and the dispersal that took place while attempting to evade "friendly" AA fire.

Raid II (Japanese designation CarDiv1/Attack Force 1) had been launched from Ozawa's "A" Force, the heavy carriers *Taihō*, *Shōkaku*, and *Zuikaku*, which made up Carrier Division 1. The aircraft of these carriers were designated as NAG 601, under Cdr Irisa Toshiie. The total strength of CarDiv 1 at the start of the battle had been eighty A6M5/Zero fighters, eleven A6M2/Zero fighter-bombers, nine Val dive bombers, fifty Judy dive bombers, and forty-one Jill torpedo bombers. In addition, dedicated search units included twelve Judy and six Jill aircraft (Tillman, *Clash*, p. 308).

As launched, Raid II consisted of forty-eight A6M5/Zero, fifty-three Judys and twenty-seven Jills, a total of 128 aircraft (see also Hata/Izawa, *Naval Aces*, p. 71). Of these, eight had to abort after launch for technical reasons; a further ten overflew their own Van Force, as a result of which two were destroyed and six had to turn back. This left a total strike force of 110 planes. (There were also two Jill pathfinders and one Judy radar counter-measures plane.) CarDiv1/Attack Force 1 was led by Lt Cdr Tarui Akira, who was commander of the *Taihō* torpedo bomber squadron; he did not survive the battle.

68. Boomhower, *Fighter Pilot*, pp. 104–10; Russell, *McCampbell*, pp. 88–99; Taylor, *Mitscher*, p. 229.

69. Buell, *Quiet Warrior*, pp. 296–7.

70. The historian Barrett Tillman states that 119 aircraft of Raid II actually reached the "target area" and only 31 returned to one of the carriers or reached the airfields at Guam; this indicates losses were 88 (*Clash*, p. 173). Hata/Izawa give a figure of 96 aircraft lost out to 128 that were launched from the Japanese carriers, indicating 32 survivors (*Naval Aces*, p. 71). William Y'Blood states that 128 planes were launched, of which 31 "returned"; the latter group is specified as sixteen Zeros, eleven Judys and four Jills. As will be explained later, by the time the survivors of Raid II returned to Ozawa's "A" Force only one carrier was available to recover them, and a few landed on one of the "B" Force carriers.

71. Taylor, *Mitscher*, p. 227.

72. Raid III was launched from "B" Force or CarDiv 2 (*Hiyō, Junyō, Ryūhō*), while Raid II had come from CarDiv 1. Raid III was designated by the Japanese as "CarDiv 2/Attack Force 1." This attack force was originally trying to home in on the so-called "7 I" sighting (reported by a scout plane four hours earlier, at 0730). However, an order was radioed to this attack force, redirecting it to the "3 I" sighting (reported at 1000), further south (Mor/8, p. 272). Apparently, fewer than half the Raid III force received the redirection message, and the rest returned to their carriers.

Total air strength of "B" Force on hand on 19 June had been fifty-four A6M5/Zero fighters, twenty-six A6M2/Zero fighter-bombers, twenty-nine Val and eleven Judy dive bombers, and sixteen Jill torpedo planes. The CarDiv 2/Attack Force 1 in Raid III consisted of forty-seven planes: fifteen A6M5/Zeros, twenty-five A6M2/Zero fighter-bombers, and seven Jill torpedo planes (Tillman, *Clash*, pp. 309–10; Hata/Izawa, *Naval Aces*, p. 81). With its high proportion of "special" Zero fighter-bombers, this force was not unlike the Raid I group from the Van Force carriers.

73. CTG 58.4, RO, 6–7/44; p. 7; Y'Blood, *Red Sun*, p. 130; Markey, *Well Done!*, p. 179. Some twenty Raid III planes actually found Task Force 58 (mainly TG 58.4) and attempted to attack. Of these, two A6M5/Zeros, four A6M2/Zero fighter-bombers, and one Jill were shot down (Hata/Izawa, *Naval Aces*, p. 82).

74. Raid IV was known to the Japanese as "CarDiv 2/Attack Force 2." It was launched at about 1100 from the carriers of "B" Force and was made up of eighteen A6M5/Zeros, ten A6M2/Zero, twenty-seven Vals, and nine Judys. The "A" Force added fourteen A6M5/Zeros from *Zuikaku* and six Jills from *Taihō* (Tillman, *Clash*, p. 177; Hata/Izawa, *Naval Aces*, p. 82).

75. The inaccurate sighting, designated "15 *Ri*," was made by a Judy (designated reconnaissance plane No. 15) from *Shōkaku*, which had been launched at 0530. It made its report at 0845, which was on the return leg of an extraordinarily long search out to 560 miles. The inaccuracy of the sighting apparently resulted from a failure to correct for compass deviation (Y'Blood, *Red Sun*, pp. 96, 104; Mor/8, pp. 271–2).

76. These eighteen planes were later engaged by two *Lexington* Hellcat/Avenger search teams about 200 miles west of Guam, and six of them were claimed shot down (Y'Blood, *Red Sun*, p. 134).

77. Y'Blood, *Red Sun*, p. 133–4; *Wasp*, WD, 6/44, pp. 7–8.

78. The detachment from Raid IV that made for Guam consisted of twenty Zeros, twenty-seven Vals, and two Jills (Y'Blood, *Red Sun*, p. 105).

79. Hata/Izawa, *Naval Aces*, p. 164; Tillman, *Clash*, p. 183; Y'Blood, *Red Sun*, p. 135. The fighters from Truk were from NAG 253, and they were apparently escorting four attack planes. This was one of the very few contributions of Vice Adm. Kakuta's shore-based First Air Fleet to the 19 June battle.

80. CincPac, RO, 6/44, p. 133. This report was actually dated 7 November 1944, after the Battle of Leyte Gulf, so it may have included an element of comparison.

81. Vego, *Major Operations*, p. 287. Point OPTION was the prearranged recovery location for a carrier air attack force.

82. Mor/8, pp. 277, 319–21; Y'Blood, *Red Sun*, p. 138.

83. Waite, "Airway," p. 21.

9. TF 58 AND THE BATTLE OF THE PHILIPPINE SEA (2):
SUBMARINES AND THE AMERICAN AIR STRIKE

1. *Albacore*, RWP/9, pp. 7–9; Blair, *Silent Victory*, p. 655–6. The original patrol reports gave time in Time Zone "I," but an hour has been added here to align them with most American historical accounts; these used the time zone of the U.S. forces around Saipan (Zone "K"). No Time Zone "J" existed.

2. *Cavalla*, RWP/1, pp. 11–14; Blair, *Silent Victory*, p. 657–8.

3. *Cavalla*, RWP/1, pp. 11–14.

4. Morison has the "A" Force carriers beginning their Raid II launch at 0856 (Mor/8, 269). A more likely timing has *Taihō* launching her contribution to the strike, forty-two aircraft, between 0845 and 0902 (Ahlberg/Lengerer, *Taihō*/2, p. 85).

5. Ahlberg/Lengerer, *Taihō*/2, p. 116. Presumably, it was these planes that Kossler spotted through *Cavalla's* periscope at 1139. This sighting led him toward the "A" Force, and his attack on *Shōkaku*.

6. For *Shōkaku*, the best analysis of damage: CF/Tully, "Sinking"; CF/TROM/ *Shōkaku*. Ahlberg/Lengerer, *Taihō*, is a two-volume account of the carrier's design, structure, and operations.

7. CF/TROM/*Shōkaku*. This was prepared by Anthony Tully in 2010.

8. This course reversal followed completion of the recovery, between 1400 and 1530, of the surviving planes from Raids II and III. For the moment there was no need to steam into the prevailing wind. Ozawa's priority was now to keep out of range of American counterattacks and rendezvous with the oilers, in order to refuel his ships for the next stage of the battle.

9. Ahlberg/Lengerer, *Taihō*/2, pp. 92–3.

10. Personnel figures for *Taihō* are uncertain. One source gives 660 officers and men lost, with "over 1,000" survivors (CF/TROM/*Taihō*). This is based on Japanese sources, and states that losses aboard *Taihō* were considerably lower than those aboard *Shōkaku*. Another source gives the total complement as at least 2,038, which would suggest about 1,400 survivors (Ahlberg/Lengerer, *Taihō*/2, p. 93). An earlier (1978) account, referencing the Japanese official history, provided a much higher loss figure: 1,650 out of 2,150 on board (Dull, *IJN*, p. 308).

11. The weakness of the escort was stressed in the post-war Japanese assessment (*JM*/90, pp. 38, 40). Seven destroyers had been lost in the weeks before the First Mobile Fleet assembled in the Philippine Sea. One "A" Force destroyer had been sunk on the final passage to the Philippine Sea. The lack of destroyers was also stressed in the British Admiralty survey of these events (*WWJ*/4, pp. 124–7). Typically, the screen of an American carrier task group in 1944 comprised at least twelve destroyers. Of the seven destroyers escorting "A" Force, four were big "Akizuki" class AA destroyers, which were perhaps less capable in the anti-submarine role.

According to Ugaki's diary there had been no anti-submarine air patrols from the carriers on the 19th (*Fading Victory*, p. 421). Both *Albacore* and *Cavalla* were forced to dive by aircraft on 18 June, but these seem to have been twin-engined Bettys from Yap (*Albacore*, RWP/9; *Cavalla*, RWP/1).

12. Details of the 0910 attack on a "Shōkaku" class (actually *Taihō*) are given in *Albacore*'s war patrol report (RWP/9, p. 11), but no sighting report to ComSubPac is recorded. There is also no record of the sighting or the attack by *Albacore* in the ComSubPac War Diary (dated 6 July 1944). Blanchard may have decided not to report immediately the location or the outcome of *Albacore*'s encounter with the carrier force, because of the risk of transmission and because he did not believe he had achieved significant damage to his target. The ComSubPac War Diary *does* record another attack on a carrier (*Shōkaku*), at 1218/19, by *Cavalla*. Later published sources seem to have assumed—incorrectly—that the staffs of both Fifth Fleet and TF 58 were aware of *both* the *Albacore* and *Cavalla* sightings and attacks (Dickson, *Philippine Sea*, p. 134; Mor/8, p. 285; Y'Blood, *Red Sun*, p. 142).

13. On 28 June, Lt Cdr Kossler and *Cavalla* were ordered back to Saipan. On 1 July Kossler had a brief meeting there with senior staff officers and was interviewed by journalists (including Robert Sherrod) (Blair, *Silent Victory*, p. 652; *Cavalla* RWP/1, pp. 19, 22, 24; Sherrod, *Westward*, p. 118). This may have partly involved an effort to obtain details of *Cavalla*'s attack, i.e. to ascertain whether a major Japanese fleet unit had in fact been sunk.

14. Blair, *Silent Victory*, p. 659. Blair's account was based on an interview with Blanchard. Even today *Taihō* remains something of mystery ship; only half a dozen photographs survive.

15. The saga of the attack and return of the *Lexington* air group (AG 16) was recounted in a classic wartime book, *Mission beyond Darkness*. The two authors interviewed many of the men who took part (Bryan/Reed, *Mission*). Basic sources on the events of 20 June: CincPac, RO, 6/44; ComFifthFlt, Initial Report, Marianas, pp. 12–13; ComFifthFlt, WD, 6/44; CTF 58, RO, 11/6–10/8/44, pp. 15–17, 57–60; CTG 58.1, RO, 6–27/6/44, p. 10; CTG 58.3, RO, 6/6–6/7/44, pp. 59–71; *Bunker Hill*, Report of Air Attack on Jap. TF, 20/6/44; *Hornet*, AR/ Marianas-Bonins; *Lexington*, AR Marianas; *Wasp*, AR Marianas; CAG 14 [*Wasp*], AAR/Marianas; *JM*/90 and *JM*/91.

Published western accounts of the events of 20 June: Belote/Belote, *Titans*, pp. 274–300; Dickson, *Philippine Sea*, pp. 139–63; Mor/8, pp. 288–304; Reynolds, *Fast Carriers*, pp. 196–203; Reynolds, *Fighting Lady*, pp. 156–68; Stafford, *Big E*, pp. 346–59; Tillman, *Clash*, pp. 201–69; Vego, *Major Operations*, pp. 289–93; Y'Blood, *Red Sun*, pp. 140–93.

16. Prados, *Combined Fleet*, p. 576.

17. Mor/8, p. 288.

18. The exposed location of the refueling point chosen by Ozawa was later criticized by Ugaki, the commander of BatDiv 1 (*Fading Victory*, p. 421). Presumably the rendezvous was chosen some time in advance to allow a rapid return by the First Mobile Fleet to the east, toward the American fleet and Saipan.

19. CTF 58, RO, Marianas, p. 54. It is unclear why Spruance and his staff assumed the damaged carrier was *Zuikaku*, rather than *Shōkaku* or *Taihō*.

20. Reynolds, *Fast Carriers*, pp. xxii, 154, 177–8, 182, 195, 236, 329; Reynolds, *Warpath*, pp. 346–52.

21. Y'Blood, *Red Sun*, p. 148.

22. CincPac, RO, 6/44, pp. 140–6; ComFifthFlt, Initial Report/Marianas, pp. 12–13.

23. The American light-carrier air groups did not include dive bombers. Aboard the heavy carriers there were 197 dive bombers in TG 58.1, TG 58.2, and TG 58.3 at the start of the battle on 11 June (and minimal losses had been suffered in the meantime). Aboard all the carriers in the three task groups were 156 TBF/TBM Avengers. A small number of Hellcats had been lost on 19 July, but the original F6F-3 strength of the three task groups had been 362.

24. Reports at the time used the terms "central" and "western" interchangeably, but the former term is more accurate. These ships (the Japanese "B" Force) were really not located very far west of the group to the south of them.

25. The number of Hellcats excludes sixteen fighters that were covering the attack on the supply groups (Dickson, *Philippine Sea*, p. 246). The CAP for the First Mobile fleet on 20 June was made up of 63 Zero fighters, of which 22 were lost (Private correspondence with Mr James Sawruk, 30 May 2024).

26. The Japanese dual-purpose 5-in/40 AA gun, designated Type 89 HA, was fitted to large ships when the fleet was modernized at the end of the 1930s; the guns could be centrally controlled by a Type 94 AA director. In June 1944 *Shōkaku* and *Zuikaku* were each fitted with sixteen 5-in/40; *Taihō* was fitted with twelve new 3.9-in/68 Type 98 guns. Japanese battleships and heavy cruisers were mostly fitted with the same basic long-range AA armament, i.e. eight 5-in/40 (4 × 2). See also Ahlberg/Lengerer, *Taihō*/2, pp. 49–62; Itani, "AA Gunnery"; Lacroix/Wells, *Japanese Cruisers*, pp. 756–7, 771.

27. *JM*/90, p. 60; Dickson, *Philippine Sea*, pp. 231–4, 246; CincPac, RO, pp. 144, 146. Actual losses to AA fire seem to have been two *Yorktown* Avengers shot down while attempting a torpedo attack against the central group. The contemporary CincPac report admits two Avengers certainly shot down, and two possibly shot down. Dickson has a table indicating that a *Hornet* Helldiver was shot down over the northern group (*Philippine Sea*, pp. 246), but no other source mentions this.

28. Clark Reynolds implied that the leader of the whole TF 58 strike was Lt Cdr Bernard Strean, CO of *Yorktown*'s VF-1 squadron (*Fast Carriers*, pp. 197–8), but this was not the case. Decisions were probably taken by the senior air commander from each of the three task groups; each would have overseen the deployment of a couple of air groups from the big carriers.

29. Cdr Shifley was CO of *Bunker Hill*'s air group, AG 8. The carrier was CVL *Chiyoda*, the battleships were *Kongō* and *Haruna*. CVLs *Monterey* and *Cabot* each contributed only four bomb-carrying Avengers.

30. The cruiser was *Maya*, which was damaged by a near miss. Some sixteen men were killed, and forty injured (CF/TROM/*Maya*).

31. The glide-bombing Avengers came from *Monterey* (AG 28) and *Cabot* (AG 31). The battleship attacked was evidently the *Haruna* (CF/TROM/*Haruna*).

32. The northern group was the remnants of the "A" Force: heavy carrier *Zuikaku*, cruisers *Myōkō*, *Haguro*, and *Yahagi*, and seven destroyers.

33. The Japanese assessment of the strength of the individual American attacks was as follows: against the northern group ("A" Force) about fifty planes, against the central group ("B" Force) about forty planes, and against the southern unit (Van Force) about twenty planes (USSBS, *CPW*, p. 243; *JM*/90, p. 59).

34. Buell, *Dauntless Helldivers*, pp. 253–5; Dickson, *Philippine Sea*, p. 246; Mor/8, p. 298; Reynolds, *Fighting Lady*, p. 157; CF/TROM/*Zuikaku*.

35. *Lexington* and *Enterprise* were the only carriers still operating the SBD Dauntless. The other heavy carriers all had SB2C Helldivers in their bomber (VB) squadrons.

36. The target was auxiliary carrier *Hiyō*. These hits by Hellcat fighter-bombers apparently occurred before the *Belleau Wood* torpedo-plane attacks (CF/TROM/*Hiyō*).

37. CF/TROM/*Hiyō*.

38. The target was apparently *Hiyō*'s sister ship, *Junyō* (Y'Blood, *Red Sun*, p. 166; CF/TROM/*Junyō*). Some fifty-three crew members were killed, and flight operations were halted.

39. The target for the *Enterprise* planes seems to have been the light carrier *Ryūhō*. In the event, that vessel suffered only minor damage from any attack (CF/TROM/*Ryūhō*).

40. On 21 June the Japanese commander of BatDiv 1 in the Van Force summarized the cost of the previous day as carrier *Hiyō* sunk, and minor damage to carriers *Zuikaku*, *Junyō*, and *Chiyoda*, to battleship *Haruna*, and to heavy cruiser *Maya* (near miss) (Ugaki, *Fading Victory*, pp. 416–17). See also *JM*/90, p. 65–6.

41. Oilers *Seiyo Maru* and *Genyo Maru* were damaged by strafing and bomb attacks. The burning *Seiyo Maru* was finished off by a Japanese destroyer at 1930, and *Genyo Maru* was scuttled during the night. The other four oilers and six escorting destroyers escaped without significant damage (CF/TROM/*Seiyo Maru*, *Genyo Maru*; CAG 14, AAR/Marianas).

42. CincPac, RO, 6/44, pp. 146–7.

43. Winston, *Fighting Squadron*, pp. 259–60. The historian Clark Reynolds did point out that "Lighted ship" was the condition for carrier night landings; the flattops had lights embedded the length of the flight deck and ramp light at either end. He also suggested that Clark, the TG 58.1 commander, took the initiative, before Mitscher (*Fast Carriers*, p. 201). Two years earlier, Spruance had illuminated *Hornet* (CV-8) and *Enterprise* off Midway after dark on 5 June 1942—the day after the main battle—while recovering a dive-bomber strike (Lundstrom, *Black Shoe Admiral*, p. 286). In any event, the extra lighting was remarkable, and certainly involved taking a considerable risk from submarine or air attack.

44. Bryan/Reed, *Mission*, pp. 91–2.

45. Dickson, *Philippine Sea*, p. 162; Tillman, *Clash*, p. 48, gives a slightly lower figure.

46. USSBS, *CPW*, p. 244; Vego, *Major Operations*, p. 291; Ugaki, *Fading Victory*, p. 414.

47. "Detailed Battle Report," in USSBS, *CPW*, pp. 244–5. The 160 included 50 U.S. planes claimed shot down in the air battle around TF 58 and Guam on 19 June, 40 planes shot down by fighters in the battle of the 20th (presumably over the Japanese fleet), and 70 by AA fire (also over the fleet).

48. *JM*/90, p. 37. This document appears to have been produced by former IJN officers in the early occupation period. The translation dates from October 1947. Other useful post-war Japanese analyses of the battle: Evans, *Japanese Navy*, pp. 278–333 [Nomura]; Ito, *End*, pp. 93–113; Okumiya/Horikoshi, *Zero*, pp. 262–5.

49. Training of carrier units at Tawi Tawi suffered because they were on "alert in progress" status for the month before 15 June.

50. *JM*/117, p. 26. This analysis was written in the early post-war period.

51. Jon Prados stressed the role of the commander of the First Air Fleet: "A key error on the Japanese side is that Kakuta failed to apprise his colleagues of the actual state of the First Air Fleet, knowledge of which might have led Ozawa to turn away or Toyoda to terminate the "A" Operation" (*Combined Fleet*, p. 574).

52. In his diary notes of 24 June 1944, Vice Adm. Ugaki wrote: "The task force [First Mobile Fleet] movements lacked speed. In spite of the fact that the operation began on the 13th [sic], and the enemy landing on the 14th [sic], it wouldn't be ready for the decisive battle before the 19th. It must be called a very slow-moving force." In a post-battle discussion with Ugaki on 28 June, Admiral Toyoda apparently stated that if the battle had occurred two days earlier the outcome would have been more favorable. Toyoda blamed the Naval General Staff for the delay of a couple of days in issuing the "stand by" order for the "A" Operation (Ugaki, *Fading Victory*, pp. 420, 424). An authoritative Japanese report written in the autumn of 1944 made the same point that the fleet movement should have been begun on 13 June rather than 15 June (USSBS, *CPW*, p. 63).

On the other hand, it is unlikely that the Japanese movement could have been made any more rapidly. Even if it had been, the First Mobile Fleet would have not been in a stronger position on 17 June than it was on the 19th. Spruance and Mitscher would not have split their forces by sending two task groups to raid the Bonins, and all four task groups of TF 58 would still have been available.

53. *JM*/90, p. 42, 66–7. According to another source, First Air Fleet officially had 1,750 aircraft, but less than half were deployed; it included only 435 planes on 11 June 1944 and only 156 on 18 June (Evans, *Japanese Navy*, p. 317 [Nomura]); Nomura Minoru served as a junior officer on the Naval General Staff in 1944.

54. MMAL, ATIS Translation No. 4, p. 7. On the continuing dominance in the IJN of the decisive-battle concept, see Evans/Peattie, *Kaigun*, pp. 479–80.

55. CincPac, RO, 6/44, p. 157.

56. Unlike the other elements, the battleships and cruisers did not in the end play a conventional role. Nevertheless, there was an expectation that in a full-scale fleet-versus-fleet action the big-gun ships might play a vital role, finishing off damaged stragglers.

57. One authoritative account of the battle remarks that "the scale of American air searches borders on negligence" (Dickson, *Philippine Sea*, p. 31) The problem was also commented on, briefly, in CincPac, RO, pp. 233–4.

58. ComFifthFlt, Initial Report, Marianas, pp. 7–8.

59. MMAL, ATIS Translation No. 4, p. 24; No. 5, pp. 9, 11.

60. CTF 58, RO, Marianas, p. 37–8.

61. CTF 58, RO, Marianas, p. 61. This report was prepared jointly by Mitscher and his chief of staff, Arleigh Burke.

62. CTF 58, RO, Marianas, pp. 37–8, 199. Mitscher was Spruance's subordinate; Spruance was required to comment on (endorse) Mitscher's reports.

63. Potter, *Nimitz*, p. 300. See also CincPac, RO, pp. 234–7; this is part of Annex B, "Comments."

64. CincPac, RO, 6/44, p. 156. By "circumstances" Nimitz seems to have been referring to the failure of some of the search planes, which should have provided the location of Japanese fleet and justified the westward movement of TF 58.

65. CincPac, RO, 6/44, p. 235.

66. CincPac, RO, 6/44, p. 235.

67. CincPac, RO, 6/44, p. 236. The battle of Cape Engaño in November 1944 did involve carriers on both sides, but the Japanese did not attempt an attack on the American fleet.

68. For the land battle in the Marianas: Alexander, *Storm Landings*, pp. 62–85; Crowl, *Marianas*, pp. 33–268; Hoffman, *Saipan*; Isely/Crowl, *Marines*, pp. 310–58; Peattie, *Nan'yo*, pp. 280–90; Shaw, *Central Pacific Drive*, pp. 231–356.

69. Buell, *Quiet Warrior*, p. 313. Sasebo was a major Japanese naval base on Kyushu.

70. *I-10* was probably sunk by destroyers *David W. Taylor* and *Riddle* near oiler group TG 50.17 (CF/TROM/*I-10*).

71. Kawamura, *Emperor*, pp. 128–34; Wetzler, *Imperial Japan*.

72. USSBS, *CPW*, p. 220.

73. USSBS, *Interrogation/2*, p. 356. But, typically, Nagano could not contemplate "being ready to throw up our hands"—surrender—as an alternative. Nagano had been ousted by Tōjō after the February 1944 Truk raid.

74. For details: Shaw, *Central Pacific Drive*, p. 355–430.

75. Spruance, "Victory," p. 550.

76. Lodge, *Guam*; Shaw, *Central Pacific Drive*, pp. 431–55. The Marines actually came ashore on Guam on 21 July, three days before the invasion of Tinian, but the fighting was more extensive and lasted longer.

77. Lodge, *Guam*, p. 159; Shaw, *Central Pacific Drive*, p. 567. The headquarters of Thirty-First Army had been located at Saipan, but at the time of the 15 June invasion, Gen. Obata had been on Guam, returning from an inspection trip to Palau. The last Japanese Army straggler on Guam, Sergeant Yokoi Shōichi, was found in 1972.

78. Lodge, *Guam*, p. 166.

79. U.S. losses in ground fighting in the Marianas were lower than those suffered in later island battles nearer Japan, after the Japanese Army changed its tactics and fought prolonged battles inland. The best known were at Peleliu (Palau) in September 1944, Iwo Jima in February 1945, and Okinawa in April 1945.

80. Craven, *Pacific: Matterhorn*, pp. 507–25, covers base construction and B-29 deployment in the Marianas.

81. Halsey/Bryan, *Story*, p. 197.

10 SUPREMACY AT SEA

1. In the action off Cape Engaño, part of the Battle of Leyte Gulf, heavy carrier *Zuikaku* and light carriers *Chitose*, *Chiyoda*, and *Zuihō* were destroyed. However, they were a decoy force and were only carrying a small number of aircraft. Many of the surface warships the Japanese fleet deployed at Leyte Gulf escaped, after the gunnery action off Samar Island.

2. Mor/12, pp. 58–60; Symonds, *Nimitz*, p. 324; Vego, *Leyte*, pp. 126–7, 343.

3. The concept is borrowed from John Lundstrom (*First Team*).

4. NHHC, "US Naval Personnel in World War II: Service and Casualty Statistics." These figures exclude personnel of the USMC and the Coast Guard. A further 2,111 naval personnel had been killed in December 1941, mainly at Pearl Harbor.

5. Spruance's terms come from Spruance, "Victory," p. 542. The final part of the Philippines campaign, the invasion of Luzon with the landing at Lingayen Gulf in January 1945, did involve a short and deadly spurt of kamikaze attacks from local bases.

6. NHHC, *DANFS/Princeton, Indianapolis*; NHHC, Notable Ships/*Indianapolis*.

7. NHHC, "US Naval Personnel in World War II: Service and Casualty Statistics."

8. No more "Independence" class light carriers joined the fleet in the period after August 1944. *Saipan* and *Wright*, two more CVLs, were not commissioned until 1946 and 1947. The older *Saratoga* and *Enterprise* served with the fleet, alongside the "Essex" class vessels.

9. Kamikaze missions also began during the Leyte Gulf battle in 1944, but numbers were small.

10. NHHC, "US Naval Personnel in World War II: Service and Casualty Statistics"; NHHC, "World War II Casualties."

11. Coletta, *Mitscher*, p. 321; Taylor, *Mitscher*, pp. 290–8. On the following day (12 May 1945), Spruance was also in personal danger off Okinawa. A kamikaze had crashed into his flagship *Indianapolis* on 31 March, and a second suicide plane hit his replacement flagship, the old battleship *New Mexico* on 12 May. Aboard *New Mexico* fifty men were killed and a hundred injured (Buell, *Quiet Warrior*, pp. 378, 388).

12. Willmott, "After Midway," p. 191. Poor intelligence exaggerated the success of the kamikazes, which in turn fed false expectations by Japanese commanders. Kamikazes did provide a "precision-guided" weapon, but one too small to sink a large ship. Conventional dive bombing and torpedo bombing attacks which *could* sink large ships (and did so in 1944 when the Americans were the attackers) had become of little use to the Japanese in the face of radar-guided F6F Hellcats and the huge barrage of AA fire; this had been amply demonstrated at the "Turkey Shoot" of 19 June 1944.

13. Spruance, "Victory," p. 555.

14. Truman, *Mr. Citizen*, p. 223. The former President also added that King "was a great Chief of Naval Operations, and he was responsible for the reorganization of the navy after Pearl Harbor."

15. Potter, *Nimitz*, pp. 401–9.

16. Leahy, a former CNO, was chairman of the Joint Chiefs of Staff and an influential advisor to the President. The five-star Fleet Admiral rank was only ever awarded to these four officers. The five-star "General of the Army" rank was introduced at the same time, when Generals Marshall, MacArthur, Eisenhower, and Arnold were promoted.

17. Buell, *Quiet Warrior*, pp. 471–2.

18. Buell, *Quiet Warrior*, p. xxx; Marder, *Old Friends/2*, p. 418. For Admiral Spruance's own views on publicity, and private criticism of Halsey, see Buell, *Quiet Warrior*, pp. 363–4.

19. Buell, *Quiet Warrior*, p 472.

20. Spruance, "Victory," pp. 540, 554–5. As Spruance added, "The foundation of our operations was logistics." One surprising omission in his summing-up was Lockhart's submarine campaign, but that was dealt with elsewhere in his talk:

"[I]t would be difficult to overestimate the part that our submarines played in bringing about the defeat of Japan" (p. 542).

21. Theodore Taylor stated that Secretary Forrestal actually offered Mitscher the post of Chief of Naval Operations in November 1945—as an alternative to Nimitz (Taylor, *Mitscher*, p. 4–5). However, a later biographer of Mitscher considered a firm offer from Forrestal to have been unlikely (Coletta, *Mitscher*, pp. 339, 360). According to Clark Reynolds, Forrestal definitely wanted an "air admiral" as CNO, but Admiral John Towers was his preference (Reynolds, *Towers*, p. 514).

22. Taylor, *Mitscher*, pp. 312–13.

23. Taylor, *Mitscher*, pp. 338–40. Mitscher was an aggressive carrier commander. He was revered by the mass of flyers who served under him, and he undoubtedly paid great attention to their welfare. On the other hand, at least one of the outstanding wartime air leaders thought that Mitscher had been behind the times; John ("Jimmy") Thach recalled him as an "old time aviator" who would not listen to advice. One example was his delay in adopting night-fighter operations (Coletta, *Mitscher*, pp. 225, 323). James Flatley, who served as operations officer on Mitscher's staff in the late summer of 1944 commented that Mitscher lacked recent flight experience and held conservative views on tactics and flight operations (Ewing, *Reaper Leader*, p. 205).

24. NHHC, "US Navy Personnel Strength 1775 to the Present."

25. Faltum, *Essex*, p. 113.

26. NHHC, *DANFS/Enterprise*. The battleship *Missouri*, now a museum ship at Pearl Harbor, was the site of the Japanese surrender ceremony, but she arrived in the Pacific too late to take part in the Central Pacific fighting. The old battleship *Texas*, preserved near Houston, also did not arrive in the Pacific until 1945. Only one of the great number of wartime cruisers has been preserved, the much-modified "Cleveland" class *Little Rock*, in Buffalo, NY; she was commissioned at the end of the war and did not reach the Pacific.

27. The NSA also set up the National Security Council and the Central Intelligence Agency. The three main armed services were placed within a "National Defense Establishment"; the Department of Defense would not be created until 1949.

28. Barlow, *Revolt*; NHHC, Peter C. Luebke, "The Revolt of the Admirals"; McFarland, "1949 Revolt."

29. Denfeld, who had become CNO after Nimitz in December 1947, was not an aviator. His only combat experience in the Pacific War had come after March 1945, when he briefly commanded Battleship Division 9, flying his flag in the new *Wisconsin*. In 1942–45 Denfeld had served as deputy chief of the Bureau of Navigation/Personnel. After the Japanese surrender Denfeld returned to Washington as chief of BuPers, serving from September 1945 to December 1947.

30. Potter, *Nimitz*, pp. 443–52. Aged 52 in 1949, Sherman was the youngest ever CNO, five years younger than Denfeld, but he would die in 1951 after a heart attack. Two prominent aviators did leave the Navy as a result of their outspokenness during the "revolt." One was Vice Adm. James Bogan, commander of a CVE task group in 1944–45, the other was Capt. John Crommelin, Air Officer of *Enterprise* during the Battle of Santa Cruz and a survivor of the sinking of CVE *Liscome Bay* off Makin in November 1943.

31. Marder, *Old Friends/2*, p. 570.

32. Rodger, *Command*, p. 543.

33. Roskill, *War at Sea*/2, p. 238.
34. The sixth armored carrier, *Implacable*, was only commissioned in August 1944. One pre-war carrier survived, the 22,500-ton *Furious*. *Colossus* and *Glory*, 13,000-ton new light carriers, were commissioned in late 1944 and 1945 and arrived in the Pacific as the war ended. The British had to use American-built escort carriers for many of their fleet operations in the Atlantic and the Indian Ocean.
35. One factor was the role of the independent Royal Air Force, created in 1918. It had been given control over naval aviation until 1937. The Royal Navy lacked the core of senior "aviator" officers, which played such an important part in the U.S. Navy.
36. Grove, *Vanguard*, p. ix.
37. Grove, *Vanguard*, pp. 410–11.
38. Madsen, *Forgotten Fleet.*
39. Five of the seven "Essex" class that took part in the Central Pacific campaign were among those fully modernized; one exception was the war-damaged *Bunker Hill*. Until 1950 carriers had "axial" or straight decks. The angled deck was first developed by the Royal Navy. It comprised a deck extension set off at an angle on the port side of the flight deck. This enabled aircraft to land and take off without moving parked aircraft; it was still possible, in addition, to launch aircraft using the conventional bow catapults.
40. A useful summary of the development of the U.S. Navy in this period, written by Norman Friedman, is in Gardiner, *Conway's*, pp. 544–633. From the 1960s the U.S. Navy also built over twenty helicopter carriers/amphibious assault ships, which were the size of World War II carriers and had straight (non-angled) flight decks. The second of the 28,000-ton "Wasp" class was named USS *Essex* (LHD-2).
41. The Soviet Naval Missile Force (*Morskaia raketnaia aviatsiia*) was the 1960s equivalent of the Kakuta's First Air Fleet. As the Soviet system collapsed in 1991, the Russians did succeed in commissioning one large conventional carrier, the *Admiral Kuznetsov*. On the whole, for most of the Soviet period, the Soviet Navy was structured as a defensive force, subordinate to the other services.

   At the time of writing, China does operate two medium-sized carriers, commissioned in 2012 and 2019; a third is fitting out. This is a work of history, and not a place for speculation or "lessons." However, the appearance of a powerful ocean-going Chinese Navy (PLAN) does still seem decades away.
42. The carrier element in the current Fifth Fleet is now Task Force 50.

APPENDIX II. THE OTHER SIDE OF THE OCEAN: JAPANESE FORCES AND STRATEGY

1. An ideal authoritative general account of the Pacific War would require a reading knowledge of Japanese. There are, however, a number of valuable treatments in English on the Imperial Japanese Navy (IJN). Evans/Peattie, *Kaigun*, provides the pre-war background, which is important for understanding wartime Japanese decisions and capabilities. Dull, *IJN*, narrates events. Prados, *Combined Fleet*, is especially strong on the intelligence side, but also includes material on the IJN still not available elsewhere.

   Hayashi, *Kōgun*, and Drea, *Japan's Imperial Army*, cover ground forces and overall strategy. Willmott, "After Midway," provides perceptive insights on Japanese naval strategy and the reasons for its failure. Wetzler, *Imperial Japan*, provides a recent analysis of underlying problems, especially as illuminated by the fall of Saipan.

Important first-person sources on the IJN side: Prange/Goldstein/Dillon, *God's Samurai*; Evans, *Japanese Navy*; Goldstein/Dillon, *Pacific War Papers*; Ugaki, *Fading Victory*; and USSBS, *Interrogation*. Early valuable post-war material prepared by U.S. government agencies with the cooperation of former senior IJN officers includes the Japanese Monograph series, especially *JM/*90, *JM/*91, and *JM/*116, as well USSBS, *CPW*.

On IJN aviation see Peattie, *Sunburst*, and Okumiya/Horikoshi, *Zero*. The online Combined Fleet/TROM database gives comprehensive details of IJN ship movements.

2. https://avalon.law.yale.edu/20th_century/decade17.asp.
3. Willmott, "After Midway," p. 187.
4. For a full order of battle see *JM/*116.
5. An earlier First Air Fleet command existed from April 1941 until July 1942 (after Midway), when it was renamed the Third Fleet. It was essentially the carrier force commanded by Nagumo.
6. Prange, *God's Samurai*.
7. On the pernicious effect of the decisive-battle concept see Evans/Peattie, *Kaigun*, pp. 129, 132, 479–80, 482.
8. USSBS, *Interrogation/*2 [Fukudome], p. 522. Prados, *Combined Fleet*, pp. 484–9, provides a positive view of Koga. See also Wilds, "Admiral."
9. *JM/*117, pp. 11, 32.
10. Prados, *Combined Fleet*, pp. 487–8; *JM/*117, pp. 10–15. The term "Z" evidently came from the historic signal flag flown by Admiral Tōgō Heihachirō at the Battle of Tsushima in 1905; this was the decisive victory over the Russian fleet. An international maritime signal for "Z," the flag is quartered diagonally with the colors yellow, blue, red, and black. To this flag Tōgō had assigned the meaning "The fate of the Empire rests on the outcome of this battle. Let each man do his utmost"— which in turn was based on a message made by Lord Nelson before Trafalgar. Vice Adm. Nagumo had flown a "Z" flag from his flagship before the air strike on Pearl Harbor. The "Y" operations were concerned with the Indian Ocean.
11. After an American carrier raid on the Gilbert Islands on 18 September 1943, Koga had dispatched a large force eastward from Truk to the anchorage at Eniwetok in the Marshalls. Under the command of Admiral Ozawa, it included carriers *Shōkaku*, *Zuikaku*, and *Zuihō*, battleships *Yamato* and *Nagato*, eight heavy cruisers and two light cruisers. The ships returned to Truk on 25 September; Koga himself had remained at Truk aboard flagship *Musashi*, with three other battleships. The second sortie came a month later. On 17 October, fearing an American attack on Wake Atoll, Koga had led an even larger force to Eniwetok, with the three carriers, *Yamato* and *Musashi* and three other battleships, eight heavy cruisers and three light cruisers; they returned to Truk without incident on 26 October (CF/TROM/*Nagato*).
12. Drea, *Japan's Imperial Army*, p. 232; Hayashi, *Kōgun*, pp. 72–3; Morton, *Strategy*, pp. 543–58, 655–60; Smith, *Approach*, pp. 87–8.
13. The admiral's portrait appeared on the cover of *Time* magazine on 8 November 1943, with the caption "Japan's Koga. Where is his fleet?"
14. Claringbould, *RO-Go*, Hata/Izawa, *Naval Aces*, p. 50; USSBS, *Interrogation/*2 [Fukudome], p. 516. The force sent from Truk to Rabaul and Bougainville apparently comprised 66 Zero fighters and 86 attack planes.

After this, heavy carriers *Shōkaku* and *Zuikaku* departed from Truk on 7 December 1943. They refitted in Kure in Japan, and then left on 6 February 1944 for a new fleet base at faraway Singapore. Light carrier *Zuihō* remained in the Central Pacific until April but served mainly as an aircraft transport. The two medium-sized (24,000-ton) "auxiliary" carriers, *Hiyō* and *Junyō* (converted passenger liners), were under repair in Japan after 1943 submarine attacks (*Hiyō* in June 1943 and *Junyō* in November). *Hiyō* departed for training near Singapore in early December 1943, and *Junyō* rejoined the operational fleet at Tawi Tawi in the southern Philippines in May 1944. Light carrier *Ryūhō* was refitting in Japan in September and October 1943, and transferred from there to Singapore and the western Pacific. "New" light carriers *Chitose* and *Chiyoda* were completing their rushed conversion from naval auxiliaries. They were in shipyards in Japan until 1 January 1944, after which they proceeded to Singapore for working up (CF/TROMs).

15. Prados, *Combined Fleet*, p. 539.
16. Prange, *God's Samurai*, chs. 12–16.
17. Prados, *Combined Fleet*, pp. 599–600, discusses late-war U.S. intelligence on Japanese aircraft production and deployment. See also Francillon, *Japanese Aircraft*, pp. 1–28, and Hayashi, *Kōgun*, pp. 70–85.
18. Hayashi, *Kōgun*, p.109; Morton, *Strategy*, p. 552–8.
19. MMAL, ATIS Translation No. 4, pp. 7–28. This document was recovered by Filipino guerrillas after the Fukudome air crash off Cebu on 1 April 1944. It was translated by Allied intelligence in Australia and made available to the American Pacific command before the invasion of Saipan.
20. MMAL, ATIS Translation No. 4, pp. 7–8; USSBS, *CPW*, p. 221. Item "1" evidently included submarine activity and the planned air raids on Majuro, Operations YU-GO and TAN (CF/"Operation Yu-Go," "Operation Tan No. 2").
21. They also specified four different types of operation. "A" was carriers with full screen. "B" was carriers operating with a partial screen, while a "main body" of surface ships undertook a separate operation. "C" was the same, but where the first strike would be made from carriers, subsequent flights would be made from land bases. "D" was surface forces without carriers.

    The plan of operations included appropriate responses when there was "danger of attack," when there was "great danger of attack," or when the enemy attack was actually taking place. It specified responses for Japanese forces in the areas actually being attacked by the enemy, and for forces in adjacent areas. General procedures for surface-force operations were laid out, as well as those for air and submarine forces.

    It was also specified that if the attack occurred in the New Guinea or the Central Pacific area the staff of the Combined Fleet would be located either at Tinian in the Marianas or at Davao in the Philippines.
22. MMAL, ATIS Translation No. 5, pp. 2–12. This document was also recovered from the Cebu crash.
23. Toyoda's appointment and the death ("in action") of Koga were announced on 5 May. Toyoda had been commander of the Fourth Fleet in north China in 1937–38, then in 1938–39 commander of the Second Fleet (also operating in Chinese waters). After that he held senior administrative posts, including Director of the Naval Shipbuilding Command, commander of the Kure and Yokohama Naval Districts, and member of the Supreme War Council.

24. USSBS, *CPW*, pp. 225–6; *JM*/117, pp. 21–4. The three documents were not available to Admiral Spruance at the time of the Philippine Sea battle.

25. USSBS, *CPW*, pp. 8–9, 226–31; *JM*/117, pp. 21–6. Although this superseded Order No. 73 (8 March 1944) and a number of other directives, it involved the same overall concept as the "Z" operations.

26. USSBS, *CPW*, p. 233.

27. USSBS, *CPW*, p. 233. Both orders were dated 3 May 1944. It is remarkable that one suggested a decisive battle was imminent, while the other referred to the coming autumn. Given the translation, the texts have to be treated with caution. The underlying reality was that the Japanese preparations were far from complete, in terms of aircraft supply, air-group training, and forward airfield construction.

28. USSBS, *CPW*, pp. 241, 260.

29. USSBS, *CPW*, p. 260.

30. USSBS, *CPW*, pp. 260–1.

31. USSBS, *CPW*, p. 260. The "regular" carrier group presumably refers to the carriers of TF 58, rather than the American escort carriers operating east of Saipan.

32. *JM*/90, p. 37.

BIBLIOGRAPHY

PART I. U.S. NAVY WAR DIARIES

Unless otherwise indicated, all primary sources cited in the notes come from a collection within the online Fold3 database: https://www.fold3.com (browse "wwii war diaries"). The collection is listed as "US, World War II War Diaries, 1941–1945." In fact, these documents all relate to the U.S. Navy, but coverage extends well beyond basic war diaries. Page references in the notes refer to "pages" in the online (Fold3) version, not pages in the original printed version or archival mark-up.

Abbreviations used in U.S. Navy War Diaries citations:

AA AR	Anti-Aircraft Action Report
AAR	Air Action Report
AR	Action Report
CAG	Commander, Air Group
CincPac	Commander-in-Chief, Pacific Fleet [and Pacific Ocean Areas] [Nimitz]
ComCenPacFor	Commander, Central Pacific Force [Spruance]
ComFifthFlt	Commander, Fifth Fleet [Spruance]
ComFifthPhibFor	Commander, Fifth Amphibious Force
CominCh	Commander-in-Chief, U.S. Fleet [King]
ComSubPac	Commander, Submarine Force, Pacific Fleet [Lockwood]
CTF 58	Commander, Task Force 58 [Mitscher]
CTG . . .	Commander, Task Group [with task group number]
POA	Pacific Ocean Areas
RA	Report of Action
RO	Report of Operations
RWP/ . . .	Report of War Patrol [/patrol number]
WD	War Diary

PART II. OTHER PRIMARY SOURCES

Abbreviations used in primary source citations *other than* U.S. Navy War Diaries (Fold3):

ATIS	Allied Translator and Interpreter Section
CARL	Combined Arms Research Library
CF	Combined Fleet
CF/TROM	Combined Fleet/Tabular Record of Movements
DANFS	Dictionary of American Naval Fighting Ships
DTIC	Defense Technical Information Center
HABS	Historic American Buildings Survey
JANAC	Joint Army-Navy Assessment Committee
JM	*Japanese Monograph*
MMAL	MacArthur Memorial Archive and Library
NA	National Archives [of the U.S.]
NHHC	Naval History and Heritage Command (Online Reading Room)
TROM	Tabular Record of Movements
USSBS	U.S. Strategic Bombing Survey
Valor	Hall of Valor: The Military Medals Database

Combined Arms Research Library [CARL] https://cgsc.contentdm.oclc.org

Current Tactical Orders and Doctrine, U.S. Fleet, USF10B

Combined Fleet [CF] http://www.combinedfleet.com

David Dickson, Bob Hackett, and Sander Kingisepp, "Operation Yu-go"
Bob Hackett, Sander Kingisepp, "Operation Tan No. 2"
Anthony Tully, Jon Parshall, and Richard Wolff, "The Sinking of Shokaku—An Analysis"
TROM [Tabular Record of Movements]

Defense Technical Information Center [DTIC] https://discover.dtic.mil

Campaign Plan GRANITE I
Campaign Plan GRANITE II

Hall of Valor: The Military Medals Database [Valor]
https://valor.militarytimes.com

Historical American Buildings Survey [HABS]

U.S. Naval Base, Pearl Harbor, Makalapa Support Facilities HABS No. HI-392 https://memory.loc.gov/master/pnp/habshaer/hi/hi0600/hi0649/data/hi0649data.pdf

HyperWar/U.S. NAVY in World War II https://www.ibiblio.org/hyperwar/USN

"Japanese Radio Communications and Radio Intelligence"
ONI Combat Narrative. "The Battle of the Santa Cruz Islands: 26 October 1942"
"War Service Fuel Consumption of U.S. Naval Surface Vessels" (FTP 218)

Japanese Monographs [JM] http://ddsnext.crl.edu/titles/31862/ items?terms=&page=0

JM/90 Operation "A"
JM/91 Operation "A" Chronology
JM/116 The Imperial Japanese Navy in World War II
JM/117 Outline of Third Phase Operations
JM/171 Submarine Operations in Third Phase Operations, Part II
JM/184 Submarine Operations in Third Phase Operations, Parts III, IV, V

MacArthur Memorial Archives and Library [MMAL] https://macarthurmemorial. org/337/MacArthur-Memorial-Archives-and-Library

ATIS Translation No. 4, 23/5/44. "Z" Operation Orders
ATIS Translation No. 5, 28/5/44. "A Study of the Main Features of Decisive Air Operations in the Central Pacific"

National Archives of the U.S. [NA]

Commander in Chief, U.S. Pacific Fleet, Current Tactical Orders and Doctrine U.S. Pacific Fleet, PAC-10, box 22, RG 38
Commander Fast Carrier Task Forces, United States Pacific Fleet, Task Force Instructions (FastCar TFI-1), 24 May 1944, box 113, RG 38

Naval History and Heritage Command [NHHC] https://www.history.navy.mil

Dictionary of American Naval Fighting Ships [DANFS] https://www.history.navy.mil/ research/histories/ship-histories/danfs.html
Mark L. Evans and Roy A. Grossnick, *United States Naval Aviation 1910–2010* https://www.history.navy.mil/research/publications/publications-by-subject/naval-aviation-1910-2010.html
H-Grams https://www.history.navy.mil/about-us/leadership/director/directors-corner/ h-grams.html
Modern Biographical Files https://www.history.navy.mil/research/library/research-guides/modern-biographical-files-ndl.html
Online Reading Room https://www.history.navy.mil/research/library/online-reading-room.html
"Antiair Action Summary" USN in WWII (8 October 1945)
"Combat Information Center Manual." CIC [Combat Information Center] Manual (RADSIX) Radar Bulletin No. 6
"Interrogations of Japanese Officials," USSBS, vols 1 and 2
"Japanese Ground Forces" ["Know your enemy"]
"Japanese Naval and Merchant Shipping Losses in World War II" (The Joint Army-Navy Assessment Committee, JANAC)
"Japanese Radio Communications and Radio Intelligence" ["Know your enemy"]
"Our Navy at War" [King Reports]
"Radio Proximity (VT) Fuzes"
"Seabee History"
"Ship to Shore Movement: General Instructions for Transports, Cargo Vessels, and Landing Craft of Amphibious Forces" [FTP 211]
"U.S. Navy at War" [King, second report]

"U.S. Navy at War" [King, final report]
"U.S. Navy" [Personnel: 1775–]
"U.S. Navy" [Personnel: WWII]
"U.S. Radar, Operational Characteristics" [FTP 217]
"War Instructions United States Fleet," FTP 143(A) (1/11/44)
"World War II Casualties"

PART III. PUBLISHED BOOKS AND ARTICLES

Abbreviations to published books and articles used in the notes:

CHSWW	*Cambridge History of the Second World War*
CPW	The *Campaigns of the Pacific War* (USSBS)
Mor/ . . .	Morison, *History of U.S. Naval Operations in World War II* (with vol. number)
USNIP	*United States Naval Institute Proceedings*
USNWCR	*U.S. Naval War College Review*
USSBS	U.S. Strategic Bombing Survey
WWJ/ . . .	*The War with Japan* [/vol. number]

For reprints, the original publication date is provided in square brackets.

Abe Zenji. *The Emperor's Sea Eagle: A Memoir of the Attack on Pearl Harbor and the War in the Pacific* (Honolulu, 2006)

Ahlberg, Lars and Hans Lengerer. *Taihō* (2 vols, Gdansk, 2003)

Alden, John D. *The Fleet Submarine in the U.S. Navy: A Design and Construction History* (London, 1979)

Alexander, Joseph. *Storm Landings: Epic Amphibious Landings in the Central Pacific* (Annapolis, 1997)

Astor, Gerald. *Wings of Gold: The U.S. Naval Air Campaign in World War II* (New York, 2007)

Baer, George W. *One Hundred Years of Sea Power: The U.S. Navy, 1890–1990* (Stanford, 1994)

Ballantine, Duncan S. *U.S. Naval Logistics in the Second World War* (Princeton, 1947)

Barlow, Jeffrey G. *Revolt of the Admirals: The Fight for Naval Aviation, 1945–1950* (London, 1998)

Beaver, Floyd. *Sailor from Oklahoma: One Man's Two-Ocean War* (Annapolis, 2009)

Belote, James H. and William M. Belote. *Titans of the Seas: The Development and Operations of Japanese and American Carrier Task Forces during World War II* (New York, 1975)

Benson, Robert L. *A History of U.S. Communications Intelligence during WWII: Policy and Administration* (Fort Meade, 1997)

Blackburn, Tom. *The Jolly Rogers: The Story of Tom Blackburn and Navy Fighting Squadron VF-17* (New York, 1989)

Blair, Clay. *Silent Victory: The U.S. Submarine War against Japan* (Philadelphia, 1975)

The Bluejackets' Manual 1944 (12th ed., Annapolis, 1944)

Boomhower, Ray E. *Fighter Pilot: The World War II Career of Alex Vraciu* (Indianapolis, 2010)

Boslaugh, David L. "Radar and the Fighter Directors" https://ethw.org/Radar_and_the_Fighter_Directors

Boyd, Carl and Yoshida Akihiko. *The Japanese Submarine Force and World War II* (Annapolis, 2002)

Bradford, James C. *Quarterdeck and Bridge: Two Centuries of American Naval Leaders* (Annapolis, 1997)

Bradsher, Greg. "The 'Z Plan' Story: Japan's 1944 Naval Battle Strategy Drifts into U.S. Hands," *Prologue*, 37:3 (Fall 2005)

Brower, Charles F. *Defeating Japan: The Joint Chiefs of Staff and Strategy in the Pacific War, 1943–1945* (New York, 2012)

Brown, Eric. *Wings of the Navy: Flying Allied Carrier Aircraft of World War Two* (Annapolis, 1987)

Bryan, Joseph and Philip G. Reed. *Mission beyond Darkness* (New York, 1945)

Buchanan, A. R. *The Navy's Air War: A Mission Completed* (New York, 1946)

Budiansky, Stephen. *Battle of Wits: The Complete Story of Codebreaking in World War II* (London, 2001)

Buell, Harold L. *Dauntless Helldivers: A Dive-Bomber Pilot's Epic Story of the Carrier Battles* (New York, 1991)

Buell, Thomas B. *Master of Sea Power: A Biography of Fleet Admiral Ernest J. King* (Boston, 1980)

Buell, Thomas B. *The Quiet Warrior: A Biography of Admiral Raymond A. Spruance* (Annapolis, 1987 [1974])

Building the Navy's Bases in World War II: History of the Bureau of Yards and Docks and the Civil Engineer Corps, 1940–1946 (2 vols, Washington, 1947)

Campbell, John. *Naval Weapons of World War II* (London, 2007)

Carter, Worrall Reed. *Beans, Bullets and Black Oil: The Story of Fleet Logistics Afloat in the Pacific During World War II* (Washington, 1953)

Celander, Lars. *How Carriers Fought: Carrier Operations in World War II* (Philadelphia, 2018)

Chambers, Mark. *Nakajima B5N "Kate" and B6N "Jill" Units* (Oxford, 2017)

Chambers, Mark. *Wings of the Rising Sun: Uncovering the Secrets of Japanese Fighters and Bombers of World War II* (London, 2018)

Chambers, Mark. *Yokosuka D4Y "Judy" Units* (Oxford, 2021)

Claringbould, Michael John. *Operation RO-Go 1943: Japanese Air Power Tackles the Bougainville Landings* (Oxford, 2023)

Clark, J. J. *Carrier Admiral* (New York, 1967)

Cleaver, Thomas M. *Pacific Thunder: The US Navy's Central Pacific Campaign, August 1943–October 1944* (Oxford, 2017)

Coletta, Paolo E. *Admiral Marc A. Mitscher and U.S. Naval Aviation: Bald Eagle* (Lewiston, 1997)

Cook, James F. *Carl Vinson: Patriarch of the Armed Forces* (Macon, 2004)

Craven, Wesley Frank and James Lea Cate, eds. *The Pacific: Guadalcanal to Saipan August 1942 to July 1944.* Series: *The Army Air Forces in World War II* (Chicago, 1950)

Craven, Wesley Frank and James Lea Cate, eds. *The Pacific: Matterhorn to Nagasaki.* Series: *The Army Air Forces in World War II* (Chicago, 1953)

Cressman, Robert J. *The Official Chronology of the U.S. Navy in World War II* (Annapolis, 2005)

Crowl, Philip A. *Campaign in the Marianas.* Series: *United States Army in World War II* (Washington, 1960)

Crowl, Philip A. and Edmund Love. *Seizure of the Gilberts and Marshalls.* Series: *United States Army in World War II* (Washington, 1955)

Davidson, Joel R. *The Unsinkable Fleet: The Politics of U.S. Navy Expansion in World War II* (Annapolis, 1996)

"Design Histories of United States Navy Warships of World War II: An Example of an Official History—USS *Independence* (CVL-22)," *Warship International*, 35:4 (1998), pp. 342–70

"Design Histories of United States Navy Warships of World War II: The Essex Class CV-9–21, 31–40, 45–47," *Warship International*. 36:4 (1999), pp. 325–98

Dickson, W. David. *The Battle of the Philippine Sea* (Shepperton, 1975)

Drea, Edward. *Japan's Imperial Army: Its Rise and Fall, 1853–1945* (Lawrence, 2009)

Dull, Paul. *A Battle History of the Imperial Japanese Navy (1941–1945)* (Cambridge, 1978)

Dyer, George Carroll. *The Amphibians Came to Conquer: The Story of Admiral Richmond Kelly Turner* (2 vols, Washington, 1972)

Evans, David C., ed. *The Japanese Navy in World War II: In the Words of Former Japanese Naval Officers* (2nd ed., Annapolis, 2017)

Evans, David C. and Mark R. Peattie. *Kaigun: Strategy, Tactics, and Technology in the Imperial Japanese Navy, 1887–1941* (Annapolis, 1997)

Evans, Mark L. and Roy A. Grossnick. *United States Naval Aviation 1910–2010* (2 vols, Washington, 2015)

Ewing, Steve. *Reaper Leader: The Life of Jimmy Flatley* (Annapolis, 2002)

Ewing, Steve. *Thach Weave: The Life of Jimmie Thach* (Annapolis, 2004)

Ewing, Steve and John Lundstrom. *Fatal Rendezvous: The Life of Butch O'Hare* (Annapolis, 2004)

Faltum, Andrew. *Aircraft Carrier Intrepid* (Annapolis, 2022)

Faltum, Andrew. *The Essex Aircraft Carriers* (Baltimore, 1996)

Faltum, Andrew. *The Independence Light Aircraft Carriers* (Charleston, 2002)

Ferguson, Robert G. "One Thousand Planes a Day: Ford, Grumman, General Motors and the Arsenal of Democracy," *History and Technology*, 21:2 (2005), pp. 149–75

Ferris, John. "Intelligence," in *CHSWWI*1, pp. 637–63

Ferris, John and Evan Mawdsley. *Cambridge History of the Second World War* (vol. I, Cambridge, 2015)

Fisher, Stan. *Sustaining the Carrier War: The Deployment of U.S. Naval Air Power to the Pacific* (Annapolis, 2023)

Ford, Douglas. *The Elusive Enemy: U.S. Naval Intelligence and the Imperial Japanese Fleet* (Annapolis, 2011)

Forrestel, E. P. *Admiral Raymond A. Spruance, USN: A Study in Command* (Washington, 1966)

Francillon, René J. *Grumman Aircraft since 1929* (London, 1989)

Francillon, René J. *Japanese Aircraft of the Pacific War* (London, 1979)

Frank, Richard. *Guadalcanal: The Definitive Account of the Landmark Battle* (New York, 1990)

Friedman, Norman. *Fighters over the Fleet: Naval Air Defence from Biplanes to the Cold War* (Barnsley, 2016)

Friedman, Norman. *Naval Anti-Aircraft Guns and Gunnery* (Barnsley, 2013)

Friedman, Norman. *Naval Radar* (Greenwich, 1981)

Friedman, Norman. *U.S. Aircraft Carrier: An Illustrated Design History* (London, 1983)

Friedman, Norman. *U.S. Amphibious Ships and Craft: An Illustrated Design History* (Annapolis, 2002)

Friedman, Norman. *U.S. Destroyers: An Illustrated Design History* (London, 1983)

Friedman, Norman. *U.S. Navy Attack Aircraft, 1920–2020* (Annapolis, 2022)

Fukaya Hajime. "Japan's Wartime Carrier Construction," *USNIP*, 81:9 (Sept. 1955) pp. 1031–7

Fuquea, David C. "Advantage Japan: The Imperial Japanese Navy's Superior High Seas Refueling Capability," *Journal of Military History*, 84:1 (Jan. 2020), pp. 213–35

Furer, Julius A. *Administration of the Navy Department in World War II* (Washington, 1959)

Gardiner, Robert, ed. *Conway's All the World's Fighting Ships, 1922–1946* (Greenwich, 1980)

Gardiner, Robert, ed. *The Eclipse of the Big Gun: The Warship 1906–45* (London, 1992)

Goldstein, Donald M. and Katherine V. Dillon, eds. *The Pacific War Papers: Japanese Documents of World War II* (Washington, 2004)

Grove, Eric. *Vanguard to Trident: British Naval Policy since World War II* (London, 1987)

Hagan, Kenneth. *This People's Navy: The Making of American Sea Power* (New York, 1991)

Halsey, William F. and Joseph Bryan. *Admiral Halsey's Story* (New York, 1947)

Hammel, Eric. *Aces against Japan: The American Aces Speak* (Pacifica, 1992)

Hammel, Eric M. *Carrier Strike: The Battle of the Santa Cruz Islands, October 1942* (Grand Rapids, 2004)

Hashimoto Mochitsura. *Sunk: The Story of the Japanese Submarine Fleet 1942–1945* (London, 1955)

Hata Ikuhiko and Izawa Yasuho. *Japanese Naval Fighter Aces and Fighter Units in World War II* (Shrewsbury, 1990)

Hayashi Saburō. *Kogūn: The Japanese Army in the Pacific War* (Westport, 1978 [1959])

Heinrich, Thomas. *Warship Builders: An Industrial History of U.S. Naval Shipbuilding, 1922–1945* (Annapolis, 2020)

Herder, Brian Lane. *World War II Fast Carrier Task Force Tactics, 1943–45* (Oxford, 2020)

Hoffman, Carl W. *Saipan: The Beginning of the End* (Washington, 1950)

Holmes, W. J. *Double-Edged Secrets: U.S. Naval Intelligence Operations in the Pacific During World War II* (Annapolis, 1979)

Holwitt, Joel Ira. *"Execute against Japan": The U.S. Decision to Conduct Unrestricted Submarine Warfare* (College Station, 2009)

Hone, Thomas. "Replacing Battleships with Aircraft Carriers in the Pacific in World War II," *USNWCR*, 66:1 (Winter 2013), pp. 56–76

Hone, Thomas and Trent Hone. *Battle Line: The United States Navy, 1919–1939* (Annapolis, 2006)

Hone, Trent. *Learning War: The Evolution of Fighting Doctrine in the US Navy, 1898–1945* (Annapolis, 2018)

Hone, Trent. *Mastering the Art of Command: Admiral Chester W. Nimitz and Victory in the Pacific* (Annapolis, 2022)

Hone, Trent. "US Navy Surface Battle Doctrine and Victory in the Pacific," *USNWCR*, 62:1 (2009), pp. 67–105

Hornfischer, James D. *The Fleet at Flood Tide: America at Total War in the Pacific, 1944–1945* (New York, 2016)

Hoyt, Edwin. *How They Won the War in the Pacific: Nimitz and His Admirals* (New York, 1970)

Hughes, Thomas A. *Admiral Bill Halsey: A Naval Life* (Cambridge, MA, 2016)

Isely, Jeter and Philip A. Crowl. *The U.S. Marines and Amphibious War: Its Theory and its Practice in the Pacific* (Princeton, 1951)

Itani Jiro, Hans Lengerer, and Rehm-Takahara Tomoko. "Anti-Aircraft Gunnery in the Imperial Japanese Navy," *Warship*, 1991, pp. 81–101

Ito, Masanori. *The End of the Imperial Japanese Navy* (New York, 1984 [1956])

Jernigan, E. J. *Tin Can Man* (Annapolis, 2010)

Jones, Ken and Hubert Kelly. *Admiral Arleigh (31-Knot) Burke: The Story of a Fighting Sailor* (New York, 1962)

Jurika, Stephen, ed. *From Pearl Harbor to Vietnam: The Memoirs of Admiral Arthur W. Radford* (Stanford, 1980)

Kawamura Noriko. *Emperor Hirohito and the Pacific War* (Seattle, 2015)

Kernan, Alvin. *Crossing the Line: A Bluejacket's World War II Odyssey* (Annapolis, 1994)

King, Ernest J. *Our Navy at War: Official Report* (27 March 1944) [NHHC]

King, Ernest J. *U.S. Navy at War: Second Report* (12 March 1945) [NHHC]

King, Ernest J. *U.S. Navy at War: Final Official Report* (1945) [NHHC]

King, Ernest J. and W. M. Whitehill. *Fleet Admiral King: A Naval Record* (New York, 1952)

Kuehn, John T. *Agents of Innovation: The General Board and the Design of the Fleet that Defeated the Japanese Navy* (Annapolis, 2008)

Kuehn, John T. "The War in the Pacific," in *CHSWWI*1, p. 420–54

Lacroix, Eric and Linton Wells. *Japanese Cruisers of the Pacific War* (Annapolis, 1997)

Layton, Edwin T. *And I Was There: Pearl Harbor and Midway—Breaking the Secrets* (New York, 1985)

Leach, Donald E. *Now Hear This: The Memoir of a Junior Naval Officer in the Great Pacific War* (Kent, 1987)

Lengerer, Hans. "*Katsuragi* and the Failure of Mass Production of Medium Sized Aircraft Carriers," *Warship*, 2010, pp. 103–21

Lewin, Ronald. *The Other Ultra* (London, 1982)

Lodge, O. R. *The Recapture of Guam* (Washington, 1954)

Love, Robert W. "Fighting a Global War," in Kenneth J. Hagan, ed., *In Peace and War: Interpretations of American Naval History* (Westport, 2008)

Love, Robert W. *History of the U.S. Navy* (vol. 2, Harrisburg, 1993)

Love, Robert W. et al. *The Chiefs of Naval Operations* (Annapolis, 1980)

Lundstrom, John B. *Black Shoe Carrier Admiral: Frank Jack Fletcher at Coral Sea, Midway, and Guadalcanal* (Annapolis, 2006)

Lundstrom, John B. *The First Team: Pacific Naval Air Combat from Pearl Harbor to Midway* (Annapolis, 1984)

Lundstrom, John B. *The First Team and the Guadalcanal Campaign: Naval Fighter Combat from August to November 1942* (Annapolis, 1994)

McFarland, Keith D. "The 1949 Revolt of the Admirals," *Parameters*, 11:2 (1981), pp. 53–63.

Madsen, Daniel. *Forgotten Fleet: The Mothball Navy* (Annapolis, 1999)

Marder, Arthur, Mark Jacobsen, and John Horsefield. *Old Friends New Enemies: The Royal Navy and the Imperial Japanese Navy* (2 vols, Oxford, 1981, 1990)

Markey, Morris. *Well Done!: An Aircraft Carrier in Action* (New York, 1945)

Marston, Daniel, ed. *The Pacific War Companion: From Pearl Harbor to Hiroshima* (Oxford, 2007 [2005])

Mason, Theodore C. *Battleship Sailor* (Annapolis, 1994 [1982])

Matloff, Maurice. *Strategic Planning for Coalition Warfare, 1943–1944* (vol. 2, Washington, 1990 [1959])

Miller, Edward S. *War Plan Orange: The U.S. Strategy to Defeat Japan, 1897–1945* (Annapolis, 1991)

Moore, Jeffrey. *Spies for Nimitz: Joint Military Intelligence in the Pacific War* (Annapolis, 2004)

Morison, Samuel E. *Aleutians, Gilberts and Marshalls, June 1942–April 1944*. Series: *History of United States Naval Operations in World War II* (vol. 7, London, 1952)

Morison, Samuel E. *New Guinea and the Marianas, March 1944–August 1944*. Series: *History of United States Naval Operations in World War II* (vol. 8, London, 1953)

Morison, Samuel E. *The Struggle for Guadalcanal, August 1942–February 1943*. Series: *History of United States Naval Operations in World War II* (vol. 5, London, 1949)

Morton, Louis. *Strategy and Command: The First Two Years*. Series: *U.S. Army in World War II* (Washington, 1961)

Mundy, Liza. *Code Girls: The Untold Story of the American Women Code Breakers of World War II* (New York, 2017)

O'Brien, Phillips P. *The Second Most Powerful Man in the World: The Life of Admiral William D. Leahy, Roosevelt's Chief of Staff* (New York, 2019)

O'Connor, Raymond, ed. *The Japanese Navy in World War II: In the Words of Former Japanese Naval Officers* (Annapolis, 1969)

O'Hara, Vincent. *The U.S. Navy Against the Axis: Surface Combat, 1941–1945* (Annapolis, 2007)

Okumiya Masatake and Horikoshi Jiro. *Zero!: The Story of the Japanese Navy Air Force 1937–1945* (London, 1957)

Olds, Robert. *Helldiver Squadron: The Story of Carrier Bombing Squadron 17 with Task Force 58* (New York, 1944)

Parillo, Mark P. *The Japanese Merchant Marine in World War II* (Annapolis, 1993)

Parker, Frederick D. *Priceless Advantage: U.S. Navy Communications Intelligence and the Battles of Coral Sea, Midway, and the Aleutians* (Fort Meade, 1993)

Patalano, Alessio. "Feigning Grand Strategy: Japan, 1937–1945," in *CHSWWI*1, pp.159–88

Peattie, Mark R. *Nan'yo: The Rise and Fall of the Japanese in Micronesia, 1885–1945* (Honolulu, 1988)

Peattie, Mark R. *Sunburst: The Rise of the Japanese Naval Air Power, 1909–1941* (London, 2002)

Perry, Glen C. H. *"Dear Bart": Washington Views of World War II* (Westport, 1982)

Polmar, Norman and Dorr B. Carpenter. *Submarines of the Imperial Japanese Navy* (London, 1986)

Potter, Elmer Belmont. *Admiral Arleigh Burke* (New York, 1990)

Potter, Elmer Belmont. *Bull Halsey* (Annapolis, 1985)

Potter, Elmer Belmont. *Nimitz* (Annapolis, 1976)

Prados, John. *Combined Fleet Decoded: The Secret History of American Intelligence and the Japanese Navy in World War II* (Annapolis, 2001 [1995])

Prados, John. *Islands of Destiny: The Solomons Campaign and the Eclipse of the Rising Sun* (New York, 2012)

Prange, Gordon W., with Donald M. Goldstein and Katherine V. Dillon. *God's Samurai: Lead Pilot at Pearl Harbor* (London, 1990)

Reilly, John C. *United States Navy Destroyers of World War II* (Poole, 1983)

Reynolds, Clark G. *Admiral John H. Towers: The Struggle for Naval Air Supremacy* (Annapolis, 1991)

Reynolds, Clark G. *The Fast Carriers: The Forging of an Air Navy* (Annapolis, 1968)

Reynolds, Clark G. *Fighting Lady: The New Yorktown in the Pacific War* (Missoula, 1986)

Reynolds, Clark G. *On the Warpath in the Pacific: Admiral Jocko Clark and the Fast Carriers* (London, 2005)

Roberts, John. *Anatomy of the Ship: The Aircraft Carrier Intrepid* (London, 1982)

Rodger, N. A. M. *The Command of the Ocean: A Naval History of Britain, 1649–1815* (London, 2004)

Rohwer, Jürgen and Gerhard Hümmelchen. *Chronology of the War at Sea 1939–1945: The Naval History of World War Two* (London, 1992)

Roskill, Stephen. *The War at Sea* (3 vols, London, 1954–61)

Rowland, Buford and William B. Boyd. *U.S. Navy Bureau of Ordnance of World War II* (Washington, 1953)

Russell, David Lee. *David McCampbell: Top Ace of U.S. Naval Aviation in World War II* (Jefferson, 2019)

Shaw, Henry I., Bernard C. Nalty, and Edwin T. Turnbladh. *Central Pacific Drive.* Series: *History of U.S. Marine Corps Operations in World War II* (Washington, 1966).

Sherman, Frederick C. *Combat Command: The American Aircraft Carriers in the Pacific War* (New York, 1950)

Sherrod, Robert. *On to Westward: War in the Central Pacific* (New York, 1945)

Smith, Holland M. *Coral and Brass* (New York, 1957 [1948])

Smith, Peter C. *Fist from the Sky: Japan's Dive-Bomber Ace of World War II* (Mechanicsburg, 2006)

Smith, Robert R. *The Approach to the Philippines.* Series: *U.S. Army in World War II* (Washington, 1996 [1953])

Spector, Ronald H. *Eagle against the Sun: The American War with Japan* (New York, 1985)

Spector, Ronald H., ed. *Listening to the Enemy: Key Documents of the Role of Communications Intelligence in the War with Japan* (Wilmington, 1988)

Spruance, Raymond. "The Victory in the Pacific," *RUSI Journal*, 91:564 (Feb. 1946), pp. 539–58

Stafford, Edward P. *The Big E: The Story of USS Enterprise* (New York, 1962)

Stafrace, Charles. *Grumman F6F Hellcat* (East Bletchley, 2011)

Stanley, Roy. *World War II Photo Intelligence* (London, 1982)

Stewart, William H. *Ghost Fleet of the Truk Lagoon, Japanese Mandated Islands: An Account of "Operation Hailstone," February 1944* (Missoula, 1985)

Stille, Mark. *Santa Cruz 1942: Carrier Duel in the South Pacific* (Oxford, 2012)

Stillwell, Paul. *Battleship Commander: The Life of Vice Admiral Willis A. Lee Jr.* (Annapolis, 2021)

Swanborough, Gordon and Peter M. Bowers. *United States Navy Aircraft since 1911* (London, 1976)

Symonds Craig L. "Mitscher and the Mystery of Midway," *Naval History*, 26:3 (May 2012)

Symonds, Craig L. *Nimitz at War: Command Leadership from Pearl Harbor to Tokyo Bay* (Oxford, 2022)

Symonds, Craig L. *World War II at Sea: A Global History* (Oxford, 2018)

Tagaya Osamu. *Imperial Japanese Naval Aviator, 1937–45* (Oxford, 2003)

Tagaya Osamu. *Mitsubishi Type 1 Rikko "Betty" Units of World War 2* (Oxford, 2001)

Taylor, Theodore. *The Magnificent Mitscher* (New York, 1954)

Thruelsen, Richard. *The Grumman Story* (New York, 1976)

Tillman, Barrett. *Clash of the Carriers: The True Story of the Marianas Turkey Shoot of World War II* (New York, 2005)

Toll, Ian. *The Conquering Tide: War in the Pacific Islands, 1942–1944* (New York, 2015)

Trimble, William F. *Admiral John S. McCain and the Triumph of Naval Air Power* (Annapolis, 2019)

Truman, Harry S. *Mr. Citizen* (London, 1961)

Ugaki Matome. *Fading Victory: The Diary of Admiral Matome Ugaki, 1941–1945* (Pittsburgh, 1991)

USSBS. *The Campaigns of the Pacific War* (Washington, 1946)

USSBS. *Interrogation of Japanese Officials* (2 vols, Washington, 1946)

Vego, Milan. *The Battle for Leyte, 1944: Allied and Japanese Plans, Preparations, and Execution* (Annapolis, 2006)

Vego, Milan N. *Major Fleet-versus-Fleet Operations in the Pacific War, 1941–1945* (2nd ed., Newport, 2016)

Waite, Elmont. "He Opened the Airway to Tokyo," *Saturday Evening Post*, 2 Dec. 1944, pp. 20–21

The War with Japan (6 vols, London, 1995)

Wetzler, Peter. *Imperial Japan and Defeat in the Second World War: The Collapse of an Empire* (New York, 2020)

Wheeler, Gerald E. *Kinkaid of the Seventh Fleet: A Biography of Admiral Thomas C. Kinkaid, U.S. Navy* (Washington, 1995)

Wildenberg, Thomas. *Gray Steel and Black Oil: Fast Tankers and Replenishment at Sea in the U.S. Navy, 1912–1992* (Annapolis, 1996)

Wilds, Thomas. "The Admiral Who Lost His Fleet," *USNIP*, 77:11 (1951), pp. 1174–81

Willmott, H. P. "After Midway: Japanese Naval Strategy, 1942–45," in Daniel Marston, ed., *The Pacific War Companion* (Oxford, 2007 [2005]), pp. 179–92

Willmott, H. P. *June 1944* (Poole, 1984)

Winston, Robert A. *Fighting Squadron* (Annapolis, 1991)

Winton, John. *Ultra in the Pacific: How Breaking Japanese Codes and Ciphers Affected Naval Operations against Japan, 1941–45* (London, 1993)

Wolters, Timothy S. *Information at Sea: Shipboard Command and Control in the US Navy, from Mobile Bay to Okinawa* (Baltimore, 2013)

Wooldridge, E. T., ed. *Carrier Warfare in the Pacific: An Oral History Collection* (Washington, 1993)

Wouk, Herman. *The Caine Mutiny* (Harmondsworth, 1958)

Y'Blood, William T. *Red Sun Setting: The Battle of the Philippine Sea* (Annapolis, 2003)

Zimmerman, Sherwood R. "Operation Forager," *USNIP*, 127:8 (1964), pp. 78–90

INDEX